SABBATH SCRIPTURE READINGS

SABBATH SCRIPTURE READINGS

ON THE NEW TESTMENT

THOMAS CHALMERS

SOLID GROUND CHRISTIAN BOOKS
BIRMINGHAM, ALABAMA USA

Solid Ground Christian Books
2090 Columbiana Rd, Suite 2000
Birmingham, AL 35216
205-443-0311
sgcb@charter.net
http://solid-ground-books.com

SABBATH SCRIPTURE READINGS
On the New Testament

Thomas Chalmers (1780-1847)

Taken from 1848 edition by Sutherland and Knox, Edinburgh
Volume 4 of 5 Posthumous Works of Thomas Chalmers
Horae Biblicae Sabbaticae

Solid Ground Classic Reprints

First printing of new edition March 2006

Cover work by Borgo Design, Tuscaloosa, AL
Contact them at nelbrown@comcast.net

*Cover image Sheep graze in a green pasture near Loch Linnhe
in the NW Highlands in Scotland. ©Ric Ergenbright. Special
thanks to Ric for the permission granted to use this image.
Go to ricergenbright.com*

ISBN: 1-59925-056-X

A New Introduction

"All history is subservient to the great work of Redemption" so begins Thomas Chalmers *Sabbath Scripture Readings*. From October of 1841 to September 20, 1846, Chalmers wrote a series of devotional-expositional thoughts on each chapter of the New Testament, starting with Matthew 1 and going to Revelation 22. It was a time of tremendous ecclesiastical turmoil, and yet in that tumultuous age, the great evangelical pastor-theologian steadily engaged in the classic Scottish Presbyterian practice of preparing comments accompanying Bible Readings for the people of God to nourish there souls on. But these are very different kinds of readings. They are didactic, to be sure, but their devotional and intercessory quality is overwhelming. The source of this difference undoubtedly resides in what the grace of God did in the heart of this man, and how this man sought to fan aflame that grace that God gave.

Chalmers (1780-1847) was one of the leading lights of the Scottish evangelical awakening of the nineteenth century. But he was a man converted to Christ only after his ministry had begun in the church! As a student of mathematics at St. Andrews University, flashes of his considerable intellectual powers became evident, and he showed interest in ethics and politics as well, but he eventually enrolled as a theological student (he had set himself on becoming a minister years earlier). He was licensed to preach the Gospel in the by the Church of Scotland at the age of nineteen, and finally (in 1802) took a charge in his native Fife, in the little village of Kilmany, not too far from the University. At the same time he became assistant to the Professor of Mathematics at St. Andrews–so much for single-minded pursuit of the kingdom!

Chalmers relied on his own native eloquence, rather than hard study, to prepare himself for the preaching ministry in those years. A few hours on Saturday evening were sufficient, he once said to an inquiring parishioner. But he was not preaching the Gospel. In fact, Chalmers' messages were the standard fare of Scottish moderatism, emphasizing the importance of moral attainments, but utterly lacking the Gospel logic required to truly aid real Christian growth, which springs from God's gracious work of conversion.

After nine years in which he endured frustrating ministry and serious illness, Chalmers finally came to understand vividly that "Do this and live" is not the Gospel, and that "Believe on the Lord Jesus Christ and you shall be saved" is the saving response to the Gospel of God, and the only real source of life transformation for the believer. Wilberforce's "Practical View" had a great effect on him. Chalmers' life and ministry radically changed. Gone were the moralizing sermons ("be good"), and in their place came faithful biblical exposition emphasizing "the utter alienation of the heart in all its desires and affections from God," and reconciliation to God as the distinct and prominent object of his ministerial labors. Chalmers said: "it was not till I took the scriptural way of laying the method of reconciliation before them" that he saw any real life change in his people.

Chalmers eventually moved to Glasgow to become the minister in the Tron Kirk and later St. John's. His legendary work among the poor and his strategic deployment of diaconal ministry were features of this decade of his ministry (1815-1823) – but proclamation of the Gospel was always the center. He preached with fire to full congregations. He was a man who knew how to communicate the truth to the common folk, and to the educated elite alike.

After serving as Professor of Moral Philosophy at St. Andrews from 1823-1828, where he was instrumental in launching the renowned "St. Andrews Six" into foreign missions, including the celebrated Alexander Duff of India, Chalmers was called to Edinburgh, as Professor of Divinity at the University. There he would train and inspire the leading lights of the evangelical awakening, from William Cunningham to the Bonars to James Buchanan and George Smeaton.

Chalmers devoted the whole of his powers of eloquence and intellect to bring to bear the Gospel on the hearts of his hearers. And to do this, he first worked hard at bringing the truth of God's word to bear on his own heart. That kind of soul-work is evident in the *Sabbath Scripture Readings*. As you read them, you will find Chalmers crying out to God in prayer, inveighing against "a factitious and freezing orthodoxy," supplying you with a guide to your own heart-work and even with words to lift up in prayer when yours fail you. These readings are not simply a testament to the vibrant evangelical religion of a great man of the past, but a living encouragement to our walk in grace—a model of how to pray the Bible back to God and of how it is to be searchingly applied to our lives. Read, savor, be humbled and grow.

Dr. J. Ligon Duncan
Senior Minister, First Presbyterian Church, Jackson, MS
Past Moderator, General Assembly of the Presbyterian Church in America
President, Alliance of Confessing Evangelicals
Convener, Twin Lakes Fellowship
Adjunct Professor, Reformed Theological Seminary

CONTENTS.

SABBATH SCRIPTURE READINGS—NEW TESTAMENT—

	PAGE
MATTHEW,	1-48
MARK,	48-77
LUKE,	78-113
JOHN,	113-147
ACTS,	147-190
ROMANS,	190-213
I. CORINTHIANS,	214-241
II. CORINTHIANS,	241-264
GALATIANS,	264-274
EPHESIANS,	274-284
PHILIPPIANS,	285-292
COLOSSIANS,	292-299
I. THESSALONIANS,	299-308
II. THESSALONIANS,	308-313
I. TIMOTHY,	313-323
II. TIMOTHY,	323-330
TITUS,	330-335
PHILEMON,	335-337

vi

CONTENTS.

	PAGE
HEBREWS, ...	337-360
JAMES, ...	360-368
I. PETER, ...	369-377
II. PETER, ...	377-383
I. JOHN, ...	383-393
II. JOHN, ...	393-395
III. JOHN, ...	395-396
JUDE, ...	397-398
REVELATION, ...	398-436

Horae Biblicae Sabbaticae.

SABBATH SCRIPTURE READINGS.

NEW TESTAMENT.

MATTHEW.

October, 1841.

MATTHEW I.—All history is subservient to the great work of Redemption; and the genealogy here presented offers to our view a series of steps conducting onward from the Patriarchal ages to Him who is the Author of Redemption. What a deep mystery is the Incarnation of our Saviour; yet without dwelling on the modus of the fact, let us look to the fact itself, as that by which a highway of communication has been opened up from the corporeal to the spiritual; and we, shrined in frameworks of clay, may be said to have obtained a sight of Him who is the very image and representation of the Godhead. We would turn aside to see this great sight, and fall down in lowly reverence before the incarnate Deity.

And under what an endearing and comforting title is it that He is first announced to us—Jesus the Saviour—and from what? He saves us from our sins—not the guilt of them only, but also the power of them.—Realize upon me, O God, the whole of this salvation. Give me a part,

both in the justifying righteousness which this Jesus hath
brought in, and in the sanctifying grace which He sheds
forth on all who believe in Him, that I may be regenerated
as well as reconciled; and that admitted to the pardon
which has been sealed by His blood, I may furthermore
be purified—and, meet for the Master's use, may become
one of His peculiar people, zealous of good works.

But there is still another title in this chapter by which
this mysterious Visitor is made known to us, and that
unspeakably precious—Emmanuel, God with us—He is
very God of whose manifestation in the flesh we here
read. He dwelt with the sons of men on earth; and in
the nature of men He again ascended to the Heaven from
which He came. What a wondrous evolution; and how
it divests the unseen God of His terrors, when He thus
steps forth on the platform of visible things, and that on
the errand to seek and to save us.

May I at length give way before the exhibition of all
this truth and tenderness, and be encouraged to lay hold
of this great salvation.

MATTHEW II.

The first approaches of Christ stirred up the hostile
passions and apprehensions of men. The work of our salvation has all the character of a struggle—and that from
its commencement to the present hour. Let us think not
then that any strange thing hath happened to us, when
we meet with deadly hatred in the world, whether from
the malice or the misunderstanding of adversaries. In
New Testament times there was a mixture of both, and
there is still; and give me grace, O God, not only to

meet with firmness and charity the visible enmity of my fellows, but to stand against the wickedness and the wiles of that higher adversary who is the God of this world, and knows well how to ply both its temptations and its terrors.

Let us rejoice, however, in the assurance, that while in the world we shall have tribulation, in Christ we shall have peace. O that I were looking more singly to Him; and O that He would arise upon my soul, and shine as the Sun of Righteousness thereon—that like the wise men when they saw the star which had appeared to them in the East, I might rejoice with exceeding great joy. I pray, O Lord, and with all earnestness, for this precious manifestation. Give me light, O God; save me from the darkening influences of sin and of the world. May I rise superior to the unworthy cares which now so deaden and depress me. O that I had the light of Christ in my heart, and that this light were reflected on all around, and more especially within the recesses of my family. This want of Christian intercourse is awful. I mourn and am in heaviness because of it.—Help me, O God.

MATTHEW III.

The historical precedency of such preaching as that of John the Baptist to the preaching of Christ and His Apostles, should lessen the antipathies of the ultra-orthodox to the admonitions of those who bid men reform their lives and refrain from wickedness *instanter*, even before they have got a full understanding of the doctrines of grace and salvation.—May I frame my doings to turn unto the Lord. May I, in reading that the kingdom

of heaven is at hand, as an argument for immediate repentance, feel that the promise of the Spirit ready to be
poured forth on the asking of it from Him who waiteth to
be gracious, is just such an argument; and couple with
this one of the most impressive images of Holy Writ—
the axe being laid to the root of the tree—and what a two-
edged weapon for plying the alternative of Now or Never:
the Spirit on the eve of outpouring if we will, to begin
and carry forward and perfect our repentance;—the axe
on the eve of being lifted if we will not, to cut us down
as cumberers of the ground. On the one side, then, is
the instrument of death in the hands of the executioner;
on the other, the baptism of the Holy Ghost to turn our
souls into well-watered gardens. O when life and death
are thus brought so near, may this hard, rebellious, and
earthly spirit at length give way, or rather now give way.
—My God, turn me and I shall be turned.

And what a wondrous evolution at the baptism of the
Saviour. The Trinity was there:—the Son receiving the
ordinance at the hands of a man; the Spirit descending
upon Him; the Father testifying by an audible voice from
Heaven.—O my God, who hast thus made known to the
world that Thou art well-pleased with Thy Son our Saviour,
be well-pleased with me for His sake. Look upon me in
the face of Thine Anointed. I am far gone from original
righteousness, but He hath fulfilled it all—He hath brought
in such a righteousness as Thou, O God, canst accept; and
such a righteousness as Thou wilt impute to the chief of
sinners, if he but venture his all upon it—a righteousness
commensurate to the full honours and rewards of eternity.
On this foundation, O God, I would lean the whole weight
of my dependence.

MATTHEW IV.

Jesus would not put forth His own miraculous powers to save Himself from perishing by hunger, but trusted for his miraculous preservation, should such be necessary, at the hands of God. Let me not do aught that is unwarrantable for the sake even of my most urgent interests, though by all the likelihoods of experience and nature they should be in the most imminent jeopardy; but be still, and settle all my confidence on Him who, either with or without visible means, can do what is best for me—against hope believing in hope—and strong in faith, giving glory to God.

But let not the subtle adversary lay hold of this good and great principle ; and transforming himself into an angel of light, seduce me therewith to a transgression on the other side—to a vain and presumptuous confidence in the Divine interposition to save me from the consequences of my own hardihood and folly. Let me not, particularly in the hope of miracles, brave the lessons and likelihoods of experience. Let me have respect to the constancy of nature; nor wantonly make trial of God, whether He will intermit or suspend it, to supplement my deficiencies or correct my errors. The law of gravitation kept the Omnipotent Saviour from casting Himself headlong, and so incurring the uncalled for expense of a miracle that the temerity might be rectified. And this very delusion wherewith Satan plied the mind of the Son of God, he still practises on us—in myself I know by one of the most destructive and deep-laid of his spells. I have no right to look for miracles of grace in behalf of my children—if myself I will not put into busy operation the means of grace.

I can pray for their regeneration; yet I do not labour and testify and teach for their regeneration. I am stricken with silence, and restrained from making utterance on the subject of their souls. The presence of one visitor will chill me, not into indifference for the eternity of those around me, but will set a seal on all my powers of expression, and wholly paralyze me through the operation of a spiritual cowardice. And yet, though I will not dare one word on the topic in society, I can in secret pour forth my supplications to God for the influence of His Spirit on the souls of those who are near and dear to me. Now, is not this a tempting of God? Is it not a presumptuous expectation that He, at my request too, will make up for my neglect of the solemn duties which belong to me both as a master and a parent?—My God, I pray not for exemption from these duties, but for boldness and faithfulness and energy to acquit myself thereof. Give me to feel more and more, O God, that religion is a reality; and put to flight the wretched scarecrows which have frightened me heretofore out of all principle and propriety.

The direct and concluding lesson of this remarkable passage is the sum and substance of religion. O for the practical supremacy of God and of His will within me— when the world and all its glory—the devil, who is the god of this world, and all his artifices—the flesh and all its besetting solicitations, would cease as hitherto to tyrannize over me. Let me prevail, O God, in thus resisting him whose works the Saviour came to destroy. To be aware of his existence and power and policy I hold is of prime importance in the work and warfare of Christianity. May the light of the gospel disperse the influences of him who is the Prince of darkness. (verse 16.) May I awaken so as that Christ shall give me this light, turning unto Him and receiving in consequence,—the promise of the Spirit being poured upon me, so as that the reign of God may be set up in my heart. Thus should I experience as the fruit of my repentance, in the immediate setting up of this power, a verification of the kingdom being at hand. (verse 17.) Give me skill, O God, as a fisher of men—the wisdom of winning souls. (verse 19.) And may I leave all in following after Christ—may I give up every thing for his sake. (verse 22.)

MATTHEW V.

Of these graces I would single out the ones mentioned in verses third and sixth, as those of which I feel the greatest sense, or perhaps only perceive the greatest semblance in my own character; and this more strongly of that in the sixth than that in the third. I am quite sure of this—the perfect nothingness of my own virtue, the utter destitution in myself of all that God can look upon with acceptance; and the desire of a perpetual longing after such a judicial righteousness as may entitle me to Heaven, and such a personal righteousness as might fit me for its happiness and its society. I am constitutionally rather than evangelically merciful. I am not sure that I mourn. There is a sense of want, but not any strongly-felt dejection because of it. And I fear at times that I feel relieved by the quarrels of such as may have leagued against me, by the dissension of enemies, and consequent weakening of their hostile combinations. My most glaring deficiencies are from the virtues of the fifth and eighth verses; and much have I to pray and watch and strive for that I may

have the charity which endureth all things, and that no
other thoughts than those of holiness shall harbour within
my heart. The two last beatitudes I may perhaps have
some share in; but on the whole I may well count all
that is behind as nothing, and press on to that which is
before.

O my God, now that I cannot be so public as heretofore, may I act as a salt and be as a light to all who
are within the sphere of my influence. Let me aim in
all things at the high Christian standard of morality—
as defined and elevated above all former standards by the
Saviour Himself. What a fell rebuke there is here on all
virulence and vituperation!—Let me indulge in these no
longer; but as much as lieth in me live peaceably with all
men. And what a high and spiritual standard of purity
is here. Let me not be deceived, but mark well the intolerance of God for this iniquity as contrasted with the
tolerance it meets both from mankind at large and in my
own feelings, which are strongly abhorrent of deceit and
dishonesty, and not so strongly of the deeds—far less of
the imaginations—of licentiousness. Let me weigh this in
the balance of the Sanctuary, and found my estimate of
its worthlessness on the declarations of Scripture and on
God's own law.

Let me be satisfied with the simplicity of "Yea, yea,"
and "Nay, nay."

These are testing precepts from verse 32 to verse 43.—
O my God, enable me to brave and to apply them.

Let me never renounce the love of kindness and of confidence even in those cases where the love of complacency
is impossible. Let me aspire to the likeness of God. And
O that I could maintain my spirituality, and avoid all

which tends to damp and deaden it. Forgive and rectify, O God.

MATTHEW VI.

November, 1841.

I cannot acquit myself of the spirit of ostentation. The charge is all the more peremptory that we are called to *take heed* lest we fall into it. If to be seen of men is the ultimate object, it is condemned; but there is an ulterior object to this in Matt. v. 16, making this therefore not the ultimate one, when our light is made to shine before men so as that they may be led to glorify God. But let us be jealous of ourselves, and take heed that we prefer not our own glory to His.

I stand in need rather of being warned against the shame of being religious than against the ostentation of it. But that is a most interesting dissuasive against long prayers and vain repetitions, which must be harmonized, however, with the direction to pray without ceasing and to pray with importunity. A prayerful heart venting forth no other than its real wishes and deep-felt necessities or desires, will in practice harmonize them.

O my God, teach and enable me to forgive: and let me herein see how indispensable our subjective state is in Christianity, and that however true it is that we are saved by the faith which apprehends aright its objective truths, yet shall we have no part nor lot in its blessings, unless that personally we realize the graces of the Christian character, and in particular forgive one another, even as God for Christ's sake hath forgiven us.

There is a sanction at least given to fasting by our Saviour, and that by the very modification which He lays upon it; and let me at least make this application of it—

cultivate a habit of general abstemiousness, and that without any abatement *thereby* in the air or manner of one's cheerfulness in society.

O my God, may my treasure be in heaven, and my conversation there, and my heart there. Translate me from under the influence of things seen and sensible to that of things unseen and eternal. Give me, O Lord, so to live above the world by living a life of faith on Thy well-beloved Son.

Such singleness of eye, of an eye bent on the good of the imperishable soul, and looking forward and beyond the ever-shifting interests of time, has a command and a clearness of prospect that is altogether lost by him who is the votary and child of this present evil world.—Save me from the darkness and deceit of carnal affections ; and let Eternity when thus made the grand aim of my existence, shed its illuminating glories over the whole field of my contemplation.

What a noble passage at the close of this chapter, and what lessons of wisdom both practical and profound. The impossibility of two affections sharing the mastery of the heart—the superiority of end to means, of life to that which supports life—the affecting and beautiful appeals to the fowls of the air and flowers of the field—the utter vanity of our cares about this world, seeing that they will not add an hour to our earthly existence, that existence the support and comfort of which form the terminating object of all these anxieties—the call upon us to place all our confidence in the God who opens His hand liberally, and knows all our necessities—the sufficiency of this day's sufferings for this day's patience, and the folly therefore of overloading the spirit with the possibilities

of to-morrow till to-morrow comes—these form the grand
considerations and premises on which the all-important
precept is made to rest—of " Seek ye *first* the kingdom
of God and His righteousness," after which, with a super-
abounding goodness that is altogether celestial and god-
like, is it promised that all the other things without
seeking or solicitude on our part will be added unto us.

MATTHEW VII.

My God, let me forget all the injuries I may have suffered, and attempt not to judge the authors of them ; but
rather let me judge myself that I may not be judged. (1 Cor.
xi. 31.) Let me grudge not against others—because the day
of reckoning is at hand, and the judge is at the door.

There is a manifest perversity and hatred of Divine
things against which it were needless to persevere, nay
dangerous to persist therein.   But should we not make
proof of this before that we abstain from trying the Christian good of others ?—May I walk in wisdom, O God, to
them who are without ; and at the same time not be
ashamed of the testimony of Christ.

What a precious encouragement in this chapter to prayer, inclusive of all men—*every* one that asketh receiveth—
and enforced by a " how much more" an *argumentum a
fortiori*, based on the strongest and most familiar of Nature's affections.—O my Father in Heaven, sanctify and
elevate the affection which I, a father on earth, have for
my own children.   When I ask for grace, surely Thou
wilt not give me a mere counterfeit instead ; and give
me therefore more than the instinctive, give me a Christian and spiritual love for those of my own family.   So

much for what we would that God should do to us; but as for what we would that men should do to us, we are not to expect from them a liberality all on one side. It must not be all asking from them without an equal readiness on our part to give and to do for them. There must be reciprocity here, and it is expressed in one of the most memorable and comprehensive rules ever delivered to the world.

O my God, let the narrowness and difficulties of the path which leadeth into life lead me to strive for an entrance there; and summon all my powers for an enterprise of strenuousness.

Are not the recipients of instruction vested by our Saviour (verses 15-20) with a judgment over their instructors? The test which He supplies them with is one at the same time of general application—" By their fruits shall ye know them."

And this test will be brought to bear upon us on the day of reckoning.—My God, let me have constant respect unto Jesus Christ as my Judge as well as my Saviour.

There is a principle and a cause within for all our actions without—the former related to the latter as the root of a tree is to its fruits, or as a foundation to the building which rises from it. O God, put the right principle within me, that I may be rooted and grounded in the faith—forgetting not that while justified by faith I am judged by works. And may these sayings of Christ sink deep into my heart. May I feel and recognise His authority in reading, as the men of that day did in hearing Him; and enable me to discern even on the face of His written word the signatures of that wisdom and weight which distinguish Him from all other teachers.

MATTHEW VIII.

A most weighty doctrinal truth enveloped in the first case which this chapter records. We have less faith in God's will than in His power to heal and save us. But He is willing as He is able. We say, if Thou wilt Thou canst. He says, I will; be thou clean.—Lord, impart to me faith.

But there are gradations in faith. In the first case we have the example of it in a nascent and imperfect form—as a grain of mustard-seed. In the history of the second case we have it in far greater strength and maturity. In the former the man believed in the power, but doubted the will of Christ to heal him. In the latter case the man believed that Christ might cure the patient who stood before Him; but more than this—believed that His word would be alike effectual though the patient were at a distance and out of sight. His was a faith not helped by the full accompaniments of sense, and which subsisted on itself alone. Lord, increase my faith—though I see Thee not may I believe. Without any aid from vision may that faith which is the evidence of things not seen have full ascendency within me. And what a precious truth, that as the faith so is the fulfilment:—" As Thou hast believed so be it done unto thee."

O my God, let me live to Him who died for me. Let me arise a restored patient as did Peter's mother-in-law, and give myself to the work of serving henceforth and for ever the great Physician of my soul.

And let me not be daunted by the sacrifice or self-denial of an unreserved submission to Christ as my Lord. Let me follow Christ at all hazards, leaving to others the

business of the world, and willing to incur every privation
in the cause of so great and good a Master. The time
may not be far off when, like Him, on earth we may not
have where to lay our heads: let us not be fearful: let
us hold fast our confidence: let us cast our care on Him
who can still alike the tumult of the waves and tumults
of the people—turning the heart of every man whithersoever He will. O Lord, calm, if it be Thy blessed will, the
agitation of our present controversies.

We war not against flesh and blood only, but against
principalities and powers. May we put on the whole armour
of God ; and under Christ as the captain of our salvation
may we be enabled to conquer all His and our enemies.

MATTHEW IX.

What Thou sayest unto the paralytic, O Christ, Thou
sayest unto all in Thy Gospel—" Be of good cheer, thy
sins are forgiven thee ;" a saying which will surely take
effect in all who believe in it, or who have the faith
which Jesus saw (verse 2) to be in the patient and those
who were with him.—Give me, O Lord, to appropriate
this saying and rejoice therein, and let the joy of the
Lord be my strength.

But, like Matthew, may I not only have faith in Christ
—may I follow Him even though I should have to leave
all—all that He bids me or would have me to forsake.
Christ is most willing to heal us, if we are willing to be
healed, and no past sinfulness of ours will stand as a barrier in the way of His mercy. Let us believe in this and
be glad : and let ours be a willing, a cordial and spiritual
obedience ; and without any attempt at sorting together

the services of bondage and those of adoption, let us cherish in our hearts that love which fulfilleth the law.

The narrative—and more especially of the miracles—continues to be impregnated with doctrine—the doctrine in particular, that according to our faith so shall it be done unto us. And as the woman felt a confidence even in the efficacy of but touching the hem in His garment, so let us even in the absence of all near or vivid conception of Him, when such manifestations are wanting, and all light save that of simple credence, all power save that of naming His name, have forsaken us—let us even in these circumstances of distance and desertion have but faith in the name, and like the woman cured of her issue, we shall be made whole.

Lord, I believe, help mine unbelief. I believe that Thou art able—what possible reason can there be why I should not also believe that Thou art as willing to save me? Open mine eyes, O Thou whose function it is to give light, that I may behold the wondrous things contained in the book of Thy testimony. And do thou, O Lord of glory, to whom all powers and principalities are subject, save me from the powers of darkness, from the machinations and wiles of the great adversary. Thy warfare, O Captain of my salvation, is on the side of all goodness and righteousness and truth. Thou camest to destroy the works of him with whom Thine enemies alleged against Thee that Thou wert in fellowship. Dispossess my heart then, O God, of its tendencies to evil. Cast the strong man, the unclean spirit out of me; and let me henceforth be possessed with that Spirit of Thine without which I am none of His.

Let me labour for the kingdom of Christ in my household, and pray for more labourers. Thy kingdom come; but for this object Thy will must be done. Let performance be superadded to prayer; and O endow me with a love for souls greater than I have ever yet felt, and with a diligence in studying for their salvation greater than has ever yet been put forth by me.

MATTHEW X.
December, 1841.

O Lord, do Thou cast the unclean spirit out of me; may I henceforth cleanse my way by taking heed thereto according to Thy word. Do Thou check the rising thoughts of sin; and grant that I may be recalled from the wretched condition of a lost and wandering sheep, and have the kingdom of heaven, even the reign of love and holiness, set up within me.

The time perhaps is coming when the work of Christianization must begin anew over the face of a land desolated of its wonted provision for the ministry of the Gospel. Prepare me and counsel me aright for such a time, O God. My own preference should be for an organization to raise the requisite supplies; and for the keeping up of a parochial system. It is clear that apart from these there is a method distinct from either of them, by which the missionaries of the present day might go forth as did the Apostles of old—providing nothing beforehand, and instead of fixing themselves anywhere, making the place of their ministrations depend on the reception they met with. But is there aught in our economics adverse to the spirit of these instructions, and might we not in consistency therewith imitate substantially these first teachers of Christianity, by walking in the footsteps of their faith and

self-denial and wisdom and harmlessness? Let it not be
in our own wisdom, O God, that we devise for Thy glory
and the good of our Redeemer's kingdom, but in the
wisdom which Thou givest. Let us be prepared for the
evil day, and so far from placing confidence in men, let
us think not that any strange thing hath happened to us,
though we meet with treachery and violence. Free me
from all anxiety about speeches and public appearances
should I be called to testify for the truth as it is in Jesus.
May I cast this care upon God, and look for the Spirit of
my Father which is in heaven. Enable me to endure
every sacrifice; and think not that the saying is yet abro-
gated—that he who will live godly in Christ Jesus shall
suffer persecution. May I be content—nay, glory in
being exposed to the same trials with my Master before
me. Raise me above all fear, and enable me to lift an
incorrupt as well as an intrepid testimony. May the fear
of God supplant every other fear; and let no temporal
calamities, however frightful, countervail the weight of
those high considerations which stand associated with
duty and eternity, and the favour of God which is better
than life, and the safety and wellbeing of the soul. But
God is the helper of all who stand up for His cause, and
why should we fear what man can do unto us? Let us
confess Him, then, before men; let us not in cowardice
or shame deny the Master who bought us; let us follow
Him through good report and evil report; let us brave
the loss of all that is dear to Nature's best affections, in
our testimony for Jesus; let us be willing to take up the
Cross, nor count our lives dear unto us; and let us not
forget that if a dark season of adversity is approaching,
we may be called not only to suffer ourselves, but to

succour others; let us be willing to distribute, ready to communicate, and more especially for the necessities of the saints, and for the moral exigencies of a land bereft of pure ordinances. What a precious consideration, that with such sacrifices God is well-pleased, and that even a cup of cold water given to a disciple of the Saviour shall not be unnoticed or unregarded by Him.

MATTHEW XI.

I would give earnest heed, O Lord, to those recorded sayings and sermons of the Saviour which He preached in the land of Judea.

And now that we live under the teaching of Christ and His Apostles, and when the knowledge thus placed within our reach is so vastly superior to that of John the Baptist, let me feel the responsibility under which I lie for the greater light that we enjoy. From the commencement of his ministry to that of our Saviour—" from the days of John the Baptist until now"—the chief doctrine was that of repentance, with the hope of a greater Prophet who was to come. Under the influence of this doctrine men strove with violence to enter the kingdom of heaven, and they carried it; and let us so strive, instead of indolently seeking. It is true that grace hath come by Jesus Christ; but still let us strive mightily according to this grace working in us mightily. (Col. i. 29.) Let not orthodoxy condemn the diligence of our efforts. Let not this diligence supersede the sense of our own nothingness, and the entireness of our dependence upon grace. And there are adversaries who will condemn us for both, at one time decrying the Puritanic strictness of our lives, and at

another denouncing our faith as the enemy of all righteousness—reproaching us alike on these opposite grounds,
even as the disciples were reproached in the days of our
Saviour. But now even as then is wisdom justified of her
children. In the face of all these perversities let us make
the most both in the way of belief and obedience of all
the light that we have—else we may incur a worse fate
than the worst of heathens; whereas, on the other hand,
if we do as we ought with the light we have more will
be given, and from a quarter whence the wise of this
world seek it not. The duteous children of a simple
faith and a simple obedience will receive a manifestation that the world knoweth not. They will be taught of
Jesus. He will reveal the Father to them.—My God, may
I participate in this process; and in the prosperity thereof may the Saviour see in me of the travail of his soul
and be satisfied.

O touch me, Spirit of all grace, into a compliance with
His blessed invitation, that so I may find rest unto my
soul. O for His meekness and lowliness of heart, and
willingness to take His yoke upon me; for there is a
yoke which His disciples must and do come under—a
burden which they all take upon them—but easy and
light because of that Love which both serves and suffers
cheerfully; because of that Grace which enables us to
overcome, and in virtue of which the commandments are
not grievous.—May I so come, Lord Jesus.

MATTHEW XII.

Ours is the religion of liberty; but let us not use it as
an occasion for the flesh. It is not we but Christ who is

the Lord of the Sabbath. Let me not therefore seek my own will or my own pleasure on that day, or rather let it be my highest pleasure to spend that day in the exercises and the contemplations of sacredness—keeping it not in the spirit of bondage but in the spirit of adoption, loving it for its opportunities, and enjoying it as a foretaste and specimen of our future heaven.

He gives a beautiful exemplification of Christian liberty in a work of mercy on the Sabbath, that work which He appears to have multiplied either on the same day or shortly after when He healed all the sick who followed Him.—My God, let me imitate this heavenly pattern of all gentleness and meekness and goodness. Let me neither strive nor cry, when instructing those who oppose themselves. Do Thou break my hard heart, and then heal my broken one. The miracle here recorded is, as usual, charged with doctrinal truth. A command was given to one who in himself was unable to obey it. But power accompanied the order. So may it be, O Lord, in the preaching of Thy word to me and mine. May Thy grace open a way for it to our hearts, and strengthen us to act upon it.

Save me, O God, from the sin against the Holy Ghost. Let me not resist the grace of Thy Spirit, lest I grieve and quench and at length provoke Him to a final abandonment. Regenerate my inner man, O God, and let me watch over the deeds of my outer man. O let me henceforth be careful of what I say. Let me beware of those hasty or heedless utterances which I have been too much accustomed to regard as insignificant. Let me bridle my tongue—so as that neither the impulses of passion shall hurry me into bitter, nor the sallies of humour betray me into idle words.

Let me enter forthwith, O God, on this long neglected discipline.

The refusal of another sign to those who had perversely and resolutely misinterpreted the sign just given, was an exemplification of that process which terminates at length in the state of being irretrievably forsaken by the grace of God.   Forbid, O Lord, that I should do violence to the incipient lessons of my conscience, and so Thy Spirit cease to strive with me.   Let not the light of Thy gospel serve but to enhance my condemnation; and O restrain my backslidings, lest taken possession of by worse influences than at the first I fall away to my utter and everlasting perdition.

And O that I not only began but maintained my relationship with Christ, so as to be acknowledged by Him as of His family.   May I keep Thy sayings, that Thy Father and Thou may love me, and come unto me and make abode with me.   (John xiv. 23.)   Even so, Lord Jesus.

MATTHEW XIII.

When my Saviour speaks let me ever be attentive to hear Him.—Save me, O God, from the withdrawing process, and give me fully to share in the advancing process which obtains under the economy of grace.   Let me give earnest heed to the things that are spoken—that, having this, more may be granted to me, and so as that I may increase in the knowledge of God, and be more and more instructed in the mysteries of His kingdom. Enable me, O God, so to apply as to find my own place in the parable of the sower, and read there what my infirmities and wants are.   How often then have I reason

to fear that I occupy a stage even behind the first class
of hearers—reading so mechanically, or hearing so list-
lessly that the word does not light upon me at all, or
become the object of recognition so much as for an instant. But even when it does, how often is it on the
understanding only, whence it slips from the memory, in
a moment dispossessed or taken away. Or when it does
make an impression on the heart or conscience, how marvellously soon is that impression dissipated among the
vanities of the world, and the sympathies of social life
with those before whom I deny Christ by my silence—
because the shame of a godly profession operates upon me
with all the influence which persecution had in former
ages. But the place to which I most gravitate, and
against which I most need to guard myself, is that of the
third class of hearers—in whom the word is choked by
weeds and thorns; because there is a depth of soil in me
for the abiding and the practical—for a fixed ruling passion which might supplant every other, or at least subordinate every other. But that soil is pre-occupied with
thorns, so as to stint the room and growth of a principle
of grace in me. If not a love for the riches of this world,
it is at least the care of this world in some one of its
varieties—sometimes a diseased and anxious feeling of
insecurity for my property—sometimes a brooding sense
of irritation at the injustice which I either feel or fancy—
sometimes a taste for occupations distinct from those
which subserve the furtherance of the spiritual life, and
at all times a general overhanging and overweening carnality. These are the several vexations of the vain show
in which I walk, and which would cheat me of my eternity.—O my God, let every plant which Thou hast not

planted be rooted up from my heart. Deposit there the good seed, and grant that—refreshed and fertilized by living water—it may bring forth fruit abundantly. Since the wheat and tares must by Thy Sovereign ordination grow together in this world, teach me to walk in wisdom to those who are without, to endure the contradiction of sinners, and do good unto all men, though more especially to the household of faith. For the growth of the kingdom of heaven in my own heart, may this weak, this little faith of mine be increased and strengthened. May it overshadow the whole man. May it germinate the deeds of new obedience, and make them to be acceptable through Jesus Christ. For the growth of the kingdom of heaven in the world, may I be a leaven for good in my family and neighbourhood, and let my light shine with a converting influence on the souls of others.—O my God, I would give up all for Christ. This day I have felt the preciousness of union with Him. May He be to me as a hidden treasure. May I abide in Him that He may abide in me and cause me to abound in much fruit. O my God, let Him be unto me as the pearl of great price—seeing that He who hath the Son hath life. May my union with Him be perfected; and give me experimentally to feel the force and significancy of those images which, though regarded as mystical by the world at large, are realized in the experience of advanced believers when they feel themselves united with Christ, as branches are with a vine, as stones with a building, whereof He is the chief corner-stone, as members are with a body whereof He is the Head. O Lord, may I be found among the good on that day when Christ cometh to make up His jewels, severing the wicked from among the just. Let me be well instructed in the mysteries of Thy kingdom, and let the word of Christ dwell in me richly in all wisdom.

Let not Christ be lightly esteemed by me. Let me honour the Son even as I honour the Father. On this last Sabbath of the year may He so shine in my heart, that even from this time forward I may prize Him as all my desire and all my salvation.

MATTHEW XIV.

January, 1842.

Herod could respect an oath, and feel what was due to the company around him, yet gave himself to the most aggravated licentiousness. Let not, O God, my sense of honour, or of any social virtue whatever, buoy me up against the consciousness of a deficient purity, whether in laxity of thoughts or actions. Let me cultivate with all strenuousness the grace of a holy abstinence from all evil propensities and evil imaginations.

And while I shun the example of wicked men, let me make a study of the character and doings of my Saviour. And what a number of lessons crowd upon us from the several passages of His history. Here within a short compass we see His compassion in healing the sick—compassion too in feeding the hungry; relieving all the varieties of actual distress, though a sound political economy in coincidence with His own example, forbids the impolicy of making certain provision for all the varieties of eventual distress—piety in looking up to heaven as the source of all our earthly blessings—and frugality in gathering up the fragments of the meal, and not suffering even that food to be wasted which He had produced miraculously and could have multiplied at pleasure.

And O what a needful lesson is given to us, by the retirement of our Saviour from the scene of beneficence to
the solitude of devotion.—Give me, O Lord, thus to alternate duty with prayer and prayer with duty.   What a sad
rebuke upon my habits and history is conveyed by this
passage in the life of Jesus Christ.   Pour on me, O God,
the Spirit of grace and supplication.   Be Thou, O God, a
very present help in the time of trouble—and more especially in the time of temptation.   Forgive, O Lord, my
transgression.   May Christ appear in the midst of this
darkness and tumult ; and so appear as to become the object not of my dread but of my confidence.   Let not my
faith give way even under a sense of delinquency, however foul and however recent.   But, O God, however bold
in the sense of pardon, save me from the boldness of presumptuous iniquity ; and let the remainder of my days be
spent in peace and holiness—in the worship and service
of the Son of God.

I feel as if a great lesson hung on the efficacy of a touch,
though it was only on the hem of the Saviour's garment.
I feel as if it corresponded to faith in His name, when the
power of conception was dull and feeble—so that we could
frame no apprehension of His person.   When I labour under the want of a lively manifestation, let the sound of
His name uphold my confidence and be as ointment poured
forth.   But, O my God, that this confidence might continue undisturbed, do Thou cleanse my heart of all regard
for iniquity.

MATTHEW XV.

The first passage in this chapter strikingly impresses the
superiority of the moral and the spiritual over the ritual

and the institutional and the sacramental. It forms a
lasting memorial against all such errors as are now revived
by the Puseyism of our day.—My God, let me keep my
heart with all diligence—that citadel and centre of whatever is either good or evil in man. Forgive the delinquency of former years; and enable me now to discharge
aright all the relative duties which I owe to those of
my own kindred. And more comprehensively still, give
me to worship Thee, O God, in spirit and in truth; and set
me loose from the influence of human authority, in so far
as it distorts or diverts or deafens the direct impression
of Thine own word upon my conscience. Let me call none
Master but Christ: and aid me, Almighty Father, in the
work of teaching others, that I may not mislead them into
error; but rather enable me to disperse and clear away
any darkening medium which may now lie between their
souls and that Bible which is the alone lamp unto our feet
and light unto our paths.

Increase my faith, O God, that therewith I might ply
Thee with my importunities and ask till I receive. O
if I had but faith as a grain of mustard seed, or as one
of the smallest crumbs which fall from the heavenly treasure which is above; and then might I ask whatever I
will till it was done unto me. But that which I ask must
be agreeable to the will of God. But He willeth me to be
saved, and to come to the knowledge of the truth. (1 Tim.
ii. 4.) Give me then, O God, this saving knowledge; and
let me obtain this blessed answer from on high—"Be it
unto thee even as thou wilt."

And let me study, and study in order to imitate, the
example of my Saviour in all things. Let me not shut
up the bowels of my compassion against actual human

suffering, but be willing to distribute and ready to communicate. Let me have the love of kindness to all. Enthrone the second law in my heart, O God, that I may be like unto Him who went about doing good continually.

MATTHEW XVI.

The credentials of Christianity are enough both for faith and for practice. Let me give myself up then implicitly to its guidance—for if I believe not the Scriptures, neither would I believe though one should rise from the dead.

And let me understand of the words of Christ that they are spirit and they are life. Let me not be deceived as Papists and Puseyites are by the literalities of Scripture. Let me beware of their leaven, as of the leaven of the Pharisees which is hypocrisy, and of the Sadducees which is infidelity. May I worship Thee, O God, who art a Spirit, in spirit and in truth.

And, O my God, reveal Thy Son to me. Give me such a knowledge of Him as is life everlasting—which knowledge cannot be given me by the flesh and blood that cannot inherit the kingdom of God. May I be drawn to Christ, and may Christ give me light. May I be made to know Him as the Son of the living God and Saviour of the world—as my Saviour. And O that I had the experience of a present salvation in the law of the Spirit of life which is in Christ Jesus making me free from the law of sin and death.

Heaven and earth must pass away ere the words of Scripture can pass away; and it is the test of a false Church, if its decrees are opposed to the essential truths of Scripture. But much that is necessary to good government and good order has been left to the Church's discretion; and while it maintains the character of a true Church by its conformity with Scripture in all that is essential, there are all those decisions on matters which have been thus left out for its arbitrement, worthy of our utmost respect ; and the sin of schism might be incurred by our separation because of such decisions. Give me, O Lord, a respect for all Thine ordinances ; and give me the wisdom to know when it is my duty to abide, and when to withdraw from the Church established in these lands—now in the midst of perplexities, and on the eve it may be of such a corruption or of such a violence as in either case would destroy her. May we be prepared, O God, to follow our Master : He renounced all on earth for the establishment of His Church. May we be in readiness for the same, for His and for its sake. May we have respect unto His judgment of us at the consummation of all things. May we savour not the things that be of men, but be willing to deny ourselves, and to take up the cross, and to make the surrender, even of our lives or our livelihoods, rather than incur damnation. Penetrate our hearts, O God, with the immeasurable worth of that soul which is imperishable ; and let the care of our eternity be uppermost in the midst of all our other cares and other calculations.

MATTHEW XVII.

O my God, let me take to the gospel attitude of looking unto Jesus—that in His face I may behold Thine own glory. May God manifest in the flesh be made manifest to my soul. And, Heavenly Father, may I be

satisfied to wait and to work for that manifestation. I
shall obtain it if I keep His sayings. (John xiv.) Let
me hear these sayings then, and observe them. Let me
take to the obvious and practicable course prescribed in
the fifth verse. Let me listen to the words of Him who
was the Son of Man and is the only beloved Son of
God, and do them. O strengthen me for this doing,
and then shall I be made with open face to behold as in
a glass the glory of the Lord, and be changed into the
same image from glory to glory, even as by the Spirit of
the Lord.

Lord, increase my faith.—Give me to experience its
power. What most of all I need to be plucked from this
carnal this earthly heart of mine is its rooted ungodliness.
Let me have that faith which will enable me to bid it
effectually away; or, in other words, which will give acceptance to the prayer of—Lord take unto Thyself Thy
great power and reign over me. Establish Thy kingdom
within my heart, and dispossess the strong man who has
so long ruled and had the ascendency there. With me it
is impossible, but with God all things are possible. Nevertheless to attain such faith, or to reach to such fervency
and efficacy of supplication—fasting would appear to be
subservient. Let me at least be temperate in all things,
and forbid that by the indulgence of sense or appetite my
spirituality should be at all damped or overborne.

And let us think of the mighty surrender which He
made, when He poured out His soul unto the death for
the world's salvation. And shall we make no surrender
as followers and fellow-workers with Him for our own salvation? Lord, I would give up all, that He may see in
me of the travail of His soul and be satisfied; and O forbid

that I should crucify Him afresh by my delinquencies.
If His disciples were exceeding sorry because of His sufferings—should not I be exceeding sorry to defeat and
disappoint the object in myself for which these sufferings
were undertaken? May I look on Him whom I have
pierced, and mourn and be in bitterness because of those
sins which were the murderers of my Lord. Give me the
godly sorrow which worketh the repentance that is unto
salvation.

What carefulness of giving offence—what accommodation to the beneficial usages of society—what respect for
constituted authorities, does our Saviour discover in the
closing verses of this chapter. I pray that in asserting
the freedom of Christ's Church I may never lose sight of
Christ's example; and O may the spirit of this passage
temper and restrain the impetuosity wherewith I might
otherwise conduct myself in the course of our present
controversies.

MATTHEW XVIII.

Give me the docility of a little child, O God, and
teach me to sit at the lessons of Thy Bible with the
humility of a scholar who feels that he has all to learn.
And O save me from blood-guiltiness. Give me an awful respect for the purity and principle of Thy little
ones, which rather than violate, let me crucify the
strongest of my beliefs, and practise a self-denial the most
vigilant and severe. Let me wound not the consciences
of those for whom the Saviour died. He came for the
express purpose of their recovery; and it is not God's will
that any of these little ones should perish. And, O Lord,
let me seek peace as well as holiness. As much as lieth

in me let me live peaceably with all men, not suffering sin upon my brother, but in anywise telling him wherein he may have offended. And O what a motive to the preservation of cordiality and good agreement among Christians in the encouragement given to social prayer. Let me cultivate the habit of Christian fellowship, O God, and guide me to the most effectual way of making good its blessings both for myself and others also.

What a splendid parable closes this chapter in behalf of forgiveness. What an indefiniteness is given to the duty, and how largely does our Saviour extend it. How closely is this duty related to the tenure of our holding upon God. What a mighty debt has been cancelled to those who believe in the Lord Jesus Christ. Even as God hath forgiven us we should forgive each other.—O Lord, enable me to forgive from the heart, knowing that faith is vain unless it is so followed up. Give me to drink in the whole spirit of this noble passage, where the most peculiar of all the Gospel duties is made to rest on the most peculiar of its doctrines.

MATTHEW XIX.

February, 1842.

Let such passages, so frequently repeated as the one at the beginning of this chapter, bring my moral sense into a more direct and vivid recognition of the guilt of licentiousness. It is obvious that it is incompatible with the kingdom of heaven, to attain which we must crucify the flesh.—My God, give me to be thoroughly decided on this matter, and henceforward to maintain the most resolute and unsparing warfare with this arch-enemy of the soul. The Bible tells of the deceitful lusts, and of the deceitfulness of sin. My God, save me from being thus deceived; and let the steady light of Thy word dissipate every treacherous illusion.

O God, let my respect to little children, and my love for them, take a direction from the example of our blessed Saviour. Let me not offend them for whom Christ died. Let me incur not their awful doom who do so, or do aught which can damage the souls of His little ones. Truly there is none good but one, that is God; yet call we Thee good, O Lord Jesus, for Thou art God; and we would honour the Son even as we honour the Father. In this passage we see not the denial but the affirmation of Thy Divinity— not a refusal of the epithet by which Thou art here characterized, but a sure establishment of the inference, that as Thou art indeed good, so Thou art indeed God. Let me, O God, know the commandments in their exceeding breadth, that I may know mine own vast and incalculable deficiency therefrom. And let me learn them, not for the purpose of conviction alone, but for the purpose of new obedience. Let me be willing and prepared to forsake all in following after Thee; and more especially let me not trust in riches, or set my heart upon them, but lay hold on eternal life, and count everything but nought for the glory which is to be revealed. And who knows, O God, but the trial of our integrity is now at hand? and I most earnestly pray both for strength and for wisdom under it. In these days of peril to our Church do Thou arm me with right and resolute principle; and let not even the dearest affections of nature lead me to swerve in the least from the onward path of uprightness and honour. I have no sufficiency in myself: make Thy grace sufficient for me. Arm me with all might in the inner man; and I pray, O God, in particular for our Church, that Thou wouldst sustain her in the midst of her sore adversities, and enable her to preserve an untainted character and entire moral weight in the midst of a crooked and perverse generation.

MATTHEW XX.

This parable applies, I think, to the call of nations, and not of individuals, though it admits of a strong individual application. Let no man take encouragement from it to postpone his repentance to the eleventh hour, or evening of his life. The answer of the labourers who were called at that hour will not avail—that " no man hath hired us." *We* have been offered that hire, and entreated to accept of it from the infancy of our days. O God, let not my repeated negligence of the many calls and the many opportunities wherewith I have been favoured, be laid to my charge. I would enter now into the vineyard of Thy Church, and within the fold of Thy reconciled children. Forgive my by-gone iniquities, O God, for they are great. Blot out, as a thick cloud, my innumerable transgressions; and save me from that sin unto death, after which prayer has lost its efficacy, and all the importunities of Thy messengers become unavailing. My God, help me. Support me in the rally I wish to make against those most formidable and besetting of all enemies—the lusts which war against the soul. Give me firmness, and give me wisdom, O Lord.

What unfaltering determination on the part of the Saviour, and that for the chief of sinners. O may I be conformed to Him in this. May I be crucified along with Him, recollecting, too, that not only my own salvation, but the salvation of others, may be implicated therein. For their sakes, as

well as my own, may I be enabled to renounce the devil,
the world, and the flesh : Thou knowest my frame : Thou
knowest my peculiar necessities : Thou knowest more especially my lack of wisdom : I pray for guidance and support,
that I may be enabled to conquer this great temptation.

I will not say that the ambition of superiority over
others is so flagrantly my constitutional vice as something
else that could be specified ; but doubtless the seed of
this, as of all evil, is within me. And I do feel annoyed
by the literary injustice which has the effect of depressing
me beneath some of my fellows. O my God, enable me to
make head against this infirmity also. Let me feel that
I have nothing which I did not receive. Let me minister
as of the ability which God giveth. Let me seek not
mine own glory, but the glory of Him who came not to
be ministered unto but to minister. And, O Father in
heaven, admit me into the number of those ransomed
ones, who become Thy children through the faith that is
in the Lord Jesus Christ.

Have mercy, Lord Jesus, on my spiritual blindness.
Translate me out of darkness into the marvellous light of
Thy gospel. Open Thou mine eyes, that I may behold
the wondrous things contained in the Book of Thy law.
Give me to know the truth, and may the truth make me
free from the law of sin and of death. In myself I am
the helpless slave of degrading and worthless passions.
Emancipate me from their vile thraldom, O God, and give
me the glorious liberty of one of Thine own children.

MATTHEW XXI.

Thy providence, O God, extendeth unto littles ; and we

desire to recognise it in every object which we meet, or which crosses our path, and in the minutest as well as greatest events of history. Give me, O Lord, to imitate the meekness and gentleness of Christ; and let me not rest my cause on the suffrages of the people, who rent the air with their hosannas now, but crucified Him afterwards. And so may we be greeted by the acclamations of the multitude in our attempts to purify and reform the Church, yet be abandoned by them in the long run. Our best earthly hopes stand associated with the rising generation; but this would point to an initial lesson of trial, the dangers and difficulties of which it is our part to brave, not because of any human dependence whatever, but on the simple call of duty, and in dependence on God.

The incident of the fig-tree has given rise to one of the most precious and important declarations in Holy Writ.— My God, what an opening is held forth to us here for the largest blessings which an immortal creature can set his heart upon! What a wide field for prayer in the sweeping term "whatsoever." Only let us understand that it is "whatsoever we shall ask, *believing*, we shall receive," and that believing is not the voluntary act by which we can fasten on aught that we list, or on aught that we may fancy or long after. Faith must have a ground of evidence to rest upon. But then on this ground how rich a variety of promises is given forth—whatsoever we ask that is agreeable to God's will we shall receive; and we know that He wills us to be saved—that He wills us to attain the knowledge of the truth—that He wills our sanctification—that He wills us to lay hold on Christ, and be reconciled unto Himself. For all these then may we pray; and, O God, let the mountain of mine iniquities be lifted off; let the clean heart and the right spirit be given to me; let the rooted ungodliness of my nature be plucked out; let my vile lusts be eradicated or overborne; and let the law of the Spirit of life in Christ Jesus make me free from the law of sin and of death.

I acknowledge Thy rightful authority over me, O blessed Saviour. Thou who art my Redeemer, be Thou also my Master and my Lord. Take pity upon me in my pollutions; and by the washing of regeneration may I be made holy, even as Thou art holy. God who at sundry times and in divers manners sent prophets into the world, hath in these last days sent His own Son. May I honour the Son even as I honour the Father. May I ever draw out of His fulness that I may be enabled to follow Him wholly, and thus be saved from the awful doom of those who shall flee to hide themselves from the wrath of the Lamb. From this wrath that is to come I would take refuge in the grace that is present and nigh unto me: I seek unto Thy grace and salvation, O Lord.

MATTHEW XXII.

Let me hasten, O God, to meet Thy call. Let none of this world's entanglements detain me from my attendance and my waiting upon God. Let me give instant response to the voice that speaketh to me from heaven, and kiss the Son while He is in the way, and lest His wrath begin to burn. And I would come before Thee, O God, with the investiture of Christ's righteousness, and of the Spirit's graces—both justified and sanctified, that I might be meet for acceptance into heaven, and meet for the joys and the exercises which are

current there. This call is now flung abroad over the
face of the world. O may it light with power on me and
mine, that they all may appear before Thee with the preparation of the sanctuary.

Give me, O Lord, the wisdom of the Saviour, even of
Him who bids us be wise as serpents, as well as harmless
as doves—that I may know rightly to divide the Word
of truth, and to protect myself from the wiles of those
who would ensnare me. More especially in this day of
trial may I be enabled to partition my regards as I ought
between Him who ruleth both in heaven and in earth,
and the authorities of this world; and whatever I am
called upon to do, may I ever carry it with just and incumbent respect to princes and governors, nor depart from
that loyalty which is the principle and the characteristic
of every true disciple of our Lord.

My God, let me strive after angelic purity here, that I
may be qualified for the angelic state hereafter. Deliver
me, if not from the presence, at least from the power of
those base lusts which war against the soul. Teach me
to renounce the low and earthly pleasures of sense for
those pleasures which are at Thy right hand, and those
joys which are for evermore. O let not sensuality, even
in its most alluring form, gain the advantage over me.
May I willingly make surrender of all that my heart has
heretofore been set upon in the life that now is, for the
sake of that higher and nobler life which awaits the redeemed in the presence of Him who is the God of the
living, and the living God.

And inscribe Thy laws upon my heart, O God. Give
me the love of Thyself; give me that love of my neighbour which is like unto the love of Thyself: and let mine

be an angelic love, which it never can be without an angelic purity.

O Thou root and offspring of Jesse, give me to know Thee more and to love Thee better. I aspire after a life of faith on the Son of God. Enable me, O Thou to whom all power has been committed, both in heaven and in earth—enable me to break my way through the entanglements of sense and sin. Give me to know Thy truth, and may Thy truth make me free. Subdue mine enemies by the omnipotence of Thy Godhead—even those enemies by which Thine own manhood was tried; do Thou succour me against them.

MATTHEW XXIII.

March, 1842.

What a lesson here of respect for constituted authorities, and how we require to be charged with the obligation of it in these times—when Church and State are opposed, and we are tempted to speak harshly or contemptuously of the powers which be. The general dissuasive of doing not as the Pharisees do germinates throughout the chapter into a number of prohibitions and warnings: First against judging others, or exacting from them according to a standard of morality which I myself fall immeasurably short of—lest I come under the remonstrance—" What hast thou to do to declare my statutes, or that thou shouldest take my covenant in thy mouth?" But first, O Lord, create in me a clean heart and a right spirit, that then I may teach transgressors Thy way, and sinners be converted unto Thee. And, O God, may I be clothed with humility—doing all for Thy and not for my glory—preferring others, and willing that they should be more honoured even in the things where I am most emulous and aspiring—in the literary credit which may I no longer idolize. And let me be most careful of laying a stumbling-block in the way of others to salvation; for though I may not with feigned words make merchandise of any, yet is there not such a thing as a prayer and an exhortation which are of uncleanness—a cloak not of covetousness, it may be, in the pecuniary sense of the term, yet of covetousness in a Scriptural and worse sense of it. And, O my God, let mine be a pure and right work of exhortation—having both for its design and its effect the real sanctification of those with whom I labour: and save me from all those factitious distinctions which would lead me to put a stress on arbitrary points, and make a sacrifice of great and undoubted principles. Purge out of me, O God, the whole leaven of the Pharisees— their hypocrisy, their pretended veneration for those great of other days, whose practices and principles we nevertheless fall short of, if we do not resist or trample on them. And above all, O God, let the winning attitude of Christ prevail over me, and soften me into a willing compliance with His gracious overtures. He *would*—it is only I who would not. May I no longer lie open to the charge— "Ye will not come unto me that you may have life." Make me willing, O God, in the day of Thy power. Let me not put forth Christ now, lest I lose my part and interest in Him for ever. O may I listen forthwith to the voice that speaketh to me from heaven—for He will at length come again, but in' wrath—the wrath of the Lamb—to those who have despised and rejected Him; and charged with blessing only to those who put their trust in Him. I would therefore flee this instant to hide me under the ample canopy of His mediatorship.

MATTHEW XXIV.

This is not our continuing city ; and in the prospect of those changes which are coming upon the earth, let me sit loose to things present, and live as if the end were at hand—looking more at the history of our times in the light of prophecy, and above all solemnized by the prospect of great and approaching dissolutions into the reflection—what manner of men ought we to be in all holy conversation and godliness ! Let me abide by what the Scriptures testify of Christ. Keep me steadfast, O God, in my adherence to the law and the testimony; let me not be carried about by every wind of doctrine ; and in the present reeling of all sorts of opinions, let me remember that it is Thy word alone which shall never pass away. Save me from spiritual declension, O God. O recover me from that hebetude of conscience and discernment which has been brought on me, as I fear, by my backslidings and my sins. Recover me from these, O God, nor let my zeal and my affection wax cold in the midst of an infidel generation. Give me to hold fast by the faith, and let me not deviate from that truth which is unchangeable. Let not the world have a hold of me ; but may I watch, and be at all times in readiness, whether for the dissolution of the present system, or for my own dissolution and final departure from it. Let me work while it is day ; and more especially, O God, let me be faithful in the charge of those souls which Thou hast committed to me. O that I had the wisdom of winning them to Christ ; and of bringing all who are near and dear to me within the fold of His mediatorship. Impress me, Almighty Father, with a seriousness of purpose and principle more adequate to the solemn importance of the things set before me in this discourse of the Saviour; and grant, O Lord, that from this time forward I may prepare both myself and my family for the futurity which awaits us. Let me not count on the delay of my death, or on any delay in the coming of the Lord, but let me be up and doing: and, O Lord, let me henceforth do all to Thy glory, and all in the name of Jesus. I should mark it well, that the servant who was cast out of the kingdom met with this destination, for deserting his duty and abandoning himself to the pleasures of self-indulgence. The specification here of eating and drinking points strongly to the obligation of temperance; and it is my earnest prayer, O God, that I may be enabled to keep this vile body under subjection; lest I should become a castaway. Through Thy Spirit may I mortify the deeds of the body and live.

MATTHEW XXV.

Let me be in readiness for the coming of the Lord. Let me not be satisfied with the empty husks of a mere external service, with but the letter and the framework of ordinances. I pray for the preparation of the inner man—for the spirit in my heart to sustain the faith and the faithfulness of a true disciple. Every man shall bear his own burden; nor will the righteousness of others, even of our dearest and nearest relatives, avail us on that day. O that the uncertainty of the time of our final summons would put us on the constant outlook, and in the attitude of leaning upon Christ—abiding in Him, that He may abide in us, and cause us ever to abound in much fruit. These are searching lessons—for it is not criminality or commission which are denounced, but only indolence or omission, wherewith conscience is generally so much at ease. It is the sleep of the virgins, it is the sloth of the unprofitable servant, which are severally reckoned with in these parables. True, he was called wicked as well as slothful ; but this should alarm us the more for the delinquency, not of positive offences, but of neglected opportunities of usefulness and mere inaction in the service of Christ. I have much very much wherewith to reproach myself. Under the impulse of a constitutional delight in activity I may have done something—but how little on the principle of glory to God, He alone knoweth. Blot out, O Lord, the fearful account of debt and deficiency which Thou hast against me. Enable me to consecrate all I have, and all I am able for to Thy service here—that I may be prepared for the high services of eternity hereafter. Spiritualize the aim of all my doings—whether for the press, or the class-room, or for the Christian good of my family and friends. It is the ambiguity of my motives which I am most afraid of—the mixture of self and of vanity, even in the seemliest of my performances—the love of ease and of indulgence—and the want of singleness, or of a single-minded devotion to the will of Christ and the welfare of human souls. Cleanse Thou me from secret faults ; and grant that henceforward I may live unto Him who died and who rose again. Thus, O God, may the powers and the opportunities which I do have be so improved, that these may come to be more largely conferred upon me, whether in the present or in a future state of existence ; and thus may I escape the doom of those who, by neglecting the required exercise of their gifts, incur the sentence of all being taken utterly away from them. Save me, O God, from the delusion, that by a negation of the good and the useful in my life, I shall only fall short of a reward. It was not the daringly rebellious, but simply the unprofitable servant who was cast into outer darkness —the place of weeping and gnashing of teeth. What a solemn representation here of the great day of account! what a call to be up and doing! what a sacred import- ance is here given to the Christian virtue of benevolence! I have sometimes felt relieved by the question of the righteous to their Judge, as implying an unconsciousness of what they had nevertheless done and were rewarded for. I am very unconscious of aught which can give me a part in their reward. O my God, work in me that I may so work as to receive the approbation of my Judge on that day. Let me do good unto all men, specially to the house- hold of faith—to those whom Christ calls His brethren, that done for them He may sustain it as done unto Him- self. Mark the dread sentence which follows, and that too not on crimes but on negations—not on evil-doing but on the want of well-doing—in accordance with the parables of this chapter. Seal home its instructions on my con- science, O God; and while I rejoice in being justified by faith, let me forget not that I am judged by works.

MATTHEW XXVI.

How unfaltering the determination of the Saviour in His enterprise for the salvation of men, with the pro- spect of treachery and crucifixion before Him. Let us not be deterred by consequences from aught that is for the good, O Lord, of Thy Church upon earth.

Let not the devices and doings of our enemies, even

though men in high places, cause us to shrink or give way in the hour of trial.

And let us pour forth of our liberality for the support of our Master's cause and honour in the world—suffering no pretexts, not even the plausibilities of a seeming and common-place philanthropy, to divert our means from this best and greatest of objects ; and in the prosecution of which it will be found that the most devoted piety and the truest philanthropy are at one.

Friends may prove deceitful and traitorous in this contest for the empire of righteousness—a cruel suffering no doubt, but the servant must not expect that he shall escape the lot of Him who, the Captain of our salvation, had to endure the desertion as well as the contradiction of sinners, and through these sufferings was made perfect.

Let us not be self-confident. The disciples of our Saviour were not so sure of their own integrity as to feel absolutely certain that they would never give way, and even so far as to incur the enormity of betraying the best of masters and friends ; and each put the question— " Lord, is it I ?" I would examine myself, I would seek the necessary grace from the Saviour, and pray that He would defend me from all temptation. Peter, perhaps, could not have betrayed Christ ; but his fortitude failed, and he denied Him. Let us not be high-minded but fear. O that my soul were fed with that precious bread of life —the doctrine of the blessed atonement, by faith in which it is that I eat the flesh and drink the blood of the Son of God, and so have eternal life.

Let me behold in these deep and mysterious agonies of the garden, the sufficiency of that expiation which has been made for sin, and the gratitude I owe to Him who

endured them.   Blessed Saviour, let me live to Thee who
thus took upon Thyself the punishment that I should have
borne ; nor let me receive this grace in vain, but perfect that which concerns me, and grant that in me Thou
mayest behold of the travail of Thy soul and be satisfied.
Give me to follow Thee in all things, and more especially
in my sacred observation of those Scriptures for the fulfilment of which Thou gavest Thyself up unto the persecutors, and suffered Thyself to be led as a lamb to the
slaughter.   Thou, most indulgent of masters, knowest our
infirmities, and when the spirit is willing, hast a kind and
pitying consideration for the infirmities of the flesh.   So
help then, O our strength and sanctifier, that we may be
fit for standing before Thee in the great day, when Thou
revisitest our earth—coming in the clouds of heaven.

O my God, I have much to deplore, and for which I might
weep bitterly.   Grant me the godly sorrow that worketh
repentance unto salvation never to be repented of.

MATTHEW XXVII.

April, 1842.

If ever called before governors for Christ's cause, then,
however deadly their intent, let me look steadfastly at
Him who has said—that as to the Master so will they
do to the servant.

Let me never betray that cause.   Nothing short of unqualified Erastianism will please our rulers.   If I stop
short of that, and repent of the concessions I may have
made, they would glory in the destruction I had brought
upon my character—while to the uttermost they would
avail themselves of all that I had surrendered into their
hands.   I pray for guidance and firmness, O Lord.

I would not idolize the multitude. I am jealous of aught like the democratic affection in the present contendings of our Church. My deference to the popular voice is grounded on the adaptation of Christianity to the popular conscience ; by which I mean the consciences of those who, after examination of character and knowledge, have been admitted to partake of sacraments. A conscientious ministry by whom the body of communicants are formed, and communicants so formed, by whom the ministry are chosen, would, with the blessing of God, act and react most beneficially on each other. But elevating our regards from the question of the Church's headship to Him who is its exalted head, what a solemn interest should be felt in the passage which records His crucifixion, or the decease that was accomplished in Jerusalem. Blessed Saviour, let me drink in the whole spirit which ought to flow from this narrative into the souls of believers ; and as we contemplate Thee, led like a lamb unto the slaughter, stricken for our iniquities, and pouring out Thy soul unto the death for us, O may our hearts respond in faith and gratitude to this great manifestation, and with the feeling that we are not our own, but bought with a price, even the costly price of Thine own precious and peace-speaking blood, may we give up ourselves unto Thee—to be ruled in by Thy Spirit, to be ruled over by Thy law. What portents followed on the death of Him who was truly the Son of God !

He made His grave with the rich. Let more of my wealth be given to the honour of the Saviour, and advancement of His kingdom.

As we view Him in the prison-house of the grave, may we know what it is to be conformed unto His death, and die unto the world along with Him.

MATTHEW XXVIII.

Let the heart of every man rejoice who seeks the Lord. The angel bade the women not to be afraid with the fear of terror as the keepers were, for unlike to them, they were seeking Jesus Christ and Him crucified. Give me, O Lord, so to seek Him that I may find Him, and then like the women shall I have great joy, along not with the fear of terror, but that of holy reverence and awe. Jesus Himself told them not to be afraid. O my God, support me not against the fears of guilt only, but against the carefulness which is so apt to prey upon me. From the place to which Thou, God the Son, art now exalted, send succour to my soul. I speak now of my sinful anxieties, for these are what I chiefly feel; and they may well convince me that my strength is small.

Let me be prepared for any measure of untruth and active hostility at the hands of those who love not the Saviour. Let me not think that any strange thing has happened to me.—My God, strengthen me with strength in my soul.

All power is given unto Christ in heaven and in earth. O may a portion of that power rest upon me. Save me, O Christ, from vain and disquieting thoughts, from the fear of worldly losses, and the broodings of apprehended injustice and provocation. Carry my mind off from myself, to the great and high contemplation of Christ and His kingdom, and the duty of seeking for its establishment both over myself and others. O how much I lack of doing all things whatsoever that Christ hath commanded. O God, help me; O Christ, be with me, even as Thou hast promised to be with Thy people to the end of the world. May I have a part and an interest in this gracious promise, so as to experience that while without Thee I can do nothing, with Thee I can do all things.

MARK.

MARK I.—Prepare, O Lord, the ground of my heart for the reception of the good seed—even the word of Thy blessed gospel. Give me to repent in the faith of Christ, that I may obtain the remission of my sins, and the baptism of the Holy Ghost. Let me not be satisfied with a mere outward purification, but do Thou purify my heart by faith—create the clean heart, renew the right spirit.

Thou, O God, art well-pleased with what Thy well-beloved Son has done for our salvation. May we be alike well-pleased with what He has done, and lay our confident hold on the everlasting life which He has brought in, that Thou mayest also be well-pleased with us for His sake. And O that the Spirit may descend upon us and strengthen us for every trial—enabling us to resist the wiles of the adversary, and to stand our ground against the violence of ungodly men—helped and strengthened, if need be, by those angels whose office it is to minister unto the heirs of salvation.

And, blessed Jesus, I would leave all to follow Thee. Make me a skilful fisher of men, and wise to win souls—specially the souls of those of my own household. Let me give time and thought to this work, even though it should trench on my ordinary occupations. Let me rightly divide this matter, O God; and labour with all prayerfulness and endeavour, till Christ be formed in them.

Let not vain imaginations, O Lord, lodge within me; and turn not only my sight and mine eyes from those objects, but my inmost thoughts from those conceptions, which stir up the lusts that war against the soul.—Heal me, Thou physician of souls; bid me arise and walk, and let that walk be in the way of Thy commandments. May I henceforth be Thy ministering servant; and let the life redeemed by Thy sacrifice be consecrated to the doing of Thy will. What willest Thou me, O Lord, to do? But what a sanction, or rather what an obligation does our Saviour's example imply—that we should pray as well as do. Let us be followers of Him who retired from the crowd into a solitary place, that after the work and labour of beneficence, He might pray; and thence went forth again on fresh scenes of activity, that after prayer He might go from town to town, preaching in their synagogues throughout all Galilee.

Lord Jesus Christ, Thou art as willing as Thou art able —Thou wilt as well as canst make me clean. O compassionate me, and heal the foul diseases of this tainted spirit; and give me to be holy even as Thyself art holy.

MARK II.

Thou God manifest in the flesh, and so the Son of man as well as the Son of God, blessed be Thy name. Thou hast not only the power but the perfect willingness to forgive sin. None, we admit, can forgive sins but God only; but Thou art God, and we desire to build our security on this contemplation, and herein to rejoice in the abundance of our peace—seeing that to meet the justice of a Divine lawgiver, there has been provided for our defence the atonement of a Divine Saviour. Give me an interest, O God, in that redemption which is through the blood of Christ—even the forgiveness of sins.

Ever blessed be Thy name that this forgiveness is offered, and with all freeness and condescension to the chief of sinners. Only let me not forget, that they who are thus forgiven, also follow Thee, and follow Thee whithersoever Thou goest; follow Thee in sufferings and self-denial, and give themselves wholly up unto Christ—to be ruled in by His Spirit, to be ruled over by His law. And not till the Spirit is put into us, and we are made new creatures, can we be moulded into a conformity with the will and example of the Saviour. The operation of grace must take effect on us ere we are made fit and willing subjects for the regimen of grace. Make the tree good, O Lord, that the fruits be good—lest the observances of Christianity, laid on the old and yet unchristianized man, should stir up the impatience and revolt of nature, and we be led prematurely to reject a discipline so incongruous with all the habits and dispositions of native and unregenerate humanity. I would therefore, O God, begin aright, and begin at the beginning with my children. I would pray for their conversion ere I overlaid them with those injunctions, in which a genuine convert alone can acquiesce. Make me wise, O God, and them willing in the day of Thy power—a day of merciful visitation to us both.

Though man was not made for the Sabbath, let not the Sabbath, therefore, fall in my reverence and estimation, but recollect that the Sabbath was made for man; and let me avail myself diligently of all its blessed services to my growth in grace and advancement both in the faith and holiness of the gospel. O give me not a sentimental but a real spiritual love for the quietness and for all the sacred opportunities of that hallowed day. Let me never forget its place in the decalogue, and how there it is shrined and set among the immutabilities of truth, and piety, and justice—these eternal and irrevocable duties of the moral law. May Thy Sabbath be my delight ; and, in virtue of its preparations and exercises, may every week find me in greater meetness than before, both for the joys and the services of that Sabbath which never ends.

MARK III.

May, 1842.

I am utterly without the power of obedience, O God, but let me not on that account withhold the effort ; let me be ever trying that in the very endeavour strength may be given to me. Neither, although thus a fellow-worker with God, let me presumptuously share with Him the honour of my salvation. He works to will as well as to do : He inspires the effort as well as strengthens for the execution. Therefore, Heavenly Father, to Thee be all the glory—Thou beginnest the good work. Carry it onward to perfection ; turn me and I shall be turned. And yet let me not forget that Thy grace worketh in me, not as in a passive and lifeless machine, but as in a purposing, willing, ever-doing creature ; and in this capacity let me know that I cannot begin too early the participation which belongs to me in the great work of my christianization. More especially it is of importance that, like the man with the withered hand, I should put forth the *conatus,* even though I should yet be without strength. And who knows but that the strength has been already given, would I only set it in exercise ? Let me, therefore, in the language of Paul to Timothy, stir up the gift that is in me ; let all that is in me, be it great or little, be stirred up to bless His holy name, and obey His holy will.

Give me, O Lord, to be impressed as I ought by the terrors of Thy law, when I listen to the demonstrations of those who are sons of thunder. Give me, also, to feel a secure refuge from these in the faith of Thy gospel, as expounded by those who are sons of consolation. The Church stands in need of the services both of her Boanergeses and her Barnabases.

And let me not be ashamed of singularity in the profession of this gospel, even though I should incur the charge of madness thereby. O save me from the hardihood of those who would thus belie even their own convictions of the truth, and cast such imputations on that system of doctrine which bears at least a creditable aspect in the eyes of the just, and the righteous, and the good. Let me feel that in so doing, I should bar the avenue to my heart of the only doctrine which by any possibility can save me, and alienate for ever that Spirit whose function it is to take of the things of Christ, and show them unto my soul, or give me that knowledge of Him which is life everlasting.

And let me remember that the great end and object, the *terminus ad quem* of the Christian doctrine, is not that I should believe as a Christian, but that I should do as a Christian ; the one is the stepping-stone to the other. If justified by faith, I am also judged by works. And let me therefore prove my affinity to Christ by doing the will of His Father and my Father, of His God and my God.

MARK IV.

Let me repeat my own special place and designation

in the parable of the sower. The ground of my heart is overspread with thorns; and it is well that for the overthrow of that monopoly which they have hitherto held over my affections, I should make the encroachment I have recently done on their former monopoly of my time. Enable me, O God, to persevere with at least half an hour of devotional exercise and meditation every day after my siesta, and may the effect be to loosen and unfix the thorns, and to eject them from the chamber of my inmost and deepest affections, and to make room there for the establishment and growth of the good seed of the word of God.   And O save me from the imposition of mere words, which present me with but the types of thought, and on looking to which, I may deceive myself with but the semblance of looking at the realities.   Forbid, Lord, my seeing only thus, so as not to perceive, and my hearing only thus, so as not to understand.   May I force my mind into an actual converse with the *ipsa corpora* of faith, that mine may be a substantial converse with the things of heaven—an actual stirring up of all that is in me to lay hold of God.   Cause me to take heed, and so to hear, that more shall be given to me.   And, O Lord, in Thine own good though unseen and mysterious way, do Thou carry on the good work of spiritual vegetation in my soul—that like unto a well-watered garden, it may be made to abound in all the fair and pleasant fruits of righteousness; and may this, the produce of Thine own spiritual husbandry, overspread the whole of my character and history—so that there shall be no place for the thorns which choke and stifle and overbear the sanctifying influences of God's truth upon the soul.

O my God, shut me up by the terrors of Thy law to the

faith of Thy Gospel. Let me never give way to the imagination that Christ careth not though I should perish.
May I understand Him differently, and so understand
Him truly. May I never forget the object for which He
came into the world, and on the fulfilment of which therefore His heart must be set—not to condemn but to save.
In Thee, O Lord Jesus, may I have peace. Do Thou hush
every wild tempest within me into a calm—be it the tempest of fear, or the tempest of wild and disorderly passions.
May I be without fearfulness, and so work the blessed assurance of the gospel in my heart, that in quietness and
confidence I may have strength.

MARK V.

O my God, dispossess this spirit of uncleanness within
me, and not this spirit only, but a legion of unholy
affections and lusts which war against the soul. May
I not only be clothed in the righteousness of Christ, but
restored to a right mind, by the emancipation thereof
from the tyranny of the flesh ; and enable me to speak of
this emancipation to others—of that great thing done for
me, in that, the law of the spirit of life in Christ Jesus
hath made me free from the law of sin and of death.

O my God, give me an earnest and heartfelt desire for
the spiritual health of my children—for their recovery
from the state of death in trespasses and sins. Assist
me, O God, in my endeavours to awaken and guide them
in the way everlasting. Bless my humble exertions in
this work, O God ; sustain me under them. Let me not
be discouraged. Lay Thy correcting and sanctifying influences on one and all of my family, that they may be

healed and live. I would pray in faith for the salvation of their souls, and say to me their father, as Thou didst to the ruler of the synagogue—" Be not afraid, only believe." But faith availeth not for the salvation of others only in whose behalf we intercede, but for our own salvation when we ask it for ourselves. Lord, I have tried many expedients and found the worthlessness of them all. Who will show me any good? Lord, lift upon me the light of Thy countenance. May the great Physician of souls lay His hand upon me; and let me not wait for those brighter and more intimate manifestations, which, however desirable in themselves, are not essential to peace. In my attempts to stir myself up that I may lay hold of Christ, give me at least to have confidence in the efficacy of His name—however dim and distant my conceptions of His person may be. Give me to touch the hem of His garment; and let me hear the joyful utterance—"Thy faith hath made thee whole; go in peace." Let me experience now the peace and joy of believing; and in Thine own good time conduct me to the higher experiences of the Christian life. Meanwhile, let me be whole of my plague —let my heart be stablished with grace. May my soul prosper and be in health. O that the kingdom of God came to me not in word only but in power—even that kingdom which consisteth of righteousness and peace and joy in the Holy Ghost.

MARK VI.

Let me prefer above all other knowledge the knowledge of Jesus Christ and of Him crucified. I would glory in His cross; I would honour the Son even as I honour the

Father. May His name be at all times to me as ointment poured forth; and believing in Christ, let me feel
Him to be precious.

Let me be without carefulness. Prepare, O God, Thy
servants in the ministry for whatever may befall them.
If pleased to sever them from the endowments of a National Church, may they go forth, doing faithfully Thy
work, and with unbounded trust in Thy Providence.
I again pray, O Lord, for the General Assembly of the
Church of Scotland, and that Thou wouldst pour on her
counsellors the wisdom which is from above. Bring their
deliberations to a happy issue; and may there be truth and
peace, and righteousness in this our day. Thou tellest, in
the history before us, of the antipathies which subsist between the Church and the world. We desire to resist
such an unholy alliance between the civil and the ecclesiastical as might subordinate the affairs of Thy kingdom, O
God, to the dictates of the secular power, and so cause the
sanctuary of Thy Church to be trodden under foot of the
Gentiles. Rather than not lift our protestations against
such a violence, may we be prepared to suffer all; and
while we pray for the reign of an ascendant and pervading charity in the counsels of our Assembly, grant, O
Lord, that they may quit themselves like men and be
strong. In compassion for the souls of the assembled
multitude did our Saviour teach them many things—in
compassion for their bodily sufferings, under the agonies
of hunger, did He bring down food from heaven by miracle,
that they might all eat and be filled. May the same spirit
be in me which was also in Christ Jesus—let me have an
eye for pity, and a hand open as day for melting charity.
But let me consider the poor (Psalms xli. 1) as well as

compassionate—of which consideration our Saviour gave forth an evidence so striking, in that He limited the number of miracles for bringing down food, while we read of no limitation in the exercise of His miraculous power in bringing down health to the diseased who met Him on His way. But what I chiefly stand in need of for the imitation of my Saviour's example, is the habit of prayer. May God cause this habit to grow on me apace; let me mix supplications with services, that I may strive mightily according to Thy grace working in me mightily; let me be of good cheer, and not be afraid as I think of my Saviour; let me take courage in the thought that it is He, and that He will be true to Himself, and that He will not deny His own meekness and gentleness and truth, and that He will be faithful in the observance of all His promises. I pray for grace to help me in every time of need. Compose the turbulence within me of those passions which war against the soul. Humble me, O God, under a sense of my infirmities; but lift me up in due time—and, as it became a calm while He made Himself known to His disciples, so may I become acquainted with my Creator, even God in Christ, and be at peace. I may not be admitted to a lively manifestation of the Saviour—approaching to that which the disciples had when they saw him with the eye of their senses; yet, in the distance and dimness of my conceptions, let me but believe, let me but touch the border of His garment, and I shall be made whole.

MARK VII.

Give me, O Lord, an unqualified reverence and regard

for Thy word. May I bring every thought of my heart to the captivity of its obedience—calling no man master but Christ only. Save me from the influence of human authority, or the fear of man which is a snare; and save me also from a vain confidence in the externals of religion. May I worship Thee who art a Spirit in spirit and in truth. Give me to render unto Thee the homage which is due to my Father in heaven.

Purge me, O God, from the secret and unseen faults of the inner man. Deliver me from the lusts that war against the soul; and, O deliver me from the vanity of distinction above my fellows. May I have a single eye to Thy glory, and not to any applause or distinction for myself, in all that I do for the service of the Church. Forgive the delinquencies of spirit into which I have fallen ; and let me henceforth discard all reference to myself when labouring for the defence of our Church against the machinations of her adversaries.

Give me, O Lord, the humble faith which so pleased the Saviour, and drew out from Him a miracle of mercy. Let me be poor in spirit, that in me the saying might be realized—of mine being the kingdom of heaven.

May God open my mouth so that I may with all courage and fidelity testify for Christ. Forbid that I should deny Him by my silence. Give me so to believe as that I shall speak, and fill my heart so with good things as that they shall overflow in conversation ; for out of the abundance of the heart the mouth speaketh. And, O my God, cause the spiritually deaf to hear, as well as the dumb to speak. Enable me to speak wisely and in season ; and may others, more particularly those of my own household, hear unto the salvation of their souls.

MARK VIII.

June, 1842.

Why should we any longer stand in distrust of the compassionate Saviour? Take pity, O blessed Jesus, on my spiritual necessities. Out of Thine own exhaustless fulness do Thou feed my soul with that which is convenient for it; and grant that I may so hunger and thirst after righteousness as at length to be filled.—Let me copy the graces of Thy example, Thy benevolence to men, Thy grateful piety to the Giver of all our blessings.

On one side of our Church there is danger of hypocrisy —the leaven of the Pharisees; on the other side of it there is danger of Erastianism—the leaven of Herod. Preserve me from both, O God. I am intimate with neither of the parties. I am conversant more with principles than persons. I begin to suspect that the intensity of my own separate pursuit has isolated me from living men; and there is a want of that amalgamation about me which cements the companionships and closer brotherhoods that obtain in society.

Restore to me my spiritual vision, O God, either instantly or gradually, as best pleaseth Thee. Work upon me this miracle of grace. I deeply feel that I cannot enlighten myself; and in the sense of my own native helplessness, I would look up to that creative power which commanded at the first light out of darkness, and which must still be put forth ere man can behold the glory of God in the face of Jesus Christ.

And let the knowledge of Christ and of Him crucified be prized by me, as by the Apostle of old, as above all other knowledge.

And let me count the cost. Let me willingly be con-

formed to Christ in His sufferings—prepared to suffer all
if such be the will of God, at whatever expense, however
sore to nature—thus savouring the things that be of God
and not of men. Save me from the adversary, who through
the medium of friends and relatives may try to seduce me
by the bland and winning suggestions of this world's ease
and this world's sufficiency.

And so in the face of every danger must we hold fast
our Christian integrity; for what is the worth of a whole
world to the worth of one's soul? And help me, O God,
against the influence of shame as well as of terror. Let
me testify for Christ, and that by words as well as works.
Why blush or be in difficulty at the utterance of His name!
Save me, O Lord, from spiritual cowardice; and let me be
instant in season and out of season for Christ and for
His cause.

MARK IX.

There is a kingdom of God anterior to that the full
establishment of which is in another state. May Thy
kingdom, O Lord, be set up within me. I pray for the
reign of God in my heart, for the light of God in my
soul. O take to Thyself Thy great power and have the
rule over me.

One of those admitted to the glorious manifestation of
the transformed Saviour tells us, that even surer and more
satisfying than such a view of Him is the sure word of
prophecy. When descending from the mount of ordinances, O let this word be a light unto my feet, and a lamp
unto my paths. Let me at least hear the voice of Thy
beloved Son, if I as yet see not His person. Let me be
effectually taught by Him now, that I may behold Him

afterwards. Let me do what He bids, and He will yet shew me greater things than these.

There was a need be for the sufferings of Christ. It behoved Him, and must have been so. Let me be armed, O Lord, with a like mind; and O give me wisdom and patience for all which Thou hast prepared for me. Let me be in readiness to do all, and to suffer all, though, if it be Thy blessed will, O God, an old age of peace and piety were a most delightful termination of my life in this world.

What pregnant sayings are given to us in the narrative of the man who had a deaf and dumb spirit. All things are possible to him who believeth; and, as the event showed, an answer was given to the prayer of faith, even in its embryo and doubtful state—so doubtful that the man while he possessed his belief, as if not sure of its reality, prayed that the Lord would help his unbelief. There is a two-fold instruction in this passage—first, to private Christians who long to be healed of their spiritual diseases; secondly, to ministers whose office it is to eject spiritual diseases from the souls of their people. Faith is indispensable to both; but it was to His disciples who attempted, but failed, to cast out the dumb spirit, that He said—This kind cometh out only by prayer and fasting. What a call to prayer on the part of ministers for the success of their work; and, besides, there is no indistinct testimony in favour of fasting, for adding to the strength and vivacity of our faith, and so to the efficacy of our prayers.

There is a marvellous slowness and obtuseness of intellect in the Apostles of our Lord, regarding the things of His kingdom, and which was dissipated not by reasoning but by the light of a simple manifestation. Have pity on my spiritual blindness, O God; open the eyes of my understanding, and give me more especially, a vivid and realizing and practical discernment of the objects of faith.

And, O God, save me from the ambition not of excelling others, but of preferment to a higher place than they in the estimation of my fellows. Mortify me to all sense and desire of personal distinction; but may I have a single eye to usefulness, to the advancement of Thy kingdom, and the glory of Thy name.

Instead of emulation, let us have peace one with another; and what an incentive to a Catholic spirit is here given by the Saviour, who bids us own a brotherhood with such as give evidence of their having something more than the name, the power and spirit of Christianity, even though they agree not with us in everything. Let me do everything to conciliate men in favour of Christianity, and nothing to scandalize men against it.

MARK X.

Our Saviour was apt to teach. So ought I, and enable me, O God, to do in more private and limited spheres what I am not so able to do now in the large and open congregation. O forgive the sins of my holy things; and blot out all the guilt I have ever contracted, by preaching myself instead of Jesus Christ my Lord.

Let me take a particular note of all those lessons which our Saviour delivers on the subject of purity. He did not lightly estimate the guilt of a transgression against this law, as I am apt to do. Quicken my moral obtuseness, O Lord, in this department of human ethics; and even should I not strongly and sensibly feel the evil of violations therein, let me resolutely keep myself from them in compliance with the authority of my Saviour.

Give me, O Lord, to feel the tenderness for the young which our Saviour manifested—and O let it be a moral tenderness. May I feel a sacred respect for the delicacies of the yet unpractised young; and above all let me have a strong sense of the worth of their imperishable souls— and grant that the magnitude of this high interest might effectually supplant and overbear all that is light or wayward within me.

There is none good but God. Yet good art Thou, O Divine Saviour—for Thou art God, God manifest in the flesh. Enable me to forsake all in following after Thee. Let me, in particular, sit loose to this world's possessions —resolved to suffer whatever losses or privations may follow in the train of my adherence to the doctrine and authority of Christ. Save me from the idolatry of wealth, and from all the sinful and degrading anxieties it might otherwise stir up within me. Be Thou at all times the strength of my heart, and at last my everlasting portion.

I feel, O God, that it is an achievement beyond the powers of my nature to conquer my affection for wealth, and my dependence thereupon. Put forth Thine own all-subduing strength upon me; crucify my desires after the things which are beneath; set them on the things which are above—the true riches in heaven—the treasure there, where Christ sitteth at the right hand of God. This were indeed a translation from the walk of sight to the walk of faith.

O that I computed and compared aright between time and eternity—between the light sacrifices here and the

hundred-fold compensations hereafter—between the affliction that is but for a moment, and the far more exceeding
and eternal weight of glory.   Give me to live by the
powers of the world to come ; and let my doings plainly
declare that I seek a country, and am looking forward to
a city which hath foundations, and whose builder and
maker is God.

And in so doing I but imitate the example and follow
in the track of my Saviour before me.   He for the joy on
the other side of death submitted to every endurance.
So be it with myself, O God.   Let me, if called, be in
readiness to give up every earthly good, and every object
of earthly affection, for the furtherance of the gospel and
its blessed designs in the world.   O that I were free of all
sinful emulations.   Let the ambition of superiority over
others be mortified within me.   Let me consider how the
Saviour humbled Himself, and how He came into the
world, not to be served but to be Himself the servant ;
and also the Saviour who gave up His life a ransom for me.
Let me seek not mine own glory or the gratification of
mine own selfishness, but the profit of many that they
might be saved.

Like blind Bartimeus I would persevere in supplicating
that my eyes should be opened—even till He who commanded the light to shine out of darkness should shine
in my heart, and give me the light of the knowledge
of His own glory in the face of His Son.   Give me to
urge this suit, O Lord, believingly, that the blessed answer may at last come, Thy faith hath made thee whole ;
and the way of life being made patent and discernible before me, I might go that way rejoicingly, with Thy word
as my guide—a light unto my feet, a lamp unto my path.

MARK XI.

This presents us with another exemplification of a providence in minute things. It is a lesson wherewith I should like to be charged.—My God, enable me thus to incorporate, or rather to animate, the sensible with the spiritual. May I see Thy regulating hand in every passing and every present object; and may I ever be ready to interpret aright Thy providence by a fit application of Thy precepts to all the events and circumstances of my history. Let me not forget that they who welcomed Christ with their hosannas, in a few days called out—crucify Him. Let me not build any confidence whatever on popularity, but through evil report and good report, may I be enabled to prosecute the even and upright tenor of my way. Meanwhile, let me not by the fear of those in authority be restrained from asserting the strictly spiritual character of the house of God. Let me render all the feeble assistance I can to the object of warding off the contaminations of secularity or earthly power from the administration of our affairs; and guide me, O Lord, aright between the corrupt influence of rulers on the one hand, and the often no less corrupting influence of the multitude on the other. That is a truly important and delightful interlude which we have on the subject of the fig-tree, and the lesson founded thereupon of faith in God. We hence learn the might and efficacy of an undeviating confidence in the act of supplicating God. O increase my faith, and perfect that which is lacking in it. Let me not doubt in my heart that what I pray for shall come to pass; but let me understand that faith is possible only in the light of evidence—just as vision is possible only in the element of material light. Blessed be Thy name, O God, for the clear evidence Thou hast poured on the best and most precious interests of our being, as the legitimate objects of faith, and therefore the subjects of hope, nay, of altogether confident prayer. In this confidence do I pray for a clear knowledge of the truth—for a full accomplishment of the great end of faith, even the salvation of my soul—for the salvation of others also, and more especially of my wife and children, and all my relatives. These are things agreeable to the will of God; and therefore things that might be asked till we receive them, that might be sought after till we find them. Remove, O God, and cast away from my heart the mountain of my ungodliness. Pluck this rooted carnality from my bosom. Translate me from the life of sense to the life of faith, that I may die unto the world, and be alive unto Him who made the world. As a proof of the necessary limitation to our faith in the asking of whatever things we may desire—if we desire to be forgiven and yet forgive not others, the prayer for forgiveness will not be granted. It is well that the limitation should lie so contiguous to the privilege here held out. The consciousness that we have not forgiven others, would, in virtue of this qualification, effectually repress our faith, when supplicating our own forgiveness from God. We are called on to have faith in praying; but we are also called on to forgive in praying. Along then with the consciousness that we forgive not, the faith is impossible; and so the twenty-third is harmonized with the twenty-sixth verse. God will forgive if we ask it in faith; yet if we do not forgive others their trespasses, neither will our Father in Heaven forgive us ours.

Our Saviour has left us an example of wisdom in dealing with men. It was not convenient or fit at this time that He should give an absolute response to the question which the scribes and elders put to Him. He replied therefore to their question by another, and by such a question as involved them in a dilemma.—Enable me, O God, to combine the wisdom of the serpent with the harmlessness of the dove; and let me understand the right application of the precept—to beware of men.

MARK XII.

July, 1842.

This a national parable, yet bears a personal application. Let me learn from it to reverence the Son of God—to honour the Son even as I honour the Father. And O that I knew what it was even to honour the Father aright—to glorify Him as God, and make His will the supreme rule of my life and conduct. Let me not incur the guilt of crucifying Him afresh by my apostasy from Him and from His ways, lest I should share in the guilt of those Jews who nailed Him to the accursed tree. Let me also learn the importance of abounding in those fruits which God requires at our hands, and by which He is glorified.—There is much in the New Testament on our duty as citizens and subjects, or on what we owe to the rulers whom Providence hath set over us—to the powers that be. My God, enable me rightly to divide the word of truth in this matter, and to partition as I ought between God and Cæsar. "Tribute to whom tribute" on the one hand; yet "we ought to obey God rather than man" on the other. How admirable is the wisdom, we had almost said the dexterity, of our Saviour's answer on this subject. Give me, O Lord, to acquit myself with the wisdom of the serpent as well as the harmlessness of the dove, in such controversies as those to which I am now called. What a blessed thing were a realizing sense of immortality! How destitute we are even of this faith, though it be faith in but an article of Natural Theology. Little do we know how deficient we are even in the first principles of religion. Give me, O Lord, the substance of things hoped for, give me the evidence of things not seen —that I may look beyond the temporal to the eternal, and live by the powers of a world to come. What a support and a cordial, amid the vexations of the life that now is, would be an elevating perspective of the magnificence and the glory and the bliss which, on the other side of the grave, await all who love the Lord Jesus Christ in sincerity! O God of Abraham and Isaac and Jacob, look down on me as on one of Thy wandering children who is seeking for a return to His Father's house, and groping the way to it. Reveal Thy Son to me; and let me henceforth sit at the feet of Him who alone has the words, and who alone has the gift of life everlasting. Convince me of my deficiency from the two great commandments of Thy law; and so convince me that I may deeply feel the need of a Saviour. When once near Him I am not far from Thy kingdom. And O may He do upon me the work of a Sanctifier or Saviour from the power of sin, as well as from the guilt of it. May He put these commandments in my heart, and write them in my mind, that, under the influence of love to Thee and love to my neighbour, I may run with alacrity and delight in the path of the new obedience of the gospel. And thou, O Son of God, who art at once the root and the offspring of David, may I

gladly do Thee homage, and the homage more especially
of my willing imitation. In all lowliness of mind may
I esteem others better than myself. May I be humble as
He was who assumed the form of a servant, and became
of no reputation. O save me from the abominations of
hypocrisy. Let me be a Christian in deed and in truth.

The treasury was for the reception of money devoted to
sacred objects; and one can perceive that for the furtherance of these we may well give all that we have. My
difficulty is in regard to the right disposal of those calls
that are made on our charity from the unknown and the
rapacious, for the supply of their physical appetencies, of
whatever sort; and I earnestly pray for a right and a
wise direction in regard to these. Here (in Ireland) do
we stand peculiarly exposed to this embarrassment; and
I pray that I may be guided safely and well through the
uncertainties of this problem. That God loveth a cheerful giver is incontestable; but I should like to have the
comfort of giving in a way that was productive of real
good to the objects of my almsgiving. This is one of
the most memorable passages in the record left of our
blessed Saviour. Let me be willing to distribute, and
ready to communicate, O Lord.

MARK XIII.

Let me not be deceived, O Lord, by false Christs—by
the mere semblance, whether of the doctrine or the character of my adorable Redeemer. May I learn of Him
at His own mouth, calling no man master, and read assiduously and independently of those Scriptures which testify of Him. Let me not be the slave of human authority,

but clear my way through all creeds and confessions to
Thine own original revelation. Give me that knowledge
of Christ, and of God in Christ, which is life everlasting.
Enlighten me more and more in the doctrine of Him
crucified ; and may I be enabled to take a confident and
intelligent hold of His covenant, and so be firmly and
surely established in the way of His salvation. And prepare me, O God, for the whole of Thy blessed will. If a
period of darkness and disaster is indeed before me, may
I know how to acquit myself in the midst of Thy coming
visitations ;—teach me the way I should go, and to what
I should betake myself. If our Church is indeed to fall
as an Establishment, let her not be forsaken by the light
of Thy countenance; and may the fruit of all her troubles
be righteousness and peace. Let me cherish more confidence than I have hitherto done in the promise of Thy
Holy Spirit, for the ready and right suggestion of what
ought to be said in the hour of controversy or examination. The answer of the mouth, as well as the preparation
of the heart, is from the Lord. O may I receive from
Thee the grace of perseverance. Although abandoned by
the nearest friends and the dearest relatives, let me not
think that any strange thing hath happened unto me.
Give me to walk in mine integrity, combining at the same
time the understanding of the man with the guileless
simplicity of the child ; and let me at last receive, as the
end of my faith and patience, the salvation of my soul.
There are great and portentous changes coming upon the
earth ; and for aught I can see to the contrary, the time
of them draweth nigh. Let me sit loose, therefore, to the
interests and arrangements of a world which, sooner or
later, shall be broken up and pass away. It is he who

doeth the will of God that shall endure for ever. Let me
ever obey, and with all diligence, Thy preceptive will; let
me ever acquiesce, and with all cheerfulness, in Thy providential will. I have been visited with a slight accident,
which confines me, for the time being, from the exercise
that I love. Let even this prove a salutary discipline;
and in all things let me have grace to say, with the full
concurrence of my heart—Thy will be done. And O that
I placed an unfaltering reliance upon Thy words; more
unfaltering and steadfast it ought to be than even on the
constancy of nature, which passeth away—whereas the
word of the Lord abideth for ever, and shall never pass
away. And let me combine watchfulness with prayer.
What Thou saidst unto Thy disciples Thou sayest unto
all; and let me therefore, as one of these *all,* both appropriate and apply. And O that I felt as I ought my present relation to the risen Saviour, who hath left a work
for His disciples below, and will return to take account
of all their performances. How little have I proceeded
hitherto on the reality of these things. How little have I
borne of respect to Christ as my Judge, or regarded Him
as a master who had put a task into my hands that I was
to execute during His absence, and for which He was to
return and reckon with me afterwards. My God, confer
that upon me which would give me all boldness in looking
forward to the day of judgment. If I had love enthroned
in my heart—the love of Thee and the love of my neighbour—then I should not need to be afraid, for then I
should be like unto God, and so meet for converse with
Him in heaven. It would form what might be termed
a wholesale security against an adverse sentence in the
great day of reckoning; and thus, on this single moral

acquirement, might I stand exempted from all those legal disquietudes which are ever and anon excited on every particular question of duty; and when the spirit of legality, instead of the spirit of love, has the possession and ascendency of the inner man.

MARK XIV.

Let me hear this testimony from the Saviour—that I have done what I could. But I deeply feel that this I have not done. O that I felt a responsibility awakened by the question—what more have I done than others? My God, let me know how to advance the honour and service of my Redeemer upon earth; and knowing this, give me the inclination and the power of doing it.

The treachery of Judas was deliberate; the flight of the other disciples was unpremeditated, and under the sudden impulse of surprise and fear. Peter's denial, too, was the result of a conflict with all his better principles; and much is to be learned from the difference of result between the two histories of him and Judas. My God, as I have eaten of that bread which is the memorial of Christ's body, and drunk of that wine which is the memorial of His blood, and so witnessed a good confession before men, let me maintain the integrity thereof, and save me from the spiritual cowardice of denying my Master in any way—of denying Him even by my silence. O enable me to maintain an upright and consistent testimony for Christ in the world, both in my walk and also in my conversation.

In these deep and mysterious agonies of my Saviour let me see the malignity of that sin for which He suffered;

and the vast, the infinite obligation under which I am laid to love and to serve Him.   O henceforth and for ever may my soul be given up in absolute and entire dedication to Him who thus poured out His soul unto the death for me.   O Lord, may the spirit overcome the flesh —may the willingness of the one prevail over the weakness of the other; so that although I feel the motions of the flesh, I may walk not after them.   May I ever conform myself to that word, in obedience to which Christ gave up His will to the will of His Father, and resigned Himself to the appointed trial, because how else could the Scriptures have been fulfilled? May I see in this passage the supreme and unalterable obligation of that word which God hath exalted above all His name.   And let me resist not evil, but without a murmur suffer myself to be led wherever it is the will of my heavenly Father I should go, for the maintenance of His truth, and the glory of His great name.

Let me not think that the servant is above his master, or that the world which hated and persecuted the one will not hate and persecute the other also.   Let me look unto Christ; and may He be my example in suffering as well as in service.   May the same mind be in me which was also in Him; and, O my God, if ever called to an examination and a public exposure before rulers and spectators, may I not give way to the anxieties against which our Saviour hath both warned and encouraged us—when He bids us not be careful what we should say, for that the Holy Ghost will teach us how to speak as we ought.

And let me profit not from the example of Christ alone, but from the example of Christ's followers—that in the language of Paul I may be a follower of them, even as

they are of Christ. But in their sins these followers stand
forth not as a model, but as a warning. Let me profit by
this too. Peter was not a follower but a forsaker of
Christ in that passage of his history which is recorded
here; and let the perusal of his fall make me to take
heed lest I fall also. O my God, humble me under a sense
of my manifold infirmities, and visit me with a constant
diffidence in myself. Let me avoid the presumptuous
confidence of Peter before his melancholy catastrophe,
and realize the experience of Paul, who when he was
weak then was he strong.

MARK XV.

Thou knowest, O God, if in the further evolutions of the
history of our Church we shall be called before the councils
and governors of this world. The servant is not above his
master; and let me not be careful, but commit myself to
Him who hath promised the suggestions of His Holy
Spirit in every such case of difficulty and trial.—Guide and
purify me in regard to Thy Church, O God.

And let me not think it strange if others be preferred
or spared, and I be made the object of persecution and
obloquy—and that too with the concurrence of the popular voice, after that I have been abandoned by this world's
friendship and general applause. And what a weight of
other endurance besides this was our blessed Lord called
on to sustain in that hour, and under that power of darkness, when to the sufferings of His body were superadded
the deep and mysterious agonies of His soul. O that my
heart were more softened by such a contemplation, and
that I knew what it was to look unto Him whom my sins

have pierced, and to mourn because of them. And let me furthermore glory in the cross of Christ; and taking up my own cross, let me be a follower in all things of Him who was meek and lowly. O that the sacrifice made for sin affected me rightly with a sense of the evil of it; and O keep me from that sinning wilfully, after which there remaineth no more sacrifice. Mayest Thou henceforth open my heart to the constraining influence of the love of Christ, leading me to love Him back again. It is my earnest prayer, O God, that I may be conformed to His death, and be enabled to suffer all for His sake.

Perhaps I should be most alive to the revilings and mockeries of the world; but Christ not only endured the cross, He despised the shame, and is now set down at the right hand of the throne of God. Let me be willing, if He so call me, to partake and to suffer along with Him, so as that from the cross I may be conducted to the crown. But, O my God, do Thou adequately impress me with the self-denials and self-abasements I should be ready to undergo, ere I can look for a preferment so exalted.

May I by faith be enabled to enter within the veil, even through the rent veil of a Saviour's flesh. Give me to have full liberty of access through the Son to the Father. Clothed upon with His righteousness may I stand with all the security of my conscious acceptance before God. O may I delight myself in this abundance of peace, and be enabled to lead others, more especially those of my own household, to delight along with me.

Truly, O my Saviour, Thou art the Son of God—the Son of God and Saviour of the world. But let me not be satisfied with rendering unto Thee the homage of my lips, but of my life and of all within me. Let Thy memory be

embalmed within my heart, and Thy name be ever as ointment poured forth. In that name may I be enabled to do
all things, and so yield unto Christ a constant ministration.

These testimonies to Christ, even from such as were
indifferent to his cause, as Pilate, and Joseph of Arimathea
—of whom at least we do not read as a converted disciple—are specimens of the remaining hold which truth
and goodness have over the consciences of men. God has
not left Himself without a witness, even in the hearts of
worldly men, as well as in the world itself. He provides
as many cordials in the way as are necessary to keep His
own from sinking under their trials.

MARK XVI.

Conform me, O Lord, to the resurrection of my Saviour.
Quicken and raise me from my state of death in trespasses
and sins. Give me to know Christ, and experimentally to
know the power of His resurrection. May I be saved by
His life; because He lives may I live also; and from the
Mediatorial throne to which He is exalted may power go
forth upon me, so as that I might be enabled to yield the
obedience of those who, made alive from the dead, walk
before God in newness of life. Let me not be affrighted
when going forth to seek Jesus of Nazareth—rather let
my heart rejoice to seek the Lord. It is an enterprise
full of hope; for he who seeketh findeth, and they who
find Christ shall find all things. My God, let me take
no rest to my soul till I have found it in the revealed and
offered Saviour. Give me to find this pearl of great price;
and let me be willing to count all things but loss for the
excellency of the knowledge of Jesus Christ, my Lord.

Lord, I believe, help mine unbelief. Rebuke this slowness, and hardness, and hebetude of spirit away from me; manifest Thyself to my soul; open the eyes of my inner man to the perception of Thy reality, and of Thy suitableness as my Saviour. O that I gave earnest heed to the word of Thy testimony, till the day dawned, and the day-star arose in my heart. My eternity hinges upon it. A most momentous alternative is placed before me: "He that believeth shall be saved; he that believeth not shall be damned." Let these statements, and more especially the last of them, shut me up unto the faith. The very threatening evinces how earnest God is for my faith. Let me take Him at His word, since He has given proof so emphatic that He will have it so. He tells me that without faith it is impossible to please Him—nay, that His displeasure will be such as to infer our damnation. If we believe not, the wrath of God abideth on us. Let me ever give in, then, to the truth of God, and be doing homage to His faithfulness—at once glorify Him and tranquillize my own conscience, thus harmonizing goodwill to man with glory to God. And O that I had experimental evidence of the power of faith in subduing my corruptions, and enabling me to resist the devil, and to overcome the evil temptations of an evil and accursed world. O blessed Saviour, I would follow Thee in faith to the place which Thou now occupiest. I would look up to my exalted High Priest, considering Him who is the Apostle of my profession. I desire, O Lord Jesus, to maintain a constant fellowship of Spirit with Thyself; and do Thou put forth upon me the hand of a sanctifier, that I may be as Thou wouldst have me, and do as Thou wouldst have me.

LUKE.

August, 1842.

LUKE I.—What a delightful representation of the Saviour's intercessory office do we behold in the prayers of the people without the temple, while the priest was burning incense within. Let all my requests to God stand associated with the name and the merits of my Saviour; and O may the incense of these merits be added to all my supplications, and so as that effect and acceptance shall be given to them. But let me pray in faith ; and in this punishment of the unbelief of Zacharias let me read the explanation of so many of my prayers having turned out to be unfruitful. My God, in the name of Christ, and for His sake, do I pray for Thy Spirit. And O that my heart were turned to my children, and that I ceased not my prayer and watchfulness till their hearts were turned to the Lord their God.

May Thy Holy Spirit who presided over the incarnation of the Saviour, may He take of the things of Christ and show them unto me, and form Christ within me the hope of glory. It is not by all the energies of nature that this supernatural birth can be accomplished—even that regeneration by which the new creature is made to arise ; and I, through the power of grace from on high, am enabled to walk in newness of heart and of life before God. This too I would ask till I received it, and seek till I found it, and knock till the door of spiritual manifestation were opened, and I were thus translated out of darkness into the marvellous light of the gospel. O may that kingdom of which there is to be no end be set up in my heart, that I may do the will of God, and so endure for ever.

What a contrast between Zacharias and Mary in their

reception of the messages from on high wherewith they were respectively favoured. Give me the faith of Mary, O God—the confidence that with God nothing is impossible; and in this blessed confidence may I never cease to pray and to look for those things which are agreeable to His will—and more especially that I and all my household shall come to the knowledge of the truth and be saved. O cause me to hunger and thirst after righteousness, and then with this good thing cause also that I may be filled.

O let this prayer of Zacharias be accomplished upon me—even that I might serve Thee without the fear of terror, yet in righteousness and holiness all the days of my life. Give me the knowledge of that redemption which is through the blood of Christ, even the forgiveness of sins; and in this redemption may I recognise the tender mercy of God. Let me see the love of the Father in sending His Son into the world to be the propitiation for my sins. Enlighten my darkness, O God; guide my feet in the way of peace; and may I wax strong in the might of Thy Spirit. Do thou, the very God of peace, sanctify me wholly; save me from the evil propensities of an evil and accursed nature; make me like unto Christ; and fulfil the declaration, that because He liveth I shall live also—because He overcame I also shall overcome, and be seated with Him on His throne.

LUKE II.

Let it ever be my rejoicing and my confidence that unto me a Saviour has been born; for this is good tidings of great joy unto all people—and why not to me as one of the people? And the good-will announced from heaven is unto men—why not to me a man? And ever blessed be Thy name, that this peace and good-will meet and are at one with glory to God in the highest. Let me dismiss my fears, even as the shepherds of Bethlehem were asked to dismiss theirs. Let me not be afraid, but only believe—forgetting not, however, that my perpetual work now should be to praise and glorify and serve God.

O let mine eyes see Thy salvation for myself. Thou hast prepared it before the face of all people. Let me as one of the people look unto that which Thou hast set before us, and be lightened thereby—looking unto Him whom Thou hast set forth as a propitiation for the sins of the world. And as a disciple of His let me hold fast my integrity; let me not give way on that day of trial which is coming upon the earth; let me count the cost and be prepared for it, taking fully into consideration that declaration of the Apostle—that all who live godly in Christ Jesus shall suffer persecution.

O may I forget not that as one of the household of faith a business is put into my hands, and let the performance of it be my unceasing care—that Christ may see in me of the travail of His soul and be satisfied; and that I may walk worthy of the Lord unto all well-pleasing. And let me imitate my Saviour in detail, as well as in the general—for without obedience in the detail the generality thereof is but in word and not in power. He who said that He must be about His Father's business is said at the distance of two verses to have been subject to His earthly parents. My parents have long left the world; and, O my God, forgive all the impatience and waywardness of my spirit towards them. And now may I testify

the sincerity of my repentance by yielding reverence unto
all to whom reverence is due.

LUKE III.

May remission and repentance be more intimately
blended with each other, not only in my Theological
system, but in my practical habits and thoughts. Thou
knowest, O God, how much I have been exercised by
the question of that vinculum which binds together the
faith of the gospel, and the repentance of the gospel.
I have felt as if, on that being cleared up, a great barrier
would be moved out of the way of my discipleship in the
school of Christ; and in the intense desirousness of my
heart for a resolution and removal of the obstacle, I have
often adopted that verse of the psalmist as descriptive of
my state—"My soul breaketh for the longing which it
hath to Thy judgments at all times." Loose this bond
effectually, O God, that I may be set free both of legalism
and antinomianism—to both of which I am liable, though
more perhaps to the former. May the crooked be made
straight with me, and the rough way smooth; and on be-
taking myself to the required obedience, for there is an
obedience required at the very outset of Christianity, may
I be made to see the salvation of God. Let not an artificial orthodoxy break or deafen the rudimental and incipient calls which are addressed to a sinner in the very act
of his turning unto God. Let me be instructed on this
by the initial directions of John the Baptist to his inquiring visitors, who asked him not what they should do to be
saved, but what they should do on their way to salvation;
and may the fruit of my doings be to bring down light from

the sanctuary, in rich dispensation from the Holy Ghost,
who is given to those who obey Him.   And what a power
of urgency lies in the consideration—that the axe is laid to
the root of the tree!   Let me tarry no longer, O God.
Let me henceforth seek Thee diligently—nor let me delay
to put faith in Thine own record, but instantly accept of
Christ as offered to me in the gospel.   I believe, help mine
unbelief.   I pray for the washing of regeneration, and for
a renewal of my spirit by the baptism of the Holy Ghost.

Be well-pleased with me, O God, for the sake of Thine
own beloved Son, in whom Thou art well-pleased.   Behold my shield, and look on me in the face of Thine
anointed.

LUKE IV.

Jesus was full of the Holy Ghost when led by Him into
the wilderness, where He held combat with Satan.   I
would pray for Thy Spirit at all times, O Lord, that I
might be strengthened and prepared for meeting the
temptations of this great adversary, so as to resist the
devil, and then he will flee from me.   And effectually
teach me the lessons of this celebrated passage in the history of my Saviour: first, when adverse events gather
round me let me maintain unshaken confidence in God,
even in the face of nature's likelihoods ; but, second, let
me not presumptuously venture on experiments of my
own in the face of nature's laws, but let me in all circumstances give to God the undivided homage both of
my reverence and trust—even to Him who hath both
established the sequences of nature, and can overrule
them at His pleasure.   Let me not wantonly violate these
sequences, for He hath ordained them.   Let me not be

dismayed when they present a menacing conjunction against me, for He can make all to work together for my good. Let me cleave therefore to Him, who is the God of Heaven and earth ; and abjure him who is termed the god of this world, and with the lying promises of blessedness and glory here, lures his votaries to their everlasting destruction.

After having put the devil to flight, Jesus went back from the wilderness to society, and there entered on the busy work of His ministry on earth, and in the power of the Spirit too—that power which is strengthened by exercise, and is given in larger measure after every new victory over the power which is opposed to it. The flesh lusteth against the spirit, and the spirit against the flesh. May I ever take side with Thy Spirit ; and give me ever to experience that greater is He that is in me, than he that is in the world.

Let me learn from the custom of my Saviour to respect the Sabbath ordinances of our land. Let me forsake not the Church-going and solemn assemblies of that day ; and O may the word of Christ ever come to me with power, whether as expounded from the pulpit, or read in the Bible. We read that ere He came to Nazareth He was glorified of all, but that in the town where He was brought up He experienced the truth of the saying, that "no prophet is accepted in His own country." Divest me, O Lord, of all vain glory ; and let me betake myself simply and resolutely to the line of duty at the bidding of conscience alone—as enlightened by Thine own revelation.

What an animating consideration in the Christian warfare, that the great Captain of salvation, who can dispossess and put to flight all the forces of the adversary, is upon

our side. Through Him strengthening me, may I overcome the flesh, and the devil, and the world.

Like Simon's wife's mother may I ever minister to
Him who hath healed all my diseases; may I minister
wisely and effectually to His Church, "inasmuch as ye
have done it to them, ye have done it unto me."

Imbue me, O God, with the active benevolence of my
Saviour. Set me on a course of well-doing; and let me lay
myself out for the wellbeing both of the souls and bodies
of men. But, O how much I stand in need of periods of
holy retirement, that my spirituality may be kept from extinction, and my strength be renewed for all the services
to which Thou callest me.

LUKE V.
September, 1842.

Well may we stand humbled and abashed at the presence of infinite purity, even when veiled in flesh, as did
Peter, when He held converse with the incarnate Deity,
God manifest in the flesh. But Jesus bade him fear not;
and let me be won by Thy love, Thou Son of God, and
enable me so to attract others also.

Thou art willing as Thou art able, O blessed Saviour,
to cleanse us from all our iniquities. Apply Thy blood to
our guilt; and let the force of Thy example be so felt that
we may become undefiled as Thou art. We desire to follow that example in its minutest details—deferring as Thou
didst to all that is yet unrepealed, and at the same time
lawful in the institutions among which we are placed;
and, more especially, retiring as Thou didst to solitary
prayer, that our duties and our devotions may reciprocate with wholesome influence on each other.

Truly, there is none who can forgive sins but God only. But Christ is God; and at His hands as our intercessor, and for His sake as our mediator and our surety, do I pray for a part and an interest in that redemption which is through His precious and peace-speaking blood.

And ever blessed be Thy name, O God, that this glorious immunity is held out to all, freely as the light of the sun in the firmament of Heaven. Thou comest not to the righteous, but to the sinner, and callest on one and all of them to repent; and Thou leadest them gently, as they are able to bear it: Thou deferrest to the preference of Thy new converts for their old wine: Thou givest them milk before Thou givest them strong meat. Begin and advance and perfect my spiritual education, O God, and conduct me onward to the higher experiences, and more difficult exercises of the Christian life.

LUKE VI.

Thou allowest Thy disciples, Lord Jesus, to do what is necessary for their subsistence on the Sabbath, but surely not to luxuriate in sumptuous festivity.

But let me proceed on the lawfulness of doing well upon the Sabbath-day; and, O that this day I could be the instrument of restoring to spiritual life the worldly and the withered souls of those who are around me.

Let me not be unmindful of the benevolence which has respect to the body, and its diseases or wants; but let my chief aim be to comfort, or warn, and in every other way to benefit the souls of others.

Let me not be discouraged by the sorrows and persecutions of a world which passeth away, nor yet fret myself because of the prosperity of enemies or evil-doers. More especially do Thou guard me against the sinful love of human applause—the ambition of that universal accept-ance and popularity which might expose me to the denun-ciation laid on those of whom all men speak well. Let it be my constant aim, O Father in Heaven, to please God rather than men ; and open my heart even to the evil and the unthankful, to the equity of the golden rule, and the generosity which pours of its abundance on the wretchedness and the wants—and this unchecked even by the wickedness—of men. Let me be like unto God— perfect, even as my Father in Heaven is perfect—in the love of mine enemies. Let me abstain from censorious-ness ; and, as the grand preparation for all that is good in my conduct, do Thou change, do Thou radically and completely change my character, O God, from sin unto righteousness, from the love of the world to the love of Him who made the world.—O my God, let me not be a hearer only, but let me hear and do. May Thy kingdom, Thine authority, be set up in my heart—and not in word only, but in power. How humiliating the resolves I make, and the non-performance which follows them ! O may I be temperate and truly humble all this day ; and in this season of prayer may I obtain at Thy hand the unction which remaineth—the living water, which, if once poured out upon me, will indeed spring up unto life everlasting.

LUKE VII.

O my God, give me the blessedness of those who see not yet believe, and who in the absence of all sensible accompaniments, find it enough that they have confidence in Thy power and in Thy faithfulness. Like the centurion who sought not the presence of Christ in his house, but believed if He would only speak the word, though at a distance from His patient, that he would be healed—so let me not say in my heart, "Who shall bring down Christ from above?" but trust in the word which is nigh unto me. Give me that faith, O Lord, wherewith Thou art well-pleased; and which if sustained in the absence either of sense or of conception, is all the more pleasing in Thy sight.

Let me imitate the compassion of my Saviour, and devote myself to the culture and observance of that pure and undefiled religion which lies in the visitation of the fatherless and widows in their affliction, and in keeping myself unspotted from the world. And give me, O Lord, to sit at the feet of the great Prophet who has risen upon the world, that I may ever be learning and practising at His lessons, and ever rejoicing in the light of His salvation.

Enable me, O God, to maintain an unswerving consistency in the face of all misconstructions. Give me the wisdom of the spiritual man, who judgeth all things, even though himself be judged and understood of no man. Let me in every good work consult my own soul; and I stand greatly in need, Almighty Father, of independence on the opinion of others in the coming deliberations of our Church. Give me the wisdom that is from above; and in that wisdom may I be enabled to hold out a faithful and upright testimony.

And give me a full faith in pardon through the blood of Christ, that not only peace but love may emerge from it. Work in me, O God, this faith with power. Grant me but this; and sure I am that sins are not wanting to be recollected and ashamed of, and for the forgiveness of which I owe an amount of love beyond all computation.

Establish this order of sentiments within me. I believe, help mine unbelief. Believing may I love—loving may I obey.

LUKE VIII.

Inverary Castle.

My danger lies both in the rock of shallow soil, and among the thorns. And do not I incur the danger of those who think they have a lighted candle within them— yet by keeping it within them, may be said to hide that candle! O for the greater frankness and forthgoing of my heart on the great concerns of eternity.

O let me not be a hearer only—let me hear and do. Give me that good and honest heart in which the seed of the gospel grows up, and brings forth the fruit of new obedience, and has for its end life everlasting. O Lord, save me from the world, and from that fear of the men of it which is a snare.

How easily, O God, couldst Thou visit me with Thy judgments, because of my unfaithfulness to Thy testimonies? To-morrow I have the prospect of committing myself to the wind and the waters.* Do Thou, O God, who couldst sweep me off at the bidding of Thy voice, interpose now to solemnize my heart, and direct the whole of my walk and conversation.

Let me be clothed, and in my right mind, O God. Make me alive to Thyself, and let my tongue speak aloud of Thy righteousness. O where is my declaration of the great things which the Lord hath done for me? Put an end to this sinful reticence, and give me to be a living witness for the truth, in the midst of a worldly generation.

O Jesus, be my helper! Loose me from the sad infir-

---

* *N.B.*—God blest us with a most merciful day.

mity under which I labour; say to me, Go in peace, and
be healed of Thy plague—the plague of a false delicacy,
which makes me ashamed of the testimony of Christ. O
for more of zeal in His cause—and not zeal only, but zeal
and wisdom together; but let me ask for this in faith,
nothing wavering. I pray, O God, for a miracle of grace
to be put forth upon me, that mine henceforth may be
not the heart only, but the history of a new creature.
Henceforward, O Lord, if it be Thy blessed will, let this
journal be kept regularly at home; and O may a vital
prosperity and blessing from on high go along with it.

LUKE IX.
October, 1842.

Should the time now be coming when, cast off from all
our present means of subsistence, we shall have to quit
the Church of our fathers, let us cast ourselves on the
good providence of God, and fulfil with all purity and zeal
the work of missionaries.

Let us not fear the great ones of earth while we prosecute this sacred vocation. God is our helper, and let us
not be afraid of what men can do unto us, who understand not the way or the work of God, while they despise
and wonder, and if they repent not, will at length perish.

O that I followed the example of Christ, who, in fulfilment of the work which His Father gave Him to do, was
instant in season and out of season—the example of Him
who blended good-will to men with glory to God, compas-
sionating and relieving the wants of the creature—giving praise and thankful acknowledgment to the Creator.
And of Him who ever alternated social duty with secret
prayer.

Let me choose the good of the soul, or life rather than death. Let me brave all for eternity, nor be ashamed of the testimony of Him who openeth and no man shutteth; and who, if I confess Him before men, will confess me before my Father in heaven.

Let that which was the theme of heavenly converse on the mount of transfiguration, be ever the theme of my faith and meditation—even that Christ died for my sins according to the Scriptures. Let me ever keep this in memory, determined to know nothing save Jesus Christ and Him crucified—sitting at His feet, and, in hearing Him, casting down all my own lofty imaginations.

O Lord, cast the unclean spirit out of me, and deliver me from those vile affections which war against the soul.

And let me not fluctuate in my purposes, so as to crucify the Son of God afresh by my sins.

Give me, O Lord, the docility and the humbleness of a little child, and check within me the ambition of superiority over others.

O for a greater union among Christians. Let us henceforth sink our differences in all but the essentials of faith and practice.

What an affecting incident, and what a noble declaration came out of it. Fill me, O God, with the spirit of my Master—of Him who came not to destroy men's lives, but to save them.

Let me count the cost of the Christian service. Let me be in readiness to forsake all for it—leaving worldly things to be done by worldly men, and giving myself wholly and without distraction, or any conflicting desire, to the cause of my Saviour.

LUKE X.

What a mighty field for the enterprise of Christian missionaries is our own beloved Scotland—even though the present apparatus of religious instruction should be kept up, and still more if it be taken down. Let us go forth, trusting in the support which God will raise up for us within the field of our labours, and dismissing all anxiety for such a provision as shall be fittest and best for us. And what wisdom as well as zeal might we learn from this passage ! There is a certain point of resistance to our ministrations at which it is right to desist from them— casting not our pearls before swine. Let me feel the Saviour's denunciation in my own conscience, and for the direction of my own case; let me think of my opportunities, and of the responsibility which they lay upon me.

Let us not joy in gifts as in graces. Let us covet that which is the best earnest of our inheritance—a real and universal charity—such a love as can only be shed abroad in our hearts by the Holy Ghost given unto us. This precious blessing, O God, Thou vouchsafest to the humble, and refusest to the proud. O Father, give me the knowledge of Thy Son ; O Son, reveal to me Thy Father, and may I ever hold believing fellowship with both.

O God, though the love of Thyself and the love of my neighbour have not been such as to avail for justification, may they grow apace in my heart for the progress and perfecting of my sanctification. The economy of—Do this and live—has been tried, and it has failed. But what under the one economy we were required to do for life, under the other we are enabled to do from life, and by the power of that life-giving Spirit, through whose blessed operation it is that we are made meet for the joys and the services of eternity. Let my charity be co-extensive with the species; and thus may I be fitted for companionship with God who is love. May the spirit of the noble parable in this chapter be fully imbibed by me, and actuate all my doings.

Save me, O Lord, from the cumbersome anxieties of this life; let them not choke and overbear the good seed of the Word of God; let them all be hushed, because overlaid by the care of the one thing needful. O that I laboured less for the meat which perisheth, and more for the meat which endureth unto life everlasting. Help me to this, O God.

LUKE XI.

What precious and powerful encouragement have we in the opening verses of this chapter, when after the Lord's Prayer He tells us of the efficacy in heaven of our importunate and persevering supplications upon earth. O God, let me never despair after this. Let me henceforward in everything give thanks, and make my request known unto God—asking till I receive, seeking till I find, knocking till the door be opened to me. In particular do I pray for wisdom, O God, and that with a special reference to the affairs of our Church and Convocation. And let it not be in the wisdom of man, which is but a semblance and counterfeit of true wisdom, but in the wisdom as well as the words which the Holy Ghost teacheth, that I may be enabled to speak in the midst of the great congregation, when engaged in counsel with my fellows in the ministry.

Save me, O God, from the hard and hopeless impenitency into which backsliders so often fall—their latter

state being worse than their first. Give me grace to know
Thy will, and to keep it.   Let this, O God, be the single-
minded purpose and determination of my soul.   O let me
be intent, supremely and exclusively intent upon this;
and let such also be the disposition and the bent of all our
assembled brethren, that the whole body of our convocation may be full of light, and so as to give forth a clear,
consistent, and right deliverance, which Thou shalt approve of, and which shall command both the respect of
our enemies, and the full consent and acquiescence of all
the good and wise in the land.

Let us marvel not though we should be hated of the
world, for the servant is not above his master.   Our enemies will try to involve us in difficulties; but give us of
Thy wisdom, and make us faithful to Thy lessons, O
blessed Saviour, and then shall they not prevail over us.
Save us from hypocrisy; save us from vain formality; let
ours be a sincere and spiritual service; and let not me,
in this crisis of our Church's history, urge a sacrifice upon
others which I would not most cheerfully share with them.
And hasten the time when all shall know Thee, from the
least to the greatest, and when the little ones—the poor
and humble of the flock—shall not be so despised.   Endow Thine own Christian people with that intelligence,
and that pure and lofty principle which will save them
from contempt; and break down all those obstacles which
are now thrown in the way of Church extension, by men
who, not Christians themselves, refuse and resist every
attempt for the spread of saving knowledge amongst the
people of our land.   Appear, O God, in the midst of us,
for the protection of Thy Church and the vindication of
Thine own glory.

LUKE XII.

My special hypocrisy is not that by which I affect, but that by which I disguise my feeling for the Saviour, so as to deny Him by my silence. O my God, relieve me from this fear and shame of man; and may I evince the strength of my faith by this test—that as I have believed so have I spoken. Give me confidence in Thy care of me; and may the Holy Ghost both embolden me to utter and teach me what I should say, whether in the parties of companionship, or in public courts and assemblies. Release me from the power of covetousness—so as neither to be anxious about what I have, nor solicitous to have more. Let me be able to devolve my own needful subsistence, and that of my family upon God—on Him who feeds the ravens, and in whose bounty the commoners of nature are made to rejoice. O let my first and foremost desires be to the kingdom of God and His righteousness, in the full confidence that all other things will be added to me. And to this freedom from care let me add liberality—laying up my treasure in heaven, and lending to the Lord by giving to the poor. O that my treasure were in heaven, and my heart there, and my conversation there: and let me ever maintain the posture of vigilance and daily waiting for the coming of the Lord. Give me the realizing sense of Him as my Master, and of my own proper task and employment as His servant, that I may be always abounding in His work.—My God, pardon and repair my grievous deficiencies; and give me so to acquit myself in the labours of Christian philanthropy on earth, that I may be advanced to a place of congenial and faithful well-doing in heaven. I have had much to warn and instruct me, and am therefore all the more responsible to the great Master of the vineyard. Qualify me, O God, for the coming warfare. Let me henceforth sit loose to the interest of a world where divisions reign, and which will shortly be the theatre of desolating judgments. Let me hold fast my integrity in the midst of them. Let me acquit myself of the faithfulness which I owe to Thee as my reconciled Father; and O if not yet reconciled, do Thou accept of me now, for Christ's sake; do Thou preserve me faultless as a disciple of His—lest when Thy wrath is discharged on the unbelievers and the impenitent I too be overtaken in a hopeless and inexpiable condemnation.

LUKE XIII.

The necessity of repentance and the opportunity for it are both here set before us. The dread consequence of our destruction will follow our want of it; and the guilt as well as the vengeance are aggravated by every prolongation of the season for our returning unto God. Ours is the impressive situation of the fig-tree let alone. Let us flee then from the coming wrath, and bring forth fruits meet for repentance.

Enable me, O God, rightly to divide the word of truth. The Sabbath was made for man, and therefore not made to suspend the exercise of his mercy and compassion—thus steeling his heart against the sufferings of others, and conflicting with the authority of the second great law. This were an abuse of the Sabbath, because fitted to injure the progress of our moral and spiritual education; but while we guard against this abuse, let us remember that the Sabbath has its use, and on the same principle of its being made for

man, we should avail ourselves to the uttermost of all its
possible subservience to the growth of our divine life, and
our progress in faith and holiness. It is eminently adapted to the highest of all objects, that of fostering within us
the love of God, which is the first and greatest commandment; and on this enlightened principle, the Sabbath law,
as being the handmaid of all the graces, is worthy of the
place which it has in the decalogue—where, shrined among
immutabilities of justice and piety and truth, it has the
rank assigned to it which belongs to the virtues of permanent and universal obligation.

May the good seed of Thy word, O Lord, with that
mighty germinating power which belongs to it, shoot up
into a tree which shall cover the whole earth, and be for
the healing of all nations. And O grant that it may
take root in my own heart, where, fertilized by the living
water of Thine own Spirit, it may overspread my whole
character with those fruits of righteousness which are
by Jesus Christ unto God's praise and God's glory.

O my God, deepen and make fruitful my Saviour's
lesson, that I should not indolently seek, but assiduously
and laboriously strive to enter the kingdom of God. Instead of speculating on the general question of the many
or the few who are to be saved, let me look well after my
own soul, and the souls of my children. May I ponder
well, and that with a view to a right and practical application, the awful consequences both to me and to them
of our neglecting the one thing needful.

O that the spirit of this earnest and affecting apostrophe
to Jerusalem were rightly to impress and influence me.
Christ would our salvation, and it is only we who would
not. O make us willing in the day of Thy power. Let

us kiss the Son while He is in the way, else His wrath will begin to burn—the wrath of the Lamb—who now beckons our approaches, a weeping and beseeching Saviour ; but will then be the avenging Judge of all who have despised the proffers of His great salvation.

LUKE XIV.

November, 1842.

After again exemplifying His view of the Sabbath, by which He evinces His compassion for the afflicted, He gives forth an injunction which marks His respect and consideration for the poor. Enable me, O God, to act in the spirit of this injunction. Give me to feel the sacredness of benevolence, and let it be my delight to visit and aid the helpless. Mortify all pride within me. Let me be lowly and free from all ambition of superiority to other men ; and now when my friends would have me to assume a higher place in the assembled Convocation of ministers, let me, while not shrinking from every fair opportunity of usefulness, die unto the applauses of this world, and seek the praise that is not of man but of God. I deeply feel, Lord, how wholly I am indebted to Thee, and how helpless I am in myself without Thee ; and, O Heavenly Father, guide me through what remains of the business of this solemn Assembly. Give wisdom, and a clear answer to the request I now make for counsel and direction. But in the midst of these urgencies let me not forget the one thing needful. Let no engagements withdraw me from this. O let me not deny godliness while contending for the outer things of the house of God ; but let me at all times deny ungodliness ; and give me at all times to live as in Thy sight, and as seeing Thee though Thou art

invisible. Let me not make excuse on any plea whatever
for not waiting upon God.

O Heavenly Father, give me to act up to the high terms
of the Christian discipleship. Put me in readiness for
forsaking all—all that is dear to nature, if called to it by
loyalty to Thine authority, and the high behests of what I
owe to God. Let me count the cost; and in the face of
all possible consequences enlist and dedicate myself to the
service of Christ. O give me that without which I shall
be cast out. Give me a thorough devotion to the service
of the one Master; and let no opposing influence seduce
me from this high calling, which is to glorify the Lord
with my soul and spirit and body, which are the Lord's.

LUKE XV.

This ranks among the noted and illustrious chapters of
the Bible; and how precious is the lesson of all these
parables! They were the publicans and sinners who were
around our Saviour, those whom He came to call, and
whom He here plies with such encouragements and views
of the goodness of God as might well lead to repentance.
To set forth the willingness of God more effectually, He
appeals to the experience of our own felt and familiar nature, in the surpassing joy that we experience on finding
that which is lost. What a touching and constraining
influence ought to lie in the consideration of that joy
which is in heaven when a sinner turns from the evil of
his way. Turn me, O God, and I shall be turned. Let the
view of Thy mercy and truth turn me. Wean me, wean
me, O Lord, from earthly things, from the husks of sensuality, and give me to set my affections henceforth on

the things which are above—that I may rejoice in the light of Thy countenance. Christ came to seek that which is lost; and the diligence, both of the shepherds and the woman, represents His diligence, His earnestness, to have us unto Himself. O may we at length give way, or rather now give way; and Lord Jesus, I am here—lay hold of me—apprehend me for Thyself. In finding me, Thou wilt indeed find that which is lost. But the most celebrated of all these is the parable of the prodigal son;—like him let me arise and go to my father. O that I viewed my God with more confidence as a father and a friend—as sitting on a throne of grace, beckoning my return, and longing after me as one of His strayed and wandering children. I have ever regarded as one of the most touching strokes in this narration, the effect on the father of his son's appearance far off, when he had compassion on him, and ran to him, and fell on his neck, and kissed him. Such is our Father in Heaven. The whole parable is designed to establish a "likewise." He will not despise our first movements towards Himself, but meets us more than half-way. He will encourage our first and earliest aspirations; and let our hearts therefore rejoice, not only when we find, but let us rejoice even when we seek the Lord. (Psalm cv. 3.) Accept of my confessions, O God, and forgive the prayerless and godless life I have led hitherto. Admit me within the precincts of Thine own spiritual family, and among the number of Thy children through the faith that is in Christ Jesus. Work in me this faith with power, and let not sin have any longer the dominion over me. O may I know what it is to be one with God. Pour on me the spirit of adoption, whereby I may at all times cry unto Thee, Abba, Father.

LUKE XVI.

How little, alas! have I felt my relationship to God—as the steward, and not the owner, of all which He has put into my hands. Let me not trust in uncertain riches, nor set my heart upon them. Enlarge my liberalities, O God: make me a cheerful giver to a greater extent than I have ever yet been: release me from the thraldom of an overweening affection for property: save me from this idolatry; and enable me henceforward to serve Thee with Thine own, to serve Thee as my alone master; and let not other lords have the dominion over me. Thus may I make myself friends by the wealth which perisheth, even friends who shall abide by me for ever—the God who loveth a cheerful giver—the Saviour who says, " Inasmuch as ye have done it unto these, ye have done it unto me"—the spirits of just men made perfect, who have gone before into heaven, and perhaps converted in the Church which I helped to raise, or by the missionary whom I helped to send forth on the work of an evangelist. How delightful to think that the humble services and contributions here might prepare for the higher services and larger philanthropies which await us there; and how animating the thought, that what we are entrusted with in heaven shall indeed be our own—for it is that which shall not be taken away from us. Let me not be deceived by the flattering estimation of my fellows, for that which might be abominable in the sight of God. Let me seek His praise, and not the praise of men—His glory, and not mine own glory. Covetousness and adultery seem often to be identified in Scripture ($\pi\lambda\epsilon o\nu\epsilon\xi\iota a$.) Let me lay hold of eternal life; let me press into the kingdom of heaven by all the strivings and the sacrifices which may be required by Him who bids me forsake all.

Then follows an illustrious parable. May I charge my heart with the lesson of it—sitting loose to this world's possession, and setting my desire on the true riches. And may Thy word, O God, dwell in me richly with all wisdom; for in that word there is a sufficiency for all my spiritual wants. It is indeed the word of life; and the remarkable averment of the Saviour would indicate that there is in it a power of evidence at least equal to what would be given forth by the re-appearance of an acquaintance from the dead. Let me esteem this word then to be better than all spoil; let me renounce the pride of life and all luxury—caring not for either the splendour or the festivities of Dives: and should coming events bring me and my children to poverty, O may the dear Bible become dearer to us than ever, and may we find its comforts and directions to be unspeakably precious.

LUKE XVII.

This chapter begins with what ought to be a most fearful and impressive denunciation. What carefulness, O God, should I observe, both of my example and of my sayings. Pardon mine iniquity, O Lord, for it is great. Save me from the fulfilment of the fell utterance in the text. Lead me to repent speedily, and flee from the evil of my ways, and so flee from the wrath that is to come. Hide me in Him who is a hiding-place from the tempest and a refuge from the storm; and O deliver me from that wrath before which no man is able to stand—even the wrath of the Lamb, when taking vengeance on those who have done a moral or spiritual wrong to any of His little ones.

And let me cultivate the charity as well as holiness of the gospel. Repentance is presupposed ere forgiveness is required for us; but with or without this condition forbearance is a universal requirement: and surely whether one or other of these virtues I, who have so much to be forgiven, should not feel the burden of them as heavier than I can bear. Thou long-suffering God, teach me to be patient to the uttermost—a patience that might have its perfect work in me, and in which, amid the annoyances and crosses of life, I may be enabled to possess my soul.

Such is the omnipotency of faith: how we should labour and pray for the increase of it! What a conquest I have yet to achieve ere in meekness I can instruct them who oppose me, and without striving, be gentle unto all men. Teach me how to rule my own spirit, O God, and to bridle my own tongue. Give me, O Lord, that faith which giveth the victory, that overcometh all things. And let me never think that I have done enough for Christ, but forget the things that are behind, and press onward.

And, O Lord, let my faith not only make me whole of my plague, but let it even work love to Him who is the Physician of my soul—that to Him I may give all the glory, and yield the grateful return of all those services by which His name might be magnified, and His cause be promoted in the world.

Thus may Thy kingdom, the reign of Thy will and Thy law, be established within me. Let me look first to myself and my own Christianity, ere I cast abroad an eye of speculation on the wide world around me.

And who knows when the day of trial will come that

is to try the whole earth? Prepare me for that day, O Lord. Give fortitude and integrity; and enable me to sustain a manful and wise and faithful part for Christ and for His cause. Disengage my affections from things present. Enable me to devote myself to Christ, and be in readiness to do all and suffer all for His sake.

LUKE XVIII.

December, 1842.

What a precious and encouraging lesson is set before us at the beginning of this chapter. What a warrant for prayer, and also for perseverance therein till its object shall have been accomplished. It implies, too, that we must lay our account with delay in the fulfilment even of our most legitimate requests, and so teaches the grace of patience as well as faith. We should wait, asking till we receive. And yet we are here premonished that, whatever our prayers shall be, a time is coming when faith will well-nigh disappear from the earth; but if the general faith of the gospel shall nearly go into extinction, it will be preceded by the decay bordering on extinction of *this* faith—that is faith in the efficacy of prayer, and so as that prayer shall be bereft of its efficacy.

O God, let me be clothed with humility. Thou resistest the proud, Thou givest grace unto the humble. Let me bow myself down to the attitude of being clothed upon with the righteousness of Christ; let me not be of the number of those who count themselves rich, and to have need of nothing; but having no confidence in the flesh let me rejoice in Christ Jesus, both as the Lord my strength, and the Lord my righteousness.

Thou only beloved Son of the Father, who art indeed

good—though there be none good but One, even the Triune God—enable me to give up all in Thy service, and for Thy sake. Strengthen me for whatever sacrifice Thou wilt at my hand. Give me to lay hold of eternal life ; and may I be ready to give up all I have, and all I am in the world, for the furtherance of that gospel which is preached to the poor, and on receiving which they obtain the only true riches. By Thy regenerating power, O God, break the force of all this world's idolatries within me, and set my affection on the substance which remaineth, on the God who endureth for ever.

Christ, the Captain of our salvation, has led the way in this course of suffering and self-denial. Put me in readiness, O God, to suffer all and lose all, even as Thou mayest be pleased to appoint for me.

My Lord and Saviour, I would importune Thy mercy. Take pity on my spiritual blindness. Give me the seeing eye and the understanding heart, through that which cures all maladies, both quieting the fears and enlightening the eyes. O for the light of the knowledge of God's glory in the face of Jesus Christ.

LUKE XIX.

It seems to have been curiosity which prompted Zaccheus at the first—his desire being to see Jesus, *who He was ;* yet it landed in the best possible result. O Heavenly Father, may my inquiries, which hitherto have been too much of a merely intellectual and inquisitive character, lead, by Thy blessing, to that spiritual revelation of Christ which is alone effectual to salvation. Let me not think myself rich, and to have need of nothing, seeing that

Zaccheus, though he did greatly more than I, was still a lost man previous to his knowledge of Christ; and seeing that it was only on the day of the Lord's visit to him that salvation came unto his house, yet let me not, with many theologians, undervalue good works done anterior to conversion. Let me forget not the precedency which John's preaching had in point of time to that of Christ and His Apostles, nor how the alms and prayers of Cornelius, previous to the mission and message of Peter to him, rose in memorial before God.

There was a something interposed between the time of our Saviour's abode on earth and that appearance of the kingdom of God which His disciples thought was to be immediate. Christ has ascended to heaven, but returns thence, and will take account of the deeds done in our body. The parable represents the present stage of God's administration. To us much has been given—alas! alas! what account can we give of the much that will be required? My God, let the moral of this parable sink deep into my heart, and give direction to the whole of my history. Give me henceforth to feel that I have nothing of my own, that I am but Thy steward—an agent for God. Whatever Thou hast bestowed upon me may I occupy in Thy service; and by the successful and right management of the affairs of Thy kingdom here below, may I be qualified for such a charge and such a superintendence in the next world as Thou mayest be pleased to confer upon me.

What an exhibition of the Saviour's tenderness is offered to us at the close of this chapter; O may it tell with overpowering effect upon my heart, which take, O Lord Jesus, such as it is, and make such as it should be. A right judicial procedure must go on both here and hereafter.

Because the Jews had not a willing ear to the representations of Christ, there was taken away from them even that which they had ; or, because they minded not the things which belonged to their peace, therefore were they for ever hid from their eyes. And so the fearful and final doom overtook them at last—a doom which our Saviour wept over, yet would not recall. O let me take this into serious application, and to-day, while it is called to-day, harden not my heart.

LUKE XX.

Give me, O Lord, rightly to divide the word of truth. It is lawful at all times to do well, even on the Sabbath ; yet, made as the Sabbath was for man, it is our part intently to keep and to cultivate the Sabbath, so as to secure the great ends for which it was instituted. While not slavish or weakly scrupulous in our observation of it, may we ever love its sacred opportunities, its quiet seasons for the study of God's Word, and for the holding of lofty fellowship with the Father and the Son. And O invest me with the grace of humility, not towards man only but towards God. Forgive all the offence I have felt hitherto at the imagined usurpation by others of the honour which I conceived myself, and myself only, to have earned. Let me complain no more, either of literary plagiarisms, or of the assumption by other men of my own schemes, and their enjoyment of the credit that they are theirs. O may I seek not my own glory, but ever rejoice when good is done or doing, under whatever ostensible leadership.

I wrote the above paragraph by a mistake of the fourteenth for the twentieth chapter of Luke. In this last, which is properly the one we have to do with at present, we have specimens of our Saviour's admirable wisdom in dealing with His adversaries—as first, when He brought them into a dilemma from which they could not extricate themselves, by putting the question respecting the baptism of John; second, (and after He had delivered a parable which smote conviction into their hearts, and made them feel as David did when Nathan told him—"Thou art the man!") by the dexterous extrication of Himself, if I may so speak, from the dilemma in which they sought to involve Him by a question respecting the payment of tribute; third, by His solution of the infidel difficulty respecting a future life, and when He elicits even from the Jewish Scriptures an argument which ought to have told on Jewish understandings; and, lastly, when after having reduced them all to silence, He closes this trial of strength by a question which He leaves them to resolve, and which should have guided them to the conclusion, that verily this is the Son of God. Lord, with the harmlessness of the dove endow us all, in every time of perplexity and need, with the wisdom of the serpent: and let us not forget the great moral lesson wherewith our Saviour winds up the intellectual contest in which He had been engaged, when He tells us to beware of those (and still more to beware of their sins) who loved pre-eminence, and sought after the glory of men; and, most emphatically detestable of all—who devoured widows' houses, and for a show made long prayers.

LUKE XXI.

This is a precious testimony to the offerings of the poor,

and may well be urged at present, when the support of
the Church is in all likelihood to be thrown on the great
bulk and body of the people. Sanctify and Christianize
all our endeavours to perpetuate a pure and free ministration of the gospel in Scotland.

Prepare us, O God, for the days that are to come, be
they days of deliverance or days of sore tribulation. Ever
blessed be Thy name for the precious encouragements
which Thou vouchsafest to Thy faithful servants. May
we abide faithful : may we not falter or be discouraged
because of the things that are coming on the earth : may
Thy Spirit help our various infirmities ; and more especially may He bear me up under the nervous apprehension
of not being able to state or to vindicate our cause should
I be called before councils or governors. May I trust
more to His suggestions than I have heretofore done—
recollecting that the answer of the mouth, as well as the
preparation of the heart, is from the Lord. And there are
other preparations for a season of impending judgment,
which I have mightily to strive and mightily to pray for,
as not giving way either to terror or impatience—the latter
being my great infirmity, whether under the malice of
enemies or the perversity of friends. In the midst of all
these disturbances let me maintain, O Lord, the self-pos-
session of my soul. Above all, let us wait for the coming
of the Son of man ; and let my constant attitude be that
of one who looketh for the Saviour. But O what need of
vigilance and self-control, and holy abstinence, and resolute exclusion of this world's vain anxieties, that, broken
loose from all the entanglements of life, I may fight the
good fight, and endure hardness as a good soldier of Christ
Jesus. Let me not be ensnared, but watch and pray that

I may be of the number of those who love Christ's appearing, and be counted worthy to stand before Him on the earth.

He is the well-beloved Son of God; and obeying the voice that was heard on the mount of transfiguration, let me hear Him. May His word dwell richly within me in all wisdom.

LUKE XXII.

January, 1843.

Save me, O Lord, from the awful guilt of betraying the Lord, and crucifying Him afresh; but give me to adorn His doctrine, and to shew forth as the fruit of my faith, a life devoted to His service and glory.

He hath gone before us unto that kingdom appointed to Him by the Father. Let us in the joyful hope of the kingdom which He hath appointed to His disciples familiarize ourselves more and more to the foretastes and the pleasures of the coming eternity. More especially may we turn to their instituted use and observance the memorials of His precious atonement—even of the body that was broken, and of the blood that was shed for us. Give us, O Lord, to be faithful to our sacramental vows; and preserve us from the dread enormity of having sat at His table, and yet abjuring our faithfulness.—Give me, O Lord, to be humble both in reference to others and also in myself. In honour may I prefer my brethren; and when I think of my own miserable weakness, may I renounce all confidence in myself, and cast my whole dependence on Him who came to destroy the work of the devil, and be the Captain of their salvation, to all who trust in Him. Protect me, O Lord Jesus, from the works and the wiles of the great adversary; and let not Satan have the advantage over me. In the name of Him who was reckoned among the transgressors, do I pray for that grace which is withheld from the proud, and given only to the humble.

O may these mysterious agonies enhance my every conception of what Christ hath done and suffered for my sake ; and also my every feeling of gratitude, that the constraining influence of His love for me might lead me to love Him back again. May I be enabled to imitate Him in suffering, and above all in prayer. Let me not be tempted, O God, above what I am able to bear. Save me from Peter's melancholy fall ; and let the believing apprehension of my Saviour looking to me from heaven, carry in it a power of warning, even as it had all the power of rebuke on the feelings of His apostle.

O may He who both gave His back to the smiters, and bore in His spirit such a weight of sore endurance—may He see in me of the travail of His soul and be satisfied.

I wait for Thy coming, Thou patient Son of God. May this rapid flight of years carry my desires onward from this passing and perishable scene to the realities of Thine eternal and unsuffering kingdom. May I love Thine appearance ; and if Thy Church is to experience for a season the hour and the power of darkness, O may I be found faithful and faultless on that day.

LUKE XXIII.

Let the servant look to his Master, and be prepared for the same treatment in this world which He had to undergo. He was called before councils and governors ; and even the multitude which had so recently rent the air with their hosannas as He drew nigh unto Jerusalem, even they rose in popular fury against Him. My God, do Thou fortify me against all the oppositions of a world lying in wickedness. Let not the terrors of power or persecution overbear me. Enable me to hold fast my integrity; and now that dangers are thickening over the Church, may her ministers be armed with right principle, and ready, in behalf of Thy cause, to do all or suffer all.

Save me, O God, from the fearful doom which came on those who perished at the destruction of Jerusalem ; and which will be repeated on those who shall perish with an everlasting destruction at the end of the world—when men shall flee to hide themselves from the wrath of the Lamb, calling on the mountains and rocks to fall upon them and cover them. Preserve me from the awful guilt of those who crucify the Saviour afresh, and to whom there remaineth no more sacrifice for sin, because of their sinning wilfully.

What an affecting example of forgiveness on the part of our blessed Lord, who lifted up not only a prayer but a plea in behalf of His murderers. Let His always be our prayer for those who calumniate or injure us, and often, perhaps always to some extent, may His be urged as a plea for them. Much, very much of the hostility which breaks out between man and man is grounded on the misconceptions of ignorance. So well might a quarrel, in possibly the greater number of instances, be denominated a misunderstanding.

Inspire me, Heavenly Father, with the warrantable confidence, that when absent from the body I shall be present with the Lord.

In all our prayers to Thee, O God, would we be mindful of the decease which was accomplished at Jerusalem. In

the name of Him who made that great atonement for the
sins of the world, do we seek forgiveness at Thy hand ;
and O may we receive a part and an interest in Him the
righteous man, who is the Lord their righteousness to all
who believe.

He made His grave with the rich. May I, O God, be
made conformable to Him in His death. As He died for
sin, may I die to sin. May the body of sin be destroyed.
May the old man be crucified with Him—even the flesh
with its affections and lusts, that all old things may be
done away, and all things be made new with me. Let
not sin have the dominion over me ; and save me alike
from the wickedness of evil deeds, and the wandering of
evil desires.

LUKE XXIV.

Let me ever hold in grateful reverence and estimation
that Sabbath which commemorates the resurrection of my
Saviour. O, on this day, may I always be enabled to hold
fellowship with the Father and the Son—honouring the
Son even as I honour the Father ; and rendering the
tribute of all my acknowledgments to Him who is God
over all, blessed for ever. Amen.

But though the Old Testament differs from the New in
that a change has been made of the Sabbath from the
seventh to the first day of the week, yet do the records of
the earlier teem all over with the facts, and doctrines, and
principles of the later dispensation. The righteousness
which is by the faith of Christ is witnessed by the law
and the prophets ; and as the hearts of the disciples
burned on the way to Emmaus, so would our hearts burn
within us, when the view of the Saviour opens upon us

in the older Scriptures, and we are made to understand the things which are testified in Moses, and in the Prophets, and in the Psalms concerning Him. What He said to His disciples then, He says to them still, "Peace be unto you." Give me, O God, to experience that whilst in the world I shall have tribulation, in Him I shall have peace—even the peace which passeth all understanding, ruling in my heart and mind, through the faith that is in Jesus. And, O Lord, give me repentance and the remission of sins—and to perfect that repentance, O endue me with power from on high. I pray for Thy Spirit, O God—for a present salvation through Him— for the spirit of love and of power, and of a sound mind. "The Lord is risen indeed." Give me to believe in my heart that God hath raised Him from the dead that so I might be saved. (Rom. x. 9.)

I see Him not—yet, believing, may I rejoice with joy unspeakable and full of glory. I worship and do Him homage as God. Lord Jesus, pour Thy blessings upon me ; and enlarge my heart to the praise of God, and to the exercise of a glad and confident and elevating fellowship with the Father and with the Son.

JOHN.

John i.—My God, deeply impress on me the lessons of this spiritual gospel, and cause me to profit by my prayers and meditations over it. O may Thy Spirit give efficacy to its words, that I may inhale their deep import, and obtain a view of their hidden glories which the world knoweth not. Cause the light, O Lord, to arise out of darkness, and shine in my heart, that the noble Scripture on which I am now entering may prove both truth and life unto my soul.

May I honour the Son even as I honour the Father—even Him who was in the beginning with God, and was God; and in whom was life, and whose life was the light of men. The before dark question—"Wherewith shall a sinner appear before God?"—has at length been resolved by Him who died that we might follow. This, we doubt not, was the chief enigma which angels desired to look into, as they contemplated the sufferings of Christ and the glory that should follow. It is by the light of the knowledge of this that many are justified. (Isaiah liii. 11.) He who hath the Son hath life, (1 John v. 12,) even that life which is in the Son; but to have this life we must see Him, and it is the light which enables us to see Him that gives life to the soul. In this Thy light, O God, may I clearly see light; and chasing away the darkness from our souls, do Thou enable us to comprehend Him.

O may we be of the blessed number of those who are lighted by the true light, that we may know Him, and knowing Him rejoice in this—that the Creator of the world and of all things is the Redeemer of men. May we have grace to receive Him as such; and receiving Him may we receive along with Him power to become and to walk as Thy children. This power turns, we are told, on our reception of the Saviour; and this reception of Him is the turning-point of all our salvation. Give us to behold His glory, that we may indeed be drawn towards Him. Thus may we be regenerated, O God—renewed in knowledge, even at the bidding of Thine own will, which can cause the light to arise out of darkness. We can only be made willing in the day of Thy power. Corresponding to the fulness that is in Christ, may we be made full, O God, of that grace and that truth which are in Him, and by which we are delivered from the curse of the law that we have violated. Thou, O God, the Father, art invisible—but Thy Son who came to us in human form was gazed on by human eyes; and He hath both declared and exhibited Thy character to the world; —He being the brightness of Thy glory, and the express image of Thy person. O make straight for me that way of access by which I, a benighted and guilty sinner, may draw nigh unto God.

Give me to behold Him who is the great Propitiation for the sins of the world; and in the act of beholding Him may I receive the Holy Ghost. Pour this living water upon me, that I may receive the spirit by the hearing of faith.

O may I receive grace to forsake all and follow after Christ. May I have my sins washed out in the blood of the Lamb. May I make an honest and guileless approach to Him—and without any reservation may I be altogether willing to do as He would have me, and to be as He would have me. May I make a right beginning; and following up the initial surrender of myself to Christ, may I experience the rich descent of Heavenly influences upon my soul. And let me not be offended because of Christ, but may He and His doctrine be highly esteemed by me and be altogether precious.

JOHN II.

Whatever the meaning of our Saviour's reply to His mother may have been, there could have been in it no disrespect to parents; and whatever countenance He may here have given to the customs of a festive occasion, there could have been in it no sanction to intemperance or excess. Let us learn from this passage the possibility of impregnating the part we take, either in the domestic or social party, with the very spirit that was in Christ Jesus. O may that spirit dwell in us—may the same mind which was in Him be also in us; and then, without asceticism or moroseness, shall we be enabled to bear our part aright through the business and the companies of this world.

In the next passage there is another and a most instructive exhibition of our Saviour—the zeal wherewith He drove the buyers and sellers out of the temple. I have not been in the habit of applying the lesson here given to the trafficking of Church patronage; but I can perceive a very close and clear application of it to the shameful traffickings in church-seats, and by which the possessors of gold and of gold rings are accommodated to the exclusion of the great bulk and body of our people. This has been the instrument of heathenizing our towns, and all for a reverence to corporations, more especially in those places where a legal provision for the ministry gave the clearest right to free, or at least to low-rented sittings, for the accommodation of the residenters in a parish. There is here the example of a Divine saying, understood not at the time, but understood afterwards— of little or no present use therefore, but of use in future— and such are many of the inspired sayings still, all the usefulness of which, or at least the greater part of their usefulness, may be yet to come, by confirming either our own faith or that of our posterity. Events that have not yet happened may give birth to new fulfilments of the Scripture prophecies; and circumstances that have not

yet arisen may give birth to new applications of the
Scripture precepts. Meanwhile, let us be very sure that
no part of Scripture has been written in vain ; and let us
view the whole of it in the spirit of docility and reverence.
I commit myself to men by my overtalking: help me out
of this infirmity, O Spirit of God. Teach me how to beware of men ; and as Christ knew what is in man, and
knoweth most assuredly what is in me, I pray for the
needful application of his needful grace, to correct all my
delinquencies and all my errors.

JOHN III.
February, 1843.

What a full and precious chapter this is ! let us seek
and strive and pray for this regeneration ; and as Paul
travailed in birth till Christ was formed in his converts,
so may we cease not from the agonies which precede this
great consummation—cease not from the toils and the
sufferings of that violence by which the kingdom of
heaven should be assailed till we have taken it by force.
We know not the way of the Spirit, but we are told the
way by which the Holy Spirit may be made ours: He is
given to those who ask Him ; and while on the one hand
we lie under the obligation of the precept—make a new
heart—we, on the other, have the encouragement of the
promise—I will create the clean heart, and renew the
right spirit ; but for which things God must be inquired
after. Let us ask *till* we receive. O that we were alive
to the greatness of the distinction between flesh and
spirit, and so to the great moral distance which we have
to traverse ere we are in a state it will do to die in. It is
by believing in Christ that this transition is effected, or

that we pass from death unto life. (John i. 12.) But how can we believe in the reality of this process which takes place, unless we also believe in such unseen and high matters as the jurisprudence of heaven, and more especially the good-will of our reconciled Father there to all who approach Him in the name of His Son—even of Him who was lifted on the cross, as the brazen serpent was in the wilderness, that all who look unto Him should live? The subjective process will not take effect on earth, unless the objective truth of heaven's purposes be apprehended by the mind—even that God sent His Son, not to condemn the world, but to save it—and this, too, from the love He bore to us sinners of mankind. O purge us from the love of darkness, and from all that evil, whether in our deeds or our desires, which turns away the eye of our mind from the Saviour, and so prevents that belief on the strength of which none of us would perish.

And O may this everlasting gospel be preached with far greater effect and extension than ever among the people, which is able to make them wise unto salvation, that they may receive the testimony of Christ, and so do homage to the truth of God who sent Him—that the reluctancy of nature may be overcome, and so fleeing unto the place of refuge for all who will, they may escape that wrath which abideth on all who reject the Saviour.

JOHN IV.

O may I know the things which are freely given to me of God, that I may live up to my offered privileges; and praying for these things in faith, may receive from on high all which is necessary to a life of godliness. More especially may the promise of the Spirit be mine—even that living water which our Saviour hath interpreted to be the Holy Ghost given to them who shall believe. Walk in me and dwell in me, O God, and let my soul be as a well-watered garden, abounding in all the fair and pleasant fruits of righteousness. Spiritualize me wholly; and grant that mine may be the intelligent worship of a subordinate and created mind to the sovereign and creative mind from whom it emanated. Save me from the vanity of forms, and from the superstitions of a gross materialism, which annexes virtue to places made with hands. And let me worship God in truth as well as in spirit; let mine be the real homage of a real desire towards God; let me not only conceive of Him aright, but let me truly and with all my heart seek after Him if haply I may find Him; and let mine be a Christianity in deed and in earnest. Thou knowest, O God, all that I am and all that I do: save me from hypocrisy, and cleanse me from secret faults, O Lord.

Let it be my meat and my drink to do Thy will. O that I really loved Thy law, and then nothing would offend me. And speed forward the progress of Thy kingdom, O Lord. Animate and direct my poor labours; and multiply the labourers, so as that there might be an abundance of reapers for the harvest of our large and hitherto neglected population. Let me not be impatient, but wait the processes which God may be pleased to institute, and at His own pleasure to prolong ere the result is arrived at. Whether my assigned function be to sow or to reap, let me ever seek not my own glory, but that of my Father in Heaven; and when I speak of waiting, let it not be the waiting of indolence, but of believing prayer. Let me do with all my might what my hand findeth to do ; but with the sentiment that duties are ours, and events are God's.

We here read of Samaritans who believed in Christ " because of His own word," and of others who would not believe except they saw " signs and wonders." I look not for miracles ; but let me give earnest heed unto the word of the testimony, and let the fruit thereof be a perpetual increase and strengthening of my faith—for if I believe not Moses and the prophets, and more especially Him who is chief of the prophets—neither would I believe though one should rise from the dead.

JOHN V.

My Saviour, I would that I were made whole. Thou great Physician, heal me ; and as withal I am weary and heavy laden—O give me rest. And let me sin no more, lest a worse thing befall. Put that in me which cannot sin, even the new nature which is altogether on the side of what is good and holy, and cannot sin. And though my old nature still adheres to me, and ever annoys me with its vile instigations, O let me not be led thereby to that sinning wilfully after which there remaineth no more sacrifice. To Thee I lift these petitions, knowing that Thou art able and willing effectually to quicken me. O do Thou will to quicken me. O may Thy Spirit, who bloweth where He listeth, sent forth by the Son, both begin and complete the great work of my sanctification. Give me while justified by faith so to work and to walk, that I may stand the ordeal of that great day when I am judged by works. Give me to pass from death unto life, from condemnation to acceptance—by believing that the Father hath sent the Son into the world; and let my spiritual resurrection here be the precursor and the pledge of my resurrection unto everlasting life hereafter. O my God, may all the evil deeds done in my body be blotted out from the book of Thy remembrance, and may I henceforth abound in those good deeds which will be found to honour and glory in the great day of account. O that, like Him whom I am bound to imitate, I sought not mine own will, but the will of God: and let me ever be reading of Him in His word. Let the Scriptures be my daily delight and exercise. And as I cannot bring down God from heaven or see Him there, let me learn of His character and way by the word which is nigh unto me—more especially, that I may know His will for my salvation, and thus find the way to life everlasting. O may His word abide in me; and may I ever be willing to come unto Him, going out and in that I may find pasture, and be nourished from His hand both in the spiritual life here and unto eternal life hereafter. Shed abroad the love of God in my heart; and henceforth may I seek to please and honour Him and Him only ;—and him that honoureth God, God will honour. And while I seek for Christ in the New, let me not forget that there is also converse to be held with Him in the Old Testament, which testifies of Christ; and very pleasant is it to read the things which are written in the law of Moses and in the Prophets and in the Psalms concerning Him.

JOHN VI.

Thy compassions are infinite, O Thou who wentest about

doing good continually. Let me care as He did for the bodies as well as the souls of men ; and let no cold-blooded economic speculation obliterate from my heart the law and lessons of the gospel.

" It is I, be not afraid." Let us look unto Thee as Thou art, O meek and lowly Jesus. Let us behold Thee with the eye of faith, and then shall we love Thee. Perfect our faith, and so shall we have that perfect love which casteth out fear.

I would labour for the meat which endureth—I would give their place of inferiority to this world's objects. And O give me to believe in Christ, whom Thou hast sent, that I might have within me the animating principle of all obedience. O give me the bread of life which came down from heaven, that I may receive Jesus and be satisfied. In Him may I find the full supply of all my spiritual wants. Draw me, O Father, to Him, that I may come, and I shall not be cast out, but—admitted to the believing sight of my Saviour—shall be raised up again at the last day. Let me be effectually taught of God, that I may not only under His leading repair to Christ, but receive His atonement, and along with this, power to walk as one of God's own children. I must not expect to see God here ; but here I may learn as much of Him and of His will as that His law might serve the part of a schoolmaster in bringing me to Christ. Let me eat His flesh, let me drink His blood, not in the letter, but in the spirit which quickeneth ; and thus receiving the atonement, Christ will be formed in me, and I shall abide in Christ.

Interpose, O Heavenly Father. Cause the scales of unbelief to fall from my eyes ; give me to behold Christ as the new and living way of access to Thyself, that I

may willingly and at once betake myself thereto—and go
to Him who alone hath the words, and who alone hath
the gift of life everlasting.

JOHN VII.

March, 1843.

Give me, O Lord, to combine the wisdom of the serpent
with the harmlessness of the dove, and to calculate aright
on times and seasons and circumstances—walking circum-
spectly.

And let me not unnecessarily expose either myself or
my purpose and affairs to the observation of my enemies.
Let me give heed to the precept which our Saviour taught,
and on fitting occasions exemplified—let me beware of men.

What a precious connexion is here set forth between
willingness to do God's will, and the intelligent view of
Christ's doctrine.   Make me willing, O God, in the day
of Thy power—that I may experience when singly bent
on doing aright, that my whole body is made full of light,
and I am thus enabled to see aright.   Let me not be deceived by plausibilities or the mere semblances of things;
but may I ever judge righteously.

Thou comest from the Father, blessed Jesus; let me
know the Son that I may know the Father also; reveal
the Father to me, O Christ, for Thou knowest Him; draw
me to the Son, O Father, and I shall not be cast out, but
shall be taught of Him who is meek and lowly in heart.

Give me living water, so as that I may thirst no more
—and that out of the treasures of a heart renewed and
enriched by Divine grace, there might flow an influence
for good on all around me.   What a noble testimony here,
and by which we are made to know that the ascension of

the risen Saviour to heaven was the precursor and proxi-
mate cause of the descent of the Holy Spirit upon earth.
He is exalted to God's right hand to give repentance.
To Him has been committed the dispensation of the Holy
Ghost—the promise of the Father: and in virtue of the
power entrusted to Him over all things in heaven and
earth, He can subdue all things unto Himself.   And whatsoever I ask in His name, He has promised that He will
do unto me.   In Thy name do we ask for grace and
strength from on high—for that Spirit which is through
faith, (Gal. iii. 14)—seeing that they only who believe receive the gift of the Holy Ghost.   Never man spake like
Jesus. He spake as one having authority, and not as do the
scribes—even they who make a boast of their law, and
because of their knowledge of the law despise the people
who are ignorant thereof.   But Thy sheep know Thy voice;
and what Thou hidest from the wise and prudent, Thou
revealest unto babes.   The rulers and Pharisees did
not believe, but the unlearned did. And so in the present day, by the tact of an immediate discernment, the
humble and illiterate are enabled spiritually to behold the
Saviour.   We hear not His spoken words, but give em-
phasis to His written words, that we may still feel and
know the Saviour's voice.   And let us not despise any of
His little ones ; but doing homage to the wisdom of a
Christian sage, though in humble life, let us look at both
rich and poor through the medium of our common Christianity ; and then shall we learn to honour all men.

JOHN VIII.

O my God, wash me from all my filthiness in the spirit

as well as in the flesh—for though in Christ there be no condemnation, and though He said, " Neither do I condemn thee"—He also said, " Go, and sin no more." Let me mourn over the infirmities of others, and restore them when I can in the spirit of meekness—considering myself, lest I also be tempted.

Let me follow Christ, and He will give me light—even the light of life. He says of Himself, that He is the way and the truth and the life. In the very truth there is a quickening and life-giving power. And if His words abide in us, (John xv. 7,) and if we take heed to our way according to these words, (Psalm cxix. 9,) to us He will manifest Himself, (John xiv. 21)—giving us that knowledge of God and of Jesus Christ which is life everlasting; and he who knoweth the Son knoweth the Father also.

Give us, O Lord, to believe—else Thy wrath abideth on us and we die. May we look unto Him who was lifted up for our offences, even as the serpent was lifted up in the wilderness, that so looking we may live—looking unto Him whom Thou hast set forth as a propitiation for the sins of the world.

O may Thy word abide in us that we may be Thy disciples indeed; and let us experience as the effect of knowing Thy truth, not only that it gives us life, but gives us liberty—for by nature we are in bondage to the power of sin, and to those hateful lusts which war against the soul. Let me no longer be the slave of these tyrants, but may the power of Christ rest on me; and then greater will be He that is in me than he that is in the world— greater will be the deliverer than the adversary and oppressor of my soul. O sinless Son of God, let me be like unto Thyself; and more especially in seeking not mine own glory. O let Thy glory and the good of Thy Church be the great and constant aims of my existence; and enable me to forget myself in the magnificence of those objects which are above me and around me. Thou prayedst for glory, but it was for the glory which Thou hadst with the Father before the world was;—it was for the investiture of the God-man with the essential glories of the Godhead; for Thou, Divine Saviour, wert from the beginning, Thou wert with God, and art God—the Great I AM—before the days of the patriarchs. And if Abraham rejoiced to see Thy day afar off, and before it had risen upon our world, let us rejoice in the light of the Sun of Righteousness who has now ascended, and with healing under His wings. Let us rejoice in the Lord alway, and again let us rejoice. Let the joy of the Lord be our strength.

JOHN IX.

The question here put stands related to the origin of evil. It was not because either the man himself sinned, or his parents, that he was born blind, but that the glory of God might be manifested. It is not the whole account of the matter that because Adam sinned and suffered we sin and suffer also. There is a higher principle involved; and the manifestation of the Divine character and glory is not only intimated in the Bible as the great end of creation, but even in the speculations of philosophers we find conjectures thrown out on the subservience of evil to the ultimate perfection and triumph of virtue—and so to the glory of Him, who at once is the fountain, and Himself the concrete or exemplar of all virtue. But in the dimness of this higher or transcendental light, how blessed

a thing it is that we should sit under the teaching of Him
who is the light of the world, or enough of light for our
position and guidance in the world—enough to illuminate
our path on the earth below, if not enough to clear up the
mysteries both of earth and heaven. Give us this light
of life, O Lord; and above all, let our eyes be opened to
the cleansing power of the Saviour's blood, that we may
at once be washed from guilt, and cured of our spiritual
blindness.

But let us be prepared for the oppositions which the
children of light, and all who live godly in Christ Jesus,
must ever experience at the hands of the children of this
world. Let us hold by Christ; and we must lay our account with the hatred and resistance of nature, as well as
with the blindness and incredulity which will distrust all
our professions, and persevere in maligning and withstand-
ing, even in the face of the clearest evidences which can be
adduced on the side of innocence and truth. Let me do
Thy will, O God, and Thou wilt hear my prayer. Give
me to say with truth—Lord, I believe; and let the effect
be that in all time coming I shall yield to Him the homage of my grateful obedience. And O deliver me not up
to the judicial blindness which comes upon those who stifle
the light that is in them; make me thoroughly aware of
the ignorance of nature: may I at least see thus much,
how blind and destitute I am in myself—as much as
might make this darkness visible—that sensible thereof
I might cast about, and be so awakened to the danger
and deficiency of nature, that Christ shall give me light.
(Eph. v. 14.) Christ proceeds on the principles of a certain
judicial administration, in dispensing to men the blessings
of light and saving knowledge; He withholds them from

those who think themselves wise and rich, and to have
need of nothing; He confers them on the poor in Spirit,
who feel the burden of their incapacity for spiritual
things. The gift of heavenly illumination He keeps back
from the proud and confers upon the humble. Make me
feel, O God, how little the light of my own mind is; and
even that little let me not abuse or be proud of, lest it
be taken away, and I be left in utter and irremediable
darkness.

JOHN X.

Give us to know Thy voice, O Lord Jesus; and enable
us to protect Thy vineyard from the intrusion of all but
the genuine expounders and stewards of the mysteries of
God; the genuine ambassadors of Him who is the great
Shepherd of the sheep.

No man cometh unto the Father but by the Son,
through whom alone we have access with liberty. He is
the great door of entry and acceptance for the sinners of a
guilty world; and it is my prayer that I may be led to
Him as the place of constant ingress when drawing nigh
not for acceptance only but also for spiritual nourishment,
that I may grow in grace and obtain the requisite strength
and guidance for all services. May I go in for the ever
needful supplies of God's Spirit, that in virtue of these I
may be helped to all duty when I go out on the business
of that world which is the field of discipline and preparation for a better world; let me grow in the spiritual life
more and more every day abundantly; and at the hands
of the good Shepherd who laid down His life for the sheep,
may I receive such grace and goodness as that He may
recognise me to be indeed one of His own. He who was

once crucified is now exalted; and O from the place He now occupies, may the Holy Ghost, sent forth by Him, accomplish in me the travail of my Redeemer's soul, that He may see and be satisfied.

Give me, O God, to know Thy Son by immediate discernment as well as by His works; let me hear and know His voice; and building myself up in my most holy faith, let me look with full assurance to that eternal life which is bestowed on all whom the Father hath given unto the Son. Let my fellowship be with both, for both are one: Christ is God, and the Father is in Him, and He in the Father. Give me thus to believe, that I may rejoice more and more in that redemption which is through the blood of a Divine sacrifice.

JOHN XI.

April, 1843.

There were certain individuals whom Jesus signalized by His more special love—as John, and Lazarus, and his sisters; let me be alive as He was to the sensations of friendship, as well as of general charity. Notwithstanding the regard He bore to all the members of the family, He subjected them to a temporary affliction, that by the illustrious miracle of this chapter He might show forth the glory of God, and cause many to believe in His name. He stayed away during the sickness, to the intent that His disciples might believe when they saw him raised from the dead. And what precious and weighty doctrine is embodied in this miracle—the doctrine of Jesus being the resurrection and the life, and also of the way in which we are made to participate therein—even by believing in Him. Though we be dead in trespasses and sins, yet upon so believing shall we be raised to spiritual life here; and though laid by natural death in the grave, yet shall we be raised to everlasting life hereafter. O my God, deposit within me this precious seed of immortality, that I may never die—that I may have my fruit unto holiness, and in the end life everlasting. I believe, help mine unbelief. The grief which made our Saviour weep may partly have been grief at the hardness of their hearts in not believing what He had just intimated of His power to raise from the dead. This we should infer both from verses 33 and 38, and also from His remonstrance in verse 40. But may we not say that there was also compassion in it—the sympathy of nature with the sorrows of nature, and by which a sanction and a sacredness are given to the sensibilities which are called forth when friends and relatives are taken away from us. Give me, O Lord, to be altogether like unto Him, who had compassion for all the suffering which flesh is heir to, and went about doing good continually, both to the bodies and the souls of men. His regard for souls shines forth also in this narrative. He prayed aloud that the people who stood by might believe that God was with Him; and many (verse 45) believed accordingly. O Lord, may I have respect unto the souls of men, and do all that in me lies for the moral and spiritual wellbeing of all who are around me.

Even the opposition of Christ's enemies turns for a testimony. And how precious the extract here given from the testimony of Caiaphas—even that Christ should die for His people, and gather into one all the children and chosen of God. When lifted up He should draw all men unto Him. Draw me, O God, that I may come unto

Christ, who will not cast me out. He is all my desire;
and give me to be assured, both by my experience of His
grace, and my faith in His promises, that He will be all
my salvation.

JOHN XII.

My God, let the honour of Christ be the aim and principle of all my doings. It is true that He will accept
what is done for His disciples as done unto Himself: and
even as to the general poor, it is the lesson of His gospel
that we should be willing to distribute. They are the
perennial objects of our perennial attention and care; but
in perfect harmony with our abiding duty to them are
those large and costly sacrifices, which either the necessities of His Church or the extension of His kingdom might
require.

Let us no longer wonder that our enemies should resist
every demonstration that we can offer of our cause, however clear or irrefragable it may appear to be in our own
eyes. The disciple is not above his Master; and what
contradiction of sinners He had to sustain, when in fell
and resolute opposition they not only withstood the evidence of a most stupendous miracle, but even would have
removed by murder him who was the subject of it from
the observation of the people.

But though the rulers were against Him, the people
were still with Him. And so it is with us at the present
moment; yet let us not be over-confident—the same
multitude who rent the air with their hosannas, in a few
days more called out to crucify Him. Let us trust not
in men, whether they be the many or the few, but let us
place our confidence in Thee alone, O God.

O prepare us for every sacrifice; make us, in the day of Thy power, willing to lose all and to suffer all for Christ's sake. May the day of our enemies' persecution, should it really arrive, be indeed the day of Thy power. Let us sit loose to the world, and to all that is in the world, counting not even our lives dear unto us, if so be that the kingdom of Christ and the good of souls are advanced thereby. Jesus was troubled, and so also may we —longing as He did for exemption from the coming evil; but like Him, too, may we concede all to the will of God. And O may we be of the number of those who are drawn to Him who was lifted up for the sins of the world. May we not walk in darkness, but be the children of light.

And we shall not abide in darkness, if we believe in Christ. Open mine eyes, O God, that the Son may be fully revealed in me. Save me from the awful doom of those whom the God of this world hath blinded. And let mine be a faithful and a fearless testimony, on the side of Him who came into the world on the errand, not to judge or to condemn, but to save. By the rejection of Him we shall be the authors of our own undoing, and our own condemnation. His unfeigned desire, and the declared will of God, are on the side of our everlasting life. If that which the Father and the Son propose to us as the savour of life unto life should turn out the savour of death unto death to us, it will be due to ourselves, our blood shall be upon our own heads, and on us will lie the charge of our ruined eternity. From this awful catastrophe, Good Lord, deliver us.

JOHN XIII.

Jesus, the same to-day, yesterday, and for ever, loveth

His own, and loveth them unto the end. Give me, O my Lord and Master, a realizing sense of Thy love. Let me feel its constraining influence leading me both to love and to live unto Him who died for me. More especially, let me imitate Thine own most gracious condescension—looking always unto Thee set forth as an example; and not satisfied with knowing, may I have the happiness of those who do Thy will. Clothe me with humility, O God; and as the faithful disciple of Him who let Himself down to the meanest offices of help and service, let me, emptied of all vanity and self, be a follower of the meek and lowly Jesus. And wash me throughly from mine iniquity, cleanse me from my sin, else I have no part in that gospel salvation which delivers all on whom it takes effect from the pollution and the power, as well as the punishment of their evil propensities and doings. If we call Him Master and Lord, let us do the things which He says. He knew both the hidden things of man's heart, and the hidden things of futurity; and by His knowledge of these, He brought first the evidence of divination, as in the case of the woman of Samaria, and the evidence of prophecy, as now, to the support of His divine mission. O grant that on the strength of His manifold credentials, I may indeed believe to the saving of my soul; and may it be such a faith that I may be able to stand against the wiles of the devil. But let him that thinketh he standeth, take heed lest he fall. The same adversary who obtained the final and decisive mastery over the wretched Judas, could also surprise Peter into, at least, one most humiliating overthrow. And he can take occasional advantage of the faithful, who are subjected in consequence to sad alternations—at some times of shame and sorrow, with the satisfaction, at other times, of victory and progress. It is thus that Paul could, after describing the agonies of the conflict, break out into the triumphant exclamation of— "I thank God through Jesus Christ our Lord." And our Saviour Himself, though without sin, had His hours of anguish, yet brightened and relieved by the " joy that was set before Him ;" and so endured the cross, despising the shame. In this very passage we read of His being troubled in spirit, and shortly after of His triumphing in the achievements and the hopes of glory. And such is the chequered mental state of all Christians in the world —troubled on every side, yet not only patient, but glorying in tribulations, because rejoicing in hope of the glory of God. Let me not forget the Saviour's new commandment—the blessed commandment of love for the brethren. O enable me to forget the grudges and heart-burnings of past controversy. Give me a well-grounded confidence in those with whom I act—that in one spirit, and with one mind, we may strive together for the faith and purity of the gospel.

JOHN XIV.

We now enter on one of the most affecting and memorable passages in the whole of the inspired record— characterized by its beauty and tenderness, as well as by its great doctrinal importance. What a remedy against tribulation of heart, that the fellowship to which we are called is not with the Father only, but with the Father and the Son. And how interesting to think of His present employment for us in heaven—that of preparing a place for us there. O may He by His Spirit prepare us for the place. Let us come unto Him who has not only

the word, but is Himself the way to life everlasting—and
the only way to Him whose favour is better than life. O
for the life-giving truth, as it is in Jesus, that I may be
saved and sanctified thereby. He who hath seen the Son
hath seen the Father, even the brightness of His glory
and the express image of His person. It doth not suffice
us to have a knowledge of the Father without a knowledge
of the Son, for then should we know only the terrors of
the Lord. O that I could realize such an intimate fellowship and oneness with Christ as subsist between Him and
the Father ; and then by thus abiding in Him I should
be strengthened for doing all things. In His name do I
ask for pardon, trusting to His promise that so it will be
done unto me ; and how delightful to reflect that by my
peace and forgiveness obtained in this way the Father is
glorified—and so the honour of the Most High is exalted
in the reconciliation of me, a miserable offender. But let
me ask for more than this. Let me ask for the love of
Christ, and such a sense of His love as might constrain
me to live unto Him and so keep His commandments.
And O for the promise of the Father—even the Spirit of
Truth, to abide with me for ever, to dwell in me and shine
in my heart, for the Spirit of consolation and of quickening, so that hereby we may know that He abideth in us
even by the Spirit which He hath given us. And let me
assiduously, and with all diligence, keep the commandments, walking in this plain way, by which I may be conducted to Christ's promised manifestations. O that I had
the Father and the Son dwelling in me ; and the Comforter
or Monitor, even the Holy Ghost, teaching me all things,
and bringing all things to my remembrance ; for how
miserably prone am I, amid the distractions of sense, to

let those things slip which concern God and His will, which
is my sanctification. Do Thou, the very God of peace,
sanctify me wholly. Let me have the peace of those who
love Thee and Thy law—that peace which keepeth my
heart and mind through Christ Jesus. Let my heart be
fixed, and not be afraid of evil tidings, because trusting
in the Lord. And for this purpose let me consider Him
who is the Apostle and High-Priest of my profession, and
to whom, now that as God-man He is exalted at the right
hand of the Most High, all power has been given in
Heaven and in earth. Let us rejoice then in this His
exaltation, while at the same time we look for His second
coming, and live in the blessed hope of being for ever with
the Lord.

JOHN XV.

This is one of my most precious chapters. Save me,
O God, from the excision of an unfruitful branch ; and
rather separate from me the most darling objects of
temptation, than that my affections should be seduced or
diverted away from Thyself. Purify my heart by faith
and by Thy word, which is the subject-matter of faith.
This cleansing power of the word is adverted to in Psalm
cxix. 9 ; Acts xv. 9 ; Eph. v. 26 ; 1 Pet. i. 22, 23.—Above
all, let me abide in Christ, let me ever be acting faith in
Him, even by keeping by Him in trust and with constant
application for His friendship and grace ; and He meeting
these habitual motions of my soul will habitually respond
to them with an unfailing and abiding faithfulness, and
so will cause me to abound in much fruit. O let me live
this life of faith on the Son of God, without whom I can
do nothing ; but with whom, and by His words abiding

in me, I shall ask all the strength I desire and stand in
need of, for doing all things. May this be my experience,
O Lord, following up the sacrament of this day, that I
may walk worthy of the sacred profession I have just
made; and that my Father in Heaven may be glorified
by the fruits of a consistent and productive discipleship
—a discipleship signalized by the keeping of all the commandments. Then will my Saviour love me; and I shall
abide in His love: and then shall I be in the Son, even
as the Son is in the Father. Rejoice over me, O my
Saviour, for good; and let me rejoice with full assurance
of heart in Thee, from whom I have received the atonement.
Let me love my fellow-men, even as Christ loved me, and
gave Himself for me; and let us serve Christ, not in
the oldness of the letter, as bondsmen, but in the newness
of the Spirit, as friends; and O may I ask of Thy grace till I
receive it, and Thine ordination of me become palpable
from my conformity to the image of Christ.   And let me
not count it strange though the world hate me; let me be
encouraged against this by the example of my Lord and
Master.   Let me have no overweening confidence in men,
but lay my account with the saying, That all who live
godly in Christ Jesus shall suffer persecution.   There is a
natural enmity, which abideth as vigorous as ever in the
hearts of the unconverted, and of which I fear we must
be prepared for another great outbreak ere the world shall
become the fair abode of religious peace and liberty.   O
Lord, may Thy Spirit, the Comforter, be poured forth to
sustain us amid all the trials which may now be awaiting
Thy Church.   Save us from our own will and our own
waywardness.   May we ever walk in the footsteps of Thy
word, and under the guidance of a wisdom from on high.

May the Spirit which proceedeth from Thee come down upon our minds, and so testify in us, that we might be led to hold forth a pure and a clear testimony to the world. Qualify me, O Lord, for bearing witness aright; and let me not be careful of what I shall say, but trust in the Holy Ghost, from whom the answer of the mouth and the preparation of the heart alike come.

JOHN XVI.

Devon Iron Works, May, 1843.

And, O my God, let me not be offended, or stumble, or be made to fall, should the enemies of the Church's freedom proceed to violence in our own day. Father, forgive them, for they know not what they do. Let me be reconciled to such dealings by the examples which have been recorded for our admonition, on whom the latter ends of the world have come. And let us not mourn or be in heaviness—at least not in despair, because of any temporary withdrawment of the Divine countenance and aid—seeing, that in His own good time and way, God will appear to vindicate His own cause, and bring forth judgment unto victory.

Meanwhile, let not the aids of Thy Spirit, O God, be withheld from us. May He guide us unto all needful truth, and inspire us with all right and necessary convictions. May we be strengthened by Him in the inner man unto all patience and long-suffering with joyfulness. And may He be our Monitor as well as our Comforter, guiding us unto all wisdom, and ever actuating our hearts with all charity.

And, O blessed Saviour, do Thou adapt Thy manifestations both to the circumstances of our lot and to our spiritual exigencies—more especially, do Thou reveal to us more

and more of Thyself. May the Spirit take of the things
of Christ, and make to our souls a clear and convincing
demonstration of them, that we may understand aright of
the sin, and the righteousness, and the judgment, which
are here spoken of. May His kingdom come, and may
we long more and more for His appearance as they whose
conversation is in Heaven, and who look for the Saviour.

There may be a season before us when we shall be cast
down, and the world shall rejoice. If cast down, yet may
we not be destroyed. May we be upheld by the promised
grace from on high, which we have so much encouragement to pray for in the name of Christ; and it will be given
to us by the Father, who is a very present help in the
time of trouble, and a very present help in the time of
temptation.

Let us but love God and all things will work together
for our good;—even the external tribulations of our history
will prove so many blessings in disguise, and will not be
able to destroy the deep inward peace in Christ which
passeth all understanding. Heavenly Redeemer, may we
be grounded and settled in the love of Thee, and not be
moved away from the hope of Thy gospel.

JOHN XVII.

What a lofty and transcendental region does this chapter raise us to—the utterance of the Eternal Son to His
Eternal Father—the communing of Spirit between the
second and first person of the glorious Trinity. The
Father is asked to glorify the Son—not with a higher
glory than belongs to Him essentially as God—but that
the God-man may be glorified with the glory which, as

God the Son, He had with His Father before the world
was. O give me that knowledge of God and of Jesus
Christ which is life everlasting. May the Son reveal the
Father to me, and then shall He who has power over all
flesh have given to me eternal life. O let the manifestation of the Spirit be added to the manifestation of the
word; and when the things of Christ are thus shown to
us, then shall we see the perfect intercommunion which
there is between the Father and the Son, and that all
things whatsoever which have been given to the Son are
indeed of the Father. More especially shall we know and
believe that His words are of God—even the words of a
real messenger from the upper sanctuary. And what a
noticeable thing it is that Christ should have prayed, not
for the world, but for the elect. He had perfect knowledge
and discrimination of the two; but it is our part to pray
for all, to pray at a venture—just as to preach the free
gospel unto all, and preach at a venture. Jesus Christ
knew thoroughly; but, as even Peter said to Simon Magus
—" And *perhaps* thou mayest be forgiven,"—well might
we say—let us pray for all, and who knows but this one
and that other may be given to our prayers. O to realize
oneness with Christ, and by the communion of saints,
oneness with each other—even such a oneness as subsists
between the Father and the Son, that we may have
fellowship not with God and Christ only, but fellowship
one with another. By Thy word, O blessed Jesus, may
we overcome that adverse world wherein Thou hast told
us that we shall have tribulation. If not taken out of
the world, may we at least be kept from the evil of it. If
in the world we are to have tribulation, in Thee may we
have peace. And, O God, set us apart, and send us

whithersoever Thou wilt, that we may be the instruments
in Thy hand for spreading abroad the truth of Thy precious and everlasting gospel—even of that which Thou
hast exalted above all Thy name.   Our Saviour, in verse
9, prays for those whom His Father had given Him ; in
verse 20, He prays for those who believe—in the one case,
for those whose election He knew—in the other, for those
to whom He assigns a personal characteristic, even faith
—that faith by the observation of which Paul knew the
election of his Thessalonian converts.   Give us, O Lord,
that ostensible union which might impress the world, and
lead them to believe ; and give us that intimate union
with the Father, and the Son, and with one another, which
our Saviour prays for.   O for the enjoyment of Thy love,
and for that holy satisfaction in God which the world
knoweth not.   May I realize the high and hidden mysteries of the Christian life.   May I attain to the riches of
the full assurance of understanding, to the acknowledgment of the mystery of God, and of the Father, and of
Christ.

JOHN XVIII.

What a lesson of submission is here given to all the
disposals and dispensations of our Father in Heaven.   The
cup which He hath put into my hands to drink shall I not
drink it ?   O God, teach me the resignation which is held
forth by this holy example, and more, if by any labours
or sufferings of mine any good is to accrue in furtherance
of the great object of the salvation of human souls, let me
look up to Him who is the Author of salvation, and walk
in His gracious footsteps ; for He even died for us—the
one man Christ Jesus died for the people.   He who was

so tender of the lives of others, and bade Peter put up his sword, gave up His own life for the sins of a rebellious and ungrateful world. O that we followed Him in His meekness, and endurance, and fervent charity; and instead of resisting as Peter would have done, if not forbidden by the voice of His Master, let us learn not to strive, but be gentle to all men, even under the cruellest provocations. And yet there was a spirit and a remonstrance, not in anger or the inclination to revenge, but under the promptings of a feeling of justice. He knew the High-Priest, for He knew all men, though Paul did not in similar circumstances; and yet this knowledge did not restrain Him from the act of expostulation, for which, when smitten, while He submitted to the wrong, He showed His sense of it. O may the fall of Peter be a lesson of caution and humility to myself. He thought that he stood, yet fell. Let me not be of those proud whom God resisteth, but of those humble to whom grace is given.

What a dreadful atrocity did these persecutors of Jesus fall into, in that they so flagrantly violated the moral while they recoiled from any freedom with the ceremonial law. Give me, O Lord, to be observant of all righteousness; and while I do the weightier things, let me not leave the smaller things undone; and, O may I remember that the cause of the Church should not be fought with carnal weapons. It is not of this world, therefore let us not fight or strive as the potsherds do with the potsherds of the earth. Let us, like our great Head before us, bear witness unto the truth, which is great, and will finally prevail. Let our conversation be where our kingdom is, even in heaven; and let us so walk in wisdom and the meekness of wisdom that even our enemies might be constrained to say—We find in them no fault at all.

JOHN XIX.

Give me, O Lord, to be imprest aright by this recital of the sufferings of my Saviour. May I therein see the greatness of His love, and feel its constraining influence, so as that I may love Him back again—yea, and live to Him who died for me. And O may the trifling injuries which I sustain be borne with the meekness and charity which shine so conspicuously in the whole deportment of Him who was led as a lamb to the slaughter. More especially, let me know what it is to take up my cross daily, and bearing it as He did, learn in all things to follow Him. Let me all the more venerate that Scripture, the fulfilment of which was so signally manifested in all the circumstances of our Saviour's death; and give me to observe the like scrupulous conformity to its sayings, as what is here manifested by Him who is at once the teacher and the pattern of all righteousness. And, O let me never forget the beautiful example of tenderness given forth in the recommendation of His disconsolate mother—nor yet the hospitality of the disciple to whose care He committed her. Above all, let me ever keep in memory this first principle of the oracles of God, that Christ died for our sins according to the Scriptures; and let the graces of faith, and hope, and love, be upheld within by the contemplation of that awful yet blessed crisis—when He bowed His head and gave up the ghost, pouring out His soul for me, and so laying the grateful burden of this obligation upon me, that I should give up my soul unto Him.

And let me well understand that my salvation is both by water and by blood—so that I might be washed not only from the guilt of sin, but also from its pollution. O may my sins be washed out in the blood of the Lamb. and also may the washing of regeneration, and the renewing of the Holy Spirit, be brought to bear upon me.

And Thou gavest Him and His cause to have favour with one, at least, of the rich in this world. We pray, O Lord, that Thou wouldst make our enemies to be at peace with us. Not many rich, not many noble, are on our side —yet Thou canst turn the hearts of men whithersoever Thou wilt; and we desire to bless Thee, O God, for the measure of countenance vouchsafed to our Church even by the affluent and noble of our day, and by the great bulk of the common people. But we desire to look beyond men, regarding them but in the light of instruments and secondary causes; and directly to Thee, O God, and to Thy will, would we refer everything that befalls us—if prosperous, receiving it with all gratitude as a kindness from heaven—if adverse, submitting to it as one of heaven's wise and righteous visitations.

JOHN XX.

June, 1843.

When the disciple whom Jesus loved (John) entered the sepulchre, he saw and believed. But blessed are they who have not seen and yet have believed. Grant me this blessedness, O Lord. Give me to believe from the heart that Thou hast raised Christ from the dead, and then I shall be saved. (Rom. x. 9.) And Christ calls His disciples His brethren—standing in common relation with Himself to "my Father and your Father, to my

God and your God." It is well to bring this into juxta-
position with the exclamation of Thomas—" My Lord and
my God." O that we were alive as we ought to the very
peculiar relation in which we stand to the God-man:
His children as God, His brethren as Himself the elder
brother of the Church, and the first-fruits of that blessed
resurrection which ushers all who partake of it into their
eternal home. Let me henceforth, and that for a practical end, make a closer and profounder study than heretofore of His person and His glory.

And give me, O blessed Jesus, that peace which passeth
all understanding—peace and joy in believing; a peace
which only cometh by the Holy Ghost taking of the
things of Christ and showing them unto us—thus causing
us to believe, even as Christ did when He showed to the
disciples His hands and His side. I can perceive a distinct authority given to the Church in the matter of discipline, in the act of Christ breathing on the apostles and
conferring the Holy Spirit upon them, and empowering
them to exclude or admit into the privileges of the
gospel.

Lord, I believe, help mine unbelief—if not by a sensible,
at least by a spiritual demonstration—if not by the manifestation of Thy body to my eye, at least by the manifestation of Thy truth unto my conscience. Let me not be
faithless, but save me from the evil heart of unbelief.
Thou art grieved with our slowness, and the hardness of
our hearts; but have compassion on it also, and forbid
that the manifold engrossments of the outer world should
destroy either the frame of spirituality or the habit of
prayer.

There is enough written in Scripture for making me

wise unto salvation. This, indeed, is the express purpose of
what is written—that I might believe, and that believing
I might have life. With a view to this precious faith, then,
let me ponder these things. Let me make a diligent
perusal of the word that is nigh unto me. As I read let
the life-giving spirit impart to me that light which is the
life of man. Let my eyes be opened to behold, and my
understanding to understand the Scriptures.

JOHN XXI.

Thou, O Lord, who thus multipliedst the draught of the
fishermen, canst multiply the converts of those who are
the fishers of men. O may the work of conversion speed
and prosper gloriously in our day. Give labourers for the
harvest, O Lord, and give to these labourers the harvest
of many souls. May this be their hire; and may they
have cause more and more to rejoice in that the pleasure
of the Lord prospereth in their hand. And O may it be
the constraining love of Christ teaching them to love
Him back again, which prompts and upholds them in all
the labours of their ministry. May their love to Christ
subordinate every other love—not only preferring Him to
all the pursuits and objects of an earthly calling, but leading
them to acquiesce in the disappointments which they may
be called to suffer in the prosecution of their own favourite
objects, and favourite ways or methods for the furtherance
of His kingdom in the world. Let me acquiesce, O God,
in the whole of Thy providential will; and not fret myself
because of the prevalent blindness or indifference to the
territorial principle, or any other principle of ecclesiastical
polity and economics on which my affections may be set.

May the love of Christ overbear all ; and seeing that if thwarted, it can only be by His permission—let me, loving Him more than my own schemes or the devices of my own heart, willingly defer to His counsel, as that which sooner or later is alone sure to stand.   I in my old age may be carried whither I would not, in the sense of being drifted along against the current of my own conceptions and wishes in matters ecclesiastical: let me acquiesce in Thy disposals, O God ; and, meanwhile, think not that any strange thing hath happened to me, but be thankful for this—"That I have not yet resisted unto blood, striving against sin." With the zeal of Peter let me not have his inquisitiveness ; but be content with my ignorance of all that is beyond or above what is written— willing to adjourn the determination of all mysteries to the day that shall unravel and declare them.—Ever blessed be Thy name, O God, for the testimony of Thine own chosen witnesses, which may we implicitly believe, and faithfully act upon.   This testimony, no doubt, was limited only to a part of the ways and the doings of Jesus— yet a sufficient part for the guidance meanwhile of our footsteps to heaven.   Let us be aware, however, that His ways are infinite, and His riches unsearchable.

ACTS.

ACTS I.—In entering on this delightful portion of Scripture, I would pray for the vivifying and illuminating Spirit, that He may guide me aright, and impress me aright, with what is there laid before me throughout its successive passages.   Let me know what the waiting attitude is ; let

me wait for the promise of the Father—not deferring my
obedience till the desired and expected grace shall descend upon me, but waiting for that grace, and this in
that very spirit of obedience which led the apostles to
Jerusalem at the bidding of our Lord, and restrained them
to it as the place of assignation, where they were to look
for the Spirit from on high. Thus, O God, may I ever be
found at my prescribed post, whether as a reader of Thy
Bible, or as an attendant on Thine ordinances, or as a doer
of Thy will—assured that it is only when in the way of
duty that we are warranted to count on the fulfilment of
Thy blessed purposes of grace and mercy towards us.
Baptize me, O Lord, with the Holy Ghost—that from Him
I may receive power to walk as one of Thy children ; and
O let me ever be looking for the Saviour, and ever bethink
myself of the position that He now occupies as my Observer and my Judge, that I may ever be doing His will, and
ever praying for His grace.

Let me forget not, that not only did the disciples obey
our Lord in going to Jerusalem, and waiting there, but
that there they continued in prayer and supplication.
His promise did not supersede their prayer, but rather
supplied them with the very topic which formed the subject of their prayer, and gave them the encouragement
and the warrant—nay, laid on them the duty to supplicate
for its fulfilment.—" For this I shall be inquired after."
And thus, O God, would we mix our prayers with our
readings and our performances, and all our acts of obedience. Thus may we be enabled to proceed from strength
to strength, and from one degree of grace and of enlargement to another, till we appear perfect before Thee in
Zion. And even on this side of death there is the appear-

ance of a great work before us, as there was for the apostles, and for which we should pray mightily that we might be strengthened and prepared. Enable me, O Lord, to take part in that ministry which is most suited to the present exigencies of our country and of our Church. Guide me to the part which I ought to take. May right agents be formed and multiplied under me. Set me, O Lord, on a productive walk and work of usefulness; and above all, as a precursor to my efficiency in the business of public Christianity, do I pray for my own personal Christianity. Uphold me with Thy free Spirit; and then will I teach transgressors Thy ways, and sinners shall be converted unto Thee.

ACTS II.

Heavenly Father, I call on the name of the Lord that I may be saved—saved by Thy Spirit's visitation from the disease of sin in my heart, saved by Thy Son's sacrifice from the punishment of sin, on the awful day of Thy coming wrath. O may Christ be at my right hand, and I shall not be moved. Let my tongue speak of His right-eousness, and my heart therein rejoice. Make me full of joy, O God, with the light of Thy reconciled countenance. May Thy Son upon His throne subdue His enemies under Him, and more especially all that opposeth itself in my heart against the saving knowledge of God, and the obedi-ence of the gospel. May that blessed influence which was shed forth on the day of Pentecost be shed on me abundantly—for this promise of the Father is not confined to the men of that day, but was to them, and to their children, and to all that were afar off, even to as many as the Lord our God should call. May Thy call, O God, be rendered effectual—so as that I may indeed repent, and receive the true baptism, even the baptism of the Holy Ghost. O let mine be a real conversion, an actual coming out from a world lying in wickedness. And I would receive Thy word gladly—and forbid that after having received a taste for its precious sayings, I should at any time fall away. O give me to be steadfast in the doctrine and worship of the New Testament. Let me have a greater taste for the fellowships of social religion. Draw me out in larger and more liberal distributions of my wealth for the good of Thy Church ; and more especially in this day of general privation to Thy faithful ministers, give me to have a heart for all, and a house for all : and let me know what it is to use the world as not abusing it, to keep within the limits of moderation, and yet enjoy within these limits. And O for that singleness of heart which belongs to those who give up all for eternity. Give me what I mainly need—the faculty of praising Thee. What I should like above all things would be to joy in God, to delight myself in God ; and for this purpose let me cherish that faith in Christ through which alone I can be admitted among His children, or have the Spirit of adoption given to me. I pray, O Lord, for daily accessions to the true Church in this land. If it be Thy blessed will may it long abide in favour among all the people ; but prepare us for the worst ; and let us marvel not though we should come to be hated of the world.

ACTS III.

July, 1843.

Let the means and the opportunities of usefulness such

as I have, be consecrated to the relief of human suffering, and to the happiness and wellbeing of men. Silver and gold I shall in all probability have less of than in former days; but, apart from these, how manifold are the channels of a most productive benevolence to others! Give me, O Lord, to study with effect the various, so as to ascertain the best ways of doing good; and O endow me with a greater love for human souls, that both by example and by direct endeavour I may be the instrument of spiritual blessings to those within the sphere of my influence. And, O God, do Thou loose my own bands—do Thou set me at liberty, that emancipated from the guilt and the power of sin, I may go forth with heaven-born alacrity in all the services of righteousness, to the praise of Thy grace: and let me ascribe nothing to any power or holiness of my own. In whatever I minister let it be as of the ability which God giveth, that in all things Thou mayest be glorified through Jesus Christ, and I be ever ready in all humility to say—Nevertheless, not me, but the grace of God that is in me. And may I remember what the channel is through which this grace cometh— even faith in the name of Christ—faith on the part of the administrators, by which they were enabled to do the good—faith on the part of the recipient, by which he was qualified to receive, and to become strong, and to be restored to perfect soundness in the presence of them all. He had faith to be healed: O my God, may I have like faith with him, and with like effect. May I be healed of all my spiritual maladies. May the Prince and the Saviour at Thy right hand give me repentance and remission by the blotting out of my sins. Turn me, and I shall be turned; and O grant me the refreshing and strengthening

influences of that Divine Spirit by whom alone it is that
I am enabled to mortify the deeds of the body, and so
to live. O may I be solemnized, and practically, so as to
proceed upon the saying, that whosoever shall not hear
Christ as their Prophet shall be destroyed; and give me
to stand in awe, and be arrested by the saying, that if
any man defile the temple of God, him shall God destroy.
Thou knowest, O God, the sin which doth most easily beset
me; enable me to cast it aside, that I may ever breathe
in the clear element of purity and a safe conscience. O
bless me by turning me from mine iniquities; and save
me from that most damning and idolatrous of all iniquities—the iniquity of a heart charged with vile affections,
and setting them on the things which are beneath; and
having no affections so set on the things which are above,
as to supplant or subordinate all the evil desires of an
evil and accursed nature. In me, that is in my flesh, there
dwelleth no good thing.

ACTS IV.

There is nothing new under the sun. As in former
days, so now, might there again be the opposition of this
world's rulers to the preaching of a pure and a free gospel
in these lands. Grant us, O Lord, the same recompense
which the Apostles had before us, so that howbeit despised
and thwarted by men in place and in power, many might
believe on the word spoken by the upright and intrepid
expounders of the truth as it is in Jesus. O Lord, may
Thy presence and power from on high be with us this
day, when assembled for Sabbath service in my own
dwelling, as we are now driven to the necessity of having

a Church in the house. O may the pure and precious doctrine of the cross be rightly and effectually proclaimed by us—even the doctrine of Him who was set at nought, even as His Headship is set at nought in this our day. May we have grace to propound Him as the alone Saviour, and earnestly to contend for Him as the alone Ruler, in whom alone salvation is to be found, and whom, whenever the authorities come into conflict, we ought to obey rather than man. Give us, O Lord, so long as it seemeth unto Thee good, the suffrages and favour of the people; but should, in the methods of Thy discipline, we be deprived even of this, give us to maintain an unfaltering adherence to Thy word and Thy will in all things, and then shall we have the praise of God, which is better than the praise of men.

In our approaches to God may we know how to blend the natural with the revealed theology, and, like the apostle, recognise God as the Lord of Creation, the great Maker of heaven and earth, and the sea, and all things; while in the same address he did Him homage as the Father of the holy child, Jesus. Fill us, O Lord, with the Holy Ghost, so that with all boldness we may declare His word, even though the kings and rulers of the earth should gather together against Him.

And, O Lord, provide us with such human helps as Thou knowest to be best for us. Give us all the popular encouragement and support which we may stand in need of. Put the grace of Christian liberality into the hearts of very many of the Church's friends; and as the fruit of powerful and efficient preaching on the one hand, grant that on the other there may be willing hearers in readiness to place at the disposal of the Church's rulers what may be expedient for the Church's good. May they on the other hand be taught to distribute wisely and well whatever is put into their hands; and give us all not to mind our own things only, but the things of others also.

ACTS V.

Put truth in my inward parts, O God. Let me deal fairly by Thy Holy Spirit; and let not the deceitfulness of sin either darken or dilute the power of His suggestions upon my conscience. Give me, O Lord, to walk in simplicity and godly sincerity, and not with fleshly wisdom, but by the grace of God may I have my conversation in the world; and I would render unto the Holy Ghost divine honours: in lying unto Him we lie unto God.

And we would now pray, if not for sensible miracles, at least for miracles of grace, that in this our day multitudes shall be added unto the Church; and without depending upon man, yet we desire to rejoice and be thankful when, through the blessing and by the permission of God, we are in favour with all the people.

We are opposed, as heretofore, by the rulers of our land; nevertheless, let us persevere in declaring all the words of life. O that they may tell with vital and converting influence upon many, and that the great and one thing needful—the salvation of souls—may be the fruit of all the varied and emulous activities which are put forth in our day. Sanctify, O God, the principle of all our doings, and let their effect be the turning of many to righteousness. Let the impellent power and motive of our proceeding be obedience to God rather than to men; yet, let not a feeling of proud resistance to man, or triumph

over him, taint and vitiate this sacred influence. How
rich in doctrine are the two contiguous verses, 31 and 32,
both as respects the second and third persons of the Trinity! Let me not divide Christ, nor put asunder the
things which God hath joined. It is the office of the
Prince and the Saviour exalted at His right hand to give
both repentance and the remission of sins. Let me equally
desire both; let me pray for both; and O may I work
mightily by strength conferred upon me from on high, so
as to perfect my repentance and perfect my holiness.
And how relevant to this process is this weighty sentence
—that the Holy Ghost is given to those who obey Him.
By the blessed alternation of performance and prayer,
give me, O Lord, to experience that in serving faithfully
I am supplied plentifully and fruitfully with grace from
Thine upper sanctuary. Let our righteousness spring up
from earth, and Thy grace look down upon us from heaven.
Prepare us both to do and to suffer. Give us to feel the
honour of bearing any part in the service of Christ and of
His cause, and let us be in readiness to give up all for
His sake.

ACTS VI.

There is much of solid and vital instruction in this brief
chapter; and first, the paramount importance of the special
work of the Christian ministry—enough to engross all the
time and attention of him who undertakes it, so as that
he should put away from him all that might distract him
from those things sacred on which he ought to meditate,
and give himself wholly to them, that his profiting may
appear unto all. Let this be more and more the spirit of
the ministers of our Church, and so that they may give

themselves continually to prayer and to the ministry of the word. What a significancy there is in the conjunction here presented of these two exercises; what a lesson to the preachers of the gospel not to trust in themselves, as if there was a sufficiency in themselves, but to derive help from Him who can alone make effectual the words spoken by man, even though they be the words of God's own inspiration. Pour, O God, the Spirit of grace and supplication on our Church's office-bearers; and while Thou providest labourers in the more high and heavenly work of heralding from our pulpits the salvation of the New Testament, we pray that all the other needful offices of the Church may be abundantly and competently filled. More especially do we pray for a sufficient supply of deacons, who might relieve the ministers of all the secularities which are too often accumulated upon them. Nor let us imagine that because the ministers should be disjoined from things secular, the deacons were to be disjoined from things sacred. They were not only required to be men of honest report, and to be full of wisdom, but also to be full of the Holy Ghost; and Stephen, one of them, was full of the Holy Ghost and faith. He is afterwards said to be full of faith and power; and while his proper official business was to care for the poor, he also set himself forth to the defence of the gospel, and acquitted himself thereof with wisdom and spirit. O God, do Thou raise up deacons for our Church, and do Thou abundantly Christianize them. A great number of the ministers have entered it; let there be a corresponding number of other office-bearers, and with the goodly apparatus of a well-equipped Church, may there be made an abundant provision both for the spiritual and the economical interests

of the people. Yet who knows but that violence and persecution may hereafter arise, insomuch that both deceit
and cruelty may be practised against us; if so, give us,
O Lord, the boldness of those primitive witnesses for the
truth; and may we be followers of them not only in
courage but in charity. Give us the serenity of conscious
uprightness; and may we not shrink from the declaration
of our faith, but at all times exhibit a pure and consistent
testimony for the truth as it is in Jesus, and for the
authority of His kingdom in the world.

ACTS VII.

Stephen was well versed in Scripture, and did homage to
its Author as the God of glory; and in reciting the obedience
and faith of the patriarchs, does homage to Him also as the
God of providence—even He who called Abraham and was
with Joseph, and presided over all the wondrous history
of the children of Israel. The worthies of the Old Testament had much to endure from their enemies, and these
chiefly their own countrymen. Such were the perversities
of God's chosen people, and such their hostile and mali-
cious treatment of the prophets and holy men of old. Let
us not count it strange should our own days witness the
same exhibition; but if the Lord be with us, as He was
with His servants under the Hebrew dispensation, who
can be against us? If He who announced Himself in the
bush as the God of the fathers be upon our side, let us
not fear what man can do unto us. As Moses fared at
the hands of his brethren so did Christ; and let us not
think that the disciple is above his master, or the servant above his lord. Men will be found still to resist the

messengers of the truth, and to resist the Holy Ghost, who hath made revelation of this truth to the world. Should violence prevail against us, let us imitate the intrepidity of the martyrs and confessors of other days. Let the glorious illuminations of faith uphold us against the terrors and adversities of an uncongenial world. Let us be strong in the faith, strong both in life and in death, because of the confidence we feel that God will keep that which we commit unto Him. May we be enabled to breathe our last in the spirit both of faith and charity, assured that God will receive our parting spirits and dying in peace with all. My God, heal the breaches of cordiality and mutual regard which now bear heavy upon my heart; and may I know what it is to be on terms of reconciliation and amity with all, even to the worst of my enemies.

ACTS VIII.

August, 1843.

Should our ministers be scattered abroad may they carry abroad the gospel along with them. May they preach everywhere, and the word of the Lord have free course and be glorified.

O that the gospel were proclaimed in purity and with power all over the land: And O that it proved to me the harbinger both of gladness and of sanctification. May it light up joy in my heart, while, at the same time, it purges out all my uncleanness. O that I were holy in all my thoughts and ways, and had that spiritual-mindedness which is life and peace.

What a lesson Simon Magus is to us. He went so far in Christianity that he is said to have believed. But the ambition of power and pre-eminence was still in him, and his heart was as set as ever on the homage of the multitude, and his own ascendency over them ; and this overlaid his Christianity, insomuch that in virtue of this wrong and overmastering affection, he was still in the gall of bitterness and the bond of iniquity.

Let me pray against every lust which wars against the soul. My God, may the vile and wrong imaginations of my heart all be forgiven me. I would pray for this even at a venture. O give me this token of my having been pardoned the iniquity of my criminal desires—that I am delivered from their power. O that my heart were kept with all diligence, and that my heart were right in the sight of God—else I have no part nor lot in the matter of Christ's salvation.

There is this contrast between the eunuch and Simon Magus ;—the one is said to have believed, but the other believed with all his heart. It is remarkable too that Simon as well as the eunuch was baptized ; but the unworthiness of his baptism must be charged on himself, and not on the administrator thereof. The responsibility lay with the eunuch for consenting to be baptized, and so also with Simon. O let me, along with my faith, have a good conscience, else how can I go on in my way rejoicing ? I do not believe with all my heart unless I give my heart entire unto the Saviour. My God, enable me to mortify all its vicious propensities—its unworthy and disgraceful passions. Thou knowest my plague, and the sin which doth most easily beset me. O wretched man that I am, who shall deliver me from the body of this death ? O that I might be enabled to thank God, because He hath given me power to be one of His own children, and so to walk no longer after the flesh but after the Spirit.

ACTS IX.

Yet Paul was an honest persecutor. He served God with all good conscience ; and should not this mitigate the resentment we feel against our adversaries of the present day ? Let me form no harsh judgment of their character, nor question the truth and sincerity of their principles, however mistaken they might be. The Saviour will espouse the cause of all who love Him—regarding the persecution of His followers as the persecution of Himself. Open the eyes of the blind, O Lord. May the scales fall from mine own eyes ; and let me not think it strange though men should malign and misconstrue and speak evil of me. It may be because they think evil ; and at all events there is no danger from this condition which still attaches to the service of Christ's cause—even the great things which its friends and advocates may have to suffer for its sake. If it be Thy blessed will, may our churches flourish more and more. May they mix trembling with their mirth. May they walk in fear and yet have comfort. Give them rest, O Lord, from their enemies round about them ; and grant such a multiplication of them, as that they beneficially fill the whole length and breadth of our land.

Jesus Christ, make me whole. Cure me of my spiritual diseases, and may the law of the Spirit of life in Thee make me free from the law of sin and death.

Fill me with the Christian grace of liberality, and that both for the bodies and the souls of men. Let me give work as well as wealth for the good of my fellow-creatures, and the reliefs of their destitution, whether in things spiritual or in things temporal. O that the sacred principle of love had full possession of my heart—not only the love which worketh no ill, but the love which longs after the increase of human happiness. Make me wisely to consider the poor, and generously, according to my means, give me to provide for them. O that when raised up my works might be such as to call forth the " well-done" of my Judge on that day, so that I may be presented and carried up alive with the Lord—even to that place where there is fulness of joy and pleasures for evermore. When I fall asleep may it be in Jesus ; when I awake in the morning of the resurrection may I be at the right hand of my Saviour. And may I experience here all the life and power of a spiritual resurrection, as the preparative and the precursor of my resurrection with the blest unto life eternal. For this may I believe in the Lord. May I lay hold on Him who alone hath the gift of everlasting life. May I receive Him, and then shall I receive power to become one of God's children in this world, and in the next to be like Him, for there shall I see Him even as He is.

ACTS X.

Let not a factitious and freezing orthodoxy shut me up against the lesson of this passage. The alms and prayers of Cornelius did come up for a memorial before God before he knew of Jesus Christ that whosoever believeth in Him shall receive the remission of sins. But without entering on this wider generality, let me take this special lesson from the example of Cornelius who prayed *alway*, of cherishing the spirit and being frequent both in the stated and also in mental acts of supplication all the day long ; and though destitute of the same means as heretofore, let

me do in almsgiving as I can, while the great direction of
my liberalities must be for the Free Church. The lesson of
prayer is further enforced by the example of Peter. Let
me be liberalized by this whole contemplation, of God
cleansing that which before was common, and taking into
acceptance those who in our contracted view might be
regarded as outcasts and aliens. There is a certain style
of evangelism which limits the gospel economy, and would
obliterate the largeness and liberality by which it is
characterized. These supernatural messages to Peter and
Cornelius carry in them a great lesson. Their ultimate
object was that these two might be brought together, and
that the words spoken by the one might enter with life and
power into the mind of the other. It was not the angel,
but Peter, who preached the gospel to Cornelius. The
angel was sent not to preach himself, but to get Peter to
preach—a most striking demonstration of the worth and
importance which are annexed to human agency in the
work of Christianization. But let us not overlook the
indispensable agency of the Holy Ghost, who fell, not on
them which heard not, but on them which heard the words
of Peter. Let me not put asunder the things which God
hath joined; but both read diligently and pray earnestly.
O for more of the Spirit of grace and supplication to mix
both with my readings and my doings. And let me
ponder these sayings of Peter—the peace by Jesus Christ
—His lordship over all—His blessed example in that He
did good continually—in His healing all the spiritual
diseases wherewith we have been smitten by the great
adversary of human souls—in His being constituted the
Judge of all—and, lastly, in the remission of our sins
through faith in Him. Seal these precious words, O God,

upon my conscience, that I may both be effectually com-
forted and effectually taught by them.

ACTS XI.

The words which Peter spake to Cornelius were the
words whereby he and all his house were to be saved. Is
there nothing which should modify the rigidness of our
theology in the historical fact, that ere Cornelius believed
or knew unto salvation, his prayers and his alms came up
for a memorial before God ? Peter, bidden by the Spirit,
affords the example of a preternatural inspiration; and
there was also an ingredient of the extraordinary in the
descent of the Holy Ghost upon his hearers, for they spake
in consequence with tongues. Yet let us not overlook the
more ordinary function of the Spirit, which is to give
efficacy to the word. O Lord, pour of Thy Spirit upon
me, that I may obtain as a grant from Thee what I cannot work out of myself, even repentance unto life. It is
Thy gift as much as faith is. The Saviour at Thy right
hand gives repentance as well as the remission of sins.
Turn me, O Lord, and I shall be turned ; draw me, and I
will run after Thee. Make me willing in the day of Thy
power.

It is by the hand of the Lord being with us that we
are enabled to believe and to turn. Yet let us not forget
the previous, if not the preparatory habit of Cornelius.
Make me careful and conscientious, O Lord ; and up to
the light that is in me observant of all Thy will ; and give
me this evidence of Thy grace having been at work with
men, even that with purpose of heart I cleave unto the
Lord : and that I may be indeed a good man, bestow

upon me the Holy Ghost and faith. It is the Holy
Ghost, indeed, who gives faith at the first; but after the
faith is given it would appear as if the disciple were
placed thereby on much higher vantage-ground for larger
and further accessions of the Holy Spirit. They that
believe shall receive of the Spirit. (John vii. 39.)   " We
receive the promise of the Spirit through faith." (Gal. iii.
14.)   Faith gives acceptance to our prayers—for it is
whatsoever we ask believingly, in the name of Christ, that
we receive; and the Holy Spirit is peculiarly and pre-eminently a gift which is promised to them who ask Him.—
Under His blessed inspiration may we be willing to distribute and ready to communicate. Pour the spirit of
Christian liberality over our land; may it overflow beyond
the support, and to the extension of the Free Church, and
even beyond this, to the spread of the gospel in the distant
places of the earth. Let every man be prompted to give
according to his ability, for the relief, if not of the temporal, at least of the spiritual necessities of all our brethren. O that the spirit and principle of a great and
a pure Home Mission were powerfully and productively to
actuate one and all of us—that lay-Christians might be
willing to give, and ministers willing to lose, for the
sake of the religion, not of their own flocks only, but
of all the population.

ACTS XII.

September, 1843.

We have here an example of the efficacy of prayer for
what might be called a temporal deliverance, though it
stood connected with a spiritual benefit to the Church.
In all things let us make our requests known unto God.

Defeat the enemies and persecutors, O Lord, of the Free Church in these lands. Vindicate Thy people's freedom; and grant that the fetters which now bind the circulation of Thy gospel may fall away or be broken in pieces. Deliver us, O Lord, from the hand of those who would enslave the souls and consciences of men; and disappoint their expectations who predict our speedy downfal, and are exulting in the prospect of their own triumphant victory over us. Let our weapons be prayer and patience; nor let either our sufferings, or our toils, tempt us away from the charity of the gospel. And do Thou pour this spirit of supplication over the land, that our Church may be strong in the prayers of many friends—based on the solid foundation of her people's faith and her people's piety. Let there be much social as well as much secret prayer lifted up in her behalf—prayer in the Church, and prayer in the closet. O that our confidence were in Thee at all times. Thou who canst smite through kings in the day of Thy wrath, wilt not leave Thy people destitute and defenceless in the hands of their powerful and high adversaries. They may set themselves and take counsel together against the holy cause of truth and righteousness, but Thou in Thine own good time wilt break with a rod of iron all those who give not God the glory. Remove every obstacle, Almighty Father, in the way of a preached gospel, that Thy word may grow and multiply in the land. Hasten the great consummation of a regenerated country and a regenerated world; and in particular, may the ecclesiastical labourers of our Free Church make such good proof of their ministry, that under them there might be a great and extensive revival in our country and in our day.

ACTS XIII.

Without any determination on fasting, let me at least beware of surfeiting, and maintain a general habit of temperance, as a help and handmaid to spirituality—removing at least an impediment in its way, though not ministering any positive aliment thereto. To obtain that aliment let me seek for it as Sergius Paulus did in the word of God; let me desire the sincere milk of the word, that I may grow thereby—sincere, free of all guile and all contamination, or of whatever would tend to transform and pervert it.

To me also is the word of this salvation sent. O let me give it right entertainment—not as the word of man, but as being indeed the very word of God. It is a message of glad tidings to me—a word of promise even to me. Give me therefore to appropriate Him for my Saviour whom Thou hast raised from the dead, and set forth as a propitiation for the sins of the world; for through this man is preached unto me also the forgiveness of sins—and not forgiveness only, but justification also—justification from all things from which I could not be justified, whether by the law of Moses or of nature. Let me beware, therefore, of neglecting this great salvation, else how shall I escape the doom of those despisers who wonder and perish?

These glorious overtures which have come to us from Heaven are limited to none. They were to the Jew first, but also to the Gentile. Draw me, O Lord, to the Saviour; enable me to close with the offered grace, and to continue therein; begin the good work, and carry it onward to perfection; let me not only be rooted in Christ but built up in Him, even to the measure of the stature of a perfect man in Christ Jesus my Lord.

The word of God has a commanding power in it, which draws multitudes to listen; yet of the many who hear and are called by it few may be chosen. Envy and opposition may arise, and persecution may succeed to popularity. Let us be prepared, O God, for the whole of Thy counsel and will in this our day. When enmity and violence arise, let us not be offended. Save us from the guilt of those who reject Thy Spirit and Thy testimony—holding themselves unworthy of eternal life. May we cast in our lot with those who are glad to hear and to glorify Thy word, and who, because ordained to eternal life, believe it. May this word go forth and prosper, and prevail over the whole of Scotland. This it will not do without the accompaniment of a fierce resistance, and that on the part of many who are seemly and honourable, and withal of chief authority and influence in our land. Let it be enough for us that we are sustained in the midst of all these outward adversities by the testimony of our consciences and the visitations of light and comfort from on high. Give us, like the disciples of old, to be filled with joy and the Holy Ghost.

ACTS XIV.

Heavenly Father, grant that I may *so* speak as that others might believe. Faith is the work of the Holy Spirit, yet a work which requires a right statement of the truth, or that the truth should be stated in a certain way. Teach, O God, the ministers of our Free Church that way; enable them to speak boldly in thy name; and give such testimony to the word of Thy grace as it falls from their lips, that a great multitude might believe; and

prepare them for opposition and violence, if it be Thy
blessed will that they should be so exercised; may they
walk warily and with wisdom, yet never desist from
preaching Thy gospel.

Give me faith, O Lord, to be healed from my disease—
at Thy word may the unclean spirit be cast out of me. O
enable me for all the services of the new obedience of the
gospel, that I may run in the way of Thy commandments,
and offer with joy and thankfulness such spiritual sacrifices as are acceptable in Thy sight. The idolatrous
veneration of men is not yet ended. Let not praise or
popularity lift us above the humility of sinful, weak, erring
creatures—subject to all the infirmities of an accursed
nature, and liable at every moment to a disgraceful overthrow; may I walk softly, O God, under a sense of my own
exceeding vileness; and, at the same time, restrain me
from the overvaluing of men. Be thou my alone master
and authority, O God; and to exalt my reverence, let
me call to mind what the orthodox and evangelical are
too apt to overlook—let me think of Thee as sitting on
the throne of nature, and overruling all her processes—
to whose creative power we refer the heavens, and the
earth, and the sea, and all things; and to whom we stand
indebted for the rain that fertilizes our ground and for
all the food that sustains us.

O confirm and increase my faith that I may overcome
the world, and learn to rejoice even in the midst of tribulations. How little have I experienced of this preparation
for heaven. I have had chastisements laid upon me, but
have not improved them. God knows my infirmities; and
He knows of a corruption on which He laid a signal rebuke, and that still cleaves to me. Make me willing, O

God, for all the discipline which Thou mayest be pleased
to lay upon me, and by which I may be schooled into a
meetness for the kingdom of God. And let the tribulations which Thou art pleased to lay upon our Church have
the effect of prospering more the gospel in our land. May
its ministers be men both of prayer and of labour ; may
the grace of God enable them to fulfil the work of God ;
and by patience and pains unconquerable, may they abundantly succeed in the work of gathering congregations
and planting many churches in the midst of us.

ACTS XV.

Let me never by a false confidence in any work of my
own mar the integrity of my justification. It is indeed
a doctrine very full of comfort, that we are justified by
faith alone; but not, as has been well said, by a faith which
is alone. It is a faith which purifies the heart, and so is
followed up by the fruits of holiness. We are saved by
grace, but yet a grace which both teaches and enables us
to deny ungodliness and worldly lusts. Let this be our
great achievement, putting off the yoke of carnal ordinances.

It is not very easy to construct the right explanation of
the apostle's decree, in that it forbids the use of blood and
things strangled, and seems to put their use on the same
rank with a flagrant immorality there also forbidden.
The question is—in how far shall we regard it as a decree
of accommodation, and in how far a rule of binding and
perpetual authority in the Church ? I pray for light upon
this question.

Give to the ministers of our day, O Lord, both the

wisdom and activity of the rulers of the Church in apostolic times—that they may counsel and govern aright; and more especially that they may associate many others with themselves in their public services. Paul and Barnabas seem to have had the benefit of many auxiliaries in their work. Give, O Lord, both the requisite ability and inclination to many of the eldership, that in our present scarcity of labourers we may draw a sufficient number from that body who might supply the want for a time, and enable us to meet the growing demand for ministerial service from all parts of the country.

I pray for our Church's unanimity, O Lord. Guide me aright in this matter, O Lord. In every good work let me consult my own soul, nor give way to the fear or the authority of man. But give me withal the meekness of wisdom. Be my counsellor at the ensuing General Assembly. O prosper its deliberations; and look with a propitious eye on the infancy of our schemes. Compassionate our difficulties, O God; and open up the path by which we might clear our way through them. Let temper, and charity, and wisdom preside over the whole of its business; and may the doings of this, our highest ecclesiastical court, be such as to command the approbation of the wise and good, and to carry along with them the confidence of the country at large.

ACTS XVI.

October, 1843.

Let us, within the limits of principle and duty, be all things to all men; and O that such was our wisdom, and such our charity, as that under the instrumentality of both, and by God's blessing, the true Churches of our land were more and more established, and that they increased in number daily.

And let all our movements be rightly taken under the guidance both of Thy Spirit and of Thy Providence. Direct us, O Lord, whither we should go; and give us a willing and attentive people, with hearts opened and prepared by the great Husbandman for the reception of the good seed of the word of God. Dispose the people to kindness towards Thy servants; and protect us from the wrath and violence of such as may be hurt or annoyed by the success of the Free Church, and the progress it might make in the affections of the community. Grant, Lord, that we might be enabled to teach faithfully and with effect the way of salvation, persevering with all courage in the work, whatever danger or opposition may arise— whether from the machinations of interested opponents, or from the fury of a deluded multitude. Prepare us to suffer all for the sake of Christ, and to take joyfully all severities and hardships that may be laid on us because of our activity in His work or fidelity to His cause. Let us ever and anon be testifying to the grace of God, as manifested in the gospel of His Son—telling all men what they should do to be saved, and pressing upon all the faith and following of the Lord Jesus Christ. O Lord, I pray for a clear and simple and direct belief in the record which Thou hast given of Him; and may I receive as the end of my faith the salvation of my soul. Let me study Thy word, that to my faith I may add knowledge. Let me have peace and joy in believing; and put a new song in my mouth, even glory to my reconciled God: and grant, Lord, such to be my conduct in the world that none might despise me; save me from all weak and unworthy

compliments or compliances of any sort—for in this I
sometimes err. Let me know when to make my stand as
well as when to give way ; nor let the interest of truth
and righteousness suffer at my hands from the failure of
such weighty and well-timed remonstrances as the circumstances of every case might require. Paul testified his
sense of the injuries that were laid upon him, and so at
times did our blessed Saviour. One might bear witness
of the evil without resisting the evil; and while principle
does not forbid, sound policy might often demand that a
firm though calm representation should be made both to
the public and to our adversaries of the wrongs that we
are called upon to endure.

ACTS XVII.

Let me compare scriptural things with scriptural, which
is in fact comparing spiritual things with spiritual. Thence
I shall gather that there was not only a " need be" for the
sufferings of Christ, in that it was so foretold in Scripture
—and all its sayings must be fulfilled—but a "need be" for
an atonement in the deep-laid necessities of Heaven's
jurisprudence, and of the divine character. Let us not
think that any strange thing hath happened to us, should
we in the present day become the objects of popular dislike and obloquy, and come under the very charge that
was preferred against the first teachers of Christianity, of
turning the world upside down, alleging against us, too,
disloyalty to the throne, and defiance to the decrees of
those courts which are constituted by law. O my God, let
me merit the eulogy here pronounced upon the Bereans.
Let me daily and diligently search Thy Scriptures, and

bring all to the tribunal of Thy law and testimony; and what I read there may I receive with all readiness.

O that my spirit, like that of Paul, were stirred within me, when—looking abroad over society—I behold the reigning idolatries which prevail in it—the idolatries of fashion and wealth and pleasure, and, finally, of science. O that I had more of Paul's intrepidity and of Paul's wisdom, and that I knew better how to accommodate and adapt my argument, as he did, to the tastes and habitudes of those whom I address.   I pray for this grace and this gift, O Lord.   And let me not leave the truths of natural theology out of my demonstration; let me begin at the beginning, and date my reasoning from such principles as we hold in common, taking my departure from the right point; and let me not be discouraged though, when arrived at the peculiarities of the gospel, almost all should be revolted—if but one or two believe.   O give me to seek, even though at a venture, and to seek till I find—even till I find reconciliation with that God on whom I so wholly and intimately depend—living and moving and having my being in Him.   It seems to me an effective scriptural argument against those Particular Redemptionists who explain away the universality of the gospel, by telling us that it only bears on some men in all nations, that Paul speaks of repentance being a call addressed to *all* men *everywhere*.   O my God, let me have respect to Jesus Christ as my Judge as well as my Saviour— let me regulate my conduct by a reference to that coming day.   *All men everywhere* is an expression which bespeaks an individual as well as national universality of offer, though not a universality of final and effectual salvation.

ACTS XVIII.

Let me be a follower of Paul in his unwearied activity for the furtherance of the gospel, and let me cheerfully resign any right of my own to a temporal remuneration for my services, should the cause of our Free Church be promoted thereby. O let not the blood of a rejected testimony from Heaven lie upon my heart ; and as far as it is my part to lift up and enforce that testimony, let me so do it as to be clear from the blood of all men. O help mine unbelief, and give me, Lord, the unspeakable comfort of all who are in my house believing along with me. And let me be intrepid of utterance when declaring the free gospel of the grace of God. Let me not be afraid, but speak, and hold not my peace.

Let me not join the voluntaries in approving of Gallio, but hold it a sacred principle, that all within their own sphere, whatever that may be, whether of rulers or subjects, are bound to consecrate all they have and all they are, to the glory and service of their Master in Heaven.

Paul exemplifies what James enjoins—" I will return again unto you if God will." Boast not of to-morrow, but say—if God will I shall do this or that. Let me subordinate all to the purposes and providence of God, nor forget that while the devices of man's heart are many, it is the counsel of the Lord that alone shall stand. His tour to Jerusalem was not a converting but a strengthening tour. O confirm me in the faith. The case of Apollos is highly instructive—eloquent and mighty in the Scriptures, and probably in a high degree useful—even prior to the more advanced instruction which he received at the hands of Aquila and Priscilla. Like him may I be fervent in spirit and not slothful in business. It is after that he was more perfected in the knowledge of Christianity that we read of his helping much those who had believed through grace. He seems to have reasoned powerfully and convincingly out of the Scriptures. Argumentative preaching is not profitless. Let all that is within us be stirred up in the service of God—reason as well as sensibility—the understanding as well as the emotions. Apollos seems to have combined both, being fervent as well as intellectual.

ACTS XIX.

How apt are we still to deal with the literalities alone of Christian truth and doctrine—adverting not to the Holy Spirit as the great and effectual agent of all saving illumination. O my God, fulfil thine own promise of giving the Spirit to them who ask it. We expect not the outward miracles of other days ; but O perform within me the miracles of Thine all-subduing grace, that I may become a new creature, and walk in newness of life and heart before Thee. And may Thy word, O Lord, be paramount with me to all other wisdom. Let all the ingenuities of human speculation, and all its curiosities, give way before the overbearing yet rightful authority of— "Thus saith the Lord." May we give up all for Christ, and seek first Thy kingdom and Thy righteousness— counting all but loss for the excellency of that higher knowledge which is only to be found in the Scriptures of everlasting truth.

Whatever we purpose may we purpose in the Spirit, or at least, with entire submission to the word and will of God ; and we would watch for Thy Spirit with all perseverance—that saved from our own waywardness our goings may be upheld in Thy paths, and our footsteps slip not. Yet let us not imagine that—walk as warily as we may— we shall be exempted from outward hostility, perhaps even to the length of violence. Human nature is ever the same; and if the cause of truth and righteousness conflict with the gain of any party, we must not think that any strange thing hath happened though their fierce opposition should be called out against it. We know that there is a powerful body who apprehend of our Free Church that by its progress and prevalence their wealth will be destroyed; and they will allege more than this in argument against us—that we are. subverting sacred institutions, and all the securities for a national religion in the land. Should tumults arise, give us the fortitude of Paul, but tempered also with the sound discretion of Paul. Enable us, O Lord, ever to walk in wisdom to them who are without; and save us from all self-seeking, or the indulgence of our own wrath or our own vanity, when called upon to fight the battles of the faith.

ACTS XX.

Let me take a lesson from the unbounded activity of Paul. O for more zeal and industry in my Master's work. Awaken me, O Lord, to a right conscientiousness in the great object of spreading abroad the knowledge of salvation; and O may I be upheld amid the fatigues of the coming winter, and be enabled both to devise and to execute aright for the theology of my students.

O that I attained to the earnestness of the apostle, who laboured in birth till Christ was formed in his converts,

and was moved even to tears in his longing desire after
their salvation. What a lesson to the ministers of the
present day—who like him should teach from house to
house, as well as publicly ; and how instructive is his own
account of the subject of his preaching ! Give me, O Lord,
to teach aright both repentance and faith to my pupils—
the guilt and depravity of nature on the one hand, the
counterpart remedy of the gospel on the other—a remedy
applied and made effectual by faith ; and O that I were
more like unto him in readiness to suffer all for the sake
of the truth as it is in Jesus. May I sit loose to the world
and all its attractions, and counting not my present life
may I give up all for my own eternity and that of my
fellow-men. O that I could say that I was pure from the
blood of all men. Humble me, O God, under a sense of
my fearful shortcomings, and exalt me by an adequate
supply of grace to make up for my sad deficiencies in
respect to faithfulness and zeal for the salvation of human
souls—how miserably behind the models of the New
Testament ! Let me henceforth make a study of frankness
in converse on the great subjects of religion—declaring
the whole counsel of God. O give me an interest in that
salvation which has been purchased by the blood of Christ,
and is brought home by the Spirit of all grace. May I
be built up by the word of Thy grace, and altogether
fitted for that inheritance which none but the sanctified
can enter. Preserve me from covetousness, O Lord. I
pray for wisdom and grace in the matter of my sustentation as a servant of the Free Church of Scotland. May I
reach the superior blessedness of the giver, and let my
moderation be known unto all men. I pray for Thy
guidance in all these matters, O Lord. Save me from

rapacity on the one hand—save me from the affectation of disinterestedness on the other; but make me really disinterested, and teach me how to steer aright between the claims or expectations of my colleagues on the one hand, and on the other what is due both to the general interests of the Church and to my own character.

ACTS XXI.

November, 1843.

Let me be a follower of Paul, both in that he committed his journeying and the wellbeing of those from whom he separated to Thee by prayer, and in that he was ready to do all and to suffer all for the name of the Lord Jesus.

O may the ministers of our Church in the present day be honoured as he was by the testimony of the Divine grace to their labours, so that they might be enabled to speak of the great things done by God through their ministry, and yet with the humility of the apostle, who said—" Nevertheless, not me, but the grace of God that is in me." Let me also follow him in his liberal accommodation to the prejudices of others—distinguishing aright between liberality and liberalism, between the accommodations of Christian wisdom and charity on the one hand, and all sinful compliances on the other. The admirable discrimination of Paul in such matters, along with his kind and considerate respect for the scruples of the weaker brethren, are worthy of all study and imitation. Along with all this, what calm and confident intrepidity when assailed with uproar and violence. Such, for aught we know, may be our lot; and it is my prayer, that it might be met with the equanimity of our great apostle. We are liable to the same misconstructions which he had to encounter—even to be reputed and reckoned with as leaders of sedition, and the fomenters of all sorts of disturbance and disorder in the land. Enable us, O God, to meet this charge with the same coolness and strength of reason that Paul did ; and meanwhile, let it be our study so to exercise ourselves as that we may have a conscience void of offence both towards God and towards men.

ACTS XXII.

Paul commended the zeal of the Jews, even when it was a zeal without knowledge ;—and such was his own zeal before his conversion. It is good to be zealously affected in a good thing, and it is my earnest prayer that, not satisfied with knowledge, I may have zeal also—an enlightened zeal towards God. He was forgiven for his persecutions, we are told by himself—because what he then did he did ignorantly and in unbelief. Let me not be content either with a zeal without knowledge, or a knowledge without zeal. Let me not only refrain from all coldness or hostility to the servants of Christ, but honour and do service to them as such—seeing that I should thus do honour and service to Christ ; and O let my sins be washed out in His precious blood.

The result of this pure and fearless testimony which Paul gave was to arouse the indignation of the Jews against him ; and this brings out his character in a fresh light. He rightly avails himself of all the civil rights he possessed for a protection against the injurious treatment they were proceeding to lay upon him ; and while he resisted not evil yet he remonstrated against it—bore testimony to the wrong, and thereby served both himself and the Roman officers. What he did was not for revenge, but prevention. He took no measures of retaliation against the chief captain for having bound him, though he anticipated—and it was well for both—the captain's having beaten him.

Yet from these bonds he does not seem to have been loosed until the morrow. There might be a certain procedure in the Roman method of dealing with an accused party which perhaps explains this. At all events, the equity of Roman jurisprudence appears in Paul being brought before his accusers face to face. Let me be without carefulness, O God, should I ever be exposed in any measure to these trials. Let me not be anxious what or how I should speak; but let my utterance and my words in every time of need be prompted by Thy Holy Spirit, and so I be enabled to speak—not in the words which man's wisdom teacheth, but in the words which are taught by the wisdom that is from above—combining the serpent with the dove, in the spirit of our Saviour's admonition.

ACTS XXIII.

O give me so to exercise myself that I may have a conscience void of offence towards God and towards men. Paul, we presume, remonstrated against Ananias with a good conscience, though, had he known more of him at the time, he would have acted differently.—My God, what I know not teach Thou me; and more especially do I pray both for guidance and grace in reference to a controversy on which I have just entered. I pray for wisdom, O Lord— first, that as much as lieth in me I may live peaceably with all men; and, second, that I may so conduct myself, as to let no man despise me. Let me abstain from all epithets of abuse, and not speak evil of dignities. Teach me, O Lord, to beware of the leaven of the Sadducees, and still more to beware of being a Pharisee in form while a Sadducee in practice. Let me no longer live as if there was no resurrection, and no spiritual world on the other side of the grave; but may I live by the powers of a world to come, and so bethink myself as to come influentially and really under the force of these solemn considerations —a coming death, a coming judgment, a coming immortality.

O that I felt at all times the cheering effect of my Saviour's gospel—and that not only to support me in the general under the prospect of the eternity whither I am fast hastening, but so as specially to bear me up amid the current trials and apprehensions of my history in the world. This would indeed uphold me amid the tribulations and menaces of a hostile world; for in Christ I should have joy—in Him I should have peace. It is well that human turbulence is so far kept in check by human law. We have to bless God for the protection we enjoy under the sanctions of civil government, which is a Divine ordinance, and has often been instrumental in lightening the hardships and trials of the Christian pilgrimage. We may yet be indebted, under God, to the principles of constitutional liberty which obtain in this country for our defence against the inroads of persecution and violence. Prepare us, O God, for all Thy will.

Paul was committed to Felix, the Roman governor; and it is well to mark the footsteps and leadings of God's providence in the history of the greatest and most gifted of all the apostles.

ACTS XXIV.

Save me, O God, from the strife of tongues; or if not, enable me in patience to possess my soul; and trusting in the promised aids and suggestions of Thy divine Spirit, may I not be careful about what I shall speak, but look up unto Thee, from whom alone cometh the answer of the mouth as well as the preparations of the heart. On Thee, O God, I would cast the burden of all my cares and all my controversies.

How well does Paul maintain the respect due to a governor—yet avoids the fulsomeness of Tertullus. What a chaste and proper introduction to his address, and how admirably he sustains it. Give me, O Lord, to cherish the hope which he here professes—even the hope of a blessed resurrection—at which may I appear in the righteousness of Christ, justified by faith alone, yet enabled to stand when judged by works; and O for this purpose enable me to exercise a conscience void of offence both towards God and towards men. But to succeed herein, I stand in need of wisdom as well as of strict regard to truth and principle. Give me the right caution and the necessary circumspection, O Lord. I pray for Thy further direction in the matter of the Montrose controversy; and do Thou so overrule all connected therewith as to bring no disparagement to the cause of our Free Church, or to the sacred interests of truth and righteousness.

When a man's ways please Thee, Thou makest even his enemies to be at peace with him. It is thus that Paul met with indulgence and a measure of kindness even from Felix. I have gratefully to acknowledge the unexpected encouragements which I have often gotten in this way—so that, even at the hands of public adversaries, have I met with a respect and a countenance for which I desire to bless Him who can turn the hearts of men whithersoever He will.

It is truly instructive to read of the topics which formed Paul's address to Felix. He spake concerning the faith in Christ, and when so doing, reasoned of righteousness, temperance, and judgment—that is, on the commandments of the law and final reckonings of the law, making use of the law as a schoolmaster for bringing his hearer unto Christ. It is true that Felix did not take the lesson; the terrors of the law only set him a-trembling, without shutting him up unto the faith of the gospel; the preaching shook him, yet did not shake him out of his iniquities, which still kept their resolute hold of him. The love of money, that root of all evil, lorded it over all the habits and affections of his soul; and it is a signal display of this passion's mastery, that, in the hope of lucre, he solicited frequent conversations with the apostle, and so braved the threatenings which had disquieted him before. Lord, save me from all self-deceit; and while from this passage I may learn how I should preach to others, O may I take its lessons personally home, lest I myself should be a castaway.

ACTS XXV.

December, 1848.

What a deadly spirit there is in persecution. And let us not deceive ourselves so as to think that this spirit hath altered, or even mitigated its native character. Lord, prepare us for the devices and onsets of human malignity; and enable us to acquit ourselves with faith and charity, whatever the treatment may be to which we

are exposed. Thou canst provide the needful counterac-
tives so as that we shall not be tempted beyond what we
are able to bear. Thou canst provide a way to escape
that we may be able to bear it. Give us the self-command, the knowledge, the freedom from all legal or action-
able offence, and the promptitude to avail himself of every
right expedient for his own protection and safety which
characterized our great apostle.

How completely apart from each other the two policies
are of the Church and of the world; and yet how so
adapted to each other as to subserve the government of
Him who worketh all in all. The maxims and spirit of
the Roman jurisprudence were on the side of Paul in the
present instance; and thus, too, shall we find the future
evolutions of our ecclesiastical history in this country, even
as we have found the present and the past, dependent on
the politics and passions of men who are not ecclesiastical
—yet all dependent on Him who holds in His hands the
whole of the complicated mechanism of human affairs.
Let us make a study of Thy providence, and recognise
Thy wisdom and power in all the events which befall us.

There are many distinct principles in operation, and
which have a controlling influence over the history of the
Church. Its doings are powerfully fitted to interest the
curiosity and many of those feelings which are merely
natural and human. We have no doubt that curiosity had
its share in prompting the desire of Agrippa to see Paul,
though his incipient tendencies towards a gospel of which
he had already heard must have had their influence.
Thou who turnest the hearts of all men whithersoever
Thou wilt canst overrule all, whether for the protection
or for the salutary discipline of Thine own children.

ACTS XXVI.

Let me imitate the courtesy of Paul, mingled, as it was by him, with unswerving fidelity and truth, without aught of the fulsome or exaggerated in his compliments. His becoming deference for rank and station is also a lesson to us. O give me the lively hope which he had of a resurrection and future life, and O that the faith of a coming immortality were more present and more influential with me. What a new colour it would give to the whole of my present existence did I realize in very truth a coming heaven when I die. Grant, O Lord, such manifestations of Thyself as might lead me to see in bright perspective the things of an unseen world; open Thou mine eyes, and turn me from darkness unto light, and from the power of Satan unto God. I pray for the forgiveness of my sins —that this barrier in the way of a blessed inheritance might be removed; and O let me never forget, that to be meet for such inheritance I must be sanctified. Ever. blessed be Thy name that Thou hast made known so clearly the instrument of our sanctification—even the faith that is in Christ. I would ever look unto Him in whom my life is—both life eternal and life spiritual. Unite me, O Lord, more closely with this blessed Saviour, that I may abide in Him and He in me, and that He may cause me to abound in much fruit. Let me repent and turn unto God, and let my turning unto Him be instantly manifested by my works—even those works which are meet for repentance. Let me frame my doings to turn unto the Lord.—Thus, by Thine own good help, may I awake, and may Christ give me light. Give me wisdom —not that which cometh by human learning, but that

which Thou hidest from the wise and prudent, yet revealest unto babes. May I be admitted into the number of
those spiritual men who judge all things, yet themselves
are judged of no man—at least they are not judged aright
by the world at large, but reputed, as Paul was by Festus,
to be mad and visionary enthusiasts. O let me not, for
the sake of being understood or respected by general
society, let me not reduce my Christianity to the standard of what they will tolerate or they will comprehend;
but let me press onward for the prize which is never
earned by the almost, but which is only won by the
altogether Christian. O to be not only almost, but altogether such as Paul was! Thou knowest my sad deficiencies, O Lord—my lack of that zeal, and intrepidity,
and thorough devotion to his Master's cause which characterized the great apostle; and in the consciousness of
which he could say—" I have fought a good fight, I have
kept the faith, and henceforth there is laid up for me a
crown of righteousness." I know my vast, my enormous
deficiency from all this, yet will I not despair—but resort
anew to the fulness that is in Christ, to the Fountain that
is opened in the house of Judah, that I may obtain remission for the past, and grace both for the present and the
future—mercy to pardon, and grace to help me in every
time of need.

ACTS XXVII.

This record of the courtesy of Julius teaches us not to
undervalue those civilities and attentions of the natural
or ordinary politeness which obtains in society, even when
they are rendered to us by those who are without. I have
much to be grateful for in this way, while I have much

wherewith to reproach myself, in that I have done so
little for the Christian good of my acquaintances and
friends. The prediction of the apostle implies a regard
on his part to the probabilities grounded on experience
and the laws of nature. It is not accordant with God's
actual economy to multiply miracles indefinitely; and
though He did honour Paul with a miraculous revelation
at this time, and also gave him the power of shaking off
the serpent from his hand, so as to escape unhurt by it,
yet He was pleased to leave the elements to their wonted
course, and interfered not for the purpose of favouring His
apostle with a prosperous voyage. When Paul spoke his
own human anticipations at the outset of the voyage
from the Fair Havens, he stated the apprehension he felt
of damage to the lives of the company; but afterwards
he spoke the word of prophecy, as received by him at the
mouth of an angel, when he told them that all their lives
should be saved—this having been communicated to him
on the very night of this address to the passengers and
crew. But perhaps the most practically useful lesson in
this passage is that grounded on the comparison of verses
22 and 23 with verse 31, by which we learn that the absolute decree does not supersede the conditions which
precede its fulfilment; but that while the one is sure the
others are indispensable. The prophecy—the announced
predestination, it may be called—of verse 22, did not
supersede the urgency of the prescription in verse 31; the
ship's company were all absolutely to be saved; and yet
unless the sailors were detained in the ship for the purpose of working it, they could not be saved. Here is a
clear example of predestination not infringing upon practice; nor should it on the large scale of Christianity

either. There is nothing, O my God, revealed to me of
Thy decree respecting my future and everlasting state;
but let me be very sure that except I repent I cannot be
saved—except I believe I cannot be saved—without holiness I cannot see God. O let me labour to make my
calling and election sure. Let me be enabled to superadd
the assurance of experience to the assurance of faith; and
meanwhile let me be of good cheer when I bethink myself
of that proffered mercy in the gospel which is held forth
to all, and which all have a warrant to lay hold of.

ACTS XXVIII.

The reception which Paul met with at the hands of the
barbarous people is a specimen of the ways in which God
opens up a path for His missionaries, and by which He
throws a protection over them. There was a natural kindness manifested to the sufferers who had been cast on their
shore, and also a certain sense of religion—natural too,
which enhanced their veneration for the apostle. Let us
take courage in Him who will not leave us defenceless in
the work of spreading abroad His truth, even throughout
the families of a hostile world. Paul here acknowledges
the courteousness of Publius, as he had done that of Julius; and it is likely that the miracles worked by him
obtained for him a harvest of souls as well as of many
honours. There seems to have been a child-like teach-
ableness among these simple people. And as Paul was
gladdened and made grateful by all these kindnesses, but
more especially by the appearance of those brethren and
friends who met him on the shores of Italy—so let us
take courage, while we thank God for all the aids and

facilities by which He encompasses our path and opens a way for us.

There was much civility manifested to the apostle from the beginning to the end of this journey. His being suffered to dwell by himself, and the free access of friends and inquirers to him for two whole years, are instances of this. We cannot but notice and admire the wisdom of his speech to his own countrymen—the acquittal of himself from all purpose of criminating his nation before a heathen power—the generality wherewith at the first he spoke of the Christian faith, and the characteristic which he assigns to it of being "the hope of Israel," so as to propitiate at the outset their attention to his further explanations. These explanations were given afterwards; and in conformity to the general practice of the first teachers, when reasoning with the Jews, there is a constant reference to—nay, the argument may be said to be dated from—their own Scriptures—persuading them out of the law of Moses, and out of the prophets. But some believed, and some believed not; and Paul explains this difference, this subjective difference, by the account which he gives of the latter class. But, as usual, he fortifies his denunciation against them by a quotation from Scriptures which themselves acknowledge. He in effect says here what he said to his countrymen on a former occasion—since ye count yourselves unworthy of eternal life, lo! we turn to the Gentiles. O God, deliver me from gross carnality. Save me from nature's blindness. Give me not only the hearing ear but the understanding heart. Destroy, O Lord, in me the covering that is cast and the veil that is spread over the face of nature. O for a more vivid and spiritual manifestation of the things of faith, that having the light of life, I may thereby be converted and healed.

Teach me, O Lord, and that with power, the things which concern the Lord Jesus Christ. O that He filled a larger space in my contemplations, and that His majesty and grace took more effectual possession of my heart. Give me to honour the Son even as I honour the Father; and let me well understand that it is only by seeking through Him that I can seek successfully or aright the "kingdom of God and His righteousness."

ROMANS.

ROMANS I.—We now enter on those Scriptures which may be regarded as the products of that illumination that descended on the apostles as the fruit of our blessed Saviour's resurrection—for the Holy Ghost was not yet given in the measure of His subsequent revelation, when Jesus Christ was not yet glorified. I pray, O Lord, that the same Spirit who dictated these Epistles may open mine eyes to a saving discernment of them; and as I ponder their blessed contents, may I be thoroughly schooled into "obedience to the faith."

And let me not be ashamed of the gospel of Christ. Let me experience it as Thy power unto salvation; and may the righteousness of faith which is therein revealed be received by me so submissively and believingly as to become my righteousness unto spiritual life here and everlasting life hereafter.

In the frightful record here given of human degeneracy let me read my own exceeding sinfulness, and that against enough of light to overwhelm me with utter confusion, and to condemn me utterly. Thou knowest my enormities, O God—my occasional delinquencies still; and, above all, the turpitude and unholiness of my foul imaginations. Purify my heart; enable me to keep in check my evil desires, if they are not to be eradicated on this side of death; and O save me from the idolatry of the creature, and let me neither set my affections on the things which are beneath, nor be afraid of men who are to die; and yet there is a natural affection, to be without which is monstrous. O sanctify my likings for my relatives and children. Save me from a revengeful or implacable spirit, and let me stand in awe of Thy judgments, O God.

ROMANS II.

January, 1844.

Let me judge myself, O God, strictly and impartially; and then shall I not be judged. (1 Cor. xi. 31.) And O let me delay no longer to avail myself of this my season of grace and opportunity, while God still forbears the infliction of deserved wrath, and still waiteth to be gracious. Let this goodness lead me to repentance; for how shall I escape if I neglect these overtures of a salvation so great and precious? Let me have respect to the day of judgment; and let not a misapplied orthodoxy deafen the impression which the view of a future reckoning ought to have upon me, when I shall be judged according to the deeds done in the body, whether they have been good or evil. I would flee from the coming wrath, and take refuge in Him who is the Lord my strength, and the Lord my righteousness; and O may I be made to abound in those works of love and holy obedience which shall be found to praise and honour and glory in that day. Make known to me my innumerable delinquencies, both from the law of the heart and the law of revelation. Convince me of sin. Shut me up unto the Saviour. May I close with Him as my surety and High-Priest, yet bear a constant and practical regard to Him as my Master and my Judge.

There is much in this remonstrance of Paul which is applicable to myself, however unlike in my circumstances to the Jews of old; for one may be skilful in the demonstrations of orthodoxy, without being practically or at all conformed to it,—make triumphant exposure of man's native ungodliness, yet feel not the burden of his own,—advocate, and with success, the sufficiency of Christ's righteousness, as our alone plea for acceptance with God, yet fail himself to lay hold of it,—expatiate on the need of sanctification, yet fall miserably short of all its graces. O may Thy kingdom come, not in word only, not in reason only, (λογος,) but in power, (δυναμις.) Let my religion be that of the heart, not in the letter only but in the spirit. May I seek not the praise of men but of God. Save me from the woful state of those who have a name to live while they are dead; and let mine be the real staple of a living and acting Christianity—not in word only, but in deed and in truth. Perfect, O Lord, that which concerns me, and form me to Thyself, that I may show forth Thy praise, that I may be altogether as Thou wouldest have me, and do altogether as Thou wouldest have me.

ROMANS III.

O my God, let me feel the responsibility which the possession of the Scriptures, Thine own holy oracles, lays upon me. I shall be judged according to what I have, and not according to what I have not. Let no sophistry dispossess me of that solemn conviction which I ought to feel and to cherish in regard to the future reckoning that awaits me. Make known to me the guilt in which I share with all mankind, and the pre-eminence of my own guilt, as contracted in the midst of clearer light and larger opportunities. Surely I have not understood nor sought after God, but have gone out of the way in following after the devices of my own heart, and have been very unprofitable, doing little if any good. Nor can I assert that my tongue has not been unruly and mischievous, or that my words have not been tinged with bitterness. And O what a stranger, both to the peace of the spiritually-minded, and to the fear of God as an operative principle. Surely my mouth is stopped; and I can allege nothing against the sentence of my entire and most righteous condemnation.

This is what the Law brings me to when sitting as a Judge; but when giving forth its lessons as a schoolmaster, the same law brings me to Christ. He hath done what the law could not do, in that it was weak through the flesh. He hath brought in a righteousness that is without the law—that is, a righteousness not coming out of our obedience to the law, but a righteousness brought in by Christ and made ours by faith. It is *unto* all—that is, offered to all, without exception; and *upon* all, or becomes the covering or investiture of all who ·believe—worn by them as their order of merit in which to appear with acceptance and honour before God. This justification is given freely, and through that redemption which all needed, for all have sinned and come short. And O the richness of the provision!—Heavenly Father, may I take thereof and be satisfied. May I look believingly to Him whom Thou hast set forth as a propitiation through faith in His blood, that He may become my propitiation, and that personally and particularly I may experience God in Christ to be a just God and a Saviour. O my God, let me draw water abundantly out of this well of salvation. O how cheerfully do I renounce all merit of my own, that Christ may be all my sufficiency and all my dependence. Let me be complete in Him, and yet without having voided the law—for not without the law to God, but under the law to Christ. O how pregnant are these verses from 21 to 26 inclusive!—My God, may Thy Spirit bring them home, that on them I may hinge my salvation.

ROMANS IV.

We may have somewhat to glory of before men, but not before God. O that I felt more my own absolute nothingness in myself, and that all my sufficiency for acceptance lies in the righteousness of Christ. Reduce me, O God, to the attitude and entire sense of my being but a pensioner wholly dependent on Thy grace; for truly nothing is due to me. I want to be divested altogether of self-confidence, and to be conclusively and for ever quit of the imagination that my works have any part whatever in my justification. Give me, O Lord, the blessedness of him whose sins are forgiven, whose iniquities are covered, and, still more, to whom the Lord imputeth—without works of his own, a positive and perfect righteousness. O for the delightful sense of all being clear with God, and for this purpose, that I had the strong and unstaggering reliance of Abraham on the faithfulness of the Divine promises. May I walk in the footsteps of faithful Abraham, and like him believe the word of God, though it should be in the face of the strongest unlikelihoods of nature and experience—and though against hope, in the hope that all which God hath said He will infallibly make good. It is a strong unlikelihood that I, a worthless and ungodly creature, should be taken into gracious acceptance by a God who is of purer eyes than to behold iniquity; yet let me do homage to God's faithfulness by believing on His word, that it is even so. It is another strong unlikelihood in the eye of nature, that this carnal and earthly heart of mine, which so cleaves to the dust, should give up its rooted ungodliness, and that I, quickened from my state of death in trespasses and sins, should, by the power of a new birth, become a new creature in Jesus Christ my Lord—nevertheless, like the father of the faithful, let me do homage to the truth of God; and, in the name of the Lord my strength, pray without wavering for that holy impregnation which is the chief of all those promises that are yea and amen in Christ Jesus. O the blessedness of that new condition which is announced in the Gospel—even that my safety and God's glory are at one—so that all is mine if I believe in Him that raised Jesus from the dead, who was given up as an offering for my offences; and now that He is an Advocate and Intercessor at the Father's right hand, there pleads for my interest and claim in that everlasting righteousness which Himself brought in.

ROMANS V.

May we verify in our own minds, O Lord, the alliance between faith and peace. Let ours be but a strong and intelligent faith, and peace will come in its train—filling our hearts and flowing through them like a mighty river. Let me have the hope of glory also as the immediate effect of faith—that thereby sustained amid the troubles of life, I may in the experience of a patience conferred on me by the love of God who giveth His Holy Spirit, have this hope confirmed by such an earnest of my inheritance as might well build me up in a confidence which will not be disappointed or put to shame. And O what a noble *argumentum a fortiori* are we here presented with, and on which we might doubly assure ourselves of the fulfilment of all the gospel promises. He who died for us when enemies, will not abandon us now that we are friends, or earnestly seeking after His friendship. But why seek as if in uncertainty any longer? Let us henceforth rejoice in Christ, as in a treasure that hath been found—and not only so, but also joy in God through Him by whom we have received the Atonement.

And let us furthermore rejoice in the overpassing grace of the second Adam, by which not only all that we had forfeited in the first Adam is made good and restored to us, but through which we are admitted to all the peculiar benefits by which redeemed are signalized above unfallen creatures—so that in this precious chapter we have another *argumentum a fortiori*, and have now a full warrant to rejoice—in that where sin abounded grace did much more abound ; and in that as sin hath reigned, grace now reigns. But it is a grace with and through righteousness—the righteousness of and by Jesus Christ, imputed to us, and constituting our right to eternal life—the righteousness, but still from and by Jesus Christ, wherewith the Spirit, which is at His giving, adorns our persons, and so renders us meet in character as well as law for the inheritance of His saints.

ROMANS VI.

February, 1844.

This is the chapter I have always fastened on as laying bare the ligament between our justification and our sanctification. The abounding grace to which reference is made a few verses before, so far from leading to abounding sin, is our guarantee against the dominion of sin over us. In Christ we died because of sin, or in Him the sentence of death has been fulfilled upon us. Our conformity to Him in His death lies in our dying to all that to which, and to which alone, we were formerly alive; and our conformity to Him in His resurrection lies in our living unto that to which we were formerly dead—in other words, we die unto sin and live unto God. O give me to crucify the flesh with its affections and lusts; and give me to live a life of faith on the Son of God. Thus, though dead, yet nevertheless we shall live. Thus, O God, may I escape the error of those who see not afar off, and forget that they were purged from their old sins, instead of which let me reckon upon myself as alive unto God through Jesus Christ my Lord. Deliver me, O God, from the reigning power of sin. May the law of the Spirit of life in Christ Jesus make me free from the law of sin and death. May I henceforth yield myself to the law of righteousness—written anew in my heart, and having its fruit unto that holiness, the end of which is life everlasting. Cast my understanding and my will, and the whole of my inner man, into the mould of the whole doctrine of Thy gospel, that coalescing therewith out and out and in all its parts,

I may be formed thereby into a living transcript of the entire Christianity of the New Testament, and so have experience of a whole salvation—freed from sin both in its condemnation and power, and walking henceforth in the security of an imputed—and in the willing obedience of an inherent righteousness. Thou art the Giver of both, and eternal life, to which both are indispensable, is wholly Thy gift through Jesus Christ our Lord—freely given by Thee, not won as wages by us ; the only wages that we have ever earned being the wages of sin, which is death.

ROMANS VII.

Heavenly Father, preserve me from these motions of sin in the members. Let me experience as the immediate effect of Thy grace in Christ Jesus, that sin hath not dominion over me. Give me to serve in the newness of the Spirit, and then shall I serve willingly, and with the inner man, counting it not enough to avoid that which is evil, but with strong affection to abhor that which is evil, and cleave to that which is good.

Deliver me, O Lord, from vile concupiscence—still more vile, that it should be excited and take occasion by Thy good and pure and holy Law. How exceeding sinful, then, is sin ; and I desire more and more to feel how rightfully I am under sentence of death by the law—even that law beneath whose lofty and spiritual requirements I have so immeasurably fallen. Give me, O Lord, to mourn not with a sorrow transient and unproductive, but with a real practical and godly sorrow—a working sorrow, even that which worketh repentance unto salvation. I am verily persuaded that in my flesh there dwelleth no good thing ;

and I desire therefore that the power of Christ may rest on me, that the good and perfect gift which cometh only from above may indeed descend upon me. O give me to delight in the law of God after the inward man ; and support me in the arduous warfare of my personal Christianity. I have often done wickedly, O Lord—brought into helpless captivity, out of which I cannot, with any strength of mine, extricate myself; and in the extremity of my wretchedness would I cry out—Who shall deliver me ? To obtain emancipation I would seek unto the Saviour, I would bring my emptiness to His fulness ; and O give me reason, as the fruit of all my prayers and all my painstakings, to exclaim with the Apostle—" I thank God, through Jesus Christ my Lord." To perpetuate and secure the ascendency of the mind over the flesh, of the law of God over the law of sin, O enable me to be temperate in all things.

ROMANS VIII.

O that all the blessings of this magnificent chapter were realized upon my person—freedom from condemnation, and freedom from the tyranny of the flesh, because that the law of the Spirit of life in Christ Jesus had made me free from the law of sin and death. Save me, O God, from the carnal-mindedness which is death, and give me the spiritual-mindedness which is life and peace. Change the enmity of nature into love for God and godliness, and grant a willing subjection of my heart to Thy law. And O let me never cease both to watch and to pray for that Spirit of Christ, without which I am none of His.

O Lord, through the Spirit may I mortify the deeds of the body, and live. Pour upon me the Spirit of adoption, and give me to experience the testimony of Thy Holy Spirit within me. There is sad straitening here in the midst of these vile bodies. Give me a well-grounded hope of that enlargement and glory, when, delivered from the bondage of corruption, I shall be translated into the glorious liberty of Thine own children. The first-fruits of the Spirit do not complete the redemption of our bodies, charged with a moral virus, from which they will not be delivered till pulverized in the sepulchre. Give me, Almighty Father, the hope that purifieth ; and O save me from the ascendency of my natural and corrupt inclinations. O may Thy Spirit help my manifold infirmities, and teach me to pray for Him as I ought. May He intercede in me, even as Christ intercedes for me, and then shall I be safe. O shed abroad that love of Thyself, to which the promise is given of all things working together for good. Translate me into the kingdom, and conform me to the image of Thy dear Son ; and conduct me, O Lord, from one step to another of that pathway which leads to the Jerusalem above. Bind me in faith to the exceeding great and precious promise, that as Thou hast given Thy Son, Thou wilt also with Him freely give all things ; and then as my faith, so will be the fulfilment. Give me a part and an interest in His blessed intercession ; and O may His love to me not only ensure His protection amid all the ills and distresses of life, but may it so constrain my love to Him, that no calamities, no terrors, no temptations, shall ever cause me to swerve from the fidelity and gratitude which I owe to that blessed Saviour who died for me, and who rose again—who died for my offences, and rose again for my justification. Give me to be strong, yea, and more than conqueror over these three great enemies to the

human soul—the devil, and the world, and the flesh. For
these things I, a miserable offender, would humbly pray,
feeling deeply and experimentally that in me there is no
strength ; yet not renouncing my confidence in that great
High-Priest, through whom it is that I obtain mercy to
pardon and grace to help in every time of need.

ROMANS IX.

O that I had the same affection for the souls of kindred
and neighbours which actuated the holy apostle. Give
me, O Lord, more and more of what may well be termed
the benevolence of faith. It is a searching test for the
reality of our faith, whether a regard for the spiritual interests of those whom we naturally love have any place in
our hearts, or any operation on our conduct towards them.
And let me also be more considerate of the Jews than
before, and of their many claims on the sympathy and
service of Christians. O that we had the self-renunciation
of Paul, and could give up even our lives, and all which
belongs to us, for the advancement of the kingdom of
Him who is very God, and over all.

Ever blessed be Thy name that Thou hast enabled me
to acquiesce in the profound mysteries of this chapter,
and yet to hold inviolate all the duties and activities
of the Christian life. I desire to receive all that is said
of God's sovereignty without reserve, and without qualification. Perhaps I may have erred in overlaying the
doctrine too much with the demonstrations that I have
attempted of its perfect consistency with the calls of the
gospel, and the obligations under which we lie to act both
upon its primary overtures, and all its subsequent require-

ments. I may have erred in recommending the adjourn-
ment of our attention to this doctrine from the earlier to
the later stages of the Christian life, and think I can now
perceive not only the perfect innocence, but even salutary
influence of these transcendental themes, as far as they
are revealed in Scripture, on the young disciple—when
called upon to " make his calling and election sure," and
when strengthened in the impression of that sure and
indissoluble connexion which has been established by the
ordination of God between a present grace and a future
glory—between holiness here and heaven hereafter. Let
me learn from this chapter a prostrate subjection of all
my faculties and feelings to God's truth and God's sovereignty. Nor let me ever forget the concluding lesson of
submission to the righteousness of God, assured—and that
notwithstanding all that had just been said before of God's
irreversible and everlasting decrees—that He who believeth in Him who brought in an everlasting righteousness, shall attain to all its benefits, and not be brought to
shame.

ROMANS X.

March, 1844.

O that I had the fervent heart's desire of Paul for the
salvation of my kindred and countrymen—a more intense
and operative affection for human souls. And let me here,
too, walk in wisdom. Let my zeal be according to knowledge and sound discretion ; and that I may the more
effectually help on the conversion of others, let my own
views be established, and more especially my entire dependence on the righteousness of Christ as my alone
availing righteousness with God. May I seek unto Him
for all that in an innocent and unfallen state I could have

gotten by my perfect obedience to the Law. And let me not strain at imaginations respecting Christ. Let me not seek for manifestations from afar, but be satisfied with the word that is nigh unto me. In the language of good Ebenezer Erskine, let me, if not regaled with *blinks*, have at least to do, and that believingly, with words. May I both believe in Christ inwardly and confess Him outwardly, and then I shall be saved. And O how precious are these *whosoevers;*—whosoever believeth, whosoever calleth, if he but call desirously, shall not be disappointed or put to shame—He is rich unto all that call upon Him. My God, give me to have a confident sense of this freeness, and to proceed upon it ; but for this purpose let me observe, faith ever cometh by hearing or by reading the word of God ; and I would therefore give earnest heed unto this word, till the day dawn, and the day-star arise in my heart. And let the like zeal which animated Paul in behalf of the Gentiles, and made him so zealous to send preachers amongst them, that they might bear the tidings of a crucified Saviour unto all nations—let the same zeal inspire us, and give vigour to all our missionary enterprises, whether for the families of our own or of other lands. O let us not abuse our privileges, so as to cause that our candlestick shall be removed out of its place. May the beautiful feet of them who preach the gospel of peace pervade the whole length and breadth of the land, and so as thoroughly to fill it, from one end to the other, with the tabernacles of the righteous ; and instead of being desolated by the judgments of a righteous God, may this the country of our forefathers be the dispenser of saving light and knowledge to the remotest extremities of the earth.

ROMANS XI.

Ever blessed be Thy name, O God, that though Thine own hidden ones be unknown to us, there may still be a goodly number of them in this our land. May this purifying and preserving salt ever abide in the midst of us— so that the kingdom which cometh not with observation may have stable occupancy here, even when irreligion and wickedness do most abound. And we rejoice in the clear and definite line of separation which is drawn by the pen of an inspired messenger between grace and works. Salvation is of grace only, and not of works at all; but still *of* grace *unto* works. May I be Thy workmanship, O Lord, created in Christ Jesus unto good works—and in the doing of which it may be my constant sentiment or saying— " Nevertheless, not me, but the grace of God that is in me." Let me ever be distrustful of my own strength and my own sufficiency; and under the deep sense of nought in myself but weakness and corruption, may I ever be looking upward for support and aid to that place whence the aliment of my spiritual life alone comes. Then shall I not be high-minded but fear, and that because of the humbling consideration that without Christ I can do nought, and that only in the faith of Him I stand. May He be made unto me sanctification; and O that the whole covenant were realized upon me, so as that not only my sins shall be taken, but ungodliness shall be turned away, from my heart. And let me not look to my own things only; but look to the footsteps, the parts of His way, as far as we can discern them, of His high and heavenly administration—and more especially to the dealing of God with His own peculiar people. Let not the mysteriousness of His counsels cast obscuration or the shadow of a doubt over the perfection of His wisdom ; but let us give all submission, and award all glory to the incomprehensible God, who inhabiteth eternity, and whose government extends to all worlds.   To this did Paul sublime his contemplations ; and in this let us be the followers of Paul.   It is good to recognise and to feel that there lie a depth and a comprehensiveness in the plans of God which are far out of sight ; and under the sense of our own exceeding inferiority and distance, let us attribute all that is good and great to Him, of whom, and through whom, and to whom, are all things.

ROMANS XII.

What a noble directory of conduct have we here!—And first and foremost, O God, give me to keep this vile body under subjection, and present it to Thee as a living sacrifice acceptable to God through Jesus Christ my Lord : and O renovate and transform me—that henceforth I may walk before Thee a new creature ; then shall I do Thy will, not of constraint but spontaneously.   Grant, O Lord, from this day forward, and during the brief remainder of my pilgrimage upon earth—grant that my life may be a continued testimony to, and representation of, that nature which Thou impressest on Thine own children, and of those actions which Thou willest them to do.   Let me ever think of myself humbly and soberly.   What reason have I for so doing ! and O that I could attain to such real and positive excellencies of the Christian character as might justify my adoption of the apostolic saying— " Nevertheless, not me, but the grace of God that is in

me." And let me know my place that I may abide in
its duties, and perform them with single-mindedness, and
constant assiduity, and with all the alacrity of one who de-
lights both generally in the commandments of God, and
specially in the appropriate business of his calling. Forgive my manifold imperfections as a teacher; and if it
be Thy blessed will, so emancipate me from all other
business as that I may wait on this high vocation without distraction, and fulfil it more adequately than I have
ever yet done.

Let me transcribe upon my own heart and life the
various graces so beautifully set before us in this chapter. Let mine be unfeigned love as well as "faith unfeigned"—the abhorrence of what is wrong, an intense
and devoted affection for what is good—kind affection
and brotherly regards to all, not seeking to please myself, or aspiring after mine own honour, but willing that
others should be pleased, and others should be honoured
before me—diligence in business, actuated by fervency
of spirit, but that a spirit in the cause of God and of His
service. It is the hope of faith which enables us to rejoice in the midst of tribulations, and strengthens up for
the arduous work of that saintly and spiritual obedience
which is here pourtrayed in many of its most prominent
features. Give me, O Lord, an effusive liberality in behalf of the poor and persecuted household of faith; and
let both my house and my heart be opened for their behalf.
Thou knowest my difficulties and the inconvenience to my
public duties that would accrue from a general and indis-
criminate hospitality. Guide me aright in this matter.
Give me a sympathy with other minds than my own—
with humanity, as such, apart from all considerations of

rank, or even of talent—and save me from all feeling of
superiority, whether in regard to mental endowments, or to
the gifts of fortune. Why should either superiority inspire
else than humble gratitude to the Sovereign Dispenser on
whom we hold for all things? And most of all do we
pray for a victory over ourselves when stung by a sense of
injury. O let us not be overcome thereby; and make it
possible, O Lord, that we should live peaceably. Let my
moderation be known unto all men. Let us ever commit
ourselves to Him who judgeth righteously, and to whom
alone vengeance belongeth. Let us be perfect, even as
He is perfect; and then shall we return good for evil—
even as He sendeth rain on the just and on the unjust,
nay, so loved our rebellious world as to send His Son for
its salvation. Let our conquest over enemies be the conquest of that charity which shames and softens, and
operates by a resistless moral compulsion, even on the
hearts of the most obdurate of men.

ROMANS XIII.

Let my conscience be clear in the matter of what I owe
to civil governors. Have I never—and more especially in
the agitations of our recent controversy—never felt or
uttered myself contemptuously toward them? Let me
put a guard over both my heart and my lips. I may
never have resisted the powers that be; but have I never
transgressed what is said in the law—that thou shalt
not speak evil of the ruler of thy people? Let me feel
the incumbent godliness of my civil obedience; and
not overlook the obligation of giving to Cæsar the things
that are Cæsar's, when contending for both the obligation

and the liberty of giving to God the things that are God's. Let me be subject, then, not only for fear, but also for conscience' sake. Let me be scrupulous in the payment of tribute—rendering a faithful account of all that is due, and not giving in to the prevalent laxity which obtains in this matter—and in the payment of debt, too, as well as in the payment of tribute, that I may owe nothing to any man, save the love which I owe to all men. O for the supremacy of this all-subduing and all-comprehending principle within me, that I may attain in all its perfection and power to the second great law ; then would I abstain from all ill to my neighbour, and on the contrary, be the positive dispenser of benefits and blessings to all within my reach.

How urgently do the concluding admonitions bear upon myself. Surely it'is high time for me to awake. My time in this world of darkness is far spent, and another world is at hand. Let me come forth on the broad daylight of a Christian practice harmonizing at all points with a Christian profession. Let me give up henceforth and for ever the indulgence of all malignant affections which vent forth in strife and envying, and the indulgence of all the forbidden sensualities. Both are works of the flesh ; but if I put on the Lord Jesus Christ, I shall make no provision, because then, not only clothed with His righteousness, but clothed with the personal investiture of His graces and virtues—the one being the guarantee of my safety, the other of my sanctification. For the perfecting of this, let me ever maintain the gospel attitude of looking unto Jesus, that I may behold the glory of the Lord, and be changed into His image, from glory to glory, even as by the Spirit of the Lord. O for such a putting on of Christ that He may be made unto me wisdom and righteousness, and sanctification and redemption.

ROMANS XIV.

This is a truly enlightened chapter, and not less signalized by its wisdom than its charity. It admits of pregnant application to many cases and questions of the present day. Teach me, O Lord, to discriminate aright, as did the apostle, that I may neither undervalue what is essential, nor lay undue stress on what is insignificant in religion. We must contend earnestly for the faith, and all the weightier matters, whether of doctrinal or practical Christianity; but why endanger unity and the peace of the Church for the veriest bagatelles? It is good to be zealously affected in all really good things; but it is not to be told how much evil has been done by zeal misplaced on wrong objects, or disproportioned to the actual worth of the topics at issue. Teach me, O God, the wisdom which is first pure and then peaceable, that I may have forbearance up to its right limits—true liberality, without its being carried onward to a wrong and hurtful latitudinarianism. Whether I do, or refrain from doing, let the soul of godliness be ever there—let all be either done or not done unto the Lord. And O that I had at all times a more solemn and practical sense of the coming judgment. In the prospect of this, let me neither be prompt to condemn others nor grudge against them. The Judge is at the door. And rather than oppose the harmless, though unimportant observations of other men, let me study to conciliate and accommodate to the uttermost. Let me, as far as in me lies, and as far as possible, or as far as consistent with positive and known obligation, be all things to all men, that my good may not only not be evil spoken of, but be all the more recommended to acceptance and good-will. And O that the great and the substantial elements of a truly religious character were to form and be confirmed within me—righteousness and peace, by being first pure and then peaceable—joy in the Holy Ghost imparting the light of Christ's salvation to my soul, and causing me to taste the preciousness of that reward which there is in the keeping of the commandments. Let me study in all things to please Christ, and advance His kingdom in the hearts of men—labouring to edify each other, and to abstain from all which might prove an occasion of sin or backsliding to any of the Lord's disciples. But whatever I do let me not dare to venture upon aught which is against the misgivings of my own conscience. Let me incur no hazard upon this ground. Let me be clearly and confidently satisfied that what I either do or indulge in is not forbidden. Let me think of that God who is greater than my conscience, and knoweth all things. To incur the risk of evil by doing that which I only suspect or fear to be wrong is condemnable on the same ground, if not in the same degree, as to incur the certainty of evil by doing that which I know to be wrong. Search and try me, O God ; and not only keep me from presumptuous sins, but cleanse me from secret faults.

ROMANS XV.

April, 1844.

Let us make a sacrifice of our own will to the great interests both of truth and charity. Let us imitate

Christ in His self-denial, and always please others rather than ourselves when it is for their profit. Let us be like-minded with Him, and so likeminded one toward another. O that we had such evidence of our having passed from death to life, even that we love the brethren; and that in the midst of their occasional perversities. On this experience we might well found a hope of glory ; and along with peace and joy in the direct exercise of believing, would be enabled, by the Holy Ghost giving us such an earnest of our inheritance, to rejoice without shame or without faltering in our thus brightened and confirmed anticipations.

Save me, O Lord, from all such partizanship in things ecclesiastical as is not essential to truth, but is injurious to charity ; and let me in meekness instruct those that oppose themselves. Let not any fancied superiority in knowledge lead me to despise even the weakest of my brethren, or in the least exasperate or disturb my patience towards them.—The being filled with knowledge will but aggravate our condemnation, if we are not at the same time filled with goodness ; under which disposition let me be willing as well as able to admonish others. Let me think how much Paul could allege by which to distinguish himself from those whom he here holds converse with—and how condescending to their infirmities—how single-hearted in his desire for their spiritual good—how unwearied in his labours for the advancement of it—how disinterested withal ; and yet with a perfect feeling of the equitable claim which those who minister in spiritual things have to a return in carnal things. He often put away from him and refused their liberalities, and was greedy of nothing from them but their prayers—their prayers for his personal safety, no doubt, but this in order to a joyful meeting with themselves, and that he might, after having got through the perils of the way, come to them in the fulness of the blessing of Christ's gospel. It is well in these seasons of disturbance and danger that we both ply our own supplications and seek for the intercessions of our brethren—both that we may be delivered from the machinations of adversaries, and that what we do for the service of friends or of the common cause may be well taken, and issue in what is prosperous and good. Here we must lay our account both with oppositions from without and divisions within. It is well, amid all these tribulations, that we have the God of Peace to fall back upon, as the habitation to which we may resort continually, and who can hide us under the shadow of His wings till all calamities be overpassed.—Deliver us, O Lord, from the strife of tongues, and from wicked and unreasonable men, that the word of the Lord may have free course and be glorified.

ROMANS XVI.

One likes the homage rendered here by Paul to the Christian philanthropy of his lay-helpers, both male and female. It is a fit and seasonable example of the recognition and courtesy that we owe to them in this our day. Let us maintain all respect and gratitude, and study every requital, to these servants of the Church and succourers of her saints and office-bearers—holding them forth, at the same time, as patterns of much labour in the Lord, and in the advancement of His cause in the world, to the adherents and friends of the Free Church. And let us well observe, that while he commemorates the services of some, he only commemorates the graces and the faith of others. Let us not limit our courtesies to them who aid us by their liberalities or services, but extend them to all such as are beloved and approved and chosen in the Lord —in a word, to all saints. Nay, let us be courteous to all, enjoined as we are to " honour all men." And O let mine be a pure and sacred affection—the love of one who, because in Christ, has crucified the evil desires of an evil and accursed nature. And for this great and indispensable achievement, may the God of Peace bruise Satan under my feet, and may the graces of the Lord Jesus Christ be with me ; and thus may I realize in my own person both the peace of the gospel and the holiness of the gospel. Thus, also, would I avoid offences, and these, too, of the most grievous description, when my universal and consistent obedience was palpable to all. Let me hold in utter abhorrence the by-ends of selfishness and hypocrisy ; yet, as far as lieth in me, as far as Christian integrity will allow, let me study to heal divisions, and live peaceably with all men—wise to do good, while innocent and unknowing of evil.

But God alone is wise, and to God alone be the glory of it : and nowhere is the manifold wisdom of God more conspicuous than in the Church, and through Jesus Christ its great Head and Founder.—O stablish me in the faith, and stablish me in the obedience of His Gospel. And what I specially desire and need to be instructed in is, the supreme place which the glory of God should have as the object of my regard, as the motive and the end of all my actions.

I. CORINTHIANS.

1 CORINTHIANS I.—O that I were indeed sanctified—
called, not outwardly alone, but effectually, to be a saint ;
and so have grace, mercy, and peace, resting upon me.
And in looking up for these blessings, let my fellowship
be with both the Father and the Son—let me honour the
Son even as I honour the Father.

As Paul prays for his spiritual children, even so would
I for the children of my own family.   One came to me
yesternight and announced herself for the first time as an
intending communicant.   I thank my God on her behalf
that this has been put into her heart.   O may it prove
the commencement and the continuance of a good work
in her soul.   May she be confirmed and graciously upheld to the end of her life, so as to be found unblameable
and unreprovable in the great day of reckoning.   O God
of faithfulness, who now calls her to this act of outward
fellowship with the Saviour, do Thou follow this up by
increased manifestations of Thine own sanctifying and
transforming power upon her heart.   And should her eye
ever light upon this page after that I am laid in the grave,
may all her purposes of devotedness to Christ be strengthened by the remembrance of a father who loves, and who
now prays for her.

My God, save our Church from divisions.   Enable me
to conduct my argument so as that peace and unanimity,
nay, fervent Christian love, shall be maintained in the
midst of us.   If there be differences of understanding, let
there be no divisions of heart amongst our rulers and office-
bearers.   But it were desirable that even differences of

opinion, as well as separations of affection, should be done away, that we may be not partially but *perfectly* joined together in the same mind and in the same judgment. Let us shun partizanship; and instead of ranging ourselves under men, let us, with all simplicity and godly sincerity, seek after the mind of God and the good of His Church, and abide thereby. And let me renounce all ambition of eloquence—the mere wisdom of words ; for it is truly awful to think that in so speaking as to set off ourselves, we might make the cross of Christ of none effect.—O may the preaching of this Cross be the power of God to me and mine, and then we shall be saved. It is not the pompous orator or disputer of this world who will carry any real or substantial victory on the side of our Church.—O purify and spiritualize her doctrine more and more. O may Christ crucified be the great burden of her sermons ; and thus may she become mighty to the pulling down of strongholds. We are not countenanced by the noble or the powerful in our land ; but if we have the foolishness and the weakness of God upon our side, we shall prevail. Let us not glory in the flesh, but glory in the Lord. Let us not make our boast of science, but seek after the simplicity of the truth as it is in Jesus. And O to be filled with His fulness, to be complete in Christ, to have a part and a possession among His unsearchable and inexhaustible riches—in a word, to be made of God in Him wisdom and righteousness and sanctification and redemption. I desire with all my heart to abide in Him, that He may abide in me—to put on Christ, and make no provision for those objects or gratifications which, however dear to nature, but perish with the using, and pass speedily away.

I. CORINTHIANS II.

O what a rebuke is here laid on those ministers who, ambitious of a name for oratory and talent, overlay the doctrine of the cross with other words than those which the Holy Ghost teacheth. Not that we are confined to the *ipsissima verba* of Scripture; but when setting the truth as it is in Jesus in any other phraseology, let it be our single aim to possess our hearers with that truth in its substance and power—at one time it may be in a homelier, and at another, in a richer drapery of language, but with no other desire, and for no other object than that in being thus all things to all men, we may save souls.—And O let mine too be the glorious determination of the apostle—to know nothing save Jesus Christ and Him crucified; let Him be my all in all; and in the work of making Him known to others, may I have a deep sense of my own insufficiency for the work. When I look to myself, may it be in weakness, and in fear, and with much trembling. But O give me to experience that when I am weak then am I strong; let me be led to the Rock that is higher than I; let me seek to the wisdom that is from above, if I aspire after the wisdom of winning souls—in the first instance, drawing from Scripture for my words; but more than this, drawing by prayer for the grace from heaven, which alone can make these words effectual, by the demonstration of the Spirit and of power, and so working faith in the hearts of men—not by the wisdom of men, but by the power of God.

Not that the teaching of the Spirit supersedes wisdom or the exercise of judgment. It fills man with wisdom, so as to make it man's own wisdom—though his own by gift alone, and not by original property, and it directs the exercise of his judgments, so that he himself, the spiritual man, judgeth all things—looks at them with his own eye, yet sees them in the light of a higher manifestation than that of nature. The operation of the Spirit no more supersedes the understanding of man than it supersedes the will of man. He worketh in us, but it is to will and to do ; He enlightens us, but it is by opening our understandings to understand. O grant unto me this higher revelation ; give me to see and to know those deep things of God which are far beyond the ken of my own faculties ; enable me to compare aright scriptural things with scriptural, that when these are lighted up by the great Revealer from on high, it may indeed be the comparison of spiritual things with spiritual. I of myself know nothing beyond the reach and compass of my own natural powers ; and not only must the objective truths be presented to me, but the recipient power must be given to me—for the natural man receiveth not the things of the Spirit of God, however nigh they are brought to him by the ministry of the word. O transform me then from the natural to the spiritual ; gift me with spiritual discernment ; enable me to look with an observant and just-seeing eye, because with the eye of a man who has been spiritualized, on all that is above me and around me ; and however misconceived or misjudged by them who are without, may I count this a small matter, but commit myself to Him who judgeth righteously. He who judgeth me is the Lord.

I. CORINTHIANS III.

May, 1844.

Even babes in Christ are still as carnal, and they are so

denominated because such a remainder of the old man
still adheres to them. We thus learn that the transformation is gradual ; but let us strive with all honesty and
earnestness to hasten it forward ; more particularly, let
us shun to the uttermost all strife and envying ; and
instead of needing to be soothed by apologetical and
complimentary offerings on the expression of my displeasure, let me endure hardness like a veteran and a good
soldier of Christ Jesus.

And, in particular, let us cease from men, and award to
God all supremacy in the great work of building up a
Church, and bringing sinners under the power of the gospel. O Lord, may we be of Thy husbandry and of Thy
building ; and, whether for ourselves or others, while we
labour with all diligence both in planting and watering,
both in casting the seed of God's word upon the soul and
in praying for living water from heaven to fertilize it,
let us ever look above our own efforts and our own prayers
to Him out of whose fulness it is that all fertility comes ;
and let us build on no other foundation than that which
God Himself hath laid in Zion. Men build variously on
this foundation. Things useless as well as things precious
may be laid thereupon. Plants which our Heavenly
Father hath not planted may have been set there by human hands ; but they will be rooted up to the laceration
and pain of him on whom they grow, if not to the ruin of
his soul. The wood, and the hay, and the stubble, will be
burnt up to the suffering of him who hath produced them,
yet he himself shall be saved. But not so if, instead of
hay, stubble, and wood, it be thorns and briars—for not
only shall these be burnt up, but the ground that yieldeth
them, (Heb. vi. 8 ;) and so in keeping with this do we here

read the appalling denunciation—" If any man defile the temple of God, him shall God destroy." O God, keep me from presumptuous sin, and cleanse Thou me from secret faults. It will be hurtful if I lay what is useless on the foundation ; but it will be ruinous if I lay what is vile. Save me from that sin which, when finished, bringeth forth death ; but save me also from all which operates, if not to the destruction, at least to the damage of the soul. Every idle word which we speak shall be taken cognizance of in the day of judgment. What a reckoning then must we undergo ?—My God, save me both from the sin unto judgment and the sin unto death. Let me offer up my body, the temple of the Holy Ghost, if I am indeed a Christian man ; let me offer it up a living sacrifice ; let me crucify its affections and lusts—yet counting it not enough that I but save my distance, let me clear away all wood, or hay, or stubble, from my personal Christianity, and also shun those carnalities which speak me but a babe. Above all, let me keep close by the Saviour ; let me hold both by the things I have and the things I hope for as coming to me through the channel of the covenant ; and view all things as mine only as I am Christ's and Christ is God's.

I. CORINTHIANS IV.

I am unable to descry the mysteries of my own spirit ; but the real character of its habits and affections, whether good or evil, depends not on my knowledge or my appreciation of them. They may lie hidden from my own observation, but the great Discerner perfectly knows them all, so as to judge them now and to adjudicate upon them afterwards. Let me not think that I shall escape the condemnation due to my delinquencies because I am myself unconscious or insensible of them. The stable characteristics of my nature will be pronounced upon by the stable and everlasting principles of justice and truth, irrespective of my knowledge as to their existence or state; and let me therefore never cease to pray that God would search me, and try me, and cause me to see if there be any wicked way in me, and guide me in the way everlasting. Who can understand his errors?—Cleanse Thou me, O Lord, from secret faults before that awful day comes, when, by the light of a resistless manifestation, God will reveal the counsels of all hearts, and vindicate the equity of His judgments before men and angels.

O may God save me from glorying in myself. Thou art the great fountain-head of all I have, and of all I am. O let this consideration put an end to all glorying and all assumption over others. Perfect within me the grace of humility; may I be clothed therewith—seeing that all which is evil in me is from myself, all which is good in me from the Lord—the giver of every good and of every perfect gift. And how far behind, how immeasurably far in graces and gifts beneath the apostles, and this from our own want of faith. What humiliations did they cheerfully undergo—pleasing not themselves, and receiving with patient endurance all the calumnies and all the wrongs that were so abundantly inflicted upon them. May I be the follower of Paul even as he was of Christ. Prepare me if need be for his sufferings, by a resolute principle of adherence to the great cause of the gospel in the world, and this grounded on the faith and patience of the saints. O let me not be satisfied with Thy kingdom in word only; may I know it in power. Give me the spirit of love, and of power, and of a sound mind; give me to feel practically and in its governing influence the truth as it is in Jesus, that I may be sanctified by that truth, and that by it I may be made free from the law of sin and death. And O let this be permanent as well as powerful, lest I be of the number of those who have once tasted of the powers of the world to come, and at length fall away. Save me from the fate of those who have the form of godliness without the power thereof—who have a name to live, and yet are dead.

I. CORINTHIANS V.

When reflecting on the excesses of depravity whereof our nature is capable, it were well to reduce the generality of the sentiment, and bring it particularly home. Thou knowest, O God, all the enormities to which I might go if abandoned to the headlong impulses of my own corrupt disposition. O that my own consciousness of this were of more effect to soften and to humble me; and when I think of the manifold delinquencies both of heart and conduct whereby I have incurred the resentment of a holy God, surely this might well disarm the resentments into which I might be hurried by the perversities and provocations of my fellows in the business of the Church. O for more of self-command and reticence, and less of a diseased appetite for human sympathy. Let me never forget the sentence of James on him who bridleth not his tongue; and how important every way is the lesson of self-restraint, when one thinks of the appalling scandals and vices into which we may be led if we bridle not the other propensities of our own evil and wofully distempered natures. The delivery unto Satan may signify excommunication—the two great divisions of the human family being made up of the Church and the world, and Satan being the god of this world. But whether this or some other explanation is to be sustained, let me always keep in mind that sin and salvation are at utter and diametrical antipodes with each other. The unhappy man of this chapter was afterwards restored, but not till after a severe discipline of repentance. My God, restore to me the joys of thy salvation, and make me glad in the light of Thy reconciled countenance ; and save me—save me from that wilful sinning after which there remaineth no more sacrifice for sins, but a certain fearful looking for of judgment.

This is a truly memorable and important rule given by Paul for the regulation of our intercourse with others. The visibly wicked of the world we may company with, but not with the visibly wicked of the Church ; or rather —for they cannot be of the true Church should their present turn out to be a permanent wickedness—we are not to company with him who, whether truly or not is *called* a brother, should he be living at the time in known wickedness. But even the men of the world, whether notoriously sinful or not, do not form a profitable, nay rather a very dangerous and withering companionship for Christ's peculiar people. There is a great difference between not shunning a man's society and cultivating that society—between a spontaneous and uncalled for movement towards him and the admittance of him into converse when the occasions of business or life require that he should move towards you, or which bring you any way together. Let me proceed on this wise and just discrimination of the apostle—not giving up such intercourse with

the world as I am necessarily involved in when prosecuting
its lawful affairs, and withholding all countenance from
those professors who disgrace the holy name by which
they are called. But let me consider myself, (Gal. vi. 1,)
lest I lapse into the condition of such as name the name
of Christ, yet depart not from iniquity.

1. CORINTHIANS VI.

Guide me aright, O Lord, on the question of law in
connexion with the doings of the Free Church. I hold
it wrong that it should have implicated the case of our
poor with law, and with its Law Committee; but give me
calm and considerate wisdom on this and every other
topic which relates to its affairs, and which comes in my
way. And save me, O Lord, from those distressful broodings which have so long and so powerfully haunted me,
which tumultuate within me even in church, and act, as
all the cares of this life do, as so many thorns which
might choke and overbear the good seed of the word of
God. And, O my God, let me be solemnized and warned
by the emphatic interdict which is here laid on the unrighteous; and it is my special concern at present to
notice, that among those who are here enumerated, *re-
vilers* have a place. O press this home upon my conscience.
Let me not strive or be a brawler. Purge out this leaven,
O God. May I keep the passover and its feast aright; and
know what it is to *forbear* and to forgive, even as God
for Christ's sake hath forgiven me. O Lord, I pray that
all bitterness, and wrath, and anger, and clamour, be put
away from me, with all malice. O my God, give me to
be harmless as a dove, and wise as a serpent. Pardon

and rectify, O Lord; and grant me experience of the efficacy of this written prayer. O enable me by next Sabbath to record its efficacy, and with the graces of a complete charity and a complete holiness, may I be enabled to assure myself as being of the number of those who are washed and sanctified and justified in the name of the Lord Jesus, and by the Spirit of our God.

Let me henceforward bear a high respect to Christian expediency; and forbid that I should ever more be the slave of those lusts which war against the soul. If I bring not my body under subjection, I myself shall be a castaway. O let me flee every dangerous fascination, and put on the whole armour of God, in resistance to it. Let me venerate my body as being indeed the temple of the Holy Ghost; nor let me ever forget the awful saying, that "He who defileth that temple, him will God destroy." Especially let me never lose sight of the truth that I am not my own, but the property and at the absolute disposal of Him who bought me. His are both my body and my spirit, and in these let me glorify Him whose they are, being alike their Maker and their Preserver.

I. CORINTHIANS VII.   *June*, 1844.

It is good to shun the first approaches of evil, and not only not to touch the unclean thing, but to keep our sight and our eyes from viewing vanity. Give me to deny all worldly lusts. Give me a self-command adequate to every encounter with the evil influences of an evil world. But let me ever when duty and circumstances allow, shun the encounter rather than brave it; and, O God, lead me not into

temptation, but deliver me from evil. With a permission
for every lawful indulgence, let me at the same time, and
though having a conscience free from all morbid scrupulosity, be aware of the mighty benefit arising from moderation, even in such indulgences as of themselves are not
criminal. In particular, whether I have stated times of
fasting or not, let me maintain such a temperance as is at
all times consistent with spirituality and study, and the
vigorous discharge of every incumbent obligation. And
let the actual allotments of providence, the existing circumstances in which I find myself—let these have their
due influence on the determination of my conduct. In
putting the question—what is the will of God ? let me not
be insensible to such evidences of His will as are supplied
by the peculiarities of the condition in which He hath
placed me, by the relations wherewith He hath compassed me around. And let me be sure to make this use
of these relations. Let me study the Christian good of
all within my reach, and more especially of those with
whom I bear the affinities of kindred and companionship.
And let me be satisfied with my lot—knowing that my
great and enduring welfare hinges not on aught which
is external, but on my keeping the commandments of
God, on my living to Him who died for me, who bought
me with the price of His own blood, and whom, therefore,
I am bound to glorify both with my body and my spirit,
which are His.

Let me sit loose to the enjoyments of this world—and
on the consideration too that the time is short, and the
world soon passeth away. Let this both moderate my
attachment to the pleasures of life, and make its disappointments and crosses fall light upon me. And thus too

shall I be freed from carefulness, so as to wait on the Lord
without distraction, and be engrossed not with trifles, but
with the one thing needful. Give me, O Lord, to be holy
in body and in spirit ; and let it be my main concern to
be so busied with the things of the Lord as to please the
Lord. And let me be steadfast on the side of all righteousness, with power from on high both to will and to do
in conformity with its dictates.

Whatever I do let it be in the Lord. Give me the comfort of knowing that my labour in the Lord is not in vain.
Let me not feel at liberty to do aught in which the presence and will of God do not go along with me. Beautify
me with Thy salvation, and take pleasure in me as one of
Thine own people.

I. CORINTHIANS VIII.

The puffing up by knowledge is finely contrasted with
the building up by charity or love. The third verse is a
highly interesting one ; and for myself I incline to the
understanding of those who conceive that God is the
antecedent to the same, or ουτος. In the first verse
the apostle had affirmed the superiority of love to knowledge, and we hold it to be in keeping with, nay a kind
of sequence or support to this affirmation—when it is said
that the love of God either implies or augments and
ratifies our knowledge of God. Acquaint thyself with
thy Creator and thou wilt be at peace with Him. Know
Him as He is—that is as love, and then wilt thou love Him
back again ; so that if this love exists, it proves a correct
antecedent knowledge of God—if you feel aright of Him,
it proves that you know aright of Him. This, if not

the view of the text, we hold at least to be a sound and Scriptural view, and full of comfort. It goes to establish how essentially amiable is God, when the loving of Him and not the being afraid of Him is the evidence of our having a true discernment of His character. Keep me, O Lord, within the limits of a sound and sober Christian philosophy. Let mine be the humility of science, truly so called. Deliver me from all imagination of my own sufficiency, and more particularly of my knowledge. Give me the docility of a little child, and enable me to manifest my just appreciation of Thy character by the love I bear to Thee; and for this purpose give me to behold Thee, the one God, in the face of Jesus Christ the one Mediator. Let me see Thee as God in Christ; and introduce me to that knowledge of, and that believing fellowship with the Father and the Son which worketh by love, and is life everlasting. And O may this love of God be abundantly manifested by my love of the brethren, and indeed of all mankind. Let all my things in which they are concerned be done with charity. O may I not offend them ; and save me from the guilt of a worthless and seducing example in the face of the unpractised young. Pardon my bygone heedlessness, O Lord—or rather let me confess my enormous culpability, the condemnation of which can only be washed out in the blood of the Lamb. But O let me not count that blood an unholy thing ; may I be purified therewith ; may I experience its sanctifying as well as its peace-speaking power ; and careful to depart from all iniquity myself, may I be alike careful to abstain from all that can be morally or spiritually injurious to any within the reach of my influence.

I. CORINTHIANS IX.

O that I could say of any that they are my work in the
Lord.   May my children be Thy children ; and make me
the instrument of spiritual and saving good to their souls.
May they prove the seal of mine apostleship.   And there
is another wisdom beside that of winning souls which I
would specially crave from Him who " giveth to all men
liberally, and upbraideth not." I pray that I may be guided
aright, both among ministers and people, in my attempts
to influence both and direct both to the most proper and
effectual methods for the support of the ordinances of the
Gospel in our Church.   I should like to have the tact
and delicacy, and withal the frankness of Paul upon
this subject, that I may both make a clear and audible
and uncompromising declaration of the principle, and yet
be so judicious in the application of it that my efforts
and urgencies may give offence to none, and meet with
acceptance and success amongst all.   Let me make no
secret of the undoubted doctrine, that they which preach
the gospel shall live of the gospel.   It is a great and
obvious consideration, charged with equity and truth of
sentiment, that men should give liberally of their carnal
things in return for the spiritual things which they receive at the hands of their ministers.   But along with the
boldness and freedom, give to our ministers also the disinterestedness of Paul.   May they do nothing to hinder
the gospel of Christ.   Though it be the clear duty of the
hearers to prevent and supply their wants, still it is their
duty also, if need so be, cheerfully to suffer want for the
sake of the gospel.   Grant, O Lord, that these two parties
may so acquit themselves as to overlap each other, and

so give room for such testimonies as Paul has bequeathed
to us respecting the liberality of some of the Churches in
his day. In all events, let the duty and desire of preaching to men the good news of their salvation be uppermost
in the hearts of our Free Church ministers. May they
feel constrained thereto by the weight of a moral necessity, and by the wo denounced on the unfaithful and the
indolent. May they humble themselves into the attitude
of servants, and win the souls of many by the grace and
wisdom of their right compliances and right accommodations. May they experience the might of the doctrine
of Christ in pulling down strongholds, and re-establish that
law of duty under Him of which in time past the people
were altogether reckless—living, as they did, without God
in the world. O that many were reclaimed from their prof-
ligacy and brutal ignorance in this way ! And, Heavenly
Father, along with our aspirations after public usefulness,
may we ever be careful of our own personal Christianity,
lest when we preach to others we ourselves should be cast-
aways. For this purpose enable us to keep under the control
of strictest principle and purity all the wayward and inferior
appetites of our tainted and polluted natures. Through
the Spirit may I be enabled to mortify the deeds of the body
and live. May I not only seek but strive to enter into the
kingdom. May I so press towards it as to take it by force.
May I struggle for the mastery ; and instead of random and
undirected efforts, may I maintain a steadfast and persevering course towards the distinct object of perfecting my
holiness in the fear of God—resolved to do all, and in
readiness to suffer all, even as Christ Himself did for the
joy that was set before Him, for the crown that is incorrup-
tible, for the inheritance in Heaven that fadeth not away.

I. CORINTHIANS X.

The Israelites who passed through the waters of the Red Sea ranked under Moses as their captain and guide to the promised land, yet fell short of it because of their misconduct in the wilderness ; and so we who have passed through the waters of baptism, rank under Christ as the Captain of our salvation, yet may fall short of the heavenly Canaan. Let us take warning by the examples recorded in Scripture for our admonition.—O give me to take heed lest I fall. O my God, let me henceforth be intent on the fulfilment of Thy will, which is my sanctification. Give me more certainly and distinctly to know my calling, that I may press toward the mark for the prize thereof. Let me not be seduced from this high walk by temptations of any sort ; and, O my God, either strengthen me for the encounter, or provide me a way of escape from them, as Thou seest to be best. Suffer me not to be tempted beyond what I am able to bear ; yet let me count it all joy when I fall into divers temptations. But there are certain things which I must flee from rather than brave—and idolatry, if not in the literal, yet in the figurative and spiritual sense, is one of these. Let me make a covenant with my eyes, and turn away my sight from viewing vanity. And let me not symbolize with the ungodly, with the men of the world, with those who, if they do not worship, at least love the creature more than the Creator. Let me not even incur the appearance of symbolizing with them, lest I thereby give offence, and either grieve any of the brethren or perhaps seduce them by an example which it is not safe for them to imitate. What might be lawful in itself had I nothing but the state of my own Christianity to attend to, might be highly inexpedient for the Christian good of others. Let charity to my brethren of mankind be ever a guiding and governing principle of my conduct ; and let all be subordinated to the will and the glory of God. Conduct me to the sublime achievement of doing all for Thy glory ; and may the comprehensive phrase of " whatsoever ye do," lead me to connect with God and godliness all the concerns of my life, all the actions of my history. O how miserably as yet have I fallen short of that glory. Give me, give me, Almighty Father, to be spiritually-minded— and then, with the enjoyment of life and peace, shall I know how to harmonize glory to God in the highest with good-will to men. Let me not seek my own wealth but that of others—nor mine own profit, but that highest of all profit to others, even their salvation.

I. CORINTHIANS XI.

The stimulus of a human example is here applied to enforce the duty of imitating a Divine example. We are called upon to be followers of Paul, even as he was of Christ—a legitimate argument therefore, and which both demonstrates the use of holding ourselves forth as patterns to our fellow-men, and the responsibility under which we lie, for the sake of others, to maintain the walk and the conversation which become the gospel of Jesus Christ. Let my light then so shine, that others seeing my good works may be led to copy them, to the glory of my Father in Heaven. And O let me not be satisfied with the mere profession of Christ as my righteousness, or of Christ as the Head of my Church, but may I so study His life

and character that I may walk even as He walked,
and that the same mind may be in me which was also
in Christ Jesus. Looking unto Him may I be made like
unto Him; but may I look unto Him not directly alone,
but to His reflected image in all His true disciples—that
I may be the follower of them "who through faith and
patience are now inheriting the promises." There is an
argument suggested by this verse for the good and the
usefulness of religious biographies.

I am taught by the next passage to give no unnecessary outrage to the customs, whether of my age or neighbourhood—such customs as, however ephemeral or however local, cannot be violated without a moral hardihood
and defiance on the part of the transgressor, and without
scandalizing the observers of the offensive exhibition. To
estimate the force of this remark, let us but think of how
much and what evil would be implied and wrought if the
men of our day were to commence the practice of sitting
in Church with their hats on, and the women with their
bonnets off. Our existing habit, which is a second nature,
would cause us to feel that it were a shameful thing in
the reckless few who dared such an innovation, and so as
to warrant the interference of the Church authorities on
the subject. There is enough of analogy between the
hats and the long hair to make the apostle's earnestness
on the subject of that liberty which he here reproves to
be not altogether unintelligible: and at all events, let me
appreciate and apply the weighty generalities of principle which occur in the course of his remonstrance—even
that the head of every man is Christ, and that the head of
Christ is God, and that of God are all things.

Give me, O Lord, in faith, and in the spiritual sense, to

eat the flesh and drink the blood of the Son of man. Give me to receive the atonement, along with its appointed memorials. In approaching the sacrament of the Supper may I so put on Christ that there would be an effectual moral barrier in the way of my fulfilling the lusts of the flesh. In coming to Him through the gate of His own ordinance may I have the sincere determination through grace to forsake all. And give me the power of self-examination. Search me and try me, O Lord, by enabling me to search and try myself. Save me from so counting the blood of Christ an unholy thing as that I should sin wilfully, or sin so as to be irrecoverably forsaken by Thy good Spirit, after which there remaineth no more sacrifice for sin.

I. CORINTHIANS XII.

July, 1844.

Give me so to recognise and feel the lordship of Christ as to prove that He has been indeed revealed to me by the Holy Ghost—even as the first Christians proved the heaven-born quality of their profession by the persecutions which they endured in maintaining it. Let us not think in despair that we have not the Spirit because not all similarly endowed by Him. He endows variously those who, by one generality already spoken of, might evince their common fellowship in His blessed influences. Let me proceed aright on the natural as well as spiritual diversities which obtain among men—assigning to each the place and function which are most appropriate to his specific qualification. Give me wisdom, O Lord, in the guidance of any conjunct effort for the good of my fellow-men ; and O do Thou fit the agents of the West Port for their respective tasks. What a noble and comprehensive sentiment comes forth of the apostle when he tells, in the course of his reasoning, that there are diversities of operations, but that God worketh all in all!—Let me ever acknowledge God in all my ways, and do homage to Him and to His as being the sole agency and power in all the varieties and throughout all the extent of universal nature.

And let me do homage to Thy wisdom in the constitution of the Church, even as Thy wisdom is conspicuous in the constitution of this great and diversified world—a wisdom designed as manifold, because having to do with infinite multitude and boundless extent. Yet as in the material workmanship one law of gravitation binds and cements and harmonizes all, so in the spiritual and ecclesiastical economy may the law of love reciprocate universally among the most distinct and distant members of the Church of the living God—so that when one suffers all might suffer, and when one rejoices all might rejoice— all in themselves apart from each other, yet with this pervading unity amongst them, that each is part of the body of Christ. Let all strife and envy and hostile emulation be thus given up, and let mutual care and mutual respect prevail in the midst of us.

Gifts are desirable and to be coveted earnestly, but graces are of far higher worth than gifts, and of far higher importance to the wellbeing both of the Church and of society. The apostle before closing his argumentation on gifts has the idea presented to him of that which is of nobler and more exalted quality, and so breaks forth into one of the most glorious effusions that ever flowed from a writer's pen, supplied from the fountain of inspiration, and issuing in such a representation or picture of the highest of human virtues as has served for the guidance and commanded the admiration of the faithful in all ages.

I. CORINTHIANS XIII.

The impression and effect of this sacred eloquence cannot possibly be enhanced by any enforcement of ours. We may re-state the lesson of this chapter, or resolve it into its particulars, but most assuredly for aught like a practical influence it is far more powerful when left to come direct from the apostle's own mouth, than through the translation of any commentator upon his writings There might, it would appear, be a faith which could remove mountains, and yet not be a faith working by love. If the former, it remains only a gift—if the latter, it is a grace. Faith, in the preceding chapter, is treated as a gift—spoken of as one of the gifts of the Spirit conferred on certain office-bearers of the Church, and restricted to these, so as to be distinct from the faith "which availeth," the faith that is indispensable to all for salvation, and wherever it exists brings charity in its train. The gift of faith without the grace of charity is but a hollow and unsubstantial accomplishment, and so are the gifts of prophecy and the understanding or knowledge of all mysteries. And so the deed of almsgiving without the spirit of love is alike valueless—even that love of which we are presented here with so noble a description. O that I were made to realize the various characteristics which the apostle has assigned to it, and in all of which I am sadly deficient—though in some more glaringly deficient than in others. How far short, for example, am I of long-suffering, and of seeking not my own, and of slowness to anger, and of patient endurance under the calumnies and the injustice of others; nay, am I free of unseemly vanity, and do I not resent the assumed superiority of others, more especially when I conceive it to be grounded on the encroachments they have made on a credit which belongs to me, and which they would arrogate to themselves? How keenly alive to literary wrongs—far more than I would if armed with the property of bearing all things. Let me grow in kindness; let me be clothed with humility; let me think no evil—or, perhaps, rather purpose no evil to any man. Is there no gleam of malignant joy that comes across me when I hear of the disgrace of those who support an adverse cause? Give me, O Lord, to know myself. Search me and try me, and root all that is evil out of me. What an insignificance it stamps on the contests and the emulations of this life, when one bethinks him of that eternity where the distinctions after which we aspire here shall be forgotten, and the charity that should subordinate all which is within us shall never die away. Let me lay up then this treasure for heaven, and be sustained amid the contempts and the imputations to which I am exposed here by a view of the mighty enlargements of knowledge and power which await me there, where all the dimnesses, and misunderstandings, and consequent mutual revilings, which take place in our controversies below, shall all be dissipated in the pure and ethereal light of those higher regions where knowledge shall be perfected, and where faith and hope shall be left behind as but the stepping-stones to the unfading charity that shall for ever remain in the paradise of God. When charity is spoken of here as greater than faith it is not because a grace is greater than a gift, for the faith that worketh charity is itself a gift; but it is because the end is greater than the means—the landing-place of more consideration than the way—the sanctification than the faith which sanctifies.

I. CORINTHIANS XIV.

Mark the distinction here made between a gift and a grace—the one to be desired, the other to be followed after. The possession of the one is a thing to be wished for, the cultivation of the other is a thing of duteous obligation. Let me ever have a higher value for charity than for all talent—and of this latter, too, let me prize the talent of useful instruction more than the powers which please or astonish, and so are more fitted to aggrandize him who owns them, and give him a more splendid reputation among men. Let me preach not myself but Christ Jesus my Lord, and that others might be saved. O let me know, and appreciate, and follow after true greatness —the greatness of being good and useful, and the greatness of ruling my own spirit; and never, O Lord, let my trumpet sound uncertainly—never let me aspire after such a language as might prove an unknown tongue to the common people. Save me from all such literary ambition; and pardon, O God, my every wrong and vain effort at the wisdom of words; but let me deal in such words as are easy to be understood. Let me preach not as a man of gifts—unintelligible to many—but as a man of grace, commending myself to the consciences of all. I would seek to excel for the good of edification, and therefore let me labour that others might understand me; and may what I say go to their consciences, and so as to manifest the searching and discerning power of the truth that is in Jesus; and thus, that even the most unlearned of hearers might be constrained to render the homage of their convictions thereto.

O my God, give me the power of ordering matters aright in the West Port; let all be peace and harmony, and no confusion there; direct all my footsteps in that undertaking; and may I more and more be made to abound in such suggestions as Thy Spirit will prompt and approve of. Let me keep all the impulses of my own spirit under the subjection of a presiding and circumspect wisdom. And more especially, O God, let me understand Thy will in regard to the right place and performances of a female agency. May their work be abundantly blessed and countenanced from on high, and have a happy effect on the families. Let me beware of mine being too much of a restraining authority; and let me seek that all things be done for edification, and all things be done decently and in order.

I. CORINTHIANS XV.

How momentous and weighty are both the truths and sentiments of this magnificent chapter. First, that faith without memory is vain—that is, the things believed are of no use to us unless they are called to remembrance and dwelt upon by the mind. Of all the articles here enumerated, let me recur with the greatest fondness and frequency, yea, ever and anon, to the precious doctrine of Scripture, that Christ died for my sins—and thus may a clear conscience, and a confident apprehension of God as my reconciled Father, be at all times upheld within me; and let me also be ever thinking of Him as my risen Saviour. And O for both the experience and humility of Paul, who so richly shared in the grace of God, and so was enabled to labour more abundantly than all his colleagues in the apostleship, yet said with all promptitude and gratefulness—"Nevertheless, not me, but the grace of God that is in me." O like him may I grow contemporaneously in humility and holiness, that with a deeper and deeper sense of my own lowliness, I may get nearer and nearer, as if by successive ascents, towards the measure of the stature of a perfect man in Christ Jesus my Lord. Let me keep a firm hold by faith of His resurrection, and be conformed thereto by a spiritual resurrection in my own soul from sin unto godliness. Verily this is a vain and miserable life apart from the glorious futurity which the gospel sets before us. Let us ever cherish this hope, looking forward to that great and ultimate evolution by which, after the present mysterious struggles between light and darkness, truth and righteousness will have the full ascendency, and God be all in all. Save me, O Lord, from the spirit of the Sadducees. Let me not seek after the company of worldly men, with whom time and the enjoyments of time are the entire and exclusive objects of pursuit or desire. Let me die unto sense, let me live by the faith of the Son of God, who will transform these vile bodies into the likeness of His own glorified body in the heavens. Having this hope may I purify myself even as Christ is pure, that the terrestrial of the first Adam may disappear, and the celestial of the second Adam be wholly substituted in its place.

And O may I not forget that he who soweth unto the flesh shall of the flesh reap corruption, and that only he who soweth unto the Spirit shall reap life everlasting. Thus may I look undismayed both upon death and upon judgment. Give me a well-grounded consciousness of the

love of God in my heart, and then may I have all boldness in looking forward to the day of final reckoning, because knowing that as God is so am I in the world, and
therefore ripening for the full enjoyment of Him in paradise. And let me not fear the Lawgiver, now that Christ
has magnified the law and made it honourable, and through
Him His disciples are sure of victory. O then let me not
be moved away from the hope of the gospel, but rooted
and grounded in Christ may I grow up in all fruitfulness,
ever abounding in His work, and with the unspeakable
but much needed comfort of knowing that my labour in
Him shall not be in vain.

I. CORINTHIANS XVI.

August, 1844.

Let me avail myself, for every fit object, of the sanction
here given by the apostle to weekly collections—they may
open for us a wide door of entry among the people for the
gospel of Jesus Christ ; but it is Thy grace, and it alone, O
Lord, which can make this great door an effectual one.
O may the alms and the prayers of Thy people ascend in
sweet memorial before God.

How beautifully does the apostle temper and harmonize
all his admonitions. Truth and fortitude are here qualified with the winning and attractive grace of charity.
How much do we need that, in these days of rebuke and
controversy, the precious combination of verses thirteenth
and fourteenth should be realized. Let us stand fast and
contend earnestly for the faith once delivered to the saints;
let us be manly and strenuous in the vindication thereof; and yet let all our things be done with charity. O
my God, teach me to steer aright between the opposite

influences which, in the present conjunction of things, might be brought to bear upon us. Let me not be over vehement and sturdy in debate, but on the other hand let me not be over soft and conciliating, the extreme to which I fear that I have too great a constitutional tendency.

He who himself declined receiving aught from the Corinthians, yet loved and honoured those who were addicted to the ministry of the saints. The people to whom he wrote were lacking in the supply of Paul's wants; and by the honourable mention which he makes of those who made up for this, he reminds his correspondents, and through them all Christians, of their duty. May the grace of liberality to Thy servants increase more and more amongst us.

Let me observe the courtesy and feel the affection of Paul towards all my fellow-Christians. And O that I had more of love to Christ—for, destitute of this grace, I am truly accursed. Work, then, O Lord, this grace in me; and for this blessed effect, let the grace of the Lord Jesus Christ be put forth upon my soul.

II. CORINTHIANS.

2 CORINTHIANS I.—Paul is pre-eminently an apostle *by the will of God;* and his comprehensive benediction of grace and peace speaks what that will is towards all to whom the gospel is sent—peace on earth, and that grace in the hearts of men here which might qualify them for an inheritance of glory hereafter. O may these blessings come both from God the Father and the Lord Jesus Christ; and let our fellowship be with both.

The God of all comfort leaves us at times to a period of tribulation and trial; and thus our lives may alternate between joy and sorrow. Let our trust not be in ourselves but in Him—that like as He raised Christ from the dead, so He, the Father of Christ, may raise us from a state of heaviness and suffering to a state of enlargement and triumph.   I am subject to great depressions and disquietudes on the subject of my West Port undertaking; but let me feel my own nothingness, and roll the matter upon God. May it emerge into promise and prosperity; and O may the spirit of prayer be shed forth on the co-adjutors in this work, that so thanksgiving might ensue to Him from whom all our sufficiency cometh.

And recurring to my own personal experience, let mine, O God, be that of the apostle, in being able to say with him what is the testimony of my conscience; and O let me henceforth, with simplicity and godly sincerity, not with fleshly wisdom but by the grace of God, have my conversation in the world.   O that I could thus at all times be off from myself, and lean the whole weight of my dependence upon God—looking to Him for the supplies of His Spirit in every time of need.   The perfection of the creature lies in the constant habit of bringing his emptiness to the fulness that is in Christ Jesus.   How . delightful the confidence wherewith we might ask that blessing which is pre-eminently termed the promise of the Father, even the Holy Spirit—might ask the presence and operation of this heavenly visitant from Him all whose promises in Christ are yea and amen. O seal us thus, and stablish us thus, even by the earnest of the Spirit in our hearts—the earnest of that heaven where Christ hath gone to provide for us an everlasting habitation, and so is not only preparing a place for us, but preparing us for the place. Give us this holy anointing, O God— the unction that remaineth. Thou art not unfaithful in Thy promises, but art abundantly willing and able to perform them, to the glory of Thy grace in us.

In this faith, and by this faith, O God, may I ever stand, and so exemplify the saying of the prophet—that the just shall live by faith. May it be a faith which not only sustains our peace, but which ministers joy to the heart—even that joy of the Lord which is strength. The law is weakness, or rather through the weakness of the flesh it cannot do what the Spirit of life in Christ Jesus can alone do, even free us from sin and death, and enable us to render unto God an acceptable obedience.

II. CORINTHIANS II.

There was a wonderful combination of firmness with softness in the character of Paul, so that while in virtue of the one he rebuked when needful with all openness and fidelity, in virtue of the other he relented and gave way to all the delicacies and sympathies of his gentler nature, when the time came for healing the wound which in the office of disciplinarian or censor he had himself inflicted. It is the most perfect human example I could name of Christian compassion and Christian courteousness, carried as far as possible—consistently with sound principle and the interests of religion, but never so far as in the least to compromise the truth of the gospel or the integrity and purity of the faith. Let me know how to blend these various elements even as he did; and while entering as thoroughly into the feelings of others with his tact and his sensibility, let me at the same time contend as boldly and as earnestly for the maintenance of the truth as did our great apostle.

Subtle and manifold are the devices of Satan—first, in luring men to some great delinquency ; and secondly, in leading them to despair because of it. In the case before us the offender who had already undergone his punishment was in danger of being swallowed up of overmuch sorrow, and Paul exerts himself to avert this danger.— My God, great and fearful are the delinquencies into which I have fallen. Blot them out, Almighty Father, from the book of Thy remembrance. Be at peace with me, O God, and restore peace to my conscience. Let me never distrust the efficacy of my Saviour's blood ; but O satisfy me with the present evidence of my being His—even that I am delivered from the power of those strong affections, the prevalence of which I have such reason to deplore. Give me this token of my having indeed trusted in Christ —my being sealed with the Holy Spirit of promise, that Spirit which not only lusteth against the flesh, but prevails over it.

There is a sweet savour of God unto Christ, both in them that are saved *and in them that perish*. There is a deep mystery in this last which we cannot penetrate—the mystery of God, not yet finished, but which will at length be so laid open that we shall know even as we are known. Meanwhile let us act on the practical declaration that God hath no pleasure in the death of the wicked, but rather that he should turn from his way and live—is not willing that any should perish, but that all should come to repentance. Here is every encouragement for present duty— whatever obscuration may now rest on the future destinies of men. Let me not meddle with matters too high for me, but be satisfied with the home-walk of a present obedience to present calls. I have no ground for complaint or for murmuring. Let me believe and obey the gospel of Jesus Christ; and then to me will His blessed message be the savour of life unto life. Amen.

II. CORINTHIANS III.

O that I were a living epistle of Christ Jesus, having the characters that are now graven on the tablet of an outward revelation transferred thence upon the tablet of my inner man. Take, O Lord, the heart of stone out of me, and make it a heart of flesh, soft, tender, and susceptible of a deep and enduring impression from Thy holy word. I am not sufficient of myself, O God, for learning even from Thine own Scriptures the truth unto salvation. Make Thy grace sufficient through Thy Spirit pressing home upon my mind those lessons of that knowledge of God and of Jesus Christ, which is life everlasting. And O give me to have the wisdom of the Spirit, and not to be satisfied with the wisdom of the letter. May the words of Scripture not only be understood in the meaning, but be felt in the life and the power of them. May I not count it enough that I know the truth—for if knowing and not doing, I shall thereby incur the greater condemnation, and the gospel will prove with me the savour of death unto death. O make me a partaker in the glorious ministration of the Spirit—that taking of the things of Christ, and showing them with effectual demonstration unto my soul, He may become unto me the Lord my righteousness, even as He is the righteousness of all who believe on Him.

Work in me, O Lord, this faith with power, that I may behold Thy glory in the face of Jesus Christ. There is a deep veil upon every natural man which intercepts from his view both the spiritual sense of Thy word and the glories of Thy character. I would turn unto Thee, O Lord, that the veil might be taken away, and so I be ushered at once into light and liberty. I would look unto Christ, that I might be made like unto Christ; yet though I do my part in this process—that is, keep looking at the Saviour, it is the Spirit, and He alone, who gives effect to it. It is not enough that I persevere in this attitude of looking. A blind man may assume the attitude and abide in it, but he cannot see; and neither can I, unless my spiritual blindness be dissipated, and the subjective power of seeing be superadded to the manifestation without me and above me. Nevertheless, let me continue in looking and looking for the Saviour, in searching those Scriptures which testify of Him, and in giving earnest heed to the word—how long?—till the day dawn and the day-star arise in my heart. Even so, Lord Jesus, come quickly. Change me into Thine own blessed image. O give me to purify myself even as Thou art pure. Let me be complete in Thee. May Christ be revealed in me. May Christ be formed in me. May He be my strength and my righteousness, and my all.

II. CORINTHIANS IV.

September, 1844.

Let me not faint, O Lord, under the toils of that ministry which Thy Providence hath put into my hands. Give me wisely to husband my strength; but let me be unwearied and most tenaciously persevering in my enterprise for the families of the West Port. Save me from all dishonesty and deceitfulness ; and let me walk on a visible platform, and in the day-light of an open manifestation. O may I find a way to the consciences of many by the godly sincerity of my conversation in the world, and above all, by the power of that gospel which the devil tries to intercept, but which do Thou, O Lord, cause to enter the hearts of those among whom I labour with power and the Holy Ghost and much assurance. May I be their devoted servant for the sake of Jesus and His truth ; and while it is my earnest prayer that Thou wouldst shine in their hearts, I deeply, deeply feel, O God, my own dependence on Thine own illuminating as well as Thy sanctifying grace. Give me a full assurance of understanding to the acknowledgment of the mystery of God and of the Father and of Christ. (Col. ii. 2.) Give me the light of the knowledge of Thy glory in the face of Jesus Christ, and in His great work of redemption. Lift the veil from my mind that it may be in darkness no longer, but that in Thy light I may clearly see light.

O that we felt as we ought the dependence and—of itself—nothingness of mere creatureship,—and the more, that the creature hath become subject to the bondage of corruption. Let me be humbled by the consideration that we are but the earthen vessels, and that that which is really treasure therein is from above—the power and the excellency being of God and not of us. Let not my present depression, then, turn into despair. He in whom is all our life and all our sufficiency is the same to-day, yesterday, and for ever ; and His servants are often degraded in the eyes of the world, and brought into a state of palpable helplessness, that it may be seen how our help is

all from on high, and that Christ is all in all. O that I
could thus believe, and that believing I could thus speak
—not fainting, because of my assured hope of a blessed
resurrection in Christ Jesus. Let this light in me so
shine before men that they too—beholding the power and
reality of faith, may themselves—by taking knowledge of
us, participate in them. And O let a sense of the coming
immortality sustain me amid all present discomforts and
despondencies—so that while my outward man perisheth
my inward man may be renewed by this bright and confident anticipation. O for a realizing sense of the unseen
futurities on the other side of death, an efficient and
practical apprehension thereof, so that I may not only
rejoice in hope of the glory of God, but may learn to
joy in tribulations also. Give me to feel the lightness
and littleness of all that is present, so that the sufferings
which are temporal may be absorbed and swallowed up in
a well-grounded hope of the happiness which is eternal.

II. CORINTHIANS V.

O that I could say with the apostle—"*I know* that I
have a building of God." Lord, increase my faith, and
give me to lay hold of eternal life. Grant that the meditations of this noble chapter—one of superlative rank in
Scripture—may have the effect of opening up for me this
glorious and ennobling prospect by leading and encouraging
me to lay hold of Christ as my offered propitiation, whom
a beseeching God hath set forth for the acceptance even
of the chief of sinners. We have much to weigh us down
in the evils of the present life, and in the corruption and
feculence of those vile bodies by which we are encompassed;

but let us be elevated by the thought that Thou hast given us eternal life in Thy Son; and to this faith do Thou add the experience which might enable us to say, that Thou hast *also* given us the earnest of the Spirit. On these grounds may we rest our confidence, O Lord, and walk no longer by sight but by faith—looking forward not with resignation only, but with desirousness, to the time when we shall be absent from the body and present with the Lord. Work in us, Almighty Father, this faith with power. Thou art the Lord of the Spirits of all flesh. May I henceforth die unto the flesh and unto the things which are beneath; and setting my affections on the things which are above, may I live by the powers of a world to come.

May I labour for acceptance both here and hereafter—and this by means of such spiritual sacrifices as are acceptable through Jesus Christ. This involves in it the obedience of works, or of the deeds done in the body; and let me not forget the Judge in the Saviour—for before His tribunal we must all appear and be reckoned with. O that His terror may persuade and His love may constrain me—persuade me to flee from the coming wrath to Him as my refuge, and constrain me both to love and live unto Him who poured out His soul unto the death for me. What a basis for the evangelical obedience of new creatures in Jesus Christ! What a mighty change is implied in our becoming Christians!—with new aims, new habits, new affections, new objects of pursuit; and yet what a free opening to this great enlargement—this vast revolution in the character and state of man. All is of God, who bestows the power to enter upon and persevere in this altogether new life; and who most welcomely, and with perfect good-will, invites us to the commencement of this new era in our moral and spiritual history. What can be more encouraging or attractive !— God Himself holding out to us the right hand of reconciliation—blotting out our trespasses—beseeching us to make it up with Him—sending ambassadors, and written as well as oral messages, into the world, full of entreaty, nay of prayer, that we should come into agreement and friendship with God. Verily, what more could He have done for His vineyard that He hath not done for it ? And to make it a sure way of access, a way to sustain us in our approaches to the Lawgiver on high, hath He instituted this double exchange between the sinner and the Saviour—our sins laid to His account, and He bearing the whole burden of them ; His righteousness laid to our account, and we admitted to the full reward of it. O let me flee to this place of safety, and take my abode under the ample canopy of His mediatorship—for how shall I escape if I neglect so great a salvation !

II. CORINTHIANS VI.

We might receive the grace of God in vain, even as we might believe in vain. (1 Cor. xv. 2.) He presses the acceptance of that grace upon us now. Now it is ours if we will. But if it be a true and real acceptance, there will and must be a present as well as future salvation. If we in very deed receive Christ, we shall receive along with Him power to be and to do as the children of God. (John i. 12.) In pressing this full and only real acceptance upon His disciples, Paul, anxious to maintain his moral ascendency amongst them, sets forth the exemplification which he and the other apostles had given of a living Christianity in their own persons. They were indeed the epistles of Christ, to be read and known of all men; and they who did thus read would learn what the gospel, in its power and reality, actually was. They indeed approved themselves as the genuine servants of God. And there behoved for the right discharge of their office to be wisdom as well as virtue; for they had to look to the right hand and to the left, and with the exercise of great discrimination, as well as the manful and resolute assertion of principle, they had to keep steadily onward in their way of labour and difficulty. And the contrast is here most strikingly exhibited between what they were in the flesh and what they were in and by the Spirit—weak of themselves, but strong in God and in the power of His might—sorrowful when they looked but to things temporal, yet joyful when they looked beyond to things eternal—poor, indeed, and with nothing, had this life been their all, yet rich and enriching others, possessing as they did that splendid reversion in the life that is to come which will prove the all in all both to themselves and to those who should receive the offer of the gospel at their hands. O may the ministers of our day thus acquit and thus approve themselves mighty in the word of Truth, because enforced by the power of God; and commanding the obedience of men to the faith, by the vivid and affecting representation which they give of its effect upon themselves, as working in them all patience and charity and righteousness.

The Corinthians were in danger from evil communications. With what a burning earnestness, yet power and delicacy of entreaty, does the apostle with a large-hearted and most desirous regard for their spiritual safety, call on them to renounce the fellowships and all the evil influences of an evil world—casting these behind them, that they might throw themselves into the arms of their reconciled and beseeching Father in Heaven. We have here the great turning point of a man's transition from death to life laid most impressively, and we may add most invitingly open to our view. Separation from idols is identified with union between us and God. There is no let or hinderance on His part, would we but choose Him as our satisfying portion, and forsake all. Let us come out then from a world lying in wickedness ; let us keep at a distance from all that is evil ; let us touch not and tamper not with temptation, and He will receive us into His household, and adopt us among the children of His own family.

II. CORINTHIANS VII.

Though we have the promises we are not therefore exempted from the precepts ; nay, the one is an argument, and the very consideration which our apostle founds upon, for urging on our obedience to the other. May I henceforward rest with unfaltering reliance on the offered privileges of the gospel, and because so resting and so relying, may I now count it and proceed upon it as my unceasing business, to perfect my holiness in the fear of God. Enable me, Almighty Father, thoroughly to cleanse myself, not from the filthiness of the flesh only, but from the filthiness of the spirit—from what good old Boston calls, speculative impurity. Turn not my sight and eyes only, but turn my thoughts from dwelling upon vanity, and give me to glorify the Lord with my soul and spirit

as well as body, which are the Lord's. How expressive is
Paul's description of his own state—" without were fightings, within were fears." I have had some experience of
the former ; and as to the latter, am apt to be visited with
certain nervous tremors and apprehensions. But let me
think not that any strange thing has happened to me. Let
me count the cost of my vocation. Let me know that in
the world I shall have tribulation, and give me to be strong
in the Lord, that in Him I may have peace : and neither
let me forget but be thankful for the many outward encouragements which God hath vouchsafed to me—for
the number and the attachment of my friends and fellow-
worshippers. But O let there be a spirit not of carnal partizanship but of genuine godliness—for it is this, and this
alone, which sanctifies our affections. The sorrow that is
not godly but of the world, worketh death—even as the
cares of life do, as well as its pleasures, choke the good seed
of the word of God. Deliver me, Almighty Father, from
such a sorrow, the sorrow of this world—from all depression of spirits connected with the loss of wealth or distinction among men. Do Thou purge even my sorrow for
sin of all its selfishness. Let it be the object of my hatred
and bitter regret, not because of its dreaded penalties, but
because of its own detested odiousness, and its exceeding
odiousness in the sight of God. Let this sorrow—the only
genuine principle of a saving repentance—be strong within
me, and manifest its reality and power not so much by
its feeling as by its fruits—carefulness in the avoidance
of all that is evil—earnest desire of a thorough clearance
from all that is vile and corrupt in this my accursed nature
—a strong sense of sin's utter unworthiness—a fearful apprehension of falling into its snares—a vehement desire,

amounting to hunger and thirst, after righteousness—a zealousness for all good works—a self-abhorrence for all the evil wherewith I am so heavily chargeable. And give me, O Lord, to be careful of the Christianity of others, as well as of my own. Let me have the comfort of knowing that the blessed faith of the gospel is forming and making progress among my friends, and especially among those of my own household. Let me see the fruits of repentance in my family, and that my children are indeed the children of God in Christ Jesus.

II. CORINTHIANS VIII.

While I pray for such liberality as is here set forth on the part of the common people, let me not forget the great and primary fountain-head of all that is good and abiding in this habit—even the grace of God bestowed on His faithful ones, and leading them onward to the imitation of our Saviour's great and wondrous example. Men sunken in deep poverty were liberal unto their power indeed, and beyond their power in the aspiration of their ardent affection for the Redeemer's cause. It is well to mark the order of precedency here from the principle to its fruit. They gave themselves first unto the Lord, and then to the help of the apostles in their great work of planting and assisting the churches—knowing that this was the will of God; and so they partook in the office of ministering to the saints. In urging the Corinthians to follow this pattern set before them by the Macedonians, he over and above sets forth the example of Christ, who though rich became poor. Give me, O Lord, to feel my wretched deficiency from this high standard. Bestow on me in larger measure and proportion that grace which Thou didst so plentifully bestow on the churches of Macedonia. Let it spread abroad more and more among the sadly deficient congregations of our Free Church. Do Thou begin it even now among the families of the West Port. Make them willing in the day of Thy power, that abounding in all that is good they may abound in this grace also. It is still but a day of small things. O do Thou brighten it onward even unto the latter day glory. Cause the poorest to take part in the fellowship of Christian charity ; and may the substantial equality be maintained among all the classes, by the rich casting in their larger gifts, and each man giving in proportion to his ability.

And we pray not only for the utmost liberality on the part of the contributors to our Church's cause, but for the utmost integrity and disinterestedness on the part of its administrators. And enable myself in particular, O God, to provide for honest things not in the sight of the Lord only, but in the sight of men. There may in all likelihood be an approaching trial for myself both of wisdom and delicacy. Thou knowest it, O God, and do Thou who givest to all men liberally of that grace and guidance which they need when they ask them in faith—do Thou prepare me aright for such an occasion : save me from affectation, save me from avarice, save me from indifference to my colleagues ; but save me also from such a deference to their interests and wishes, as that I should give in to any proposition which might offend the Church, or give occasion for its adversaries to speak reproachfully. Grant me that *bonhommie* with my coadjutors which so obviously subsisted, and which is exhibited in this chapter between Paul and his coadjutors ; and within the sphere of my own proper influence and management, may I be enabled to direct aright the services of my friends, and powerfully to stimulaté and turn to its most beneficial account the favourable disposition of our churches to the cause of righteousness and truth.

II. CORINTHIANS IX.
October, 1844.

O that the people of our Free Church were in such for-wardness of mind as that it were superfluous for me to write to them as touching the sustentation of a ministry for the families of our land. Let the duty of giving be better understood, and more felt and acted on in this our day. In this department, too, of Christian obedience, let the duty—even as all duty should—be our delight. And God is not unrighteous to forget our work and labour of love. Let us sow bountifully and we shall reap bounti-fully; yet let it not be in the mercenary hope of a re-ward that we let forth our liberality on the objects of Christian benevolence—though it be indeed a precious de-claration, and must have been made for the purpose of in-fluencing us, that " he that giveth to the poor lendeth unto the Lord." Yet in the very exercise of this grace of li-berality, in the very keeping of this commandment, may we experience that there is a great and an immediate re-ward. Let the heart be fully upsides with the hand in these dispensations, that as we have purposed in the one so may we give with the other. Let us never forget that it is the heart which God looks to, not the *opus operatum*, not the work, but the will that prompteth the work. To give with a grudge or by constraint is not well-pleasing. It is the cheerful giver whom God loves; and

O the blessedness of the righteous—for over and above the pleasure felt in the instant of well-doing, is it followed up by the rewards, both of Providence and Grace—a larger heartedness within, and often the increase of outward means for a larger dispensation. God not only strengthens the principle, but generally increases the fruits of righteousness, in return for every exercise thereof that is well-pleasing to Himself—not only making us more willing than before, but more able than before, for every good work. Christian benevolence awakens the thanksgivings and the prayers of those who are the objects of it, in behalf of their benefactors ; and they receive an answer to these prayers, in larger supplies both of the disposition to give and of the wealth which empowers them to give more abundantly. But whether the hundred-fold more even in the present life shall be rendered to us in this way or not, the promise will be substantially accomplished, if in the end we have life everlasting, and here are made rich in faith, and morally or spiritually, if not materially rich in good works. O that a sense of God's unspeakable gift in sending to us the Son of His love, who submitted Himself to death for us all, made us more alive than heretofore to the weight and magnitude of our obligations—that we may give ourselves back again to Him, and consecrate all we are and all we have to His will and service.

II. CORINTHIANS X.

There are some first-rate and most precious memorabilia in this chapter. What more affecting, for example, than the characteristics here assigned to our Saviour—His meekness and His gentleness. Let me, in considering

Him who is the Apostle and High-Priest of my profession, (Heb. iii.,) dwell especially on these winning attributes of His mild and compassionate nature—that therein I might have confidence and joy.   And let me, in imitation of Him who was lowly in heart, cast down all my lofty imaginations, and sitting at His feet with the docility of a little child, be taught of Him who alone can reveal the Father to me, (Matt. xi. 27-30,) bringing every thought into captivity to the obedience both of His revelation and of His will.

Let me not trust to myself that I am Christ's, but let me trust objectively to His precious declarations and promises.   Let my confidence go outwardly upon the Saviour; and O for the experience of those early Christians who, when they first trusted in Christ, were thereafter sealed with the Holy Spirit of promise.   In personal converse with my fellow-men I often give way to a certain facility of which I have afterwards repented.   Let me cherish a great reliance upon the issues of my own deliberate judgment, and in every good work consult more than I have yet done with my own soul.   I feel as if I could do more good by my written than by my oral and conversational pleadings or testimonies.   Let me walk humbly with God, and so far independently with man, as to be free of that fear and excessive deference towards him or his opinions which might prove to be a snare.

Let me hope that I am now disabused of the false confidence which might be suggested by the comparison of myself with my fellow-men.   Even on the ground of this comparison there is much to humble me, and when I look at the patience, and the courteousness, and the hospitality, even of unconverted men, there is great reason why I should feel abashed, and put the question to my conscience—what doest thou more than others? But the radical and effectual measurement of my pretensions is to bring them direct to the standard of the Divine law, and learn from thence my wretched deficiencies from the true and absolute rules of righteousness, and how far I have fallen short of the glory of God. Elevate me, O Lord, from the terrestrial to the celestial contemplation—from the moralities of an earthly to those of a heavenly and Divine citizenship—that I may learn how far, how infinitely far, I am deficient, as well as how much, how superhumanly much, is to be done, ere a child of nature can indeed be transformed into a child of God, so as to become the heir and the joyful expectant of a blessed immortality. Surely all boasting of ourselves, or of our labours, should be thereby put to shame and silence. We will glory only in the Lord. Increase our faith in Him, and this will enlarge our desires, both for the copying of His example and the doing of His will. Raise us, O God, to this higher platform. Stablish us in Christ, that rooted and built up in Him we may attain to the fulness of the stature of perfect men in Christ Jesus our Lord, and so that He may see in us of the travail of His soul and be satisfied.

II. CORINTHIANS XI.

Endow me, O Lord, with the watchful concern felt by Paul for the pure Christianity of his converts; and give me also the delicacy and the wisdom which marked all his attempts on the sympathy and conviction of his fellow-men. O that I had a similar concern—amounting even to jealousy, for the religious state of those of my own household; and what a pregnant expression of the rightness of

that state, even the simplicity that is in Christ! Give to
me and mine, O Lord, the simple trust in Him which
brings down the Spirit as the earnest of our inheritance
hereafter, and which also works in us here a simple and
an entire devotedness to the will and glory of the great
Emanuel. Save us from the contaminations—whether
of false opinion or of a spirit of worldliness; and let no
plausibility seduce us from the direct and obvious simplicity of the truth as it is in Jesus. O deliver me from
the hateful and debasing idolatry of those who would
make a gain of godliness. Emancipate me from all that
is wrong and selfish on the question of remuneration for
my services in the Church; save me alike from avarice
and from the ostentation of its opposite; and give me that
just sense of what is due to my colleagues on the one
hand, and to the opinion of the public on the other—that
I might steer aright among the influences which act upon
me on both sides; let me beware of a deceitful influence
in either direction, and while I would cut off occasion of
reproach from whatever quarter, O be Thou the Being
with whom I have to do, walking in simplicity and godly
sincerity before Thee—having respect unto God rather
than unto man. Save me from all that is evil under the
guise of what is good—from the deceitfulness of sin—
from the temptation of that cunning adversary who can
gloss over his own service with the semblance of righteousness as well as of pleasure. O what a humbling representation is here set forth of the labours and trials of this
great apostle. Let me take the lesson to myself, and
contrast the picture here given with my own selfishness,
my own love of ease, my own impatience under the crosses
and contradictions to which I am exposed; how ready to

sink under discouragements, and to faint when aught that is adverse or annoying befalls me. There was a substratum of piety and prayer to sustain all the toils, and burdens, and endurances which were laid on this manful and intrepid warrior in the cause of God—who fought the good fight, and kept the faith. So be it with me, Almighty Father; and let me experience the truth of the blessed saying, that " they who wait upon the Lord shall renew their strength—they shall walk and not be weary—they shall run and not faint." What was it that enabled Paul to say—" I can do all things?" The glorious and instructive answer is—" through Christ strengthening me." O may He, the Lord my righteousness, be also the Lord my strength.

II. CORINTHIANS XII.

Doubtless pride was not made for man. The most exalted of our kind have been the most exempted from it. Let him that glorieth glory in the Lord—there being nothing in himself which he did not receive—so that when the gift or the grace is withdrawn from him, he, in the humiliating lesson of his own inherent weakness, meets enough to mortify and abase him. We have nought to speak of but our infirmities that the power of Christ may rest upon us, and that grace be conferred which is given only to the humble.

Then follows a most instructive paragraph. Paul was left to make the whole discovery of his own nothingness. A temptation bore upon him against which he had to pray, for that in his own strength he could not have prevailed. And how pregnant with inference is the answer that was given to him—not a removal of the temptation, whatever it may have been, but grace and sufficiency from on high.—My God, Thou knowest the sins which do most easily beset me. Extirpate, if it be Thy blessed will; but if sin must dwell in the house, may it not be master in the house. Let believing and constant supplication be my refuge, so as I may experience that when I am weak then am I strong. Give me, O Lord, to realize this mystery—this great secret of practical godliness; and may I ever, in going forward to duty, look upward to Him from whom cometh down every good and perfect gift. Make Thy grace, O God, sufficient for me, perfect Thy strength in my weakness.

What a noble testimony here to the reality of the Christian miracles. But it is with the moral and not the argumentative lesson that we at present have to do; and O that I had grace to imitate both the glorious disinter-- estedness of Paul and his intense devotedness to the good of human souls.

And what a tenderness of godly jealousy did he feel for his converts; and what an enumeration here both of the vengeful and the licentious passions of our fallen humanity.—My God, let them not have the dominion over me. I have just risen from a sacrament: I have made the vow.—O help me to pay the vow. Humble me, O God, under the sense of my former most disgraceful relapses. Keep me, O God, within the bond of Thy covenant. The sins and iniquities of my past life—and these, too, in the face of solemn and repeated sacramental engagements—do Thou remember no more. Take unto Thee Thy great power and reign over me, and strengthen me with all might in the inner man, that strong in the grace which is in the Lord Jesus, I may obtain the victory over all the frailties and corruptions of my accursed nature.

II. CORINTHIANS XIII.

November, 1844.

Give me, O Lord, to realize the experiences of the apostle, who when he was weak then was he strong. Give me this proof, O Lord, of Jesus Christ being in me —that when most sensible of my infirmities, and most constrained to pray because of them, then am I most richly supplied with aid from above, by the power of Christ being made to rest upon me. This were indeed a most satisfying demonstration of my part and interest in the promises of His gospel, the best and most decisive evidence of my being in the faith. Let me therefore examine myself—first, as to the sincerity and singleness of my aim to be an altogether Christian; and secondly, as to my success in the prosecution of that aim—for the want of this success would indicate either the defect of a hearty and devoted good-will, or a failure either from my ignorance or neglect of those expedients which are pointed out in the Bible, and placed within my reach for the advancement of my sanctification; and which ignorance, or which neglect, must infer a want of faith in the efficacy of these expedients. Give me then, O Lord, to show my faith by my works, and to examine myself by the test which our blessed Saviour lays down, when He says— " By their fruits ye shall know them." May these fruits, O God, evince that I am not one of the αδοκιμοι, or, as it has been translated, "reprobates." And in these fruits may I abound more and more, growing up unto the measure of the stature of a perfect man in Christ Jesus my Lord. Save me, O God, from the withering and congealing influences of that orthodoxy which, in putting down all human perfection under the legal economy, would depress our efforts and aspirations after that perfection for which we are bidden to labour under the evangelical economy. There is such a perfection toward which we ought incessantly to aim, however short we may fall of its attainment. Give me, O Lord, this perfection of an entire and devoted will, this honest dedication, this simplicity and godly sincerity, this singleness of endeavour, to make good—not with fleshly wisdom, but by the grace of God—the prize of my high calling, so as to stand perfect and complete in the whole will of God.—My God, help me onward to this great achievement. And O may the closing benedictions of this epistle have upon me their adequate fulfilment; but in order that the God of love and peace may be with me, let me feel the comfort of this gracious representation of my Father in Heaven; and let me study as far as lieth in me to be at peace with all men; and let my affection for others be a holy affection, and then will it be like the love wherewith God loveth us. Let no vile admixture of the corrupt and the carnal be present so as to vitiate or unhallow this love; and O may I have the full manifestation and experience in my soul of the grace of the Lord Jesus, and the love of God, and the communion of the Holy Ghost.

GALATIANS.

GALATIANS I.—May this blessing from the Father and the Son, as pronounced by the divinely authorized apostle, be fully realized upon me—grace as including both a graciousness towards me and the fruits of it, and peace as including both the removal of God's displeasure against

me and of my enmity against God.   And let me never
forget the purpose of my Saviour's death, when, with a
love that it were well if we could more enter into and
appreciate, He gave Himself for our sins.   It was to deliver us from this present evil world, from the wrath that
impends over it, and from the wickedness that so abounds
in it.   Neither let me forget that this was agreeable to
the will of the Father; and that it was not only Christ
who so loved us as to pour out His soul unto death, but
it was also the Father who so loved us as to send His
Son to be the propitiation for our sins.   Let us keep
steadfastly, and without the least deviation, by this glorious gospel.   Let us contend earnestly for the faith once
delivered to the saints; and more especially let us never
falter or decline by ever so little from the precious doctrine, that by grace we are saved.   Keep us, O God, so to
abide in this doctrine that Christ may abide in us, and
make us fruitful in every good work to do His will.

O reveal Thy Son in me—for "no man knoweth the
Son but the Father."   May I be so taught of God as to
be drawn unto Christ.   But neither knoweth any man
the Father save the Son, and he to whomsoever the Son
will reveal Him.   Therefore would I sit at the feet of
Jesus Christ, as the alone Teacher who can so acquaint
me with my Maker as that I may be at peace.   He is the
alone way and truth and life—my all in all for salvation
and the real knowledge of God.   No zeal and no profi-
ciency in any system of faith or righteousness apart from
Him can at all avail me.   Give me, O Lord, the unction
that is from on high of the only eye-salve by which I can
see—for it is not flesh and blood that can teach me these
things, but only Thy Spirit, who taketh of the things of

Christ and sheweth them unto the soul. The natural man
discerneth them not, neither indeed can know them. O
that I were visited with the heavenly and divine illumination whereby Christ is savingly apprehended; and renouncing all confidence in the sufficiency of reason as if
it superseded the need of a special revelation subjectively
to myself, as well as of a general revelation objectively to
the world, O that I were so taught and so transformed
by the inward working upon me of the Holy Ghost as to
make it manifest to all men that I have been indeed with
Jesus, and as to cause my light so to shine before men, that
others seeing my good works may glorify my Father who
is in heaven.

GALATIANS II.

Save, O God, the Free Church of Scotland from all the
perversities and mismanagements of the ecclesiastical
somewhats of the present day. But passing from the
narrative to the doctrine of this chapter, what an essence
and condensation of gospel truth have we in its closing
verses! Altogether it is a most precious epistle; and
precious beyond all estimation is the main lesson of it—
not merely and generally justification by faith, but by
faith without one particle or the slightest alloy of human
merit—thus placing our dependence before God on the
compact and homogeneous foundation of Christ's righteousness, free from all pollution or admixture of any
righteousness of ours. There is a great principle involved
in the rejection of that tittle and iota against the admission of which as an ingredient in the matter of our valid
and legal plea for heaven the apostle contends and pro-
tests so earnestly. Let me not, O Lord, even by the

gentlest leaning towards works for my right of acceptance
with God, let me not waken up the old covenant, the law
of " do this and live," against me—else I shall make myself indeed a transgressor, and make Christianity the
minister to me of a grievous and irreparable condemnation.   May I no longer be tremblingly alive to the law
as my judge, but gratefully and most desirously alive to
God as my benefactor, and the great exemplar and
patron of all righteousness—so as henceforth to give myself to this His will, even my sanctification.   And O what
depth and substance in this matter, too, we are here presented with.   Crucified with Christ, nevertheless alive—
with Him dead for sin, so that the law has no further
claim upon us ; and dead to sin, so that I no longer live
in opposition to the law, but in conformity therewith, and
find that in the keeping of its prescribed duties there is
a very great reward—and this because Christ liveth in me,
because grace and not sin hath now the dominion over me,
because spiritually risen with Him who is the Lord my
strength, I am inclined and enabled for all His commandments.   That this may be realized upon me, give me to live
a life of faith, and let it be the appropriating faith which
can say that Christ loved me and gave Himself for me.
On this footing would I now close with the Saviour, and
on this footing live by Him through time and through
eternity.—Work, O God, this faith in me with power ;
and when I lay hold of Christ for that righteousness
which He hath brought in, and which cometh not by the
law, give me to experience that the grace which justifies
also reanimates and renews me—so as that henceforth
I should enter on the new life of the new creature in
Jesus Christ my Lord.

GALATIANS III.

Let me look unto Jesus, and with unfaltering confidence in the efficacy of His death as a propitiation for my sins. And O what a precious result : it is in this attitude, persevered in expectantly and prayerfully, that I may look for the illapse of the Spirit upon my soul—by faith in the word read or heard, and not by the works of the law. The Spirit is given to them who believe, (John vii. 39 ;) and the promise of the Spirit (verse 14) is received through faith. O let me never work for a righteousness by the law ; but with simple reliance on the atonement and righteousness of Christ may I be enabled, by the shedding forth upon me of the Holy Ghost, to abound in all those fruits of the new obedience against which there is no law. Let me dispose of all my legal terrors and anxieties by casting the burden of them upon the Lord, and He will sustain it. Let me flee from the curse of the law unto Him who was made a curse for me, and so hath redeemed me from that curse—having Himself borne the penalty, having Himself given up His life a ransom for many. I pray for the faith that will appropriate and apply this great transaction, with all its benefits and immunities, to my own soul. Thus let me stand disengaged from the law as a covenant, dead unto it, that I might live in the Spirit, (verse 2,) and so live unto God. (ch. ii. 19.) The giving of the Law from Mount Sinai did not obliterate or change the character of that promise which was given to Abraham centuries before ; and it has come down to us in the same unencumbered and unconditional form in which it was made to him. Let us be strong in the faith as he was—let us, against hope, believe in hope as he did—

let us not stagger at the promise any more than he, but place the same unfaltering reliance with him on the faithfulness of God; and thus walking in his footsteps we shall be admitted along with him into the family of God's own children. Yet may the uses of the law be still realized upon us; may it shut us up unto the faith; may it act as a schoolmaster for bringing us to Christ; may it convince us of sin, and so constrain us to the Saviour. Teach us, O Lord, how wofully deficient we have been from the standard of its requirements, and so how deeply we are involved in the curse and condemnation of its broken commandments—so that we may make our escape from the law, which is the minister of death, to that gospel which can alone give life and liberty to the soul. Give me, O Lord, from a child of wrath to become one of Thine own reconciled children; and may I not only be found in Christ, but may I put on Christ—and then will I make no provision for the flesh to fulfil the lusts thereof. His power will rest upon me—and justified by faith, so as to have peace with God, He, the very God of peace, will sanctify me wholly.

GALATIANS IV.

December, 1844.

There could not be a more distinct and decisive transition, or one that more satisfactorily bespoke our being on the right way, than to advance from the spirit of bondage to the spirit of adoption, or from a servile to a filial and confiding obedience. O for the experimental realization of my being indeed under the glorious law of liberty, even the liberty of God's own children; and this will take effect when brought to be not under the law—that is, not under the old law, but under grace.—My God, emancipate my slavish heart from the dominion of weak and beggarly elements, yet so as that I shall not use my liberty as an occasion for the flesh. And let not my discharge from the legal obligation of days and months and times and years so far set me at large as that I should forego the advantage arising from the stated distribution of my hours, or as that the Sabbath should cease to be prized by me for its opportunities of sacredness. May I love Thy Sabbaths, and then in keeping them I shall but observe the law of liberty. Liberty consists in the doing of that which we like best; and then is it perfect liberty when our likings are towards the things which are best —best of all when directed to Him who is the best and the highest of Beings. What a mighty change in our subjective nature, when love to Him is throned in supremacy over all the inferior desires and appetencies of man; and it is a change brought about by our believing regard towards that great objective exhibition which Christianity holds forth to the world—even Christ crucified, and this to redeem us from the condemnation of a violated law. O then may we receive Christ, even by believing on His name—(John i. 12)—and then along with Him shall we receive the adoption of sons. O for the experience of such an outpouring of God's Spirit upon my heart as that henceforth I shall call Him, Abba, Father. Let me wait and watch for this. Let me resolutely aim at this. Let me act a desirous faith on the words of God's own testimony, and persevere in giving earnest heed thereunto till the day dawn and the day-star arise within me. Let me be zealously affected for this, and let not this first and greatest object be supplanted by zeal for aught which is inferior to this. Let me rejoice therefore in God my Saviour. Let me abound more and more in all the fruits of a willing and so a free and fearless obedience. Let me break forth into the exclamation of the psalmist—(Psalm cxvi.)—"Lord, I am Thy servant, Thou hast loosed my bonds, and I will offer to Thee the sacrifices of thanksgiving." And though in the world I may have tribulation—for all who live godly in Christ Jesus shall suffer persecution—yet in Him may I have pleasantness and peace.

GALATIANS V.

A rich chapter, wherein the evangelical doctrine effloresces into evangelical practice, and is full of fruit. We are called upon to stand fast in our Christian liberty—only let us not use that liberty as an occasion for the flesh. And for this purpose, O God, do Thou renew our will, do Thou make us willing in the day of Thy power for that which is right; and then, if liberty consist in doing what we will, we shall indeed manifest the most glorious of all liberty by our abounding in all righteousness and goodness and truth. Our service of those whom we love is the service of perfect freedom; and so it forms no infringement but a confirmation of the best and the highest liberty, when we "by *love* serve one another." And this habit of the soul and of our history we can only reach through the "faith which worketh by love." Let us pass then from the law which will lay upon us the yoke of an inextricable bondage, if we seek to be justified thereby, to the law of love, at the bidding and under the impulse of which we shall do those things against which there is no

law. Were I but well-founded in the right principle the
right practice would instantly emerge from it. Did I but
through the Spirit wait for the hope of righteousness by
faith—this new hope would germinate a new affection and
a new life. The Spirit begins with faith, but He does not
end with faith ; and O give me to realize that fair assemblage of graces and accomplishments which are sure to
adorn every character that is under His fostering and fer-
tilizing influences. The principle which He asserts is one
of universal warfare against all that is evil. He lusteth
against the flesh, that though we feel, yet if we walk
in the Spirit, we shall not fulfil the lusts of the flesh.
Save me, save me, O God, from the licentious, and what
I pre-eminently stand in need of, from the wrathful affections of this carnal and accursed nature ; and O give me
to abound more and more, not in temperance only, but in
meekness and gentleness, and long-suffering. Give me
to ponder well those decisive sentences—that if I do the
works of the flesh I shall not inherit the kingdom of
God ; and that if I am Christ's, I have crucified the flesh
with its affections and lusts. Enable me, O God, to stand
the trial of these authoritative and withal most searching
criterions. Let me but do that which in one word is comprehensive of the whole law—let me love my neighbour
as myself ; then shall I have that in me which worketh
no ill, and—what, alas ! I am mainly deficient in—I shall
not strive, but be gentle unto all men—meekly instructing
them who oppose themselves.

GALATIANS VI.

Thou knowest, O God, with what justice and force the

consideration of my own delinquencies should lead me to
deal mildly and mercifully with those who have lapsed
into sin.   Give me at the same time to discriminate between the being overtaken in a fault and the full determination of those whose hearts are set upon evil, and so
sin deliberately and wilfully ; yet let me be far more
patient than hitherto in bearing the burdens of others.
O how grievously deficient here ; for with what intolerance
and impetuosity have I often bid the communications and
concerns of others away from me.   At the same time let
me carefully abstain from laying upon others the load of
my own obligations, but fully acquit myself of all for
which I am responsible.   More especially am I here told
to be liberal in the sustentation of him who ministers for
my benefit in holy things.   Grant, O Lord, for the sake
of Scotland and of its Free Church, that this truly Christian principle may be more widely diffused, and more
generally acted on.   And what a preparation for this and
for all the duties which I owe both to the brotherhood of
my own Church, and to society at large, did I, instead of
making provision for the flesh which perisheth, make provision for the Spirit, that He may enrich me by those
graces of character which form the treasures in Heaven
which shall not be taken away.   To sow unto the Spirit
let me obey Him, and He will be given to me, (Acts
v. 32 ;) let me be faithful in the use of His lesser gifts and
He will bestow larger ones, (Matt. xiii. 12;) let me so prize
Him as to pray for Him, and He will be granted to me.
(Luke xi. 13.)   Thus strengthened we shall walk and
not be weary, we shall run and not faint—looking to the
joy set before us.   Thus enriched we shall do good with
every opening for it unto all men, and particularly to our

fellow-disciples in the Lord—adding charity to our brotherly kindness.

For this noble superstructure let me have a firm and deep foundation in that which God Himself hath laid in Zion—not in the vain observances of a ritual now passed away, but in that glorious atonement, by faith in which the world loses its charms, and we die unto the world—so as to effect an entire personal transformation that makes us new creatures in Jesus Christ our Lord. O give me deep and right views of doctrine, and then shall I walk according to the right rule, and have peace with God, and mercy to pardon the innumerable sins and shortcomings that while in this body I am ever falling into. But let me bear about with me the dying of the Lord Jesus Christ, and His grace will be with my spirit, His life be made manifest in my mortal body.

EPHESIANS.

EPHESIANS I.—What substance and what spirituality are condensed in this precious epistle!—and in this chapter particularly, what influences and connexions are pointed out between the celestial and the terrestrial—between the purposes of God in Heaven and the products óf these upon earth—between those originating principles in the upper sanctuary which gave birth to Christianity, and its actual fruit in the hearts and among the habitations of men. At the outset of his address to the Ephesians, the apostle speaks of their character and of their spiritual endowments; but he instantly refers these to the primitive

election of God, which election at the same time determined
not their future glory alone, but their present graces of
love and holiness.   His predestination is the source and
fountain-head of all, and His glory, even the glory of
His grace, is the end of all ; yet this larger connexion
between the prime and the ultimate does not exclude
from his view the nearer connexions which obtain among
the intermediate terms of this great moral and spiritual
process—our union with Christ, our acceptance in Him,
our redemption through His blood, even the forgiveness
of sins, and all through the medium of our faith in the
Saviour after that we had heard of Him, after which
again cometh the sealing of the Spirit who is the earnest
of our inheritance.   And accordingly it was not till after
he had heard of their faith and love that he gave thanks
on their behalf—inferring their election from their graces,
instead of premising their election in the eternity that
was past, and thence inferring their blessedness in the
eternity to come.   Hence, too, the fervency of his prayer for
things present to them, as the pledge and the preparation
for things future—the enlightening Spirit, the knowledge
and hope of heaven's glory, the working of that mighty
power which achieves the regeneration or spiritual resurrection of those on whom it is put forth.   He prays not
merely that they should know these things, but that they
should know them experimentally—and this requires
the operation of a Divine energy like unto that by which
Jesus was raised from the dead ; and such as is the glory
of His exaltation, so in our measure and according to our
proportion will be the glory of ours—for we are the fulness of Christ, the partakers of His victory and of His
triumph over the powers of darkness.—My God, realize

these things upon my soul; and while I thus pray for
myself I would, in imitation of Paul, intercede for others
also—more especially for those of my own kindred, that
their understandings too may be opened, that they also
might be made the subjects of a new creation, so as that
we shall share together in a common meetness for the inheritance of the saints.

EPHESIANS II.

There is no falling off in this chapter from the richness
which, generally and throughout, characterizes the whole
of this truly dense and precious epistle. We have here the
regenerative process described from its beginning to its end,
and so as to inform us both of the *terminus a quo* and the
terminus ad quem. It took up with us at the first when
we were dead—dead in sin and worldliness, and under the
power altogether of the great spiritual adversary—sunk
in a death that was universal; for we were all by nature
"the children of wrath," and all the children of disobedience. We have here, too, the principle which originated
the process—the rich mercy and great love of God, and
kindness towards us, through Jesus Christ—the channel
for the conveyance of that grace by which, and which
alone, we are saved; and though while by grace it is
through faith, yet is it still altogether of grace, for this very
faith is the gift of God.—Work in me, O Lord, this precious faith, that I may be quickened and live with Christ;
and not only have part with Him in the inheritance of
heaven, but even now be partaker with Him in the converse and character of its holy citizenship. Give me, O
Lord, to see what Thou hast shown—even the exceeding

riches of Thy grace.   Neither let me forget the Rock out
of which I am hewn; for truly my salvation is not my work.
If I am indeed one of Thy chosen ones, it is not because
I have worked, but have been worked upon, and so made
Thy workmanship, and created by Thee in Christ Jesus,
the alone foundation on which I would build, both for a
right and a rightness.   And let me remember that though
salvation be not of works, still it is to works, and that
these works are as much a matter of ordination as is the
eternal life for which they qualify and prepare us.   We
were aliens from the family of saints and believers as well
as from God, the Father of this spiritual family.   Truly
we lived "without hope and without God in the world;"
but how blessed is that access whereby we are brought
nigh—even through the blood of Christ, which let me
ever recognise and refer to in all my approaches unto
God.   It is He who, travelling in the greatness of His
strength, has broken down the middle wall of partition,
not only between us and the living Church, but between
us and the living God.   To unite us with the one He has
removed the ceremonial law, it being all fulfilled upon
Himself; to unite us with the other He hath removed the
enmity of the Lawgiver, He having magnified His whole
law and made it honourable.   And now that peace is
proclaimed unto all, let us enter upon the offered reconciliation; let us draw nigh with all boldness and in full
assurance of heart; let us company much with them of
the household of God, building on the foundation of
Christ, not only rooted in Him but built up in Him.
And, O Lord, remedy a grand defect in my habit: let
me have more of fellowship with others; provide me
with a Christian acquaintanceship; let mine be a social

religion, that not only through the Spirit I may have free access to God, and have God dwelling in me, but that through the same Spirit I may be related to my brethren, and sharers in a common grace, even as parts of the same building are to each other. May I behold the realization of a spiritual Church among my friends and fellow-Christians in the world.

EPHESIANS III.
January, 1845.

In this digressive chapter we have all the fulness of the apostolic mind, and the digression indeed may be regarded as a sort of lateral efflux, or off-shooting at another part of the brim, out of that very fulness—opened in a manner characteristic of Him at the touch of a single word, which let forth a side-stream that suspended for a while the one which he had previously and directly been pouring forth. The word, the suggestive word, which acted as a turning point, and caused the apostle to deflect from his course, was " Gentiles." This drew him aside to the consideration of the mystery—the thing before unconceived of and unknown—even the admission of the Gentiles to all the privileges of a common and equal participation with the Jews in the promises of Christ—in the hopes here and enjoyments hereafter of that inheritance in heaven which "fadeth not away ;"—a mystery this coeval with God's purpose from the beginning of the world, but now only revealed in full manifestation by the Spirit to the prophets and apostles of that age. And Paul was the chosen and chief instrument for carrying this glorious design into effect ; he was pre-eminently the apostle of the Gentiles ; and from this higher development of the Divine counsels he represents the economy of the Church as a fit subject of contemplation to other and higher orders of being, for displaying to their view the manifold wisdom of God. O give me a part in this glorious enlargement, thus extending to all, and through Him by whom God created all things—even Jesus Christ, by faith in whom it is that we have boldness and access with confidence to God, and whose name we might assume, to whichever branch, whether Jews or Gentiles, we belong of the great human family. O God, let me have the experience of this great and purchased blessing—let me have the subjective experience of it, even the experience of being strengthened in the inner man with might by the Spirit, and of having Christ to dwell in my heart by faith. Let me have that love in my heart towards Christ and His people which Christ beareth for His own—a love given to me out of God's fulness, and so enabling me to comprehend somewhat both of the depth and the extent of that love which He bears to our sinful world, and which He proclaims in a message of reconciliation, not confined to one tribe or district, but designed for every creature, and carried abroad among all nations. These things we pray for from God, in His peculiar capacity of being the Father of Christ, whose love passeth knowledge, yet the knowledge of which we are invited to share in. O may He work in me effectually, and far beyond what I can either seek for or conceive ; and to God in Christ be all the glory.

EPHESIANS IV.

O my God, do Thou uphold my goings that I may walk in the truth, and walk worthy of Thee unto all well-pleasing. Let me know my vocation, and that Thou hast not called me to uncleanness but to holiness; and O give me the humbleness, and the meekness, and the peaceableness of the gospel, with the forbearance of that charity which endureth all things: And I most earnestly pray for the progress and the perfecting of Christian unity—for which purpose grant that I may ever study to repress all those controversies which relate not to the essence of that faith for which we are required to contend earnestly. What an objective oneness there is in the character and realities of the religious system, and more especially in the ever-living God. O may His pervading and harmonizing Spirit unite us in the prosecution of the one great object of a Christian Church; and however diverse its offices and ministries might be, let us, holding by the one Head, co-operate without emulations, or heart-burnings, or arrogance of any sort, even as do the members of the natural body—for the edifying of the body of Christ. Having the unity of the faith let us all, professing one and the same truth, speak that truth in mutual and common love, each for the others; and O may we thus be enabled, both by a cordial and an ostensible unity, to draw many accessions from the world that is lying without, and thus grow both in extent and in vital quality. And give me to embody, O Lord, the representation of individual Christianity here set forth—renouncing all fellowship in spirit or in practice with a world lying in wickedness, and alienated from the life of godliness. May I prove my conformity with Christ and with the truth that is in Him, by the crucifixion of the old man with his affections and lusts, and by the resurrection within me of the new, created after the image of God in righteousness and holiness.   Give me a thorough renovation of spirit, and let this have effect on my outward life and conversation—more especially in the avoidance of all deceit and of all sinful anger.   There is an anger which is not sinful, but even this let me not cherish or keep up, but may both it and its various effusions be henceforth put away from me.   And O let me not forget the terms by which I hold on God, even His forgiveness of me in Christ, and let me so forgive others.   And I pray for a more evangelical seasoning of my speech ; and let all that is malignant or licentious, or even unprofitable, be henceforth dissevered from the converse I hold with my fellowmen, that I may be the minister of grace unto their souls, and so grieve not that Holy Spirit who is ready to make efficient all the instrumentality which I can put forth with the honest purpose of benefiting either my own soul or the souls of others.

EPHESIANS V.

There is a pure and right outlet for all the original tendencies of nature ; and more especially there is the affinity to those of our kind, not of licentiousness but of love—holy, spiritual, evangelical love, a love by which we become like unto, or the followers of God, and to the cultivation of which we are called in terms of endearment, but not the endearment of an affection carnal and unhallowed.   And O what a persuasive influence is thus brought to bear upon us, that we may be led to the love of our fellows—even the love which Christ bore to us, as manifested in the blessed atonement, the incense of which arose in sweet smelling savour unto God.   How closely faith and feeling are here blended together; and thus let me ever warm my heart by a believing contemplation of the truth as it is in Jesus, even of Him crucified. And O may the love thus awakened cast out every base and inferior affection. I pray for this great moral revolution in my soul. Let the true light germinate that right love which supplants the ascendency of those degrading lusts by sowing unto which we shall reap corruption and forfeit the good of our eternity. Let the fruit of the light given by that Spirit who taketh of the things of Christ and showeth them unto me, be in all goodness and righteousness and truth; and while cleaving to that which is good, let me abhor that which is evil.—My God, let me be diligent, and give myself watchfully to the great work of my sanctification—understanding this to be the will of God concerning me. And just as the gospel provides for us holy love as the appropriate outlet for those tendencies which might otherwise have broken forth into gross and grovelling licentiousness, so does it provide elevating and exhilarating joys in the direction of sacredness for those other tendencies which might otherwise have found their indulgence and their vent in debasing intoxication. Let me not then be drunk with wine, but be filled with the Spirit, and have joy in the Holy Ghost —that true melody of heart. Let me be grateful to God and humble towards my fellow-men. And O that I had that love for the nearest of my relatives which Christ bore to His Church—a love that had for its most earnest object the salvation and sanctification of her soul—a love which led me to be as intent on her spiritual good as on my own: and let me therefore pray for grace, that we may walk together as heirs of the grace of life, and that our prayers may not be hindered. The days are evil—for many things occur to break in on the great work of preparation for heaven. Let me therefore gather up all the fragments of time I have, and clear out as much more as I can for the one thing needful, for the growth of grace and the perfecting of holiness.

EPHESIANS VI.

Teach me, O God, the deportment I should observe in regard to my children. Let me refrain from the wrath which provoketh wrath, and which may not only irritate but also discourage them. Let mine be a calm and steady and practical regard for their souls ; and let this be the manifest principle of all my dealings with them. And let me be observant of my duty to my superiors— not as unto them so much as unto the Lord. More particularly, should I be reviled and denounced by any of the upper classes as a disturber of the peace, let me not in retaliation say or do aught that is fitted to undermine the reverence due to station and rank in society ; but though unknown to them and unacknowledged by them, let me, in the sight of God and under the impulse of His will, do all that in me lies for strengthening the cement of mutual service and good-will among the various orders of the commonwealth. Let me endure hardness as a good soldier, through Christ's power resting upon me, and because strengthened by His might in the inner man ; and let me know the strength of my enemies, so as that I may calculate aright on the requisite preparation of force by which I might withstand them. In particular, let me be aware of the skill, and power, and virulence of the great adversary—the strong man who would fain keep his hold of me—the roaring lion who goeth about seeking whom he may devour. Let me put on the requisite armour of defence and resistance, fighting him who is a spiritual foe with spiritual weapons. When assailed by his fiery temptations, let me bethink myself of the trueness of God's sayings all round, so as that I may be impregnable on every side; and may Christ's righteousness be the plea on which I withstand every attempt of Satan to have the dominion over me. And by the faith which overcometh the world, let me prevail over all the urgencies of sense and time wherewith the god of this world is incessantly plying me; and let the hope of salvation be my helmet of protection against all those evil influences which would defile and unfit me for heaven. And let the word of God in the hands of that Spirit for whom I should watch and pray with all perseverance—let this word be my weapon of defence against that world which is the instrument wherewith the devil ever tries to annoy and subdue me, even as he did the mighty Saviour who repelled and overmatched him with quotations..from the oracles of everlasting truth. Thus, by the help of God—the God of peace—may Satan be bruised under our feet. And in fellowship with the Father and with the Son, may I have experience of the apostolic benediction of love from God and from the Lord Jesus—and so I shall, if but the precious faith of the gospel be stablished and strengthened within me, even the faith which worketh the love of the Lord Jesus Christ in sincerity.

PHILIPPIANS.
February, 1845.

PHILIPPIANS I.—This, too, is a most precious epistle.
May its opening benediction of grace and peace be abundantly fulfilled on me—and that both from the Father and
our Lord Jesus Christ, with whom may I be admitted to
close and confiding fellowship. Teach me, O God, the
same affectionate concern in the Christianity of others
which the apostle Paul had ; and O may his prayer in
behalf of his disciples be realized upon myself. Begin the
good work of grace in my heart, and carry it onward to a
full performance. Shed abroad in my heart the love of
God ; and let mine be an intelligent affection for the
things that are above—mine being a religion of knowledge and of judgment, so that I may prize things in the
proportion of their real worth ; and with the sincerity of
my intentions mix up so much of the palpably right and
reasonable as to silence and satisfy those who might otherwise be offended. Fill me, O God, with the fruits of
righteousness ; and let me ever keep by Jesus Christ,
who is the germinating principle of them all, and by God,
whose glory is the end of all. And O that Christ and the
advancement of His kingdom were the great objects of
my existence and of all my doings. Should His gospel
be furthered thereby, let me rejoice in the oppositions and
sufferings which I may be called upon to endure. Give
me fully to share in the catholic spirit of Paul, who could
rejoice even in the contentions by which the knowledge
of the gospel was spread abroad among men. Give me
boldness in this cause. Thou knowest my longing desire
for peace and retirement in my old age, but let Thy

Providence and Word be my guides ; only let me have the
well-grounded hope of being with Christ when I depart
from the world ; and then, O God, let my work here, and
the time of my departure hence, be not as I will but as
Thou wilt. O let my conversation be such as becometh
the gospel, and may I stand together with the fellow-
labourers at my side, striving earnestly both for the purity
and for the extension of the Christian faith. Grant, O
Lord, that there might be more of unity among those who
love the Lord Jesus Christ. Give them to love each other,
and so to present a steadfast and unyielding front against
all the adversaries of truth and righteousness. There
may be yet much to suffer, and many strivings to be gone
through, but let us know how to rejoice even in the
midst of tribulations ; and if faith be a gift, if it have been
given us to believe in Christ, let us thankfully receive it
as a gift also, should we be called on to suffer for His
sake. Let us not count on our discharge from this warfare.
Let us think of Christ and His apostles before us ; nor
look for the servant having either greater privileges or
greater exemptions than his master. God in His own
good time will appear on the side of His own people, to
the triumph of the righteous, to the disgrace and utter
discomfiture of all their enemies.

PHILIPPIANS II.

In this pregnant chapter we first see how the faith and
fellowship of Christ lead His disciples to a fellowship with
each other. The consolation in Christ stands associated
with the comfort of love—and that of love not to Him
only, but to all for whom He died. The sympathy of a

common feeling towards Him leads to a common and re-
ciprocal agreement both of heart and mind among themselves.   And O what a noble application of the high doctrine of our Lord's divinity—not argued here, but affirmed
and proceeded on and made the foundation of a most
beautiful practical lesson, even that of mutual condescension.   O my God, let me honour the Son even as I honour
the Father; and on His humiliation give me to found
the grace of humility; and in the deliberations of the
Church more particularly, let me feel how monstrous a
thing it were to seek my own glory, but let me exclusively mind not my own things but the things which best
conduce to the stability and extension of our Saviour's
kingdom in the world.   Let me learn from this glorious
passage both to bow at the name of Christ and to maintain a lowly deportment among my fellow-men.   There
are many provocations to an opposite conduct, but let
me tremble to encounter such temptations in my own
strength—tremble even as the child would do to let go
the support of his nurse's hand; and lean as He would
on that God who can alone work in us effectually both to
will that which is right and to do that which is right.
And what a precious application here, too, of another
high doctrine.   God works in us to set us a-working, not
that we may stand by and do nothing, but that with the
utmost vigilance and fear—lest we should forfeit His aid—
we may work out our own salvation.   And O what need I
have of the succeeding precept to " do all things without
murmurings and disputings."   My tendency is to discharge invectives on the perversity of others, and to brood
over it.   Teach me, O Lord, to do what is right, but with
a perfect freedom from that wrath which worketh not the

righteousness of God, and abstinence from all grudging, seeing that the Judge is at the door. Thus may it be that my good shall not be evil spoken of, even in the midst of a crooked and perverse generation. Enable me to shine as a light in the midst of it ; and O my God, while labouring to demonstrate the methods of extending Thy Son's gospel, spare me the mortification of finding that all seek their own things, not the things of the Lord Jesus. Forbid, Lord, that there should be a wrong or wilful lack of service anywhere ; but if there should, do Thou raise up many Epaphrodituses, who might supply that lack. Grant that many might arise who shall minister to the wants of our gospel-labourers—and this not so much for their sake as for the sake of the gospel itself. Let such be the kindness and consideration for each other among all the members of the Free Church of Scotland, that when any has cause to mourn all might mourn, and when any rejoice all might rejoice along with them.

PHILIPPIANS III.

This is one of the most notable chapters in Scripture. O that it were transcribed on the fleshy tablet of my heart, then would I rejoice in the Lord ; and the repetition of His name would at all times be like the pouring forth of ointment—ever fresh and ever savoury. Let me ever stand aloof from His enemies, and from all the workers of evil ; neither let me be of the number of those who would compound their own merits with the merits of Christ, but having no confidence in myself, while rejoicing in the Lord Jesus, may I in this two-fold attitude of humility and dependence, receive of that Spirit by whose influences

I may be enabled to serve and to worship God. I feel that unlike Paul I have nothing to boast of; and that on his example I might build an *argumentum a fortiori* for leaning wholly and exclusively on the righteousness of Christ. Let me be found in Him, let me have faith in Him—counting all that is in myself to be nothing or worse than nothing; let my whole aspiration after a righteousness be towards the righteousness of Christ. Begin, O Lord, this confidence within me, and let me hold fast this beginning of confidence even unto the end—that great may be my recompense of reward. Conform me, O God, to His death; and give me, O Lord, not to shrink from suffering for His sake: Above all, may I experience the power of His resurrection within me, by myself being raised to newness of life here, and so as to have part in the resurrection of blessedness from the dead hereafter. Sure I am that I have not attained to perfection; but I would press onward to apprehend the holiness, even the perfection in holiness, (2 Cor. vii. 1,) for which Christ lays the hand of a sanctifier on all who believe in Him. Bring me into fellowship, O God, if it be Thy blessed will, with some who are thus minded, that I may tread the path to heaven along with them, likeminded in our hopes and our aims, and holding with them that common sympathy which binds together the citizens of the same inheritance, and expectants of the same Saviour. O God, let me participate with the holy apostle not in his pursuits only but in his griefs and aversions—more particularly to those who disgrace the holy name which they bear by their sensuality and their earthliness and their unhallowed enjoyments. Let us fight with all earnestness against the power of sin here, that we may be

everlastingly delivered hereafter from its hateful presence.
It dwells in these vile bodies—may it not have the dominion over them.   It is an inmate of the house—may
it not be the master of the house.   May the power of
Christ's resurrection be effectually put forth on us, by the
working of which our vile bodies shall be transformed to
the likeness of His glorious body—for this He is able
to do, in virtue of the power committed to Him as God-
man when he rose from the grave—all power both in
heaven and earth.   He is able to subdue our corruptions,
and cause grace to prevail over all the infirmities and
pollutions of our accursed nature.

PHILIPPIANS IV.

Here, too, are things unspeakably precious.   But first
let me remark the overflowing affection, the φιλαδελφια,
of Paul for his fellows in the gospel, whether as disciples
or helpers—the fit companion of that joy in the Lord
which he so emphatically recommends.   May that joy
be my strength ; and in the contemplated nearness of the
world wherein it is to be perfected, let me sit loose both
to the griefs and the pleasures of a world that passeth
away—a moderation this which I am not to hide in a napkin, but make known unto all men by my doings, being
such as plainly to declare that I seek a country.   Let me
be especially moderate in my sense of injury from others,
seeing that the Judge is at the door.   And what a coun-
teractive would these lessons prove to all diseased anxiety
about the things and interests of the present life.   But
we are told to be careful for nothing—not even then for
the interests of the soul and of eternity, in as far as

this would imply an unhappy disquietude and distrust respecting them.   In everything, and more especially in things of spiritual and everlasting concern, let us make our believing requests unto God, and mix thanksgiving therewith, because of the mercies and hopes and experiences of the gospel.   And O what a blessed consummation—the peace of God—a peace through Christ which passeth understanding, even as His riches are unsearchable, and His love passeth knowledge—a peace which pervades and takes possession of the whole man, keeping our hearts and minds, so as to pass through us like a mighty river, and cause us to delight ourselves greatly in its abundance.   (Isaiah.)   And, *finally*, as it were the conclusion of the whole matter, the landing-place or *terminus ad quem* of Christianity, are we called on to make a study of all those graces and moralities whereof there is here given so beautiful an enumeration—and this that our doings may in themselves have an inherent excellence, and form a goodly spectacle for the homage and admiration of observers, so as both to adorn the doctrine of our Saviour, and to attain the great end of its revelation to the world, even that our characters might be perfected, and we be thoroughly furnished unto all good works.   And still the fruit of righteousness is peace—a blessed privilege which attaches at the first to our faith in the imputed righteousness of Christ, and is afterwards fostered and confirmed more as we grow and make advances in our own personal righteousness.   Give me, O Lord, to imitate Paul in his contentment, and in all his various welldoing ; and O give me to realize his experience as here announced in one of the weightiest and most memorable of our Scripture sayings—" I can do all things through

Christ which strengtheneth me." He is at once the
source of all our new obedience, and the medium through
which it is acceptable to God—of sweet odour and well-
pleasing to Him, because perfumed by the incense of the
merits of His own beloved Son. It is thus and through
this mediatorship that we obtain acceptance for our works
as well as for our persons. May the people of the Free
Church, O God, do by their ministers as the Philippians
did by Paul; and out of Thine inexhaustible riches may
all their need be abundantly supplied, even as Thou hast
promised. Glory to God in the highest—grace unto all
the brethren.

COLOSSIANS.

March, 1845.

COLOSSIANS I.—This, too, is a most delicious epistle,
abounding in pregnant clauses, and redolent all over of the
very essence of the gospel. After the usual benediction,
which may God fulfil upon myself, the apostle gives
thanks for the hope, or rather the thing hoped for, and
laid up in heaven for his converts. He infers this futurity
of blessedness from their present faith and love; and O
give me the assurance of glory hereafter from the work of
grace in me now. The Colossians had a most warrantable
hope at the first, or so soon as they believed the word of
truth in the gospel; and they had a farther and confirming hope afterwards, the grounds of which were patent to
others—to Paul and Epaphras, as well as to themselves
—even the fruit which they brought forth, and the love
felt in their hearts, and manifest to the eye of observers.
They had both the hope of faith and the hope of experi-

ence. Give me, O Lord, a part and an interest in the
prayers of this chapter; give me spiritual discernment;
give me to grow in the knowledge of Thyself, and to walk
worthy of Thee, so as to please my Lord, and abound
more and more in the works which He requires of me.
Strengthen me, O Lord, and more especially for patience
and long-suffering, that I may even glory and rejoice in
tribulations: And let me share in the thanksgivings as
well as the prayers. Let me cherish the assurance of at
least my judicial meetness for heaven—of my translation
from the right and power of the adversary to the lordship of Christ over me, and of my part in that redemption
which is through His blood, even the forgiveness of sins.
And to stablish and strengthen my faith still more, let
me dwell on the greatness of Him who is the object of it
—who created and sustained, and was before all things,
the Lord of the universe of nature, as well as Lord of the
Church: and well did He earn this latter pre-eminence,
when He rose from the dead, after that by His blood He
had made peace between God and man, and reconciled
our race of aliens to the Lawgiver whom they had offended.
Once enemies we are now friends; and He will present
me holy if I continue in the faith grounded and settled,
and not be moved away from it. Keep me steadfast, O
God. Sustained by the hope of the gospel may I rejoice in
afflictions; and O may Christ be formed in me the hope of
glory. O give me to be perfect in Him, and enable me to
realize the co-operation here set forth between the human
and the Divine agency. May the work of God in me set
me a-working. The more strenuously the Spirit works in
me, the more strenuously do I work. I labour and strive
in the proportion of His working. Let me be taught on

this matter in all wisdom. Let me learn the respective parts of God and man in the work of regeneration. Let me know what it is, in the prosecution and the perfecting of my holiness, to be a fellow-worker with God—depending on Him as entirely as if He did all—labouring as diligently as if I did all—combining God's sovereign grace with man's active service—man striving mightily according to God working in him mightily.

COLOSSIANS II.

Along with his devotion to the cause of Christ, Paul bore in his heart a proportionally intense affection for its converts. Give me, O Lord, to enjoy what he so much desiderated for the Christians of his day—an intelligent as well as a believing fellowship with the Father and the Son. May Christ be made unto me wisdom ; and for this purpose let me become a fool that I may become wise— renouncing my own philosophy, and all its alluring imaginations, that I might receive Christ with the simplicity of a little child, and submit myself with entire docility to His guidance, keeping on the way which He has pointed out for me. He hath loosed my bonds : let me be His servant, walking on His prescribed path, and offering the sacrifices of thanksgiving. If I thus keep His sayings, to me will He manifest Himself. Let my faith prompt obedience ; let my obedience stablish me in the faith. Let me bring at all times my own emptiness to the fulness that is in Christ Jesus. And O that I could be made experimentally to realize the connexion between the initial production and the consequent growth of my Christianity—between my burial with Christ and my resurrection to His glorious likeness

—between the forgiveness which cometh by the redemption that is through His blood, and the quickening operation of that Spirit through whom I am raised from my state of death in trespasses and sins, and enabled to put off the old and corrupt man, who heretofore has lorded over me. And that I may attain to this, let me look fully and with unfaltering faith on the finished work of my Saviour—on His entire cancelment of the debt that was against me, and on the total discharge from all count and reckoning which I have gotten at His hands, or which at least He holds out for my instant acceptance. Lord, I believe, help mine unbelief. May the glorious power of Christ rest upon me. May I be made to participate in His victory over the evil one. May the strong man within be conclusively and for ever dispossessed ; and may I from this time forward overcome, because greater shall He be that is in me than He that is in the world. Thus equipped—thus provided with spiritual armour from on high—thus emancipated from all the freezing legalities which but nurture and uphold the spirit of bondage, may I henceforth, keeping my hold on Christ, both as the alone Head of His Church, and as the fountain of all holy influences, serve Him in the spirit of liberty. Let mine be altogether a spiritual service—the obedience of the affections and of the heart, which if really enlisted will send forth not only a purer but far more abundant obedience upon the history. Save me alike from the drudgeries and the hypocrisies of a vain formalism. Let mine be a spontaneous and enlightened service, emanating from that well of living water which springeth up in the heart of regenerated man, and efflorescing into all the graces and virtues of the Christian character

COLOSSIANS III.

Give me, O Lord, to undergo this glorious translation,
even of being buried with Christ, so as to be dead to all
old things and to the world, and to be risen with Him,
so as that I may live in newness of life. Let me henceforth aspire upwardly, and with my affections thither-
ward, and away from earth, that I may fetch all my
spiritual nourishment from above, even where Christ
sitteth at the right hand of God, and whence, out of
His fulness, He gives all that is necessary for a life of
godliness. We would seek to be thus saved by the life
of Christ—(Rom. v. 10)—saved from the unfruitful works
of darkness, and all the abominations of a carnal and
accursed nature. Give me to feel, O Lord, that the prohi-
bitory sanctions against sin are in every way as strong
and decisive under the economy of the gospel as under
the economy of the law. Let me therefore put off all sin,
whether sensual or social, and die alike unto the malignant and the licentious affections of the old man. Give
me a regeneration which has its root in saving and spiritual knowledge, and its issue in all the virtues of daily
life. I pray, O Lord, for truth in the inward parts; and
did I receive Christ in truth, so as to become a new creature in Him, there would be no fraud or falsehood in my
dealings with men. And as Thou hast told us what to
put off, so dost Thou also tell us what to put on, and to
put on too as the elect of God. These high doctrines of
regeneration and election, when rightly understood and
applied, do not sublime the Christian above the graces of
everyday character, but originate and make sure the existence of them. O Lord, give me to abound more and

more in the fruits which are here enumerated—in humble-ness and meekness and forbearance. Let me forget all my quarrels, and henceforth forgive from the heart all who may ever have injured or offended me. If God have en-tered into peace with me, I may well be at peace with my fellow-men, from whom I have never sustained the wrongs and the provocations of my rebellion against my rightful Sovereign in the heavens. Let this peace of God, then, towards me regulate my disposition towards my brethren of mankind. With the charity of Christ's Spirit give me to be rich in the wisdom of Christ's word; and let mine, O God, be a joyful Christianity, which effuses itself in glad and grateful acknowledgments that might be heard by others to their instruction and encouragement in the ways of the divine life. Unseal my lips, O God; give me to be more open and pronounced in my testimony; put grace into my heart, to the overflow of all that is good and gracious in my conduct. Teach me a universal obe-dience in the name of Christ, and to the glory of the Father. Let the religious and the relative virtues keep a rapidly advancing pace with each other in my character. O may I never feel bitterness against her whom it is my part to love, even as Christ loved the Church. Enable me fully to sustain the parts of the Christian husband and the Christian father, doing all heartily unto the Lord.

COLOSSIANS IV.

Enable me, O God, not only to give my servants that which is just and equal, but to deal equally with the lower classes in general—forgetting not, more especially, the moral benefits and attentions which are due to men

as men, and that all are servants of the same Master in
heaven.   On the strength of this common relationship of
rich and poor to the God who made them, O may I be
guided aright in my endeavour to bring up the poorest
and most profligate of our land to the exalted position of
being not only the servants but the sons of God.   Pour
on me, O God, the spirit of grace and supplication; and
may I watch as well as pray with all perseverance, mixing
my grateful acknowledgments with my devout and unceasing supplications to the great Parent and Preserver
of men.   And let me never forget in prayer my applications for power from on high on a preached gospel, and
that the ministers thereof may be guided in their great
work of winning souls.   I furthermore pray not for wisdom to them alone, but to myself, that the brief remaining time I have in this world may be employed to the best
advantage, both for the profit of my own soul and for that
of others.   More especially may the time spent in company be laid out for Christ, and not lost in the common-
places and frivolities of ordinary conversation.   May my
speech be leavened with religion, and yet be adapted to
the peculiarities and the needs of every man, so that all
offence may, when possible, be shunned, yet many be won
to the faith and the following of Jesus.   Let me also
imitate Paul in those cordialities of kind and Christian
affection which he effused upon his brethren in Christ
Jesus; and, O Heavenly Father, supply me with fellow-
workers in the great cause of His Church and kingdom in
the world.   Make me a sharer in all the good characteristics which are here enumerated, and in all the blessings
which are here invoked.   Let me be faithful in the service
of Christ and the ministry of His word.   Give me the

discernment of states and spirits, and may I know how to speak the word of comfort in right season unto others, and how also to acquit myself as a help and a comfort both to the Church and its ministers. But above all, O God, as the crown and consummating gift of Thy grace, make me perfect and complete in the whole of Thy will. Let not my zeal overbear my heedfulness, nor my heedfulness repress my zeal—that I might make full proof of my Christianity as a man, and of my ministry as an office-bearer in the Church of God.

I. THESSALONIANS.

1 THESSALONIANS I.—The address is to a Church characterized as being in God the Father and the Lord Jesus Christ ; and this is a modifying consideration when we come to apply the statements of any of the New Testament epistles to a congregation of ordinary hearers in the present day. Mark the gratitude of Paul for the graces which he here enumerates as characterizing these his correspondents and converts. It was through the medium of their faith and love and hope—these three great virtues of the Christian character—and through this only, that he knew them to be the elect of God. Give me, O Lord, thus to make my calling and my election sure. O may the gospel come to me not in word only but in power and in the Holy Ghost and in much assurance—assured objectively of the power that lieth in the blood of the everlasting covenant, and of my welcome thereunto—assured also subjectively by my growth in grace, and my abounding more and more in the will of God. Hereby

may I know that I know Him savingly and aright, even
by the keeping of His commandments. And give me also
to know how to mix with the cares of life the precious
and alleviating and sustaining comforts of the gospel, even
as did those Thessalonians, who, while they received the
word with much affliction, did it in joy of the Holy Ghost.
Thus may I exemplify the power and beauty of the Christian faith. Turn me from the idolatries of the world;
turn me unto Thy service; and may mine be something
more than adherence to a doctrine or a name. May I not
only recognise Thee to be the true, but intimately feel
Thee to be the living God—that I may address Thee at
all times as a real and living object of contemplation, that
I may worship Thee, who art a Spirit, "in spirit and in
truth." Still, while in these vile bodies, we cannot do this
as we would: there is a drag and an incubus upon us
which weigh us down to carnality. We groan, being bur-
dened, and have to wait for the time of our coming enlargement, when emancipated from every incumbent load,
we shall serve God without frailty and without a flaw.
We have to wait for the redemption of the body; or, as
put here, we have to wait for the Son of God from heaven, (Philip. iii. 20,) who will change our vile body, that
it may be fashioned like unto His glorious body. He who
hath delivered us from the wrath that is to come will
accomplish for us another great and glorious deliverance,
even from the corruption which still cleaves to us, and
will continue so to do while we live in the present evil
world. (Gal. i. 4.) Let me never forget the co-ordinate
importance of these two deliverances. Doubtless He gave
Himself for us to deliver us from the wrath to come; but
He also gave Himself for us to deliver us from the present

evil world. And His resurrection from the dead has a special bearing on this last deliverance. He makes us to be spiritually the partakers thereof: because He lives we shall live also. The Spirit is now given, because Christ is now glorified; but having only yet the first-fruits of the Spirit we have much to long for. (Rom. viii. 23.) We have not yet reached the consummation of the glorious liberty of God's own children, but let us with patience wait for it.

I. THESSALONIANS II.

April, 1845.

O for the revival of a zealous apostolic spirit among our ministers—such a spirit as Paul manifested. What dangers he underwent—with what perfect integrity did he acquit himself of the Christian message, not as pleasing men but God—with what an upright conscience he could make his appeal to the great searcher of hearts—how nobly superior both to avarice and the fear of man—nay, how thoroughly disinterested, to the length of forbearing even his right to a maintenance from his disciples. Truly he discharged his solemn and responsible trust with all fidelity; and how gracefully did he blend with all the more strict and cardinal virtues of his sacred office all the gentleness and mild affection of a tenderly attached friend to the people among whom he laboured. O may we be enabled to follow this noble man's example, and also to fulfil his exhortation to walk worthy of God and of the calling that we have received from Him. May His kingdom begin with us now in peace, and righteousness, and all the fruits of the Divine Spirit; and may the hope of coming glory have the purifying influence ascribed to it by the apostle on our hearts and lives. (1 John iii. 3.)

O may Thy word, Almighty Father, be received by us in faith, and work in us effectually. To this faith may we add virtue—fortitude—such a readiness as the Thessalonians had to brave all the persecution to which we might even in these times be exposed for our testimony to the truth as it is in Jesus. O that I had more of what Paul so abundantly possessed—an appetite for and enjoyment of what might be termed social Christianity. I have marvellously little the experience of this—a certain delicate or sensitive recoil from the subject with many, which I have been in the habit of stigmatizing as satanic. Satan hinders me not from the outward opportunities alone of religious converse, but from that force and freedom of spirit which should carry me forward to a full entertainment of the subject with my fellows.—O my God, give me to set my delight here on the excellent ones of the earth, that I may be prepared for the perfect enjoyment of their and my presence before Jesus Christ at His coming; and draw close the affection and the affinity between Mr. Tasker and the families of the West Port. Do thou plentifully endow him with the graces and gifts of the apostle Paul. May he have many souls for his hire; and bestow Thy guidance on him and on all the other associates in the good work of attempting to reclaim an outcast population to the light and obedience of the gospel. O may the attempt be a successful one, and may he, in particular, have many for a crown of joy and of rejoicing in the great day of account.

I. THESSALONIANS III.

I pray, O Lord, for a thorough establishment and comfort

in the faith—comfort objectively, when I look to the truth
of God in the word—comfort subjectively, when I look
to the work of grace in my own soul.   I pray for a more
intimate and abiding union with Christ, and then shall I
look unmoved on such afflictions and trials as, for aught
I know, are yet awaiting me.   Thy will, O God, be done.
Whatever the outward tribulations might be, let me
inwardly grow in faith, and charity, and more especially,
in love to the brethren, or affection for all good men.   O
may a goodly number stand fast on the day of visitation
which is coming over the whole earth ; may the Lord's
people acquit themselves like men, and hold up their
unflinching testimony in the midst of an adverse world.
Give us the animating consolation which Paul felt when
he beheld the firmness and steadfastness of the brethren ;
and grant me more of that social and Christian sympathy
with others which might lead to a mutual confirmation of
each other's faith and each other's purposes.   And much
do I need to have my own faith perfected—supply, O
God, that which is lacking.   May this great central and
presiding grace grow in me exceedingly, and may all the
dependent and derived graces grow in me proportionally
along with it.   More especially may I grow in that
charity which, as the end is greater than the means, is
greater even than faith ; for, O what a sad deficiency in
Christian fellowship—in fellowship one with another,
which I pray that I may increase and abound in, for the
want of it and of the affection which prompts to it is one
of the most grievous under which I labour : and it is not
only in love for the brethren that I fall so lamentably
behind ; let me have love not only for man as a Christian, but for man as man, and then shall I have love to

all men. Nor is this love incompatible, but is here conjoined with holiness—nay, with holiness as the effect and
the end of it. Give me, O Lord, this holy love, this love
untainted and unblamable, because free of all that is
unhallowed, unmingled with any base or vile affection
which wars against the soul. And O that in virtue of
these blessed endowments I were found worthy to stand
before the Son of man at His coming—which great event
I desire to look, and to wait, and to be prepared for. Let
my mind be but established in the faith of verse 2, and
my heart will be established in the holiness of verse 13—
the one being the commencement, the other the great
end of Christianity. Perfect, O God, that which concerns
me, that I may be ready, and ready even now, for I know
not on what day or at what hour the Son of man cometh.
What an observer Paul was of Providence, and what a
constant feeling of dependence thereupon. " Now God
Himself and our Father, and our Lord Jesus Christ, direct
our way unto you." In all my movements upon earth
may I ever thus be looking upward both for grace and
guidance from heaven. May the times and the opportunities be ever studied in connexion with the will of God,
and with the indications given forth by His word, and by
the events of that experience and history which He over-
rules according to His own purposes and His own pleasure.

I. THESSALONIANS IV.

Let me count all that I have yet attained as nothing,
and less than nothing. Give me to walk so as to please
God, and to abound therein more and more. Deliver me
from the power—nay, from the presence of every foul

imagination. May I be enabled to keep my heart with all diligence, remembering that without purity and principle there I cannot see God. May I know how to check the first onset of unhallowed desire; and may the covetous affection, in the sense which it seems to have here and in other scriptures, may it be kept effectually in check, and not only be stript of its dominion, but may it be refused all dwelling-place within me. May I know my calling. May I give to holiness its right and high place in the system of my Christianity—heaven itself, and not the means only of my entrance into heaven—the essence of eternal blessedness, and not merely the token, and far less the purchase, of that blessedness. O give me to conform to the whole scheme of that redemption which Christ came to effectuate, and for the fulfilment of which there behoved to be not merely the rendering of a sacrifice, but a dispensation of the Spirit, even that Spirit which, now that Christ is glorified, is plentifully bestowed from heaven and poured forth on all who put their trust in Him. Let us not slight òr despise that grace of inward chastity which it is the office of the Spirit to work into our souls;—indeed the very essence of Christian virtue seems to be holy love, love one to another, with a pure heart and fervently. He who loveth not knoweth not God, neither has been taught by Him; but as in verse 1, so in verse 10, to please Him therein let us increase more and more. Let us realize the blessedness of Him who is the giver, and labour so as to have lack of nothing, and thus to shun the necessity of being a receiver. What a lesson to all, and more especially to the great bulk and body of the common people. May this lesson be taught them faithfully and fearlessly;

and O that the adherents of the Free Church, consisting
mainly of the lower classes, were thus to signalize themselves so as to obtain the credit and toleration of society
at large.—My God, make me more alive to the affections
of Christian fellowship that the comfort of these closing
verses may be more prized by me. Animate this cold
and selfish heart of mine with the charities and sympathies and all the companionable feelings of the gospel
of Jesus Christ. And O give me a more realizing sense
of the coming resurrection and the coming immortality.
Let me wait in faith for the coming of the Lord. Let not
the lowering adversities which hang over the Church of
Christ sink me into helpless and hopeless despondency,
but look onward to the time when those dark and menacing troubles shall all be ended, and so we shall be
ever triumphant and happy because ever with the Lord.

I. THESSALONIANS V.

O God, keep me in readiness for the coming of Thy
Son. Let me not fall asleep in the arms of a delusive
security, but give me to be broad awake to the great
realities which are above and before me. O let me work
out my salvation with fear and trembling, and having
on at the same time the gospel armour of faith and hope
and charity. Let me cherish the hope of salvation;
and let me live up to this glorious privilege here, that
hereafter I may live and be for ever with the Lord. And
give me, Almighty Father, to evince the purifying influence of this Christian hope: blot out the remembrance
of all my grievous delinquencies; and henceforth let me
be sober and vigilant, as becometh one who has been

taught that the work of preparation for eternity is the great work and business of our lives. And O let me not be engrossed with a desire after my own comfort and the cares of my own sanctification alone, but may I know how to edify others, and to lift in their hearing both a fearless and a fruitful testimony for the truth as it is in Jesus, and for the duty of so living, that whether in life or death we shall be altogether His.

And, O God, do Thou pour upon all professing Christians, and more especially on those of the Free Church, a spirit of greater liberality for the support of Thy blessed gospel; and not only may they be kind and respectful to their ministers, but may they ever be at peace among themselves. Let their esteem for their pastors be founded on esteem for their work, deeply seated on a right and true estimate of the worth of the soul and greatness of eternity. And what a precious collection of precepts have we in the latter half of this chapter. Give me, O Lord, to be intrepid in warning others—to be gentle in the ministration towards them of support and comfort—and patient towards all men. Let no provocation call me to that which is evil, but let me ever follow that which is good, both towards the brethren and towards all. I would joy in the Lord, and may that joy be my strength. I would pray with a constant aspiring and upward tendency towards God. And under every visitation, whether prosperous or adverse, I would that gratitude should always predominate, and have the victory in every trial or change of circumstances. And what a blessed conjunction is here of the Spirit and the word, in that I should quench not the one and despise not the other. Guide me, O Lord, in all my researches after the right and the true—that I may know what to reject and what to hold fast by. And for the credit of my profession, let me abstain not from evil only but from the very appearance of evil—regardful not of the inherent merit only of my conduct, but of its effect on the safety and spiritual condition of other men. And O what a precious conjunction is there here between peace and holiness. He is the God of peace who sanctifies wholly; and O may this process take full effect upon me, upon body and soul and spirit, so that I may be found altogether blameless in the day of the Lord. Thou hast promised this, O God; and we not only plead but we trust Thy faithfulness for the doing of it. Give me the intercession of many Christian friends. Give me an affection without taint or impurity for them all. Give me diligently to peruse and fruitfully to ponder on Thy gracious word; and may the grace of the Lord Jesus both enlighten me in the knowledge of Thy Scriptures, and cause that in the comfort of them I may have solid satisfaction and hope.

II. THESSALONIANS.

May, 1845.

2 THESSALONIANS I.—This is a short but withal a most sententious and weighty chapter. The Church of the Thessalonians is said to be in the Father and in the Son, and a joint benediction from both is pronounced upon it —being placed as every Christian Church is under the Mediatorial economy. O let me be individually in God and Christ, from whom may grace and peace descend upon me, that my charity may be made to abound, and my

faith to grow exceedingly. And give me, O Lord, to have patience under all the tribulations to which Thou mayest be pleased to call me, or persecutions, if these are to be revived in our latter days. As manifestly as God is righteous so manifestly will He distinguish between the enemies and the faithful disciples of His Church on the day of reckoning. Deliver me, O God, from the fearful vengeance which awaiteth the former. Give me the saving knowledge of Thyself, and the obedience of the faith to the gospel of Thy Son, that I may be numbered among His saints on that day, and that He in me may be glorified and admired. But how can He be glorified in me save by my abounding in the fruits of righteousness? Do I thus abound? Can I be said to adorn Christ's doctrine, though called to adorn it in all things? Can I be counted to walk worthy of this calling? God hath called me from uncleanness unto holiness, do I walk worthy of such a calling? Does my light so shine before men, that in me, or in my good works, men are led to glorify God here? Or are the graces of my character such that they will be found to praise and honour and glory in the great day of account? Alas! alas! how much do I stand in need of the prayers of others—how much I ought to pray for myself, that God would fulfil in me all the good pleasure of His goodness, that He would work in me to will and do of His good pleasure, that He would work in me a faith of such power as to overcome the world and all the vicious affections of my heart as well as habits of my life—in one word, that He would form me to Himself, so as that I might shew forth His praise. Thus and thus alone can the name of the Lord Jesus Christ be glorified in me and I in Him—

an effect that can only result from the operation of the grace of our God and the Lord Jesus Christ upon me. O that I more deeply and constantly felt the need of this grace—that I were ever looking up for the supplies of it from the sanctuary above—that such a spirit of prayer were given me as might bring it down upon my soul—that combining self-renunciation with entire dependence upon God, I realized the experience of His own saying—that while He resisteth the proud He giveth grace unto the humble.

II. THESSALONIANS II.

One day is to the Lord as a thousand years, and a thousand years as one day. We are apt to magnify the present, its symptoms and prognostications, and yet what we now regard as immediate may, in the counsels of Him who maketh not haste, have to wait the evolutions of centuries. Yet there is a palpable and immediate duty laid upon us in this chapter. We are here told of a man of sin, against whose delusions we are called upon to guard, and by whose authority we must not be enthralled, else we shall be deceived into all unrighteousness. Save us, O Lord, from falling away, lest we share in the perdition that waiteth upon the great apostasy. We hold the usurpation of Rome to be evidently pointed at, and therefore let us maintain our distance, and keep up our resolute protest against its abominations. But may we not forget that there are other usurpations in the Church of Christ; and let us not be led away by the spell of great names in theology, even though on the side of Protestantism. We do very strongly feel that the controversies and confessions of the reformed Churches have given a cast to the doctrine of Scripture which has to a great extent transformed it from the pure and original model. Deliver us, O Lord, from the magic power of Antichrist in all his forms, and give us the love of the truth that we may be saved. Meanwhile let us wait the coming of our Lord who will destroy all adversaries, and will dissipate every darkening influence by the brightness of His appearance. In His light we shall clearly see light. And I desire to cherish a more habitual and practical faith than heretofore in that coming which even the first Christians were called to hope for with all earnestness, even though many centuries were to elapse ere the hope could be realized : and how much more we, who are so much nearer to this great fulfilment than at the time when they believed. And whatever obscurity may rest on the prophetic matter of this chapter there is much of clear principle bearing upon present duty. Let me especially remark that the unbelieving of the truth is brought in as a counterpart to pleasure in unrighteousness ; and that on the other hand the belief of the truth is bound together in indissoluble alliance with the sanctification of the Spirit—both in fact being essential constituents of our salvation, and wanting either of which we shall have no part or lot in that glory which is to be revealed. Let us stand fast, therefore, by the word of the apostles, and not by the corrupt traditions of after ages ; neither let us stop short at the Bible, but hold converse with the living realities which are set forth there. May the Father and the Son take up their abode with us, and may the fruit of their blessed manifestations be our establishment in all truth, and in the practice of all righteousness.

II. THESSALONIANS III.

The word of God does not suffice for the conversion of men but through the Spirit of God; and therefore to the preaching of the minister there should be superadded the prayers both of the minister and people. Let me supplicate the blessing of God on the services of the West Port, that the word may have free course there and be glorified; and that all the evil influences of the unreasonable and the wicked may be averted from the operations which are going on in that place. Work faith, O Lord, more especially in those whose Christianity should be most instrumental to our success. And O do thou establish this counsel of my heart, and preserve me from all which might mar either my own spiritual prosperity or that of the families among whom we labour. Let me love God—let me wait patiently for His Son from Heaven. How identical is the benediction here with the direction of Jude—"Keep your hearts in the love of God, looking for the mercy of Jesus Christ unto life eternal." The spiritualities of this great apostle did not shut out—they sustained and gave impulse to the moralities of ordinary life; and so he passes from the love and faith which have the heavenly and the unseen for their object—he passes on from them to rebuke the disorder and idleness of those who, trusting to the charity of the Church, sought to live without labour. It was a very noble exhibition of Paul that he worked with his own hands, and this for the sake of example to his converts; and here, most of all, do we observe a striking coincidence between the lessons of the New Testament and those of political economy; and the precept is alike decisive with the example—a precept, therefore, which should be freely and fearlessly urged on the bulk and body of the people.—My God, let me not be weary in the work of faith or labour of love, but be steadfast and immovable in the business which lies upon me to do. Let me do it with all my might—rebuking faithfully when I ought, yet affectionately withal—seeing that while called upon to warn the unruly I am further told that all my things should be done with charity. I pray for the peace and the grace which form so frequently the theme of the apostle's benediction. God is the God of peace—and how highly it is estimated in the gospel of Him who is our great Peace-maker! When the Lord is spoken of in relation to this precious blessing it is in the form of an invocation—that He might give us peace always by all means. When man is spoken of in relation to the same, it is in the form of a direction—that as much as lieth in him he should live peaceably with all men. May the benedictions of this genuine epistle of Paul be abundantly fulfilled upon me and upon mine.

I. TIMOTHY.

1 TIMOTHY I.—May Christ be my hope as He was Paul's. May Christ be formed in me the hope of glory—that blessed fruit of the mercy by which I am forgiven, of the reconciliation by which I have peace with God; and O may I have the grace which sanctifies, as well as the mercy which pardons, and then shall I be enabled to realize the apostolical test for the strength and the reality of my hope—even that I purify myself as God or as Christ is

pure. Save me, O God, from all useless expenditure of strength or of zeal on idle and vain controversies. Let me seek the great and proper end of Thy commandment, which is that the law of love be established within me. If my faith be unfeigned, if there be truth in my inward parts, if I obey that truth from my heart, sincerely, and with my conscience deponing thereto—out of such placid and peaceful and prolific springs will there issue that blessed fruit of the Spirit, even the love which worketh no ill, and so a love which fulfilleth the law. May it be to me a glorious law of liberty, and not a law of bondage or restraint—such as it is to those desperadoes in wickedness who stand in need of its terrors to overcome and keep them in order. The efficacious teaching of the sound gospel will powerfully and persuasively disincline me from all wickedness. But to make this reformation good, let me have the faith and the love which is in Christ Jesus. Let me remount to the first and fundamental doctrine of salvation by Him. Let me receive it as a faithful saying and worthy of all acceptation—that He came into the world to save sinners. Blessed words! and O how encouragingly precious—that His is a salvation which reaches even to the chief of sinners. While emboldened by the example let us furthermore imitate the humility of Paul. Let us acknowledge with him that we are not only great but the greatest of sinners. Let us lie low in the depths of our own self-abasement, and in time we shall be exalted through Him who is the wisdom of God, and the mighty power of God, unto salvation. Then shall we, in the enjoyment of peace and good-will from Heaven, be enabled with the apostle to ascribe glory to God in the highest—to the King eternal, immortal, and invisible.

But that we may be upheld in this attitude of confidence
when looking upwardly to Heaven, we must war a good
warfare upon earth; we must maintain the integrity of
our allegiance to Christ as our Master and Lord. Along
with our faith we must hold a good conscience. These
work admirably into each other's hands. But, on the
contrary, if we put away the one the other will be destroyed. It will be found of disobedience that it darkens
our spiritual vision, that it hides from our view the
glory of God in the face of Jesus, that it gives Satan
the advantage over us—so that he blindeth our minds,
and intercepts the light of the glorious gospel of God
from shining unto them.

I. TIMOTHY II.
June, 1845.

These intercessions for all men are in keeping with the
perfect freeness and universality of the gospel; and the
order here given for them should not only prove most encouraging to all who are interested in the souls of their
relatives and friends, but most encouraging also to all
who are intent on their own individual salvation, yet
stand in doubt of God's good-will to themselves. For
what a warrant is here given not only to prayer in behalf
of others, but to confidence in our own behalf. God
willeth all men to be saved, and to come to the knowledge of the truth. What a large, and liberal, and comprehensive view does this give us of God's declarative will
in favour of the whole world. Let us ask then both for
ourselves and others till we receive, let us seek till we
find, let us knock till the door be opened to us. With
what alacrity and perseverance should we do so, when

told, as we are in this passage, that it is good and acceptable in the sight of God our Saviour.   And what a mighty
prop to our assurance in this exercise, when thus led to
associate with it the thought both of the one God and the
one Mediator.   Let not our hearts be troubled—we believe
in God, let us believe also in Christ.   When thus employed
let our fellowship be with the Father and with the Son ;
and when we think of the guilt, whether of ourselves
or others, let us think of the ransom given for all, and
so to be testified in due time as to clear up all the difficulties into which men most unnecessarily and unwisely
plunge themselves on the question of general and particular redemption.   Let us keep by the plain duty
here enjoined upon us—pray everywhere and for every
creature, in the spirit of faith towards God, and of forgiveness towards all men. (Matt. vi. 14, 15.)   Thus shall
we pray without wrath and without doubting.   And let
us not forget the other proprieties of the Christian life
which cluster around the main lesson of this chapter—
loyalty to kings and magistrates—a quiet and peaceable
life in all godliness and honesty—the lifting up of *holy*
hands, which implies a careful avoidance of all impurity.
It is thus that *in like manner* the women are enjoined to
be modest in their apparel and demeanour, and to be
adorned not with gorgeous or expensive clothing but
with good works.   The subjection of the woman is here
set forth as one of the undoubted and incumbent proprieties of the Christian life ; and whereas in the general
doctrine of the Fall there is a mysterious obscuration over
the whole proceeding, yet are we presented here with an
obvious equity, in that the woman had a harder measure
of retribution dealt out to her because she was the first

offender, and the chief transgressor in the sin of Eden. One likes the recognition of a plain principle associated, as here, with this transaction—the pledge as it were of a full and satisfactory development in a future state, when it will be seen that just and true are all the ways of the King of saints.

I. TIMOTHY III.

To desire the office of a bishop is synonymous with that preference which we often witness on the part of aspirants for the office of the ministry. It may often proceed from a secular ambition, but often also from an affection to the cause of Christ, and the good of human souls. It is often a genuine and right desire, and should be fostered by encouragement and aid. I feel the rebuke of those characteristics which are here set forth on the essential properties of a good bishop, because I feel how greatly deficient I am in several of them.

How instructive, too, is the value annexed to general reputation; and we further meet with the repetition of a former testimony to the alliance which obtains between faith and a good conscience. We conceive it to be another trait of the preternatural sagacity of the Bible that it has stated the preparatory virtue that lies in good deaconship, as if it were an effectual school for a still higher office in the Church of God. The timidity which shrinks at the first from the proposal of an eldership, and the manner in which it is at length got the better of by experience and training in the lower and less formidable office—these are what I have so often observed, that I have been led to remark in this instance, too, a most interesting coincidence between the deliverances of God's word and the actual findings of human life.

I am inclined to attach the pillar and ground of the · truth to the mystery of godliness in the last verse, which is indeed a most pregnant one, and one of the highest theological importance. Let me be one of the world who believes on Him to whom the Spirit gave such convincing attestation of His indeed being God manifest in the flesh.

I. TIMOTHY IV.

Give me, O Lord, to walk worthy of Thyself unto all well-pleasing, and herein to abound more and more. And more especially do I pray for a deep and practical sense of that holiness to which I am called.—May I know what it is to keep my heart with all diligence, and to maintain that inward purity without which I shall not see God. Let me abstain alike from uncleanness and covetousness, and enable me to mortify both—even the lust of the flesh and the lust of the eye. May I remember that by a process of vicious indulgence the conscience is seared; and may I live in a fearfulness of this fatal calamity. Let me mix up with all my enjoyments a grateful sense of Thee as the Giver; but let me mix up with every gratification both prayer and the ministry of the word—so that when using the world I may not abuse it. May I be stablished in the faith and exercised unto godliness. Let my trust be in the living God, who is the Saviour of all men, and under which endearing title I may be well encouraged to place upon Him that reliance personally for myself which will assure me that He is specially my Saviour. And, O God, called on as I have been to teach others, let me stand forth

as an example to others, and that not in the purity alone
of which I have been just now speaking, but in all the
graces of an upright and holy conversation. Give me the
charity to bear aright, and withal the wisdom to govern
aright. I stand urgently in need of wisdom from on
high; counsel and console me, O Lord; put the gifts of
wisdom and strength within me; and let me stir them
up so as to meet the great and perplexing difficulty by
which I am at present exercised. And I pray not for
myself alone, but for him who labours in holy things
among the families of the West Port. Prosper, O Lord,
his meditations upon thy word. Let me ever rejoice in
the endowments which Thou hast been pleased to bestow
upon him. Do Thou guide and encourage him, O Lord.
May he be enabled to wait upon Thee without distraction;
and let him so minister, that not only his own profiting,
but the profiting of those under his charge, may appear
unto all. O may he not only be himself saved, but may
he be the instrument of salvation to many; and may both
he and I be carried in safety and at length with triumph
to that prosperous consummation for which we are jointly
labouring. May these difficulties shut me up to prayer.
Draw near and comfort me, O God. O that I could walk
in wisdom; I would trust in Thee, and lean not to mine
own understanding. Do Thou, O God, establish the
thoughts of my heart.

I. TIMOTHY V.

Enable me to rebuke both in wisdom and in charity,
and, moreover, with all purity. What a pertinency and
wisdom shine forth even in the minute clauses of Scripture!

In my treatment of a people let me have respect unto their duties and incumbent virtues, and do nothing to undermine these. What a powerful apostolic sanction we have here for a moral and disciplinary administration. And let me here note also the goodness and the acceptableness before God of those pieties and charities which belong to the domestic relationship. Give me a comfort and a confidence which have been sadly disturbed by our controversial and systematic theology—a comfort and confidence in the doing of Thy will; and let me further understand, that a failure in my obligations towards those whom God hath given me, renders my faith, or the profession thereof, of no effect—inasmuch that if wanting so far in the relative duties as to neglect the care of provision for my own household, I am reckoned with as one destitute of the faith, nay, as worse than an infidel. There are virtues enumerated here which I would do well to appropriate as lessons for myself—hospitality, liberality, a carefulness to maintain all good works, the resistance of all unlawful pleasure, of all self-indulgence, and more particularly the love of ease, and of idle or mischievous gossiping. Let me bear a high respect to the office-bearers of religion, and do them justice in carnal things—careful at the same time of their reputation and honour. I may here remark, that while called upon to rebuke with all gentleness at the commencement of this chapter, I am also called upon to rebuke the open transgressor with all fearfulness. Give me, O Lord, the requisite boldness, but save me from partiality. Let me at all events, and however difficult I may find it to deal with the sins of others —let me not partake of these sins, but keep myself pure. O if I were as temperate as I ought to be!—There is a

liberal indulgence, but there is also a strictness of obligation in the ethics of the gospel.   O that I could keep by
the line which separates scrupulosity from excess, and
that my regimen were determined by the sole consideration
of health for God's service—a regimen never violated or
broken in upon by the temptations of immediate gratification.   Above all, let me look forward to the coming
judgment-day—the day of the revelation of hidden things.
Let me not feel at ease because of the secrecy of aught I
do which is evil.   The time is coming when the worst
abominations—those which, if known, would overwhelm
the delinquent in shame and confusion, and banish him
from society—shall at length be brought to light.   On the
other hand, while called upon to make my light shine before men, let me not do what is good to be seen of men,
or for the sake of their applause ; but let me ever prefer
to the praise of men the praise of God.   The disclosure of
all things is at hand, to the everlasting contempt of the
wicked—to the exaltation and triumph of the righteous.

I. TIMOTHY VI.

O my God, conform me in all respects to that doctrine
which is according to godliness.   Give me to understand
that the wholesome doctrine of our gospel comprehends
more than the mere dogmata of our faith—in the treatment of which we may do little better than dote about
questions and idle logomachies.   May I, both for myself
and for others, proceed on the value in which I ought to
hold the practical teaching of the New Testament ; and
first, let me be an apt and proficient scholar in the precious
lesson of contentment and freedom from all covetousness.

Give me to feel aright the vanity of this world's possessions; and whereas I am apt to feel nervous when visited
by a sense of the insecurity of deeds and dispositions
and documents of property, let me henceforth be forti-
fied against all these distracting and degrading anxieties, by a trust in the living God, who giveth me all
things richly to enjoy. Let me neither aspire after the
riches which I have not, nor set my heart on the riches
that I have. Save me from that ambition which so often
is the parent of many sorrows—from that love of money
which is the root of all evil. Give me well to understand
that one might err from the faith in other ways than by
an erroneous and mistaken view of the doctrines of Christianity, that he might so err by his practical disregard
of the lessons of Christianity—for then does he put away
from him a good conscience, the readiest way by which
to make shipwreck of faith. O give me to flee all evil
things, and to follow after good things; and thus it is
that the good fight of faith is maintained—by another
sort of controversy than that of intellect or argument—by
a controversy with the love of the world, and a firm resistance to its manifold temptations. Of the things we are
required to follow after, I feel my especial need of patience
and meekness. If I do the things of this blessed enumeration I shall never fall, but secure the eternal life
which I have laid hold of.—O my God, forgive my grievous delinquencies from these, and henceforth let my
light, so often tarnished hitherto, shine with purer and
brighter lustre before men. O let me be strenuous and
diligent to be found without spot and blameless, till
that day of which the Father knoweth—even He who is
invisible, and to whom let all the power and glory be

everlastingly ascribed. O may I henceforth sit loose to the world, and make friends in heaven of its mammon of unrighteousness—rich in good works, and liberally diffusive to others of God's manifold bounty to myself. Thus let me lay up store in heaven ; let my heart be there and my treasure there—transferring my interest as it were from the present to the coming world, and in the act of relinquishing my hold on the life of sense, laying hold on life eternal. Such a practical habitude will be my best preservative against errors concerning the faith, and thus shall I avoid the babblings of vain controversy, and the oppositions of the science which has darkened theology by words without knowledge.

II. TIMOTHY.

July, 1845.

2 TIMOTHY I.—The gospel of Jesus Christ is the promise of life through Him. God hath given unto us eternal life, and this life in His son. Give me thus to believe, seeing that it is the word of Him who cannot lie. And therefore would I pray with all confidence for the grace that sanctifies, the mercy that pardons, the peace that allays all my disquietudes ; and let me maintain that pure conscience—that conscience void of offence, without which faith will be shipwrecked ; and if my faith be unfeigned my conscience will be pure. And O along with the faith of Paul, let me have the sympathies of Paul and his Christian fellow-feeling for others. And I pray for the increase not of my personal only but of my family religion—watching over the souls of children, for whose faith unto salvation I do most earnestly pray. And let Thy

gifts within me be put to busy use and exercise, and be
stirred up by the forth-putting of zeal and honest endeavours on my part to their proper application. Save me
from fearfulness; save me from the spirit of bondage.
Shed abroad in my heart the love of Thyself by the Holy
Ghost. Give me to walk as one of Thy children, and give
me the wisdom that puts all the spurious folly and fana-
ticism of weak religionists away from it. What a mighty
endowment, what an elevation of Christianity, when the
Spirit of love and of power and of a sound mind is conferred on us. Let me lay account with tribulations, and
let me have power and fortitude from on high to encounter
and to bear with them. Save me from shame in testifying
for Christ and for His cause—ever deferring to Him as
my Saviour, in whom alone I have life and immortality,
through the blessed election of the Father, to whom I pray
for conformity to the image of Christ, for the death of
sin in my heart, and for all the power and vitality there
of a spiritual resurrection. Let me not be discouraged
by sufferings, but let me, in the assurance of the Lord
being my strength, commit to Him the safety and guidance of my soul—to Him who is at once the Shepherd
and the Bishop of souls. I know Him to be able for this,
and why should I have any doubt of His willingness?—See
in my soul, O Christ, of the travail of Thy soul, and be
satisfied. And I desire to hold fast the form of sound
words, not by argument alone but in love—not alone in-
tellectually and controversially, but in charity and all
affection. And O may I remember not only that the
Holy Ghost is the author and the restorer of all spiritually
good things, but that I keep them and put them into
exercise, stirring up His gifts by a power and a habit

which He alone can impart, and He alone can sustain in me. All is of grace; and through its operation it is that I am strengthened with all might in the inner man unto all patience and long-suffering with joyfulness. When I suffer from the desertion, or the misusage of friends, let me be thus strengthened, O Lord—thinking not that any strange thing hath happened to me, but praying like Paul for a reward for his friends, and also praying for as well as practising forgiveness to all mine enemies. Help me to these achievements, O Lord.

II. TIMOTHY II.

What a pregnant direction—to be in the grace that is in Christ Jesus! What an intimation here of the diligence of the Christian life, and yet in an entire dependence on another strength than our own! May God teach me practically to realize this combination, and to experience that when I am weak then am I strong. And O give me to endure hardness; let me not murmur or grudge or repine, but let me vigorously, and with all the passive fortitude of a good soldier, meet whatever troubles or provocations God in the exercise of His holy discipline might be pleased to lay upon me. Let me be disengaged from earthly cares and earthly objects in the glorious task of fulfilling the great end of an immortal creature. May I obtain a crown of righteousness, by means of the righteousness of Christ become mine, and the grace of Christ preparing me for an inheritance of glory. In pursuit of and preparation for the next life, let not the cares of this life distract or embarrass me. And O may our ministers be freed by the liberality of their people from those anxieties which tend to distract them in the service to which they are called. And let us not think that any strange thing hath happened to us because we are called to endure and to suffer;—Christ suffered before us, but was afterwards exalted. In like manner, if we suffer or even die for Him, we shall hereafter live with Him. He will be faithful to all His assurances, though we should be faithless and unbelieving. But let us, on the contrary, keep by Him, adhere to Him and to His cause, brave all dangers and difficulties for His sake and for the sake of the diffusion of that word which will fulfil its own object in every place whither it is carried, be it for the salvation of the elect or the condemnation of those who reject and despise it. And O give me, Almighty Father, to keep by essentials, and not spend my strength in vain and unprofitable controversies. Give me the wisdom of rightly dividing the word of truth, one part of it from another; and also of rightly distributing to each a word in season, making a study of its varied adaptations to the varieties of human experience. Let me refrain from idle and unnecessary questions, often leading to dangerous heresies; and may I hold it enough to be sound in the weightier matters both of the Christian faith and the Christian practice. I may deceive myself, but God cannot be deceived. He knoweth them who are His; and we may know whether ourselves are of that number by realizing this palpable test, even that we depart from iniquity. God knoweth how to discriminate between the precious and the vile.—My God, let me henceforth utterly renounce those sinful desires and affections which must be renounced by all who are Christ's in deed and not in name only; and let me make my calling and election sure by the busy cultivation of all the Christian graces—praying with a pure heart unto God. And O may I know how to minister all needful rebuke with gentleness. O pour the spirit of repentance upon him to whom I have lately spoken in the language of condemnation. O recover him from the deceitfulness of sin, and give him repentance to the acknowledging of the truth. Guide me, O Lord, to the right treatment of his case ; and give me the wisdom, which I sadly want, of managing as I ought the affairs of men.

II. TIMOTHY III.

Inverness.

How much there is in this chapter which should go to my conscience, and operate with all the force of conviction there! I am a lover of my ownself, and if not disobedient to parents, I have been impatient of their manifold infirmities. I fear that the matters of public engrossment have so far occupied my heart as to impede the full flow of family affection there. Furthermore, I have been heady and high-minded, and how sadly a lover of my own will and of its earthly objects more than of Him who made me and made all things. O give me the power of godliness and then all would be well. What a wretched account of a mind that is " ever learning and yet never able to come to the knowledge of the truth !" Next to this is the state of that man who is constantly laying at the foundation, but does not go beyond the first principles of Christianity, so as to go on unto perfection.—O my God, enable me to be a follower of Paul even as he was of Christ. How miserably short I am in all kinds of charity, long-suffering, and patience. And where has been the persecution which I have suffered in consequence of my will to live godly in Christ Jesus? Has there been no sinful conformity to the world; and is not the very acceptance which I experience at the hands of nearly all—including men decidedly of the world and not of God, a call upon me to examine myself, and see whether there is not a grievous want of that godliness by which all who are in Christ Jesus must be characterized—seeing that He who justifieth the ungodly also turneth away ungodliness from their hearts. O by means of these blessed Scriptures may I become wise unto salvation—and so I shall if I read them in faith. Enable me to give earnest heed unto them, till the day dawn and the day-star arise in my heart. What a blessing to know that all Scripture is given by inspiration from God, and that all is profitable. May I find it profitable unto me, and in the various ways which are enumerated—more especially for reproof and correction and instruction in righteousness. What a practical thing out and out is Christianity!—It would seem as if the doctrine which stands first in order were the fountain-head out of which came forth the other blessed effects of scripture-teaching here put down—and very much according to that natural process by which the mind passes onward from one step in the march of reformation to another—being first reproved for its delinquencies and errors; secondly, turned from them by the conviction that leadeth to correction; and then, proceeding forward from ceasing to do evil to learning to do well, from the negative to the positive, from the correction to the instruction in righteousness. Let me forthwith enter on this journey, and prosecute it to the landing-place of being perfect and thoroughly furnished unto all good works. What a distinct and impressive view is given here of the great end, the *terminus ad quem*, of Christianity!—It is that man should be restored in character and habit to the state in which he was anterior to the fall—to the image in which he was created —to that righteousness of the inner man which would send forth upon the outward walk and history all the fruits of righteousness. May I prosecute this as the great design of my being, which is to glorify God and to enjoy Him for ever.

II. TIMOTHY IV.

Tillichewan.

What a solemn charge ; and by what dread sanctions of enforcement is it pressed home upon our observance ! O that I were more faithful to human souls, and more instant at all times to exhort men, without shame and without fear, that they should mind the things which belong to their peace. Let me not be afraid of men, nor be carried away by a deference either to their feelings or their views, from a full and free exposure of the truth as it is in Jesus. There is a spurious, and I fear a fashionable orthodoxy, regulated by the cadence of the form of sound words, but averse to the sound doctrine which is according to godliness, and which teaches men to live aright as well as to think aright. But let me make full proof of my ministry, and O that I could say with Paul, " I have fought the good fight."—My God, enable me henceforth so to exercise myself that before death comes I may be warranted to speak in the language of a triumphant assurance, comprehending in it both the assurance of faith and the assurance of experience. Save me, O Lord, from the love of the present world, and put in its stead the love of Christ and of His appearance. I would wait for His coming, with my conversation in Heaven, and · all my hopes and interests there. I have no such commission as Paul may have had, to predict a retribution on Alexander who had done him much evil. Let me imitate him, therefore, not in such a prediction, but in the prayer that God would forgive those who had forsaken Him : and let me at the same time study myself, and enlist others to the extent of my influence, to be profitable unto the Church. Deliver and preserve me, O God, and this not from outward enemies alone, but preserve me in a condition of meetness for the inheritance that is above ; and for this purpose, let the Lord Jesus Christ be with my spirit, for unless I have the spirit of Christ I am none of His. Bestow this grace upon me, O Lord. Purify my heart by faith, and enable me to purify myself even as Christ is pure.

TITUS.

August, 1845.

TITUS I.—Give me the faith, O Lord, that I may therefrom gather the truth of my election ; and O may the doctrine which I profess be indeed a doctrine according to godliness. How blessed the security for eternal life, when linked with the assurance that He who hath promised it cannot lie. Let me so believe that the truth and faithfulness of God may be thus upon my side ; and in trusting with all my heart to these, may I feel how immutable the guarantee, and how strong the consolation. O may the precious benedictions of the apostle have their fulfilment upon me—the grace that sanctifies, the mercy that pardons, the peace of a confiding fellowship with the Father and with the Son our Saviour. Yet let not the spiritualities of religion unfit me—rather let them stimulate and prepare me for the outward business of the house of God. My earnest prayer is for a well-ordered and efficiently working machinery in the Free Church of Scotland. And let me not hold it enough that a right order be set up in the Church, but give me to set up a right order in my family. The apostle connects a capacity for household with that for ecclesiastical government, and therefore let me never cease to labour till Christ be formed in the hearts of my children. And O that I better observed the apostolic gentleness which becomes a teacher and office-bearer in the Church. May I know what it is to abstain from striving, and to instruct in meekness. I err sadly in this respect—impatient of contradiction, wayward and greatly wanting in the wisdom of meekness. Let me hold fast good doctrine ; but it is not by intolerance, or by an intolerant manner, that I shall convince the gainsayer. On this matter I have much to learn ; and I do pray that I may carry it with all humility and long-suffering, as well as with sound judgment, in order that my views, so far as they are consistent with truth and the word of God, might make way among my brethren. The apostle had men to deal with who might naturally and readily have provoked his anger, yet, for the very purpose of making head against them, has he exhorted to be not soon angry. There are others beside the Cretans who might well provoke a resentful as well as indignant feeling, yet let the sharpness of my rebuke have nothing more in it than moral indignancy—let there be no personal resentment in it; still it is worthy of remark that we have the apostolic sanction, not only for rebuking but for rebuking sharply in such cases. There is a warrant for being angry, but not too soon: it is only after they have held out against a gentle and affectionate remonstrance, and held out long against it, that we are entitled to take up the language, not of rebuke only, but of sharp and indignant rebuke.—O my God, let me at length be practically and powerfully impressed by the repeated testimonies and demands of Thy word on behalf of purity. Purify my heart by faith, for if the heart be not pure there will be an overflow of evil; and in the midst of all my seemly professions I may be hurried onward to such doings as might redound to the disgrace and scandal of the Christian name in the world.

TITUS II.

Sound doctrine is here made up of the moralities of human conduct. Let me be temperate, O God, and not given to much wine. Would it be looked upon now-a-days to be a doctrinal sermon, or would not the soundness of the preacher be suspected, were he to give forth a textual exhortation from the clause of "keepers at home"? What a precious characteristic for young men, to be sober-minded! Doctrine is here the act of teaching, which should be performed with all gravity and sincerity. What a testimony to the religious importance of the common and everyday moralities of life in these exhortations to servants, when told not to answer again, and not to purloin—and this that they may adorn the doctrine of God our Saviour. And what a noble representation is here given of the gospel of the grace of God, in that it teaches us to live aright by teaching us to look aright. Our habitual attitude should be that of looking unto Jesus—and what a view is here given of the purpose for which He died! He gave Himself for us, no doubt, to expiate our sins, but the ulterior, the terminating purpose, was to turn us from sin unto righteousness. He died to redeem us from guilt, but this with a view to something beyond, even to our personal sanctification, and that we should become zealous of good works.—My God, let me for the accomplishment of this object be a fellow-worker with my Saviour; let His will be my will; let me be purified from dead, and still more, from wicked works, to serve the living and true God; and let me henceforth serve, not in the oldness of the letter, but in the newness of the Spirit. O let me remember that Christ's people are a peculiar people; and let it not be said of me, "What doest thou more than others?" And hitherto too little, greatly too little has been my looking for Christ, my waiting for the appearance of Christ—an expectancy so often enjoined on the first Christians, and still more incumbent upon us. Surely there is nothing in the world as it now is that should so detain and engross our affections as not to long for another world, for the new heavens and the new earth wherein dwelleth righteousness. And is there not here an express affirmation of the divinity of the Son? It is Jesus Christ who is both the great God and our Saviour. The appearance for which we are taught to look is the appearance of the great God, even our Saviour Jesus Christ. Let me honour the Son even as I honour the Father; and let my hope be grounded on the knowledge and belief of a Divine Saviour

TITUS III.

Obedience to magistrates is the incumbent duty of every Christian—insomuch that the spirit of evangelism and the spirit of radicalism are at antipodes the one to the other. And O what a noble characteristic, and how precious in this our day, is readiness to every good work, especially on the part of Christian laymen—it being more the part of the Christian minister to give himself wholly to the work of the ministry. But, to my humiliation be it spoken, how urgently do I stand in need of the golden precepts contained in the second verse. There is a strong provocative to evil-speaking and brawling which now acts and stirs within me.—My God, let me not give way to it. Let me know how to combine gentleness with firmness. I pray in this matter for Thine especial grace and guidance, O Lord ; and let me observe this meekness not to brethren only, but to all men—so as to walk not in wisdom only, but in the meekness of wisdom to them who are without. And the argument for thus deporting ourselves, even to the unconverted, is the recollection of what ourselves at one time were. This forms a strong appeal upon our charity, and is mightily strengthened by the consideration that these poor aliens are now, what we once were, deceived. But there are other characteristics of the natural state which might well alarm me, and fill me with the apprehension that I am yet carnal. Am I never foolish ? do I ever give way to divers lusts and pleasures ? or am I altogether free of envy ? or do I never so conduct myself as to justify the hatred of others, while there is hatred to others in my own bosom ?—O my God, save, save me conclusively from these—and this in the only way possible, by the descent of a powerful appliance from above, even the washing of regeneration and the renewing of the Holy Ghost. If these have ever been shed upon me at all, O may they now be shed far more abundantly, and so that my conversion might become far more palpable to myself, and I be warranted to say—"Hereby know I that I am in Him, even by the Spirit which He has given to me." And let me ever keep fast hold of the precious truth that by grace I am justified, and that not by my own works of righteousness, but by the love, and kindness, and mercy of God I am saved. It is only thus indeed that I am a rightful heir of the blissful immortality in heaven. Let all this be affirmed constantly, in order that they who believe should be careful to maintain good works, both for what is necessary and what is profitable, avoiding, on the other hand, those vain controversies which are unprofitable. Teach me, O God, so to divide the word of truth that I may be able to define the limits of heresy, and not indulge in laxity or latitudinarianism. *N.B.*—We are bidden love those that hate us, and greet those that love us.

PHILEMON.

PHILEMON.—This exquisite epistle is not without its important practical lessons. It came from Paul when a prisoner to his convert Philemon, and forms a most beautiful pleading in behalf of the runaway slave whom the apostle had lately gained over to the faith. It begins with the language of benediction and compliment to Philemon, who was the master of this slave. Let us learn from the

subject-matter of the prayer on his behalf, that the most
effectual method of communicating our faith to others is
to make it palpable or known to them that, because in
Christ, we abound in all good works and graces. Paul
had no doubt of Philemon's generosity, and therefore
would not lay what he wanted upon him in the form of
an injunction, but in the form of a request. And so,
with inimitable grace and delicacy, he put himself as
Paul the aged and in prison, and in this attitude be-
seeches him to receive Onesimus—taking him into forgiveness, and not only so, but on the footing of a Christian
brother, to be cherished with all affection, and loved by
him both in the flesh and in the Lord. This latter distinction I have always looked upon as highly instructive.
It gives a religious warrant to the love that we feel for
others naturally ; and it blends with this the love that we
feel for their Christianity—that love for the brethren
which is one evidence of our having passed from death
unto life. The one is love in the flesh, and the other love
in the Lord ; and Onesimus was at one and the same
time the object of both. Paul, by beseeching rather than
enjoining, and by offering payment to Philemon for the
value of his slave, seems to acknowledge his right of property in Onesimus. Certain it is that the extreme aboli-
tionists of the present day greatly overshoot the mark, and
go beyond the New Testament, when they make slave-
holding *per se* a bar to communion. Christianity will
undermine slavery, even as it will put an end to war ;
but it does not seem to have issued an authoritative
enactment against either ; and in the history of the
Church there have been both Christian soldiers and
Christian slaveholders. Nothing can exceed the tact and

courteousness of this communication—a perfect model of the gentleman blended with the Christian. The politeness of modern society is in many respects the embodiment of the Christian graces. It may, and generally I fear is, the body without the spirit; but that it should express what it does is in itself an homage, the homage at least of its forms to the substantial virtues of the gospel of Jesus Christ. When I contrast such a chivalrous exhibition of so much generosity and so much gentleness, as is here made, with the rudeness of the age, I cannot but look on the outpeering quality of this epistle before that of all other specimens which have come down to us, as another and most interesting contribution to the evidence, daily accumulating upon our view, in behalf of the Divine origin of our faith.

HEBREWS.

HEBREWS I.—I enter on this epistle with a deep sense of its importance, and earnest prayer that God would bring home its precious views with the light and confirmation of His Holy Spirit to my understanding and heart. And how unspeakably glorious is the representation here given of the Almighty Saviour, and of His sufficiency for the work of our redemption. Let me honour the Son even as I honour the Father; and as I am told that he who hath seen the Son hath seen the Father also, let me study the character and doings of Jesus Christ, that I may thereby increase in the knowledge of God. And O what security should it give to our faith, when we think that He who upholdeth all things by the word of His

power did by Himself purge our sins. Let me rejoice more
and more in my contemplations of the dignity of His person,
and of His transcendent superiority to all that is created.
The angels are infinitely beneath Him, for He is the everlasting God. And when I read of the moral ascriptions
which are here given to Him, let me ever look unto Him
that I may become like unto Him—like unto Him in my
love of righteousness and hatred of all iniquity. It is
most interesting to observe that *because* of these characteristics God had anointed Him with the " oil of gladness."
There is such an oil in the very essence and constitution
of every virtuous nature. And mark how He is called
both Son and Lord, and that the highest ascriptions of
Deity are given to Him—these quotations from the Psalms
proving that He who in the Old Testament is set forth in
terms the most unequivocal, as being the very God, is
identified in the New Testament with Jesus Christ our
Saviour; and thus proving Him to be " God manifest in
the flesh." The unchangeableness and the eternity of
this high and holy One are impressive, contrasted with
the ephemeral and evanescent character of all earthly, or
rather of all created things; for both heaven and earth
shall wax old and perish, but He is the same always, nor
shall His years at any time fail. And such also is His
superiority to the highest of created intelligences;—the
angels are but ministering spirits, whereas the Son is at
God's right hand—a Prince and a Conqueror as well as a
Saviour. It is an incidental revelation, but a very interesting one, that angels somehow or other minister to the
heirs of salvation. They rejoice in their conversion; they
are ranked with the spirits of just men made perfect,
(ch. xii. 22, 23,) who compass us about as a cloud of

witnesses; and here they are represented as helping us onward upon our course heavenwards. With such a magnificent contemplation as this why should my spirit sink under the pressure of earthly disappointments, or droop and be in heaviness because all is not congenial or satisfactory among my fellow-men, or in the business of the Church below? Let me take refuge in higher things, and look upwardly where Christ sitteth at the right hand of God.

HEBREWS II.
September, 1845.

Let me give earnest heed to these things, that I may both retain them in my memory and be ever observant of them in practice. Let the dignity of the messenger constrain my attention to the message; and seeing that it is the message of a great salvation, how can I escape if I turn with neglect or indifference away from it? When one thinks of the gospel brought down from heaven to earth by the eternal Son of God, what a call on the sinful men of earth to entertain it!—My God, do Thou effectually rebuke the light esteem in which I have hitherto held it, and let me never forget that to make it but the subject of an occasional regard is to approach the habit of those who view the Cross of Christ as foolishness or a thing of nought, and of whom we read that they will infallibly perish. Let me henceforth be not only more solemnized, but more influenced and operated upon by the thought— that as Christ has done so much and suffered so much for me, I should for Him be ready to give up all that is dear to life and nature. O may He from this time forward be my all in all—the object of my full and intent and persevering regard, and for whom I am in readiness to do whatever He would have me, and to suffer whatever He would have me. He was humbled and died for me, and became perfect through sufferings. Let me not think it strange that I should partake in these, even as He Himself partook in the state and nature of our wretched humanity. Let me lay my account therefore with the great and manifold tribulations through which it is that we must enter the kingdom of God. Let me hold it enough that all is over after death, and that this last enemy is destroyed by the Captain of our salvation—so that on quitting the body we are ushered into His presence, and live for ever with Him in glory.—My God, do Thou conform all my views and all my habits to this great and heavenly contemplation. Let me henceforth look on the reconciliation as perfected, and put myself into the hands of Him "that sanctifieth," that I may be one with Him in holiness, and be purified even as He is pure. He is both merciful and faithful, and withal able to perfect that which concerns us. He knows our frame, and is experimentally acquainted with our sufferings and trials. He is like unto us, and views us in the light of brethren, and hath a most perfect sympathy with us in all our temptations and all our cares. Blessed Jesus, we implore Thy succour in the midst of all our sorrows, and all our struggles with the devil, and the world, and the flesh—so that on us may be fulfilled the saying—" Because I have overcome ye shall overcome also."

HEBREWS III.

What a pregnant direction it is that we should consider Christ both as the Apostle or Messenger who brought to

us the knowledge of our great salvation, and as the High-
Priest who died an atoning sacrifice to make it good.
And what a testimony also to the divinity of Christ, in
that He is here represented as worthy of more glory than
Moses, on the ground that He was the builder of that
house or economy where Moses was only a servant; and
that the Builder of all things, and so of that house—even
Christ, is God. And we are Christ's house, we are of God's
building and God's husbandry, if we hold fast our confidence and the rejoicing of our hope firm unto the end.
What a warrant and encouragement have we here, not for
faith only but for a joyful faith!—Let us therefore rejoice
evermore. But see also how the faith and the obedience
are, if not identified, at least implicated, and that by indissoluble connexion with each other. The evil and har-
dened heart of unbelief arose through the deceitfulness of
sin, and led to a departure from the living God. They
with whom He was grieved were they who had sinned;
and they by whom He was provoked, and of whom He
sware that they should not enter into His rest, were they
who believed not. We thus see how inseparably it is that
belief and obedience, that unbelief and sin, go together.
Each is stated as if indiscriminately to have been the
cause of God's displeasure with the children of Israel; and
the consequence of either or both was that most of that
generation entered not into rest, but their carcasses fell
in the wilderness. It is remarkable that to harden not our
hearts is held as if tantamount to holding fast our confidence—synonymous, if not in word, yet in effect and reality. Let us then be steadfast in the faith. Let us repair
to Christ as at the first; and as the fruit of this perennial
habit or exercise, let us rely upon Him and rejoice in Him

even unto the end. The faith and the feeling will give mutual support and strength to each other—the faith that is opposed to unbelief—the feeling that is opposed to hardihood. To save our departure from the living God, let us abide in Christ, and be made partakers of Him, and He will abide in us, so as to sustain at once both our faith and our obedience. And O let me not be insensible to the call of "to-day," that I may no longer postpone the good work either of faith or of repentance. Let it be remarked that "some" might signify a small or a very large proportion of the whole. It is said that some, howbeit not all, who came out of Egypt by Moses did provoke God: certainly not all—for both Caleb and Joshua were faithful, and got both an entry and an inheritance in the land of Canaan. Let them be examples to us, that we may shine as lights in the midst of a perverse and crooked generation.

HEBREWS IV.

Let us fear lest we fall short because of unbelief—let us fear lest we fall away from the faith of the gospel. There is a fear which might co-exist with faith ;—the two are not incompatible. By faith Noah, moved with fear, prepared an ark ; and Paul told his converts that because they stood by faith they were not to be high-minded, but fear. (Rom. xi. 20.) What is this fear then, and what is the object of it ? A fear—not lest the promises should fail, but a fear lest we should fail of confidence in these promises. A fear—not lest God should fall from His faithfulness, but a fear lest we ourselves should fall from our faith : a fear lest we should let go our hold of that which

supports us is the very fear which will constrain us to
keep fast our hold; and thus it is that there is a fear
which shuts us up unto the faith, and which leads us to
keep by it all the more steadfastly and determinedly.
And so the conclusion of the argument is, not to feel
boldly in ourselves—that were a boldness the very opposite of the fear which is here enjoined upon us—but to
come boldly unto the throne of grace, that we may obtain
not mercy only, but grace to help in time of need.   The
fear is lest we should be moved away from our dependence on this grace or on these promises—whether by the
pleasures of the world, as the children of Israel when
they looked back with longing eyes upon Egypt, or by
the trials of the world, even as they were by the trials of
the wilderness.   Keep me then, O Lord, from all the
vain securities of earth and from all proud confidence in
myself, for Thou resistest the proud; and O let the end
and aim of my labour be my entry into rest—sweet, and
pleasant, and gladsome rest.   This is in truth a weary
world, full both of fatigue and tribulation; but let this
shut me up unto Him in whom even now I may have
peace here, and if I hold the beginning of my confidence
steadfast unto the end, in whom I shall have both peace
and glory hereafter—a better rest than Joshua, the Jesus
of the Old Testament, secured for the children of Israel—
that better rest, even a heavenly, which the Jesus of the
New Testament hath secured for all His people.   And
lest we should fall by unbelief, let us give earnest heed
unto the word of the testimony—that word which is able
to make wise unto salvation—that word which contains
within itself the most piercing and powerful manifestations
of its own truth—that word which so discerns us as to

make us discern in its characters both of force and of omniscience, the hand of the divinity which formed it—that
word on which if we but gaze intently, and intelligently,
and desirously, the day will at length dawn and the day-
star arise in our hearts.   We look unto Thee, O blessed
Jesus, to whom this word gives testimony.   O for a more
realizing sense of Thy truth, and Thy tenderness, and
above all, of Thy sympathizing humanity.   Thou knowest
both my trials and my necessities, for Thou hast undergone and Thou hast felt them all.   O succour me and
save me; and give me in the midst of my various difficulties and oppositions to have both the guidance and the
grace on which I feel that I am altogether dependent.

HEBREWS V.

Christ had compassion on the ignorant, though not
like the earthly high-priest so compassed with infirmity
as to need a sin-offering for himself, but made Himself a
sin-offering for the people.   And in the mysterious sufferings which He underwent He uttered cries and prayers
unto God, and was trained in the school of affliction,
learning obedience thereby.   Let me submissively and
unquestioningly take these informations from the Bible,
and turn them to personal application; let me lay my
account with suffering; let me be submissive and resigned
under it, so as to work patience and the wisdom of experience.   May the obedience of Christ be a pattern to
teach me obedience, and more especially obedience to
Himself, that I may reap the eternal salvation of which
He is the alone author.   And to be the author of my
salvation, may He be the author and finisher or perfecter

of my faith, that I may receive as the end of my faith the salvation of my soul. And let me never disjoin faith from obedience; so that without the scrupulosities of a sensitive and extreme orthodoxy, I may be as ready to award the blessings of the New Covenant to those who obey Christ as to those who believe in Him — two characteristics which are inseparable, and ought never to have been so conflicted the one with the other as they have often been amid the strifes of religious warfare. Let me especially imitate my blessed Saviour in that He glorified not Himself. May I seek not my own pleasure but seek the good of Zion; and seeing that He, the same yesterday, to-day, and for ever, so humbled and subjected Himself for our sakes, give me, Almighty Father, to learn of Him who was meek and lowly in heart, and then should I find rest to my soul. I have much, I should almost say everything, to learn that is to be had in the school of Christian experience. When did I ever verify the distinction between milk and strong meat? Have I ever been taught the first principles of the oracles of God, and still more have I proceeded any way beyond them? Have I not been tarrying for years at the place of breaking forth? and where are the sign-posts which mark my distinct progress from one stage of the Christian journey to another? Have my senses been at all exercised by reason of use to discern between good and evil? or have I not been satisfied all the while with the kingdom of God in word, while a stranger to its reality and power? Give me, O Lord, to make a real business of my Christianity; and then shall I be experimentally as well as doctrinally skilful in the word of righteousness.

HEBREWS VI.

October, 1845.

Let me not tarry at the first principles of the Christian faith, but leave them in the sense of proceeding on them, and thence going on unto perfection. Surely to proceed on a truth is a higher homage to its certainty than constantly to be proving at it, and to be always laying at the foundation without rising above it to the work of building up the superstructure. Instead of laying again and again at the foundation of faith towards God, we are required to build up on our most holy faith. (Jude 20.) By leaving the first principles, however, it is not meant that we should lay them aside; but having once learned them so as not to need being perpetually taught them over and over again, to hold them fast as the indispensable roots of a progressive vegetation. Let us hold fast the beginning of our confidence even unto the end. And what are the principles which are worthy of being thus held? They are here enumerated; and substantially they may be stated as lying in repentance and faith, and the doctrine of our being cleansed from the pollution as well as guilt of sin, as signified by baptism, the emblem of the washing of regeneration; and the doctrine of the new creature growing up in all the graces and accomplishments of the Christian life, as signified by the putting on of hands, the emblem of our renewal and endowment by the Holy Ghost; and finally, the doctrine of our bodily resurrection hereafter, as well as our spiritual resurrection here; and last of all, the doctrine of a judgment to come that is to fix the state of our eternity. And we shall go on unto perfection, the apostle says, if God permit—for He may withhold His Spirit; and hence let us fear and tremble lest we should grieve and resist and finally quench this high and heavenly agent within us; for what an awful catastrophe to the backsliders who have advanced so far and then fallen away.—My God, heal me and restore me, and let me never again give offence to Christ by offending any of His little ones. O let me abound more and more in the work and labour of love towards the saints of our Lord; and instead of receding, may I press forward with all diligence, so as to attain to the full assurance of hope unto life everlasting. Let me not be slothful, O God, but maintain the faith and patience of those just men made perfect who have gone before me. And that my subjective Christianity might thrive and make progress, let me ever cast a fixed and steadfast regard on the blessed truths of objective Christianity—more especially on the faithfulness of God, who hath not only said but sworn, that He will bless all the spiritual children of Abraham. O how precious a thought that God wills us to have a steadfast and strong faith in Himself; and that because of this willingness He hath given us not only His assertion but His oath. How strong the consolation, and how immutable ought to be our confidence, seeing we have so full and firm a warrant to lay hold of. Carry, O God, the eye of my mind within the veil, where Christ sitteth at Thy right hand clothed in all the honours of an unchangeable priesthood. Let this be the anchor of our souls both sure and steadfast—this our faith grounded and settled so as that we shall not be moved away from the hope of the gospel.

HEBREWS VII.

We may not stand in need of the argumentation here

set forth with the design of reconciling the Jews to that change of priesthood which took place when the economy of the law gave place to the economy of the gospel. But there is an enduring and most invaluable lesson bound up with this reasoning of the apostle, and such as should in-crease our faith in the efficacy of Christ's mediatorship. And what a blessed conjunction are we here presented with—in that He should both be King of righteousness and King of peace! In Him mercy and truth have met together, righteousness and peace have kissed each other. O may both these inestimable blessings be made sure to me through the sure and eternal and unchangeable priesthood of Christ. Let me be so washed in His blood as to be cleansed not from ceremonial but from all spiritual defile-ment—and so as to be meet for the participation of an endless blessedness in heaven, when I shall be for ever with the Lord. On the strength of that better hope which is now brought in, I would draw nigh with all confidence and liberty of access unto God. Give me to feel and to rely with perfect faith on the firmness of that suretiship which has both the saying and the oath of God to estab-lish it. And there is not only all faithfulness to be ascribed to this mediatorship, but all power. Christ is able to save to the uttermost. He addeth intercession now to the atonement which He hath already made once for all. What a blessed apparatus of reconciliation with God!—He who pleadeth for us at God's right hand is om-nipotent to save—and willing as He is able. Save me then, O God : save me both from the guilt and the pollu-tion of my sins, and fulfil on me that saying—" because I live ye shall live also." Let me consider Him who is the Apostle and High-Priest of my profession. Let me dwell in thought on the characteristics here assigned to Him—holy, harmless, undefiled, and separate from sinners. And may I look at these not for the purpose only of confirming my faith in the efficacy of His atonement, but for the further purpose of copying the virtues of Him who is set forth as an example as well as a propitiation : " Be ye therefore holy even as He is holy." Give me the love which worketh no evil, and not the avoidance only but the utter abhorrence of all that is evil ; and let me come out from amongst them, and be separate from sinners even as He was. And to make good this full exemplification, let me not only look to the display of His character while on earth, but let me look to Him now as exalted in the heavens whence He bestows the sanctifying Spirit on all His followers.

HEBREWS VIII.

O that we considered effectually and aright the august representation which is here set before us—Christ sitting on the right hand of the throne of the Majesty in the heavens—a minister of the true tabernacle—the glorious and primeval exemplar showed to Moses in the mount, and after which he framed the sanctuary that was set up beneath for earthly rites and earthly services. Give me, O Lord, richly to partake in the benefits of the better offering, the better covenant, the better promises. Now that the shadow has passed away, and the substance has been placed within our discernment and our reach, let me look upon it with the eye of faith and be satisfied. Let me contemplate Him who is the Apostle and High-Priest of my profession, the great Mediator, who poured out His soul as an offering, and whose precious blood is the blood of a covenant that is everlasting, and all whose promises are yea and amen. The gifts which were offered according to the law are but the feeble resemblance of that unspeakable gift made known to us in the gospel—even Jesus Christ our Lord. And so the first covenant has given place to the second, under which, instead of the ceremonial purifications of the former, we are promised a better and a higher purification.—My God, may I have an experience within of the fulfilment of this covenant in my soul. Put thy laws into my mind, and write them in my heart; enlist my affections on the side of the new obedience of the gospel; and give me to feel how essentially my personal salvation from sin is bound up with the great scheme of restoration to the favour of God. Give me, O Lord, that knowledge which Thou alone canst teach. Deliver me from the narrowing influence of human lessons, and more especially of human systems of theology. Teach me directly out of the fulness and freeness of Thine own word; and hasten the time when, unfettered by sectarian intolerance, and unawed by the authority of men, the Bible shall make its rightful impression upon all, because—the simple and obedient readers thereof—they call no man master but Christ only. Teach me, O God, to regard the scheme of salvation more than I have done hitherto under the aspect of a covenant having Thy faithfulness for its guarantee, and all that sense of security associated therewith which we feel in the stipulations of an engagement or bargain.—O my God, do Thou take up Thy habitation in my soul that I may walk as one of Thy children, and be Thou a Father to me; and in the name of Christ, who is the surety and Mediator of this new and better covenant, do I pray that my sins and mine iniquities Thou wouldst remember no more.

HEBREWS IX.

What a precious chapter for the morning of a communion Sabbath, in which are set forth the efficacy of that atoning blood which is represented by the sacramental cup, and the worth of that sacrifice which I am this day to commemorate. May my conscience, O Lord, be this day thoroughly purged from the guilt of all those rebellious and unprofitable works that were done when I was in a state of death—dead in trespasses and sins; but may I never forget that I am thus emancipated for the purpose of going forth to the service of the living God. On this day may I be enabled to say in truth—"Thou hast loosed my bonds;" and henceforth may I be Thy servant, even Thy servant—offering up the sacrifices of righteousness, and calling on the name of the Lord. The way into the holiest of all is now made manifest, and more especially in the solemn ritual of this day is Jesus Christ evidently set forth crucified before me. May I draw nigh with full assurance of heart; but for this let me not hold it enough that I have an objective confidence in the blood of the everlasting covenant, let me draw near with a true heart, a heart sprinkled from an evil conscience, and a body washed with pure water. The salvation of the gospel is a salvation both by water and by blood—the washing of regeneration and renewing of the Holy Ghost, as well as through the righteousness of Christ made ours by faith. Let me henceforth have full peace of conscience in the contemplation of Christ's atoning sacrifice, and

look up to Him now in heaven where He appears in the
presence of God on behalf of His own, and whence He
sends down upon them the grace that both illuminates
and sanctifies.   Give me, O Lord, to be thoroughly
grounded and settled in the truth that Christ died for our
sins according to the Scriptures; but instead of always
laying at the foundation, let me forthwith build upon it
—that reconciled by the death of Christ I may be saved
by His life, or from the place which He now occupies
receive the needful sustenance for my spiritual growth
and wellbeing.   He is made unto me redemption, but
let me not divide Christ: He is made unto me sanctification also.   Let this work of grace be progressing in my
soul, and then may I look forward with boldness to the
day of judgment.   Let but the love of God be shed
abroad in my heart, and then shall I have confidence in
the thought, that as He is so am I in this world.   Then
may I look for Christ without the apprehension of sin
being laid to my charge—seeing that He hath borne away
its guilt from my person, and washed away its pollution
from my heart and life.   Thus will He appear to His own,
without any reckoning with them because of sin, but unto
their complete and everlasting salvation.   Amen, O God.

HEBREWS X.

November, 1845.

My God, give me to feel more conclusively at rest on
the ground of Christ's one and perfect sacrifice than I
have ever yet done.   May my conscience be at length set
at liberty, freed from the bondage of guilt, and so emancipated for the services of taste and of willingness, rendered to God in the spirit of adoption.   May I now regard

myself as sanctified and set apart unto God as one of His peculiar people, who has come out from a world which lieth in wickedness. And there are means and agencies set up by the economy of the gospel sufficient for this consummation—even for the perfecting of those who have accepted, and to whom now He is all in all. Because He liveth we shall live also; and from the place of glory to which He is now exalted does He send down those heavenly influences by which He prepares many sons for glory. Let us seek for the law of God in our hearts; and from henceforth ever cherish a most entire confidence in the efficacy of that atonement which Christ hath made for us. Let us with full assurance of faith and all boldness in the blood of Jesus, draw near by the new and living way of His rent flesh and His consecrated priesthood, with our hearts sprinkled from the stain of a guilty conscience, but withal our bodies washed with pure water. The two must go together—the unwavering faith which rests on God's promise, and the purification by which, in person and character, we are made holy and fruitful in good works. Here follows the efflorescence of that practical Christianity which emerges from its well-laid principle. And what an awful testimony is here against Antinomianism!—Save me, O God, from the wilful sinning which infers the certainty of damnation. Give me so to know the truth as that the truth shall make me free, and sin may have no longer the dominion over me. O Lord, may I well understand that Thine is a holy salvation, and that if I pervert it into an encouragement to sin there remains the dread alternative of a sorer punishment and heavier condemnation. Give me to have all boldness in prospect of the coming judgment, instead of

that fearful looking for it which belongs to them who count the blood of the covenant an unholy thing. May I stand in awe and sin not, lest I fall into the hands of Him who is the God of vengeance. There is a salvation; but this so far from superseding judgment will aggravate and make it all the more terrible—for how shall we escape if we neglect, and how much more if we abuse, the great salvation? Mark how faith is identified with obedience—elements which the controversies of the Church have arranged in hostile conflict and placed so widely apart from each other. It is the confidence which hath great recompense of reward, and it is after doing the will of God that we receive the promise. The reward and the promise here are the same; and the confidence is the knowledge that our labour in the Lord shall not be in vain, and so we are kept steadfast and immovable therein.

HEBREWS XI.

Faith may be contemplated in two aspects, either as belief in the faithfulness of a promiser, or as a realization of unseen things; and both are exemplified in the instances of this chapter. Give me faith in the invisible God, and give me to please Him by my homage to His truth. Let me ever rise from things sensible to their unseen Creator. In opposition to the influences of this visible world may I believe that Thou art—in opposition to the self-constituted orthodoxy of human systems, may I believe that Thou art a rewarder, aye and a rewarder of diligence too—of diligence in seeking after Thee, if haply we may find Thee. Noah realized things not seen as yet, and his faith moved him with fear—a fear of the coming

destruction, against which he provided with all assiduity at the bidding of God, and so became heir of the righteousness which is by faith.   Give me this faith, O Lord, that I may attain unto this righteousness; and further enable me to realize that victory of faith over sense, of which we are here presented with so many illustrious specimens—as by Abraham who both trusted in the promise and looked for the city which hath foundations, and Sarah who also trusted in the promise of what to the eye of nature was a great unlikelihood, and with her husband did against hope believe in hope—he, it is said, (Rom. iv. 21,) being fully persuaded that what God had promised He was able also to perform, and she judging Him faithful who had promised.   They both trusted in God, and cherished a realizing sense of what they did not see, or only saw afar off—and so did they seek a country.   Uphold me, O God, in the attitude of a pilgrim and stranger looking forward to an inheritance on the other side of death, and declaring plainly that both my treasure and my heart are there.   Give me, O Lord, to be so persuaded as to embrace the promises—not only believing but desiring, so as to have all my efforts directed to the attainment of that better country which God hath prepared for His own.   And O that I could walk in the footsteps and the faith of him who was in readiness to offer up all that was dear to nature at the bidding of God; like him may I show my faith by my works; and like all the patriarchs, may things future and beyond the ken of present sight have the ascendant over me as over Isaac, who prophesied of things to come, and Jacob whose benedictions had respect unto distant things, and Joseph who looked to Canaan, then afar off, as his own resting-place and the home of his posterity; and above all, Moses who made surrender of all pleasures and treasures, because he looked to a future recompense, and endured as seeing Him who is invisible. And if those of a remote antiquity, who saw only through a medium of distance and dimness, were thus enabled by the power of faith to maintain their firmness and integrity in the face of the most dreadful persecutions and fiery trials, how great is the responsibility under which we lie, who live in the full noontide of a finished revelation! Thou knowest, O God, what sufferings are yet in reserve for us. If it be Thy blessed will, do Thou avert the judgments which hang over our country; but if not, and we have to pass through the ordeal of famine, and pestilence, and insurrection, grant that when Thy judgments are abroad upon the earth we may learn righteousness.

HEBREWS XII.

This epistle, like all the others, effloresces towards its conclusion from principle to practice, from the truths of the Christian doctrine previously laid down to the moralities of the Christian life. Let me feel the control of the higher spirits now looking over me. O for my deliverance from the sin which doth most easily beset me, and for a patience like that of my Saviour, to whom I should look continually. I have not as He did resisted unto blood; and wherefore so easily transported from charity and long-suffering by the lesser crosses and contradictions which have too grievously annoyed me? O that I received everything as from the hand of God, and the discomforts laid upon me as the tokens of His love— then should I rejoice when I fall into divers tribulations.

Let me view all as from the hand of God, as a message from Him—and then let it be felt as my chief concern to put the right interpretation thereupon. O may the troubles of life be so improved and sanctified as to minister the peaceable fruits of righteousness to my soul. Let me do all my things without murmurings and disputings, and so follow peace with all men; for they are from the perversities of others, whether real or fancied, that my trials chiefly spring. Grudge not one against another, the Judge is at the door. And then besides this peace with all men, what an emphatic testimony is here given to the indispensableness of our being holy before God. This holiness is that, without which—the *without* referring to the holiness singly and apart from the peace—without which no man shall see God. O Lord, let me be diligent in keeping my heart and in turning my eyes from vanity, lest I fall short ; and the root of bitterness which Thou knowest to be in me, shall spring forth to my own grievous trouble and the defilement of many. This would indeed be selling my birthright to an eternal inheritance for a wretched morsel—sacrificing to the delight of a moment the good that is imperishable. Let me not be deceived, or think that under the economy of grace there are not terrors as appalling as were ever exhibited at the ushering in or under the economy of the law. It is true that the blood of sprinkling speaketh better things than the blood of Abel, yet like his will it cry for vengeance if I count it an unholy thing. God is a consuming fire to all who are out of Christ, and tenfold more so to those who, professing to be in Christ, name His name yet depart not from iniquity. The cloud of witnesses referred to at the beginning of the chapter is greatly reinforced

and added to in the end of it, for besides the spirits of
the just made perfect, we have the angels, and Jesus the
Mediator, and God the Judge of all. We have come not
to the visible Sinai, but to the unseen things of faith,
which should tell more powerfully upon us; and the voice
now not heard by the sensible but the spiritual ear, is that
which, besides shaking the earth as at the giving of the
Law, will shake the heavens also. O let me receive the
truth, not as by the mere reading of an article or a doctrine, but as by the hearing of a voice; and, my God,
give me grace to stand in awe and sin not, but serve
Thee acceptably with reverence and godly fear.

HEBREWS XIII.

Let this evidence of my having passed from death unto
life—even that I love the brethren—brighten more and
more in my heart and upon my character. Let this
brotherly love not only continue but increase with me;
and I do fear that I have been too suspicious of strangers,
and therefore not so mindful of, not so hospitable to them
as I ought to have been. Would I confide more I might
fall in with specimens of real Christianity that I would
otherwise exclude from my attentions and regards. Let
me think of my own liabilities to exile and suffering, and
lend a helping hand to those in adversity, specially if
they be of the household of faith. But O save me from
the wiles of that subtle adversary, who, transforming himself into an angel of light, can, under the guise of mine
being a Christian love, turn it into carnal licentiousness.
Save me from all filthiness of the spirit as well as of the
flesh. Give me a sound respect and observance for all the

hallowed virtues of domestic life, and save me from the covetousness which in Scripture stands so often allied with another vile affection. Let me not fear the artifices or attempts of grasping men, but trust in the living God who hath given me all things richly to enjoy. And O that a living Christ were more the object of my steadfast contemplation and faith and practical regards than a fluctuating Christianity. Would I but cultivate the habit of believing converse with Christ as a person, then through His grace and Spirit dwelling in me, there would be that element of unchangeableness within which would save me from the endless tossings and turnings of many a vain question, grounded on the too prevalent view of Christ not as a person but a doctrine. There is something very instructive in the contiguity of verses 8 and 9, and the contrast set forth by them. Let us seek for stability, not in the literalities of an outward observance, but in the spiritualities of the inner life, and the duties of moral and lasting obligation—as devotion to Christ and non-conformity with the world, and the spirit of pilgrims looking onward to and seeking after immortality, and thankful, joyful love to the God who first loved us: and over and above these unseen graces, let us practise the liberalities of Christian benevolence, making that sacrifice of selfishness which is pleasing to God; and let us obey, and remember, and generously aid in supporting, those who have the rule over us in the Lord. And O that I were more alive to the responsibility and the reckoning under which I lie for the souls of others, especially those of my own household. I pray for a good conscience and an honest procedure in this and in all things; and, O Lord, may I have the happiness of a fulfilment in the benediction

of the apostle. Make me perfect, O God. Turn me
to Thyself. May I walk worthy of Thee unto all well-
pleasing. And may I count it not enough that I pray
for these things, may I watch for them—nay, may I
work for them—and this with full respect to that blood
through which alone I can lift up a plea or prefer a cove-
nant-right for mercy, and with full respect to that Spirit
who alone can work in me to will and to do according to
Thy good pleasure. And so may Christ be all in all ;
and to Him be the entire glory ascribed both of the
redemption and sanctification of His followers.

JAMES.

JAMES I.—This is a truly delicious epistle !—may the
Lord improve the study of it for the good of my soul.
How precious its very first lesson, by which I am bidden
to rejoice when various trials come upon me : of these I
have more than my average share at this moment. May
I encounter all these in the spirit of faith, even a faith
that worketh patience : and may I do more than endure,
may I even welcome these tribulations in the spirit of
confidence in Him who is both a very present help in
the time of trouble, and a very present help in the time
of temptation. Let me roll all upon God ; and how urgently do I stand in need of the further admonition, that
my patience should be perfect and entire. And not only
do I lack patience, I lack wisdom ; and I hereby pray
most earnestly for guidance as well as grace from the Father of lights, and that He may give me liberally, without
upbraiding me for all my bygone waywardness. Increase

my faith, O God; give me singleness of eye; save me
from the vacillations of those who halt between the two
services of sin and of the Saviour; let me rejoice even in
the humiliations of defeat; let me endure these and all
other trials, for the joy that is set before me in the crown
of life which fadeth not away.—O my God, let me not be
deceived into the imagination of a resistless force in any
of the temptations which assail me, so as to ascribe them
to a power above and beyond myself. The evil thing to
be resisted is in me, and it is not the temptation but the
grace that resists and overcomes the temptation which
cometh from above. Let us look upward then for every
good and perfect gift, that our patience may be perfected,
that our faith may be perfected. Give me, O Lord, to
receive with meekness that word which, at the bidding of
Thy will and in the hands of Thy Spirit, can make a new
creature of me. Thou hast promised—and Thou art faithful and unchangeable and true to Thy word—Thou hast
promised Thy Holy Spirit to them who ask Him. In all
meekness and lowliness would I wait for His illapses, O
Lord. In this attitude let wrath be unknown. I am
miserably given to this in the contests of opinion respecting what is best for the Church's good; but it is not wrath
which worketh any good thing. O may the word sink
deep into my principles and purposes, that I may do it:
and in passive submission to God's word let my own
word, whether the word of dogmatism or resentment, be
kept under restraint; and let me feel the rebuke here laid
upon the unbridled utterances in which I have hitherto
indulged so loosely and so largely. Let me not be deceived, but give evidence of mine being a genuine Christianity by my charity and my holiness.

JAMES II.

December, 1845.

Let me abhor all partialities and preferences in things sacred. Let me look to man simply as man, and proceed on the essential equality of human souls. The respect of persons is one of the most grievous obstacles in the way of a universal scheme for the Christian education of the people. The judges here spoken of are they who make the evil thoughts of others the subjects or matters of their judgment, but who, because men of evil thoughts or evil affections, are evil-thinking and evil-inclined judges themselves. O my God, do Thou pour forth a larger and more liberal spirit on the ministers of our generation. Give them the zeal and the affection of real home missionaries; teach them to respect the Christian rights of the poor; and in all their devisings may the greatest amount of gospel instruction, with a view to the greatest amount of salvation, be their great and regulating principle. Teach me, O God, to love man as man; and above all endue me with a more intense and far more practical affection for human souls. Let me not fall into the transgression of neglecting the poor because poor—for this were a transgression of the second law; and though it should be only one instance, give me, O Lord, to feel the guilt and the danger of one known and allowed sin. Let mine be a universal obedience, or an obedience which fully and honestly aspires to this. Let me remember that though now emancipated from the law of ritual observances I am placed under the law of love, which is the law of liberty; and give me to feel, O God, that by even one transgression of this, because of Thy law, I am in fact an outlaw, and liable to the sentence of my offended Judge. More especially do I offend against the law of love, when I withhold mercy from the poor, and so will he be judged without mercy who showeth no mercy. Give me the blessedness of those that are merciful, in that they shall obtain mercy. Let me abjure all that security which Antinomians would associate with a faith without works. Though justified by faith alone, let me remember that it is not by faith being alone, or by a faith which is alone.—My God, may I show my faith by my works, and when tempted to the opposite of this, do Thou prove unto me a very present help in the time of temptation. Let not Satan prevail; may I resist him that he might flee from me. Save me from my besetting sin, O God, and let not any sin have the dominion over me. May I find an increase of my faith with every new act of obedience, and may that faith be perfected, or attain its end, or reach its proper consummation and landing-place, by working love, and yielding all the fruits of righteousness, so that I may both be justified by a faith yielding works, and stand a reckoning upon works produced by faith.

JAMES III.

These two verses in connexion are pre-eminently applicable to myself—not perhaps in that I have the mere ambition of rule, but that I have strong convictions of what is best for the government of the Church; and when these are thwarted I do give way to unbridled utterances of dissatisfaction and complaint. Could I but bridle my tongue I should be able to bridle my whole body.—Give me this perfection, O Lord, else my religion is vain. (ch. i. 26.) And O that I could restrain my effusions on every occasion, too, of real or conceived personal injury, and give up my cause in silence unto the Lord, committing myself to Him who judgeth righteously.—" Grudge not one against another, the Judge is at the door." I pray for the government of my tongue ; what mischief might ensue from its unchecked effusions !—Save me, O Lord, both from the anger which impels and the inconsideration that allows it free scope and indulgence. Give me more especially to feel the identity of the first and second laws. If I love God, how can I have but that love to my neighbour which worketh no ill ? O that I had the consistent and universal grace which would lead me to breathe congenially in the element of a universal love—such a love as would endure all things, and more especially the contradiction of my fellows ; and such a love, as superior to the feelings of provocation and resentment, would enable me to overcome all my adversaries by heaping coals of fire upon their head. Let me conquer by kindness and· humility ; and then shall I have part in the sayings— that he who humbleth himself shall be exalted, and that the meek shall inherit the earth. But to rectify the efflux let me rectify the fountain whence it proceeds ; or, in other words, keep my heart with all diligence, and so repress or make my escape from those broodings which are so apt to arise and tumultuate within me. O for the meekness of wisdom—it cometh only from above. The tongue, it is said, no man can tame. The impellent force that gives rise to all its unruly ebullitions no man can subdue ;—but all things are possible with God.—Save me from strife and envying. It is not the wrath of man which can work out the cause of truth or righteousness : Thou knowest, my God, how grievously I err in this department of my affairs. Let me know how to combine firmness with gentleness, and how so to conduct myself as that no man shall despise me, and yet that all my things shall be done with charity. May I have the blessing of the peace-maker; and as much as lieth in me live peaceably with all men. O that I could make escape at all times from the thoughts which irritate and disquiet me, or bid them away at pleasure from my heart. I long for retirement—I long for quietness. My God, let me have more of converse with Thyself as I lessen my converse with my fellows. Give me, if it be Thy blessed will, an old age of piety and peace, yet of Christian usefulness withal. O that I were endowed with more of self-command; but what I chiefly want is the charity of the gospel, for were this within me in sufficient strength it would enable me to endure all things.

JAMES IV.

These need not be the fightings of ordinary war, but the fightings of civil or ecclesiastical debate—the war of opinions in regard to the best management, whether of a Church or of a commonwealth. I have had much to exercise and try me in this sort of controversy, and I would do well to search with all vigilance and jealousy, and see whether there be not the pride and the heart-burnings of a rivalship for any sort of distinction or superiority which do insensibly mingle with the operation of better and brighter motives in my proposals for the good of any of our institutes. I do hope that there is not much to soil the patriotism of my efforts for the Christian and educational wellbeing of my countrymen; yet lest there should, let me pray, and pray aright, not for the victory of my own will and way over that of others, but for the establishment of what is really most beneficial and best. Let me not give in because of the overwhelming majorities opposed to me. Let me make no surrender of God's cause in compliance with men who seek ease or emolument, whether for their neighbours or themselves. Let me not for the sake of their friendship betray any right principle or any right expediency, the adoption of which were conducive to the spread and furtherance of the gospel. O let me act on and avail myself of the precious encouragement here given to cast myself with all submission and in all humility upon God. It is one of the Bible's weightiest sentences—that He resisteth the proud and giveth grace unto the humble. Let me carry it with all humility both towards Him and to my fellows ; and cleansing both hand and heart from everything evil, let me draw near unto God in dependence on the gracious promise that He will draw near unto me, to guide me by His wisdom, to quicken me by His Spirit. Give me singleness of eye, O Lord, simplicity and steadfastness of purpose ; and if I am to be in darkness or despondency for a season, let me commit to God, who is best judge of the due time for it, the care of my deliverance and at length my exaltation. Above all, let me commit my grievances unto the Lord in silence, without casting blame or obloquy upon others. The Judge is at the door ; grudge not therefore the one against the other. And let me refrain from boasting.—Have I never spoken too confidently and too exultingly of the prospects both of the Free Church and of the West Port Mission ? O that I could in every calculation admit as the overruling and indispensable element—the will of God. I desire to walk softly, and to think soberly, and to maintain a habitual reference to Him who, if not acknowledged and not sought after, will stamp an impressive mockery on all our swelling anticipations. Let me empty myself, that all grace might be poured upon me out of the fulness of Christ. Let me be a fool that I may become wise.

JAMES V.

Should riches increase let me not set my heart upon them, but act as a faithful steward of the good which has been entrusted to me. O may these riches be so used as that they shall witness for and not against me; and forbid that in the treasuring up of them I should be treasuring up wrath upon myself in the last days. Give me to be merciful, and save me from that love of pleasure which is opposite to the love of God. And O that mine eyes waited more for Him, and that His love were shed abroad in my heart. I would both pray with importunate perseverance, and yet wait with patience. O let my hope and my affections be centred on the Lord Jesus Christ; and may I not be weary nor faint in the keeping of His words, that to me He may manifest Himself. What need I have—what imminent and humiliating need—both to watch and to pray for the regulation, or better, the extinction, of that wayward, headlong, and tumultuous propensity to grudge against my fellows, more especially against those with whose views and practices I have to come into conflict in the management of our public affairs. Let me commit myself unto Him who is the Judge of all, and the day of whose final awards is coming so speedily.—O my

God, forgive the ebullitions of my resentful impatience, in the fresh recollection of one of which that occurred but three days ago, I now feel a sore compunction. And, meanwhile, let me be patient in the thought that a day of clear understanding and settlement is at hand. O that till that time comes I had the grace of endurance—satisfied with the utterance of my testimony for what I think right, and not thrown into a state of violent or agonizing disappointment, because the testimony has failed of success. And let my utterances be given forth with perfect temper and calmness—they will be all the more impressive if they are so. I may not attempt to enforce them by an oath, but neither should I enforce them with undue vehemence; better than this were the simple deliverance of yea, yea, or nay, nay. May such be my deportment to my fellows; and whatever my state of temperament or affection may be at the time, let me give a sacred direction to it, going with it to God—in prayer when I am sad—in aspirations of gratitude when I am joyful. Let me both intercede for others and crave the intercessions of the faithful for myself. I stand urgently in need : I have committed many offences—the good Lord forgive them all. O give me the faith that availeth for the success of prayer; and also give me, good Lord, the humility and frankness to make the penitential avowal of my faults in the hearing of those whom I have injured or offended. O that I were privileged to save a soul from death. There is one dear friend whom I have attempted to convert from the errror of his way.—My God, aid and direct me in the next attempt which I purpose making soon. Guide my heart and my pen to such words as shall prove to be words in season and of power.

I. PETER.
January, 1846.

1 PETER I.—I pray for faith as the gift of God, and as that which is exceeding precious—being indeed that which availeth. (Gal. v. 6.) And O that my election were made sure to me by my palpable sanctification through grace, and by the peace of my conscience through the sprinkling thereupon of the blood of Christ.—And believing that God hath raised Him from the grave, may I have the well-grounded hope of salvation. (Rom. x. 9.) May I experience the power of faith in sanctifying and saving me; and laying hold on eternal life may I link therewith all my joy and all my expectation.—Let this sustain and lighten me amidst all the darkness of this world's adversities. May the consideration of Him who is the Apostle and High-Priest of my profession, (Heb. iii. 1,) inspire me with love and gladness, and an elevating sense of superiority to the ills and crosses of my journey here below, even till I receive, as the end of my faith, the salvation of my soul. And let me no longer lightly esteem those things which even the angels desire to look into: and O that such high and heavenly contemplations were followed up by a suitable and corresponding practice. May the hopes of the gospel purify, (1 John iii. 3,) and may they sober me. Enable me, O Lord, to dismiss my evil lusts, and to be holy in all manner of conversation. Let me be careful to maintain good works, for by works I am judged. And O what an argument for holiness, to think of the quality of that by which we are redeemed—even the blood of Christ, as of a lamb without spot and blemish—foreordained from all eternity by God, and now

manifested for us. Let us make the required use of this manifestation. The object of it is that our faith and hope might be in God. The predestination is God's—the revelation, with all its lessons and influences, is ours. Let us yield obedience to the truth thus made known to us ; and the effect will be love, not only to God in whom we trust, but to the children of God, the love of whom is like unto the love of the Father. O may that word which endureth impress—which it can only do through the Spirit, (verse 22)—those doctrines by the faith of which I am saved ; and thus, with the Holy Ghost as the agent and the Bible as the instrument, shall I be born again. Let me give all diligence then to the study of its precious contents ; and let the effort be animated by prayer, that to me it may be a life-giving word, forming me into a new creature. And what a seasonable reflection for this first Sabbath of the year is that of the apostle on the evanescence of all flesh. The glory of man is perishable —it is the glory, as it is the word of God, which alone abideth everlastingly. Wean me, O God, from a world which passeth away, and all the lust thereof.—Give me to do Thy will, that I may abide for ever. (1 John ii. 17.)

I. PETER II.

Enable me, O God, to lay aside all the evils which are here enumerated, and more especially evil-speaking ; and as a babe is nourished by milk, so may I be nourished by Thy word. Give me to drink the milk of consolation, and taste that the Lord, even Jesus Christ, is indeed gracious. May He no longer be to me but a dead or nominal doctrine, but a living Head, in whom I have life, and by whom I am enabled to offer up acceptable spiritual sacrifices. O may I be built into and form part of that spiritual temple whereof He is the chief corner-stone. Let me cherish a full reliance upon Him, for then I shall not be disappointed or put to shame ; and to me, O God, may He be exceedingly precious, and His name like ointment poured forth. O may I never be offended in Christ ; but as one of His peculiar people, called out of darkness into His marvellous light, may I show forth His praise and adorn His doctrine in all things. Let a sense of the mercies of God constrain me to present my body a living sacrifice to the living God, and thus prove to the world what the acceptable and perfect will of God is.

And let the first fruit of this sacrifice be a crucifixion of the flesh—a denial of self in those evil affections which war against the soul. Thus may I by this and other good works shine before men, and so as that they may be led to glorify God ; and may I live peaceably with all men—in particular, with men of authority and office—by demeaning myself as a quiet, and orderly, and obedient subject before them ; and whatever I do in this way let me do it from a religious principle and for the Lord's sake—thus blending my loyalty to the sovereign with the operation in my heart of both the first and the second law. Thus shall I combine the honouring of all men and love to them of the household of faith, with loyalty to the king and the fear of God.

Forgive my impatience, O Lord, when made the subject of any wrongous infliction, whether by word or deed. When suffering injustice let me know what it is quietly to commit myself to Him who judgeth righteously. May I think what Christ hath suffered for me in spite of all my neglect and provocations. Let me not be satisfied with believing in what He did. May I do as He did. What a trial of my faith—when reviled to revile not again! Bridle, O God, this impetuous and ungovernable tongue of mine—else my religion is vain. The Judge is at the door; and by Him all questions will be soon and right-eously settled. Let us follow His blessed example who abstained from all threatening; and on the great day of our atonement suffered Himself to be led like a lamb unto the slaughter. The single clause of—" by whose stripes we were healed," carries us back to the fifty-third chapter of Isaiah, and tells us that when He bore our sins in His body on the tree, it was a penal death which He endured, for then He bore the chastisement of our peace.

I. PETER III.

There is a lesson here for husbands as well as wives. Let my conversation be such, O God, as shall win souls to Christ. Give me, too, the ornament of a meek and quiet spirit; and let me here see the value which God has for character irrespective of what may be called its mercantile worth, or as an equivalent for heaven in the light of what we had earned and won a right to by our obedience. This is utterly excluded by the constitution of the gospel; but while the mercantile worth of all our virtues put together is of no account or estimation whatever in the balance of the sanctuary, yet is their moral worth as highly reckoned and had respect to by God as ever. And accordingly this ornament of a meek and quiet spirit is in His sight of great price. O direct and enable me to honour, and so to live with her whom I am commanded thus to do—that we

may walk together as heirs of the grace of life, and that
our prayers may not be hindered. And let these social
virtues have a wider scope than within the limits of my
household ; let them go forth upon all with whom I have
intercourse in society. Teach me to bridle my tongue,
and be courteous unto all—to be patient under calumny
and injustice, and cherish all the kindly and compassionate feelings of a nature renewed after the image of Him
who, when He was reviled, reviled not again. And what
an example for us to follow when suffering wrong—to commit ourselves unto Him who judgeth righteously. These
are high but they are also indispensable virtues for every
Christian, and we see that the Judge who is above takes
the same cognizance of them, and makes the same distinction between the good and the evil under the new dispensation as under the old. O that we were fully unfettered from all which has the effect of distorting and
deranging the Christianity of the Bible in the artificial
systems of human orthodoxy. Let us learn from verses 15
and 16, that we shall have no reason of the hope that is in
us without a good conscience. There must be the answer
of a good conscience towards God ere we can hope for our
own individual salvation—not as having yet attained to
all obedience, but as now willing and resolved in the
strength of divine grace to prosecute all obedience, even
unto perfection. And let us never separate what God
hath joined. Let us ever be looking in faith to the truths
of objective Christianity, as well as steady to maintain
a good conscience in the things of subjective Christianity.
In particular, let us ever fix our eye upon Christ as the all
in all of our judicial righteousness before God, without
which we should never have been brought nigh. In con-

forming ourselves to His death, let us put away the filth
of the flesh; and let us be saved by His resurrection
through the quickening of that Spirit wherewith He can
subdue all things unto Himself.

I. PETER IV.

Resolve me, O God, against all sin, and help me to put
on the whole armour of God, that I may achieve the victory
over it—seeing that by the crucifixion of the flesh, by its
being made to suffer even unto death, sin is ceased from,
because sin is destroyed. Thus do we become conformable
to Him who suffered and died for us; and thus do we
live no longer to our own lusts, but to the will of God.—
My God, enable me to renounce all the deeds and devices
of the old man, and to break from every sinful conformity
with a world lying in wickedness and ungodliness. It is
a small thing to be judged of man's judgment: He who
judgeth me, and to whom I must shortly give an account,
is God. And seeing that the day of reckoning is at hand,
let me be sober, watchful, prayerful—having respect at all
times to Him in whose presence I am so soon to appear.
And give me charity, O Lord. I think myself to have
been injured and misused by certain persons, both in regard to the matters of the Church and to my own private
concerns. Give me the charity that will throw a veil over
this, and that will also restrain me from all transgression
of that law of love which worketh no ill to one's neighbour. O that my hospitalities were more subservient to
the good of edification, and that I grudged not the expense of those offerings by which real good might be done
either to the souls or the bodies of men. And whatever

I do let me remember that I have nothing which I did
not receive : whether it be wealth, or influence, or talent,
all is from God, and from His manifold grace, and for the
right use of which all who enjoy them are responsible.
How it would chasten a vain complacency in our own
ministrations did we but minister as the stewards of God.
Help me, O Lord, to have paramount respect unto Thy
glory at all times.   I am so fearfully deficient in these
higher spiritualities that I may require heavier judgments to discipline me into these than have ever yet fallen
upon me.   However severe and however unjust, let me
not look on it as strange.   It is a mighty alleviation to
sufferings of all sorts when made to feel that they are but
the common lot of humanity, and still more the common
lot of the faithful, appointed in wisdom and love for their
trial and their growth in grace.   We should thus rejoice
in the midst of tribulations, committing our cause to Him
who judgeth righteously, taking care that we thus commit
ourselves to Him in well-doing. (ch. ii. 20.)   Let the spirit
of glory rest upon us.   Let our religion impart to us an
elevation and a sense of its greatness.   Let such be our
knowledge and understanding of God as to make us feel
that in being called by Him we have been called to glory
and to virtue.   And O what a consideration it is, what a
warning and argument for our utmost strenuousness in
the divine life, our highest efforts and aspirations after
the excellencies of the gospel, to be told, as we are here,
that the righteous shall scarcely be saved.   Judgment
begins with the Church, and ends with the world.   Let
me flee from that world, and from all ungodliness, that I
may not rank with them who obey not the gospel of God.
But O may I forget not that though naming the name of

Christ, and in the bonds of the covenant, I must be careful to maintain good works—careful, and that to the uttermost, in departing from all iniquity.

I. PETER V.

Burntisland, February, 1846.

Give me, O Lord, an assured hope of the coming glory ; and grant that with this hope I may purify myself even as Christ is pure. And O endow me with an ardent and disinterested affection for human souls. Deliver me from the power of covetousness, and let what I do in Thy service be done spontaneously, and from an inner principle of godliness—not for filthy lucre. Save me also from the love of power ; and O grant that my light may shine before men. Let me have a perpetual respect unto Christ as my Judge, and that I may stand before Him with acceptance grant that now He may be the Bishop and the Shepherd of my soul. And O that I were clothed with humility—humbling myself before God, and humbling myself also before men, and might receive in consequence both a present grace and a future exaltation in God's own time and way. Let me cultivate the precious and peace-giving habit of casting all my care upon God, and in the confidence that He cares for me ; but while looking upwardly to Him with full assurance of heart, let me not forget the vigilance, the caution, the self-command—the necessity for all which is so obvious when I look around me among the temptations of the world, and consider the power and skill of him who is the god of the world. God may destine me for sufferings during the remainder of this my journey ; avert it, if so be Thy blessed will, O God ; yet if needs be, let me be sustained by the glory that followeth the comparatively light afflictions of the present life. The Captain of salvation was made perfect through sufferings, and so perhaps may I.—My God, I pray for the wisdom that may preserve, and for the fortitude that will bear me up under all which Thou mayest have appointed for me. Let me be steadfast in the faith. Let me stand in the true grace of God, my Father in heaven, to whom I would ascribe all power and glory everlasting. Give me, O Lord, a pure and holy affection for all the brethren in Christ Jesus; and in Him may I have peace, though in the world I shall have tribulation.

II. PETER.

2 PETER I.—A truly rich and precious chapter, beginning with the mention of a precious faith—a faith obtained by men, and so given by God, (Eph. ii. 8); and the object of which is the righteousness that the Father will accept, and which the Son hath brought in. May I obtain this faith, O Lord, and that knowledge of God and of Jesus Christ the fruit of which is peace, and all the privileges of the Christian salvation. Call me, O Lord, to glory and to virtue; make me a partaker in the great and precious promises of the gospel—more especially of that godly nature which ever strives against the flesh, and secures our escape from its corruptions by securing for us the mastery over them. There is assuredly nothing in the faith of the gospel that should supersede our diligence. On the contrary, we are required to give all diligence, and this for the purpose of making additions to our faith.

And how precious the additions are which are here set
forth. Give me to realize, O Lord, this fair and lovely
assemblage of graces ; and more especially those of which
I stand most in need, as being opposed to the sins that
most easily beset me—the temperance, the patience, the
godliness.—Thus may I abound in the fruits of righteousness ; and knowing these things may I make good the
happiness of those who do them. Let me not prove by
my lack of Christian obedience, and of all its virtues, that
I see but a little way into the design of the great Christian economy under which I sit—to make me perfect in
character, and deliver me from all my old sins, and furnish
me thoroughly for all good works. It is by giving diligence, in fact, to make sure of these things, that I give
diligence to make my calling and election sure, for if I do
these things I shall never fall away—but both justified by
faith and judged by works shall have the " Well done,
good and faithful servant," pronounced upon me, and so
be taken up with abundant entrance into heaven. But O
my God, how miserably behind am I still.—Perfect that
which concerns me. I need to be constantly kept in
remembrance of these things, for unless I do keep them
in memory, nay, and proceed on them, my knowledge
is vain, my belief is vain. (1 Cor. xv. 2.) Let me be so
stablished in the truth as that I shall persevere and
walk in the truth. (2 John, 4 ; 3 John, 4.) What a sure
guide Scripture is, and how noble the testimony of Peter,
who tells us that faith in Christ as made known to us by
the word is a safer and better guide than the sight of
Christ as revealed in glorious and supernatural visions.
What reason then had Peter to feel the importance of
taking measures for perpetuating among his disciples the

knowledge and remembrance of these things—an endeavour which was carried into accomplishment by those precious additions that he himself made, as an instrument of God's Spirit, to the word of prophecy. Let us give earnest heed then unto this word—and how long?—till the day dawn and the day-star arise in our heart, which of itself, indeed, is a very dark place, but which God, who commandeth the light to shine out of darkness, will shine into if we but hearken diligently unto him, and wait for the promised manifestations that come, yet come through the Scripture from on high. What an attitude both of exertion and expectancy is here prescribed to us—the exertion of all our faculties in the perusal of God's holy word, yet the expectancy of that Spirit from above who alone can open our understandings to understand it; for He who inspired the writers must also enlighten the readers of the Bible—who must be guided not by their own private interpretations, but by the revelation of the Spirit through the word, even as the inspired penmen were guided in the original construction of that word not by their own will, but wrote as they were moved and directed by the Holy Ghost. The patent way to a saving illumination is the persevering and prayerful reading of the Bible.

II. PETER II.

Let me not underrate the mischief of heresies, and particularly those which relate to the person and work of the Saviour. To deny the doctrine of the atonement is to deny that He bought us. There is a more direct moral offence in the merchandise which these false teachers practised on the victims of their delusions. Save me, O God,

from the love of filthy lucre; and also keep me sound in
the faith. But, O my God, how much is there in this
passage of Scripture to touch me with conviction and
seriously to alarm me!—Let me reflect on the severity of
God: He delivers the godly out of their trials, but where
is my practical and ascendant godliness, and have I the
abhorrence that Lot had against the licentiousness by
which he was surrounded? Do rivers of water run down
my eyes because men have forsaken Thy law?—My God,
where is my sensitive recoil from evil thoughts and evil
imaginations? and where the habit or the principle that
would lead me to make it a duty and matter of strict and
watchful conscientiousness that I should shun all the sights
and influences which tend to inflame the passions and
pollute the heart? Let me recollect the historical evidences of God's inflexible opposition to all that is evil,
and take the lesson suggested by those fears or those
movements of conscience and recollection which either
Thy word or Thy providence may have awakened. Henceforth I would fear alway, so as not only to abstain from
all impurity, whether speculative or practical, but also
from any impetuous or froward invectives against rulers
and public men. Make me both humble and holy, O
God. What an awful description of the moral helplessness of men—" that their eye cannot cease from sin!" Let
me enjoy the comfort, O Lord, that though I feel the
motions of the flesh I walk not after the flesh. But I
must aim at more than this—even to check the first motions, to keep my heart with all diligence, to turn my
sight and eyes from viewing vanity, to glorify the Lord
with my soul and spirit as well as my body, which are the
Lord's. Give me above all things, O Lord, most carefully

to abstain from giving offence to Thy little ones. Let me never forget the awful judgments denounced upon those who vitiate the hearts or the principles of others. Give me, O Lord, to feel the danger of backsliding; and do Thou not only spread a veil over all my past iniquities, but save me, save me from ever relapsing, else the latter end will be greatly worse than the beginning. Let me recollect the desperate and irrecoverable condition of those who fall away—insomuch that the call for vigilance is as great in advanced as in early life. Save me from a false security, or from thinking that I shall stand or keep my ground independently of earnest heed or habitual prayer. Let me from this time forward start on a resolute course of self-command and the careful avoidance of all that can either pollute or secularize me. May I thus realize the habit of prayer without ceasing, and of working out my own salvation with fear and trembling, yet in dependence on Him who worketh in me both to will and to do.

II. PETER III.

Newliston.

Let not knowledge suffice, or faith suffice. I must keep in remembrance, and call to remembrance, the truth by which I am saved, else I have believed in vain. (1 Cor. xv. 2.) Let me be ever mindful of that system and body of truth, which is built on the foundation of the Apostles and Prophets, Christ Himself being the chief corner-stone. Make me aware, O God, of the danger of these latter times. Let me not fall asleep in the false security of a constant and imperishable nature, to the exclusion or disownal of Him who seeth the end from the beginning, and to whom the mighty periods of this world's history are

but the brief evolutions or stages of a progression that will
see out the present economy of things—at length to pass
away and be replaced by the higher and better economy
of those new heavens and that new earth, wherein dwelleth
righteousness.   Let me look with intent earnestness, and
busy preparation for it, to the day of the coming of the
Lord.   Let me flee from the coming wrath to the hope
set before me in the gospel.   Let the goodness of God,
not willing that any should perish, lead me to repentance ;
or, if not drawn by the force of this consideration, let me
be driven by the terrors of that dissolution which is to
come on the materialism now around us.   If not saved
with compassion let me be saved with fear—the terrors
and threatenings of Thy law shutting me up unto the
faith of Thy gospel.   Let me prepare for the land of uprightness by a life of uprightness.   Let me qualify for the
everlasting habitation by cultivating even now the spirit
or the principle which dwelleth there.   Let me be diligent to attain the immaculate character of Paradise, that
I may be fitted for its joys.   And let the very God of
peace sanctify me wholly, so as that I may be found unblamable and unreprovable in the great day of reckoning.   God hath indeed suffered long with me: He hath
spared me to the evening of life.   Let me make no further tarrying, O God ; and save me from the doctrinal speculations which would mislead from practice, or at all stifle
and overbear the urgencies that should lead to an active
prosecution of the new obedience of the gospel.   Save me
from the errors of transcendentalism in Theology ; and
uphold my feet in that plain though narrow path which
leadeth to life everlasting.   Give me, O Lord, to persevere
with steadfastness in the faith and holiness of the gospel.

Let me not hold it enough that I grow in knowledge, give me also to grow in grace—remembering that I have not the real knowledge of our Lord and Saviour Jesus Christ if I do not His commandments. (1 John ii. 4.) Let me not then be led away. Let me not fall into sin by falling into the error of those wicked men who, under the guise of evangelism, practise, if they do not profess, a deceitful Antinomianism. May I, on the contrary, adorn in all things the doctrine of the Saviour. May He be magnified in my body and in the whole conduct of my present life. May His glory be manifested now through my abounding in much fruit, and may I be preferred hereafter to the celebration of His glory among the choirs and companies of the celestial. Thus now and ever may He be the theme of my highest praise, that Christ might be magnified in my life, magnified in my death, and magnified in my resurrection and final blessedness through all eternity. Amen, amen.

I. JOHN.

March, 1846.

1 JOHN I.—We again meet with John the apostle, and can perfectly recognise his identity with John the evangelist, his gospel and his epistles being marked by the same intensity of feeling, the same depth of sentiment, which breaks forth, not into argument like Paul for the object of producing conviction, but into strenuous asseveration—the product of a conviction already felt, and by which a kindred feeling is awakened, and on the strength of internal evidence and the inherent power of truth, most

legitimately awakened in the heart of the reader. And so he lays on his testimony to the reality of Christ the whole force which lies in the concurrence of all the senses. Life is said to be in Him at the beginning of the gospel, but here He is termed the Life itself—eternal life, which, O my God, I desire to lay hold of, even by laying hold of Him —for he who hath the Son hath life, and he who hath not the Son hath not life. May I know what it is, O God, to have fellowship with the Father and with the Son ; and O that I knew with whom of Thy spiritual family upon earth I could hold fellowship. How marvellously little I enjoy of what may be called social religion, or the sympathy of mind with mind, each actuated by the common faith and love of the gospel. May the light of the upper sanctuary beam directly upon my soul. In God's own light may I clearly see light. Make me glad, O Lord, by the shining of Thy countenance upon me ; and give me even now a foretaste of that fulness of joy which is at Thy right hand, of those pleasures which are for evermore. But there is a walk associated with, nay preparatory to, this high spiritual illumination. Direct me, O God, to this walk, and uphold me therein—a walk of truth and uprightness and perfect openness, so that my moderation and other virtues might be known unto all men—a great step, one should imagine, to a day-light fellowship with those of my own kind, and conjoined in this blessed chapter with a higher fellowship. There is a remarkable concurrence of two affirmations in these verses, out of which a most important doctrinal conclusion might be drawn. If we walk in darkness we lie, and yet if we say that we sin not we lie. There are sinful motions of the flesh, even with those who walk not after the flesh. The children of light do in this world sin, but sins unto death are different from the spots of God's children. For the blotting out of these, there must be a daily recurrence to that blood which cleanseth from all sin, and cleanseth thoroughly.—My God, let me be thus cleansed: and O what a provision has been made for the repentant sinner's confidence, in that beside the mercy of God we, on the strength of Christ's death and righteousness, have the faithfulness and justice of God to appeal to. Let me flee then into this haven of perfect security; let it be my refuge and my hiding-place at all times. Forgive and cleanse me, O God; cleanse me alike from guilt and from pollution—and ward off sin and Satan from my soul. Let me no longer be deceived by the imagination of any strength or sufficiency in myself; but let me look up to the very God of peace, that He may sanctify me wholly, and that henceforth I may put off the unfruitful works of darkness, and put on the armour of light.

I. JOHN II.

It says everything for the morality even of the most peculiar doctrines of the gospel—that those stated in the last chapter are here said to have been written in order that we might sin not. Yet with all our strenuousness against sin, we do sin; and so Jesus must be ever and anon resorted to as our advocate with the Father; and let no one scruple to confide in Him as such, seeing that He is set forth as an offered propitiation for the sins of the whole world. But, again, we have not the saving knowledge of Christ if we keep not His commandments—insomuch that without this obedience we utterly deceive ourselves in thinking that we know or believe of Him aright. The decisive test of our being in favour is the love that we bear to Him.—O shed abroad this love in my heart ; let me abide in Christ that He may abide in me, and cause me to abound in much fruit, and then shall I conform to my profession, and do as I say—by walking as He walked. How the privileges and the precepts of Christianity alternate the one with the other in this rich passage !—One of the most illustrious of these precepts is the love of the brethren—no new commandment in respect of its obligation, not even in respect of its delivery in a written law, for we have it expressed in Lev. xix. 18 ; but new in respect of motive and the enforcing power of that truth which now shines upon the world in the blessed doctrine of Jesus Christ—even that He hath given Himself for us an offering and a sacrifice to God. Let us walk in love then, as Christ also hath loved us ; and save me, O God, from the hatred of any one—whatever his provocations or injurious usage might be. Let the babes in Christ rejoice in the forgiveness of which I have now written, and in the freshness of their first and early love to the Father in heaven now reconciled to them. Let the young men in Christ rejoice in the walk and work of that obedience of which I have also written, and wherein they have as yet gone on so prosperously. Let the Fathers in Christ bear witness along with me of what they have seen and heard, whether in His own person or the works and testimonies of His immediate followers, that we may rejoice together in that fellowship of which I have written, even the fellowship of our common recollections and common faith. These things have I written that their joy might be full, and let them joy accordingly. But let them

love not the world—for all its special affections are opposite to the love of Him who made the world.   The doing
of His will is both the evidence and the strengthener of
this love.   Let me work assiduously that I may love fervently—not slothful in business, but fervent in spirit,
serving the Lord.

O God, may an unction from the Holy One preserve
me from all the errors and perverse tendencies of the
present day.—More especially let me honour the Son
even as I honour the Father.   Let me continue in fellowship with both, keeping a fast hold of the promise of
eternal life; and this will best mortify the lusts of a
world that passeth away.   And O for the anointing which
remaineth—the teaching that cometh not from man nor
by man, but by the Holy Ghost—not only to impart
truth to our souls, but also the life and principle of all
acceptable obedience.   May we be like unto Christ, and
then shall we have confidence in the day of judgment.
Let us so do the righteousness which He did that we may
know of our regeneration, and so have a hope that maketh
not ashamed.

I. JOHN III.

Shed abroad Thy love in my heart: give me power to
become one of Thy sons: bid me stretch forth the
withered hand to lay hold of Christ as my elder brother,
that I may be one of Thine own peculiar people, known
and chosen of God, however unknown or misunderstood
by the world.   By looking unto God we are made like unto
God; and when we shall see Him as He is, or face to face
in heaven, then shall our likeness be perfected.   Let us
raise our upward regards to Him now; let us look unto

Jesus, that in proportion to our clear view of Him even
here we may even here be impressed by a resemblance;
and cherishing the hope of that resemblance being com-
pleted in heaven, may we meanwhile purify ourselves
even as He is pure. Without this there is in us neither
a genuine hope nor genuine faith. By the law is the
knowledge of sin; and seeing that Christ was manifested
to take away sin, let us never understand this high function of His but in the most comprehensive sense of it, as
taking away both the guilt of sin and its power. The
whole effect of our abiding in Him is to make us abstain
from sin. The whole effect of our seeing Him in whom
is no sin, is to expel sin from ourselves; so that in as far
as we sin it is because then we are not abiding in Him—
then we are not looking to Him. If we do righteousness
genuinely and truly, we shall do it in the spirit of an
honest endeavour after all righteousness, a resolute warfare against all sin; else our righteousness is not like
unto His, for in Him there was no sin. Sin comes from
another source than from the Son of God, who came to
destroy the works of him who is the agent and the fountain-head of evil. Whatsoever is born of God leadeth not
to sin—that germ will yield no such fruit; it cannot
from its very nature, and the quality of Him from whom
it sprung. And thus are the two classes of men—the
children of God and the children of him who is the father
of lies—discriminated from each other. Righteousness
and love, or the want of them, are the specific marks.—My
God, open my heart on this day, and amid my present
special occasions, to the love of my brethren. And let
me not confine this affection to believers: Christ laid
down His life for us when we were enemies. Let me

strive, then, to love even the whole of mankind—man as man; and give me, O Lord, to abound more and more in that affection for all, and specially for the household of faith, which constitutes an evidence so palpable of our having passed from death unto life. What a condemnation is here pronounced upon hatred! what a capital punishment awaits him in whom it abideth!—O my God, let me be compassionate to the needy, and ever act on the inseparable alliance which obtains between the love of God and the love of our neighbour. Save me from every subtle delusion. O may I act in a present urgent affair so as that my heart shall not condemn me and I have confidence in God. I ask for wisdom to guide me on this special occasion; and I ask for the ever-enduring principle of charity. Enable me by grace to keep these blessed commandments—even to believe in Thy Son, and to have love for His disciples, as also for all men. Let me weather this trial; and give me therein, O God, the triumph and the victory. And what a truly noble consummation if, as the result of it, I can verify the mutual inhabitation of Christ in me and me in Christ, and say with the apostle—that we know that He abideth in us, even by the Spirit which He hath given us.

I. JOHN IV.

This is a truly precious chapter. Let me not overlook any of its separate lessons—as Christ's atonement for us by suffering in the flesh, and the Spirit's power in us, by which we are enabled to overcome the world, and attain the mastery over him who is the god of this world—the spirit that worketh in the children of disobedience. Give me, O Lord, the spiritual discernment which cometh from above, whereby I might distinguish the true from the counterfeit, and have that saving knowledge of God and Christ which is life everlasting. But there is a pervading and predominant lesson which stamps its leading peculiarity on this whole passage—the priority of God's love to us, and in our own moral nature the priority of our faith in God's love of us to our love of Him back again. It was not because we loved Him, but because God loved us, that He sent His Son into the world a propitiation for sin. O let us know and believe this. (verse 16.) Let us look on God as love; let the barriers of our hard and sluggish unbelief at length give way; let us see God as He is, and then shall we feel to Him as we ought. Our love will follow in the train of our faith, without which indeed God's love to us would be as powerless in calling forth any response of gratitude as if it were a nonentity. It is no reality to us but by our belief that it is real, and then does the faith of verse 16 work in us the love of verse 19—we love God because He first loved us. Perfect this love in me, O God, that I may look without dismay to the awards of the coming judgment, and this because of my consciousness that as God is love so am I animated and possessed by this blessed spirit of charity. Thus may I be freed from the fear of terror, while the fear of deepest reverence remains with me. But let me not forget the test and the evidence of my love to God—even that I love my brethren of mankind. Save me from self-deceit or delusion in this matter, O God; and let me not count it enough that I love as the world does—love them who love me. True, I should love God because He loved me; but the love of man to me ought not to be the pre-requisite to my love of him. It may be to the love of gratitude, and his virtues may be indispens-

able to my love of moral esteem for him; but neither
should be waited for, that I may have towards him the
love of kindness or the love of compassion—even that
very love wherewith God loved sinners who were yet His
enemies, when He sent His Son to seek and to save them.
May such be my love to my fellow-men—a love that can
stand its ground against all their perversities, and all the
hostility or injustice which I may suffer at their hands.
Thus alone can I be perfect even as my Father in heaven
is perfect, who is kind to the unthankful and the evil, and
sendeth His rain on the just and on the unjust. Plant
within me, O God, this sacred and steadfast and enduring
charity—the love not of emotion but principle, watered
by the dew of heaven, and rooted and grounded within
me by the faith of the gospel.

I. JOHN V.

Let me not look on faith as an easy and natural exercise of the mind, seeing that one must be born of God ere
he can really believe that Jesus is the Anointed of God.
Give us, O Lord, to feel the identity both of the love and
the honour which we should render to Father and Son.
He who loveth the Father loveth the Son; he who honoureth the Son honoureth the Father. There is a love
for men in the flesh, and a love for them in the Lord—
the one a natural the other a gracious affection. (Philem.
16.) The same person might be the object of both; and
it may require therefore a discriminative test by which to
determine whether the love we bear to one has respect to
him as a child of God or a brother of the species. The
test is here given. If we love and obey God, then our

love to His children is to them as His children, which
does not at the same time exclude the other, it being a
grievous deformity of character when we are without natural affection. Let me not be deceived, O God, by counterfeit graces. Give us not a stone for a loaf, a scorpion
for an egg, a serpent instead of a fish. Enable us to test
aright our love to Thee by our obedience, and our love to
others by doing all and suffering all for their sake. And
let us experience the possibility, nay, the facility of our
Christian duties—not that in themselves they are within the reach of nature's performances or powers—but
that the strength which raised Jesus from the dead also
quickens and enables us for the whole work and warfare
of the Christian discipleship. Give us, O Lord, the faith
that overcometh. Give us to aspire after the whole of
Thine offered salvation—the atonement which is by the
blood of Jesus—the sanctification which is by the living
water of God's Holy Spirit. There is a perfect harmony
between the three elements—of our salvation from the
punishment; of our salvation from the power; and our
consequent salvation from all the defilements of sin. O
give me the inward witness—even a faith so vivid that I
may be conscious thereof. May I be effectually chidden
out of unbelief by the thought that I thereby affront
God, charging Him with falsehood. And O what a large
and free salvation is that for which He requires our faith
—even that He hath given us eternal life. How it brings
His glory and our greatest comfort to one!—And let me
ever look unto Him in whom my life is, and with a deep
sense of the alternative, that he who hath the Son hath
life; he who hath not the Son hath not life.

Let my faith grow exceedingly, each element thereof

acting upon another, each lower step advancing me to a higher one. Let this growth be alimented by prayer; and what an ample warrant for this, in that we might ask whatever is agreeable to the will of God. He wills me to be saved, and to come to the knowledge of the truth—(1 Tim. ii. 4)—nay, He wills this for all men. And yet there is a limit to our faith, if we see one to have sinned unto death; but not seeing this, and we have not the discernment of spirits which prevailed in those days, let us pray at a venture—let us intercede for all. For aught we know, he in whose behalf we pray may not be irrecoverable. Certain it is that whatsoever is born of God sinneth not, and whosoever is born of God sinneth not unto death. Keep us, O Lord, from the power of him who is the god of this world. Form Christ in us. May He the true God dwell in our hearts by faith. In the recognition of Him who is true, may we be preserved from all idolatrous homage to the things of sense and of time.

II. JOHN.

April, 1846.

2 John.—There is a love founded on a common appre-- hension of the truth between mind and mind, and a mutual acknowledgment of that truth in each other; but in counterpart to this there is an alienation of affection that takes place, when there arises the suspicion or imagination of an error, and, more particularly, when it amounts to the conception of a heresy. I believe that at this moment I labour under a suspicion of this sort; and I feel a consequent distrust and perhaps even dislike of me as the effect of it.—My God, give me to walk aright

under this visitation—to walk in the truth even when accused for dereliction of or hostility to the truth. Guide
my thoughts aright, and along with these my feelings and
my conduct aright. Let all things be done with charity,
even while I quit myself like a man. Give me, O Lord,
to experience in mind and heart the precious conjunction
of truth and love. Give me the unction that is from the
Holy One—the anointing which remaineth ; and then not
only shall the truth dwell in us and be with us for ever,
but we shall be grounded and settled in love—that first
and foremost of the Spirit's fruits. But let me not forget
that God's commandment is not barely that we should
walk aright, but in order to this, that we should walk in
truth. The commandment includes both the truth and
the walk. Give me, O Lord, the love of the truth that I
might be saved. How intimately love and truth are
blended together in this epistle !—we are commanded to
walk in truth—we are beseeched to love ; and this love
is said to lie in our walking after the commandments.
And all is here urged on the ground that error is abroad
—error so deadly as to involve in it the denial of Christ,
even amounting to its being an antichrist. To deny that
Christ came in the flesh is to deny the literal sacrifice
made by Him for the sins of the world—analogous to
the denial spoken of by Peter, regarding those who denied
the Lord that bought them. (2 Peter ii. 1.) This is a
damnable heresy ; and let us mark the reiterated testimony which the apostle gives as to the importance of
right doctrine—nay, the sanction which he confers—if not
on our hostility to, at least on our alienation from, all those
who bring not the right doctrine along with them. With
such there should be a suspension of all intercourse, at

least of all hospitality.   Give me, O Lord, to conduct myself aright amid these various elements and various considerations.   Let me not undervalue doctrine, and not only
seek earnestly, but contend earnestly for the faith once
delivered to the saints—else I may lose the things which
I have wrought, and fall short of a full reward.

III. JOHN.

Henderland.

3 JOHN.—To love in the truth is a counterpart to that
alienation which ensues on matters of doctrine, and which
when conceived to be vital, does give birth to a serious
estrangement between man and man.   If not in fancy
only but in fact vital, then this love in the truth does
legitimize, if we may so express it, we shall not say the
counterpart hatred, but the counterpart alienation that
often takes place on such a difference breaking out.   The
apostle, in his Christian love for Gaius, obviously wishes
him a prosperity distinct from spiritual prosperity; and
this gives a sanction to the value we feel, whether for
ourselves or others, in behalf of temporal things.   But,
my God, prosper me above all in spiritual things.   Give
health to my soul—spiritual health here, as the earnest
and preparation for my eternal wellbeing hereafter; and
as the fruit of a right state within, let all be right that is
visible in my walk and conversation.   Give me to walk in
the truth and to be faithful in all my doings, whether for
the Church at large or towards the individual members of
it.   And open my heart more than hitherto to those Christian visiters from a distance who come on their errands
of philanthropy.   Guide me aright in my attentions and

conduct towards such ; and let me forget not the hospitality
that is enjoined in another part of the New Testament.
O give me to feel my stewardship, and to act accordingly.
Let me lay out more than hitherto for the Lord Jesus,
and clear my way to a larger devotedness and liberality
than I have yet attained to.   Divest me of all love for
pre-eminence.   Let my efforts and aspirations be towards
God's glory and not my own.   In honour may I prefer
others, and be clothed with humility, without at the same
time letting any man despise me.   What have I that I
did not receive ; but what I have received let me lay out
for the good of others—not hiding my talent in a napkin.
Save me from the spirit of exclusiveness.   Make me
readily to acknowledge and receive Christians of all denominations, if satisfied that they are Christians indeed.
Let not my soul enter into the secret of those who, in
the spirit of an illiberal sectarianism, would reject the
approximations which are now making to a greater unity
both of sentiment and of outward profession than has
obtained in Christendom since the days of the Reformation.   There are some of our aspirants for ecclesiastical
distinction who, in this respect, too, would act the part
of Diotrephes, who would neither symbolize with those of
other denominations besides his own, nor allow others to
do so—and this, too, in the spirit of an ambition for pre-
eminence among those of his own narrow views.   Let me
rather, like Demetrius, and without sacrificing the truth
itself, study to have a good report of all men ; or, like
Gaius, cultivate the habit of charity to strangers.—My
God, Thou knowest what my infirmities are.   Help me
by Thy good Spirit, that I may not only be well reported
of men, but that my record may be on high.

JUDE.

JUDE.—With all my dislike of a certain ultraism in our Church, let me not forget the obligation of contending earnestly for the faith—one leading and pre-eminent article of which I hold to be justification by faith alone: and yet the first deviation from the faith which our apostle here specifies, and most dwells upon, is the converting of God's grace unto sin, as if the doctrine of our Saviour were not a doctrine according to godliness and all purity. No doubt the denial of Jesus Christ, whether in His person or work, is also noted; but what is chiefly insisted on is the practical abuse of gospel mercy. Preserve me from all such abuses, O God—from vile lusts, from covetousness, from insolence, whether in thought or speech, against the authorities whether of Church or State. They are probably the ecclesiastical dignities which are here referred to ; but how aptly may it often be said that in speaking evil of them we speak of what we know not, we meddle with matters too high for us ? What fearfully expressive images are here made use of—clouds without water, or having the semblance and the promise of what is good, whilst utterly void thereof—carried about of winds, the sport of every incitement—trees having the leaves of profession but all the fruits of righteousness either withering or wanting—twice dead, the death in trespasses and sins before entering the Church, the sins unto death of the irrecoverable backslider after it—stars of brilliancy and conspicuousness it may be, wandering here and there, but soon to be extinguished for ever. Save me, O God, from such a moral and spiritual

catastrophe as this. Root out my sensuality and give
me Thy Spirit. Let me henceforth be habitual and diligent in practising that lesson of the inner man, the truly
important one which is here given, for keeping my heart
in the love of God. Let me build myself up both on the
securities and sanctities of the faith—looking for mercy,
yet praying for holiness—fearing God, yet hoping in His
mercy. Thus the exercise of faith, and the presence of
its objects to the mind, keep alive the gratitude, while
the most holy character of these objects waking a kindred
character in us, ensures the process that by looking unto
God we become like unto God. Let the terrors of the
Lord, so forcibly depicted in this chapter, keep me back
from the ways of destruction—let the winning love and
compassion of my Saviour maintain me in constant adherence to Him, so that I may abide in Him continually.
To Thy wisdom, O God, would I refer the whole conduct
of my soul. Keep me from falling, and present me faultless before Thy throne. Thus shall I indeed be preserved
in Christ Jesus ; and while on myself there would be
realized the two clauses of the Bethlehem proclamation—
Peace on earth and good-will to men—the last clause of
" Glory to God in the highest" would have its illustrious
verification.

REVELATION.

REVELATION I.—This is a glorious chapter, and one that
I have ever valued for the strength and clearness of its
attestations to the Divinity of Christ. But let me first
remark on the decisive announcement here given to the

authorship of this prophecy, and also to the vast and urgent importance of the prophecy itself. Let me read it, O God, and O do Thou enable me to apply it aright, and this under the solemn impression that the time is at hand. Give me, give me, O Lord, to keep and well to observe, both discerningly and earnestly, the things which are written therein.

And now let me here note the concatenation of evidence which there is for the Godhead of our Saviour. One who is distinct from Jesus Christ, even God the Father, is spoken of as He which is, and which was, and which is to come. Again, One, in verse 8, even the Lord, announces Himself as one which is, and which was, and which is to come—thus identifying Himself, in the attribute of eternity at least, with Him who is read of in the fourth verse. Again, in verse 11, One announces Himself by a voice which is heard behind him as Alpha and Omega, one of the clauses of description given of Him who puts forth the utterance of verse 8. And to do away the last and the least remainders of uncertainty, we have both the sight and hearing of the apostle, fixing it down that Jesus Christ is indeed the personage of verses 8, 11, and 18; for He says of Himself what is said of Him in verse 11, that He is the first and the last; and further says, "I am He that liveth, and was dead"—thus completing the proof that Jesus is indeed the Alpha and the Omega, the beginning and the ending—the Almighty (verse 8); and so the mighty God, (Isaiah ix. 6,) as well as one in eternity with the everlasting Father. O may He who is the Prince of the kings of the earth be also unto me the Prince of Peace. Give me to take part in the song of eternity—"Unto Him that loved us, and washed us from our sins in His blood." O may I be made a king and a priest of His. May I never forget, but ever feel, that my sins pierced this blessed Saviour, that He was wounded for my transgressions, and bruised for my iniquities, that the chastisement of my peace was upon Him, and that with His stripes I am healed. As He suffered for me, O may I not be unwilling to suffer for Him— nor count it strange that I meet with tribulation, even as John did, and this at a very advanced age. Let me acquit myself rightly under all the visitations of God. Let me live under the control of Him whose eyes are as a flame of fire—the eyes of a Discerner and Judge, and whose eyelids do try the children of men. But yet He saith to every true disciple—Fear not, He liveth, and we shall be saved by His life ; saved from that hell and that second death of which He has the keys, and to which He will consign all the adversaries and all the neglecters of His great salvation. And I pray not for myself alone, but for the Church whereof I am a member. May our candlestick never be removed out of its place ; and may the candles therein burn purely and brightly, both for the enlightenment of our people, and for sustaining the ardour of their zeal in the cause of truth and righteousness.

REVELATION II.

May, 1846.

This is a searching chapter ; and these addresses of our Saviour should not only put every Church, but every individual upon his trial. He who knoweth what is in man tells the angel of Ephesus what He knows both of good and evil in His Church. I have worked and laboured somewhat, and feel strong indignancy at what I hold to

be evil, and have persevered under many discouragements
in my attempts to settle a gospel ministry among the poor,
and all this under a deep sense of the power of Christianity when brought to bear on the popular mind—and it
may be for the sake of Christ's name.   But has it been
for the sake of Christ Himself, or the love I bear to Him,
not as the bearer of a certain name, but as a real and
living personage ? I am quite sensible of my constitutional
activity, of my keen and sensitive recoil from what is
morally wrong in public men, of my philosophic tendencies
to carry out the likeliest experiments for the good of
society ; but might not all this be apart from affection for
the Saviour, or even affection for the souls which He died
to save ?—My God, search me, try me, begin again with
me the work of a real and radically sound repentance ;
and give me brighter evidences of my state, than even
that wherewith Thou hast concluded in favour of the
Ephesians, and from which I derive to myself some degree of comfort—even that I hate many of the things
which Thou hatest.   I am still in the midst of the battle ;
give me, O Lord, the conquest and the victory, that I may
eat of the tree of life, and be translated into the paradise
of God.—My God, I know not what trials are in reserve,
either for my Church or myself individually.   Certain it is
I have not suffered unto blood as did the primitive Christians, nor even materially the loss of wealth, as these
Smyrnites had, yet who though poor were rich.   But prepare me for the worst : only enable me to hold fast by the
faith and name of Jesus, that I may inherit life and not
be hurt of the second death.—My God, who piercest asunder even to the thoughts and intents of my heart, Thou
great Discerner of men—save me from the Antinomianism

that would turn the grace of God into lasciviousness ;
make me earnest for all sound and vital doctrine—hating
its opposite ; and thus may I know what it is to have,
even now, that secret of the Lord which is the foretaste
of those yet unknown treasures in heaven, the very conception of which is unknown to all who are untaught by
the Spirit of God.　And O grant, Almighty Father, that
I may grow in grace, and that mine may be a progressive
Christianity.　But even though it should, let me not be
satisfied with my own solitary state—let me beware of
tolerating corruption in others, and more especially that
corruption which recommends and so spreads itself to the
destruction of many souls.　Let me feel the control of
Thine omniscience, in that Thou searchest the reins and
the heart, and canst penetrate into the inmost thoughts and
affections of every one.　May I hold fast and persevere
unto the end.　May I be in Thy hands an instrument for
bringing the gospel of Thy Son to many, and at length
be rewarded by an ascendancy over men's spirits for their
good ; and be admitted to shine in the firmament of Thy
glory for ever.　Let these things heard by the ear sink
deep into the heart.

REVELATION III.

Craigholm.

My God, how descriptive this, regarding the Church of
Sardis, is of myself—a name to live, while I am well-nigh
if not altogether dead.　O, my God, strengthen for me,
or rather strengthen by me, the things which remain—
give me to be more watchful than hitherto.　My works
are not perfect, and to instance but in one thing, has patience had its perfect work in me ?　I would renew, O God,

my repentance before Thee ; and at the same time hold fast my faith, or the rejoicing and confidence of my hope, lest sudden destruction come upon me. Give me to confess Christ before men, that He may confess me before the Father and His angels. Give me, O Lord, of the blessings and the promises which Thou here holdest forth to the Church of Philadelphia. Mine is indeed but a little strength, if any at all. I have adversaries and I pray for charity towards them. In as far as I am right and they are wrong, give them to see and, if Thou thinkest meet, to acknowledge their error. I will not pray for their humiliation but for their amendment. Bring forth my judgment unto light, and my righteousness as the noonday. Save me from the trials that are too heavy for me, and give me to overcome. Prepare me for the land of blessedness and everlasting peace—where enemies cease from troubling, and the weary are at rest. And my closing prayer from these verses, my prayer to Him who is unchangeable and true—to Him who is not the beginning but the Beginner, not the first created but the Creator, not the first originated but the originator—for though to Him is ascribed a Sonship, His is an eternal Sonship, and without Him was not anything made that was made— my prayer to this high and holy One is that He would save me, both from the character which is here denounced, and the curses which, if not reformed, will most assuredly be fulfilled upon it. Save me, save, O God, from the lukewarmness of the Church of Laodicea. I have a zeal about things pertaining to God, but where is my zeal for God Himself? I may be a zealous assertor of the doctrine that has come out of His mouth ; but where is my zeal for God as a being—for the living God? And I am actuated by the strong conviction that nothing will make society right but a diffused Christianity—yet where, alas! is my warm and zealous affection for human souls, or for Christ, the real personal Christ, who is the alone Saviour? It may be that I am not cold; but assuredly I am not hot. My only comfort is that I do not say of myself, and most assuredly do not feel of myself, that I am rich and have need of nothing. I would cry unto Jesus. May the chastenings that are now upon me yield this peaceable fruit, ever taking unto Him both as the Lord my righteousness and the Lord my strength—my righteousness wherewith to be clothed, my wisdom also by which I might see. O the blessed universality of the saying—If *any* man open. Lord, I would open my heart, and welcome with outstretched arm Thine admittance there. Enter into convivial friendship with me, O Christ. Give me to overcome as Thou hast overcome. And let all these warnings be not only heard by the ear, but sink deep into the heart. Amen, amen.

REVELATION IV.

We now come to the outset of what we properly understand by prophecy, or rather the preparation for it, in the gorgeous representations of this chapter. What the inspired man saw he saw in the Spirit—the throne and Him who sitteth on the throne, and the celestial dignitaries around it, with the insignia of grandeur—for crowns of gold were on their heads. There is a mystery which might be variously and plausibly explained—but still a mystery to me, in the seven Spirits of God. But let me be satisfied that it should abide so—for what is man, to

intrude into or pronounce upon the things not seen by
him? We understand not the apparatus of this glorious
vision, nor can we tell whether the four living creatures
are symbolical or real; but we understand, and should be
solemnized by the articulate utterance that is here ascribed to them, the invocation which they ever and anon
lifted, and which in one brief but comprehensive sentence
sets forth the holiness, and the sovereignty, and the omnipotence, and the eternity of God. Glory, honour, and
thanks were rendered unto Him; and let us, even in this
land of darkness afar off, join in the solemn celebration.
Give me, O God, a constant and profoundly admiring
sense of Thyself. Let us keep by Him day and night,
and may I know what it is to maintain the habitual frame
and feeling of godliness. Let there be a deep infusion of
gratitude in all my sentiments and all my services of the
Deity; but for this faith—and faith too in the gospel of
His grace—is indispensable. Train me, O God, by the
services on earth, to a communion with the saints in
heaven. Be more to me than a name, or an abstraction,
or a doctrine. May I bear a practical regard to Thee as
to a God who liveth—as to the living God. And as the
elders cast their crowns before Thee, O may I seek not
mine own glory, but render all unto Thee, and seek Thy
glory alone. Give me to feel that nothing is mine, but
that all is Thine; and if I have received all, wherefore
should I glory as if I had not received it? Thou art
worthy, O God. Clothe me with humility. Give me
henceforth to demean myself in all meekness and lowliness among my fellows, and to feel thoroughly and at
all times that I am but a derived and dependent creature. O that I felt the intimacy of my relationship to

God as altogether the product, and at the entire disposal
of His hand. Let it be remarked that He who sitteth on
the Throne is represented in this chapter as God the
Creator, and that no reference is made in it to the Lamb
of God.

REVELATION V.

This is a truly noble and instructive chapter, and
views of deepest interest present themselves on the comparison of it with the preceding. The book containing
the prophecy could be opened and read by none but the
Son of God, who was also the Son of man, here called the
Lion of the tribe of Judah and Root of David. O blessed
Jesus, in whom are hid all the treasures of wisdom and
knowledge, the whole Bible is to me a sealed book; but
do Thou unseal it to the eye of my mind, and open mine
eyes to behold the wondrous things which are contained in
it. But what to me is of chiefest concern in this passage
is, that here the Lamb of God—not spoken of before,
is represented as placed in the very same situation and
surrounded by the very same objects with the Lord
God Almighty in the preceding chapter—even He who
created all things, and for whose pleasure they are and
they were created. This Lamb that had been slain had
seven horns and seven eyes; and these are said to be the
seven Spirits of God, which, in the former description,
(ch. iv. 5,) were the seven lamps of fire burning before the
throne. What a mysterious union and incorporation and
identity is here! There God is on the throne, and sat; here
Christ is in the midst of the throne, and stood; there the
seven Spirits of God are lamps of fire burning before the
throne; here they are the seven eyes of the Lamb. Let

us view with holy and humble reverence this triune representation of the Father, Son, and Holy Spirit; and
still more, to compensate for the sublime obscurity of
such a contemplation, let us rejoice in the unequivocal
testimonies here given to the Godhead of the Saviour.
Let us specially note the identity of those ascriptions
given to the Lamb that was slain, and to Him by whom
all things were created: "Worthy is the Lord God Almighty—(ch. iv. 8)—to receive glory, and honour, and
power," (ch. iv. 11;) and "Worthy is the Lamb that was
slain to receive *power*, and wisdom, and strength, and
honour, and *glory*, and blessing." (verse 12.)   And as if
to identify or conjoin the Father with the Son, it is
again said in verse 13—"Blessing, honour, glory, and
power be to Him that sitteth upon the throne, and to
the Son, for ever and ever."   I would cherish the thought
of Christ's divinity : I would mix the consideration of His
person with His work—that I may behold in the deity
of Christ the completeness of that redemption, the efficacy of that atonement, the regenerative power of that
grace by which the restoration of the human family is
carried into effect.   And there are other precious things
in the Scripture now before us!—What a song is that
which was raised by the four and twenty elders, or rather
by the redeemed saints or spirits of the just made perfect!
—May it be the song of my eternity ; may I close now
with the Redeemer; and, appropriating His propitiation,
be able to say that He has redeemed me to God by His
blood; and thus may I begin the song on earth, to be
perpetuated above and through all eternity.   The odours
here spoken of are said to be the prayers of saints, perfumed by the incense of a Saviour's merits.   (See ch. viii.

3, 4.) Let it further be observed that all angels, and
every creature in heaven or on earth, or under the earth,
is represented as celebrating the great event of our redemption by their homage to the Lamb that was slain.
He who liveth for ever and ever is alike the all-powerful
God in ch. iv. 9, and the Lamb that was slain in verses
13 and 14 of the present chapter. Christ was God
manifest in the flesh.

REVELATION VI.

I cannot enter here on the interpretations of this prophecy, which, however uncertain or controverted they
might be, affect not the importance or the preciousness
for edification of many sentiments and passages in the
Apocalypse of John. It is to these that we must confine
ourselves ; and therefore, without touching on the national
movements which are predicted under the four first seals,
let us remark how the history of the world is made subservient to the history of the Church—so that at length
the vindication and reward of God's own people are sure
to come round after, it may be, many vicissitudes and
many trials. God will ever avenge His elect at last ;
and even those of them who have suffered wrongfully,
though they may not have resisted unto blood, will have
ample redress and reparation awarded to them. Let us
meanwhile wait patiently for God's day of reckoning. Even
the worst afflictions, being for a moment, are but light
when compared with the exceeding and eternal weight of
glory. Let us therefore be prepared to do all and to
suffer all that God might permit to be laid upon us ; if
it be for the name of Christ and the word of God, then

happy are we. He is a holy and a true God who judges
the earth; but are we ready for this solemn account?
My God, confer upon me that, in the conscious possession
of which I might look on with boldness to the day of
judgment. (1 John iv. 17.) Shed abroad in my heart
the love of Thyself by the Holy Ghost, and having the
love of Thee I shall have the love of my neighbour also ;
or, in other words, shall be conscious that as God is so
am I in this world, for God is love. But O, on the other
hand, what an awful expression—the wrath of the Lamb!
and how manifold are the transgressions by which I have
most rightfully incurred it. Enable me, enable me, O
God, to take hold of Thy covenant ; let me not count the
blood of that covenant an unholy thing. Save me from the
catastrophe of fleeing from the face of Him who sitteth
on the throne, and calling on the rocks and mountains
to hide me from the fury that shall be rained down on
them who obey not the gospel of our Lord and Saviour
Jesus Christ. Let me flee now unto Him as my refuge.
Instead of then fleeing to be hid from Him, let Himself
now be my hiding-place from the storm. Let me flee from
the coming wrath, and for refuge to the hope set before
me in the gospel ; but where, alas ! is the purifying influence of that hope ? Thou knowest, O God, what a weak—
nay, what a wicked—nay, what a detestable creature I
am. I call out—"Unclean, unclean." Heal my backslidings ; deliver me from the power of my inborn and
yet obstinate corruptions ; let me be temperate in all
things ; let not sin have the dominion over me. I pray
to be rescued both from present disgrace and from future
damnation—for I am exceeding vile, O God, and cry for
Thy mercy on me, a miserable offender.

REVELATION VII.

June, 1846.

With what facility could God let loose upon us those mighty elements which He alone can restrain !—It is of His mercies that we are not destroyed. Now is the season of His forbearance, yet I doubt not that a fierce and awful tempest is awaiting us.—But He knoweth His own ; and the events both of nature and history are made subservient to their advancement and final blessedness. Seal me, O God, unto the day of redemption ; and, meanwhile, deliver me from the machinations of him who is termed the prince of the power of the air, and the god of this world. Give me, O Lord, to join at length that mighty throng of the exalted in heaven, and to share with them in the invocations of a common worship to God and to the Lamb ; and let my fellowship now be with the Father and with the Son, and let me do homage to the Son in all my approaches to the Father. O grant that I may join in the beatific song of eternity.—Enable me, O God, to lay hold of everlasting life ; and elevate me to the prospects and the preparations of a high calling. But where is my meetness ?—how shall I attain to the heavenly state then, if now I am not heavenly-minded ? No doubt I have had my tribulations, but have they had any other effect than to work in me that sorrow of this world which worketh death ? Where has been my patience—even that patience which worketh experience and is the precursor of hope ? Where has been the sanctified use of my afflictions ; and have not I, after the repeated chastenings of a wise and salutary discipline, lapsed into sin again—nay, into the very sins and abominations for which I had been so grievously punished both in my conscience and my fears? All this I confess, O God, and would wash it all out in the blood of the Lamb; and having thus made my robes white, prepare me, O God, for the whole of Thy will, whether it be to do or to suffer for Christ's sake; and sustain me in the midst of all my light afflictions and annoyances, by the prospect of an exceeding great and eternal weight of glory. What blessedness in heaven! O may I serve Thee here, that day and night I may serve Thee there in the temple of Thine own immediate residence. May I dwell everlastingly with God, by whom every desire of my mind, then righteous and pure, shall be satisfied, and every painful visitation shall be warded off from my person. Give me to drink, there, of the elixir of immortality from the living fountains to which my Saviour shall conduct me, and to eat of the leaves of those trees which shall be for the healing of the nations. There, and in the midst of Thine unsuffering kingdom, no grief shall be experienced, but all sorrow and sighing shall flee away. O may my heart now be there, and my conversation there.

REVELATION VIII.

This silence of half-an-hour in heaven has long struck me as one of the highest sublimities in Scripture. I forget the explanation—as I indeed do of almost all the various and particular prophecies, for which I have no memory whatever, though I very recently read Elliot's "Horæ Apocalypticæ," and consider it as one of the ablest expositions I know òf this part of Scripture. I shall not therefore attempt any interpretations of the unfulfilled prophecy here; but there is enough of the obviously good and impressive to furnish materials for instant reflection. How

precious, for example, to be told of the angel with the
golden censer; and of the incense that was given to him
which he should mix with the prayers of all saints. (Luke i.
8-10, and Rev. v. 8.) Let me lift up all my prayers in
the name of Christ, that they may rise to the throne perfumed by the incense of His merits, and so with a sweet-
smelling savour which shall make them acceptable to
God. O Jesus, my intercessor and advocate at the right
hand of God, may I lean more upon Thee for everything.
—May Thy Priesthood and Mediatorship occupy a larger
space than hitherto in my habitual contemplations and
thoughts. I desire the habit of a confiding reference to
Thee at all times for acceptance, for peace of conscience,
for strength, and for guidance as well as grace, that I may
not only be taught but upheld and carried forward in the
way wherein I should go. Let me but have my personal
interest in Christ secured, and then I may possess my soul
in patience under all the coming judgments and desolations that are in reserve for our earth. Wars and revolu-
tions, I believe, await us. O grant of me and mine that
we may be safe within the ark of the covenant. Give me,
O Lord, a more practical realization of these things: may
I be a Christian in deed and in truth. And why do I not
so close with the Saviour as to claim Him for my own, to
lay my confident hold on the propitiation He has made for
the sins of the world,—after which I would joy in God,
and feel constrained by Christ to live unto Him, to obey
and glorify Him in all things? Make good this transition for me, Almighty Father.—Translate me out of darkness into the marvellous light of Thy Son's gospel; may
this gospel enter my heart with the demonstration of
the Spirit and with much assurance; may I take Jesus

Christ at His word, and no longer be afraid, but only believe. Stablished upon this foundation I might view
unmoved the calamities which are to befall our world, unmoved by any fears for my own personal safety, however
much it should concern me to pray for my fellow-men,
and labour by converting them to the faith of Christ—to
ward off from as many as possible the woes that are to be
fulfilled on the impenitent and unbelieving.

REVELATION IX.

The fifth trumpet, I understand, ushers in the rise of the
Mahometan power ; and the sixth, if I recollect right, its
decline and overthrow. This seems to interpose a long
period between these contiguous soundings ; but without
stopping to consider these interpretations, let me seize
only on those topics which admit of a moral and spiritual
application.—And first, we see the respect which, in the
dispensation of His judgments, God bears to the safety of
His own sealed ones. We read elsewhere of God shorten-
ing the period of a general and wide-spread calamity for
the sake of the elect, and here the destroyers are charged
to confine their inflictions to God's enemies and the
enemies of His Church. Again, we are told that the chastisements which had been sent abroad upon the earth, and
the plagues by which many had been killed, proved inef-
fectual as lessons or warnings to those of God's adversaries
who had been spared. Let both the first and the second
of these passages tell upon my own heart and conscience.
In reflecting upon the former I would pray that I too
may be counted worthy of escaping those things which are
to come upon the earth. Have regard, O Lord, to me

and mine in the great day of Thy retributive visitation. Grant me, O Lord, the requisite protection against the plagues and inflictions of that day; and like as the destroying angel in Egypt passed over those houses which had their doors sprinkled with the blood of the Paschal Lamb, so may I be sealed unto the day of redemption, having the conscience sprinkled with the blood of Christ, and my soul so cleansed by the washing of regeneration that I may be reckoned among the sealed and the sanctified ones of the Lord. Again, in reflecting on the latter of these two passages, would I pray that when Thy judgments are abroad upon the earth, I as one of the inhabitants thereof may learn righteousness. The inefficacy of such judgments on mankind in general has been strikingly manifested in our own time, and more especially when contrasting the alarm and apparent seriousness which impressed many spirits at the period of the French Revolution, and which yet seem to have been dissipated, nay, displaced by much infidelity, or at least by as widespread an ungodliness as before, when the danger was overpast.—My God, let me and many others in our land be led both by Thy word and providence to a deep, stable, and solid repentance, so as that we may stand with acceptance before the Son of man at His coming.

REVELATION X.

The seven thunders must have been sounds of articulate utterances, and such as the apostle could have written down. Let me acquiesce in the obscuration which, in virtue of their not being written, rests on the Millennium and on all the details of it. It is not for us to pry into what God hath thus expressly prohibited from passing into a revelation for men in our stage of the world's history; but there are words of great significancy and of mighty import and application to us in this chapter. The oath of the angel standing on the earth and the sea, and the brief but weighty description of Him by whom it was sworn, form one of the most emphatic deliverances in holy writ. Let me ever do homage to God as the Creator of all things. How often is He lost sight of even in this capacity—familiar and easily apprehended though we imagine it to be? A simple but strong sense of God, as of Him who made myself and made all things, would give a new habit and complexion altogether to the spirit within me; and then within the compass of this solemn adjuration, we have the consummation of time, as an element that should abide no longer—bringing us to the border of that sublime speculation which respects both time and eternity. But let me take on the practical impression, unequal as I am to the metaphysics of this high question. Thou, O God, who madest the world, livest for ever and ever, but the world will pass away. May I renounce the world for God, choosing Him as the strength of my heart and my everlasting portion. And what a pregnant expression here is the mystery of God—a mystery to be finished in the days of the voice of the seventh angel. This might only mean the accomplishment of things, before hidden things, set forth in the old prophecies, " as He hath declared to His servants the prophets;" still there is a time coming when we shall know even as we are known—when the whole enigma of God's work and God's administration shall be cleared up, and the difficulties now resting on sin and death, and all evil—these now

inexplicable secrets of the Divine policy—shall be fully
resolved, and the song be lifted up of—"Just and true are
Thy ways, Thou King of Saints." I wish that my friend,
Mr. Foster, could have adjourned some of the difficulties
which exercised him to the day when all things shall be
made manifest. I greatly wish that he could have restrained his speculation on the duration of future punish-
ments, and acquiesced in the obvious language, or at least
the obvious practical lesson and purpose of Scripture upon
this question—which was to cut off every pretext for
postponing the care of their eternity from this world, and
to press home on every unsophisticated reader of his
Bible the dread alternative of—now or never. Meanwhile,
we repose in the general conviction that God will be vindicated in all His dealings with the creatures whom He
has formed. There is an unexpected analogy between
sin and the act of the prophet's obedience to the angel;
sin is sweet to the taste, sweet in the mouth, so that we
roll it under our tongue, but when finished it bringeth
forth death. Let us alike resist all present temptations
because of their future consequences, and resolutely acquit
ourselves of all present duties notwithstanding of future
consequences, and in defiance of all the pains which might
attend our performance of them.

REVELATION XI.

July, 1846.

There are various interpretations of this chapter, which,
as usual, I have forgotten, and let me therefore fasten
upon its practicalities. Let me first then observe how
wide the distinction is between secularity and sacredness
—the one within the precincts of a guarded and select

territory, the other without and abroad over the face of a world lying in wickedness. O may I keep myself unspotted from this world, and forget not that the love of it is opposite to the love of the Father. And let me here also see the utter alienation which obtains between the children of this world and the children of light, nay the fierce hostility of the former to the latter, and the triumphant feeling which pervades the hearts of the ungodly when the cause of serious religion meets with a check, or for the time with an overthrow; but it can only be for a time, for it will at length be set upon its feet again, and Christianity will become the reigning power and predominant interest throughout the whole earth.—And destruction will overtake its enemies; but we must lay our account with times of peril and commotion, for which we should prepare by supplication to the Father of lights, and a conversation even now in that heaven whence we should be looking for the Saviour. Meanwhile, let me not be forgetful of the words of this prophecy, but in obedience to the solemn warning which ushers it in, let me cast an observant eye upon its pages, as reflected it may be by Providence in the events of our coming history. O may I be counted worthy to stand before the Son of man; and let me not be discouraged by the frustration for a season of all the attempts now making to regenerate our earth, but even in the midst of most adverse visitations lift up our heads, for that our redemption draweth nigh. What a moral victory will then be achieved for the world, when its kingdoms shall become the kingdoms of the Lord and of His Christ!—O for a similar victory of the good over the evil principle in my own person; for in the microcosm of every single man there are precisely the same elements

at work and in war as throughout the species at large.
Take unto Thyself, O Lord, Thy great power and reign
over me—destroying the principles and forces of the old
man, and setting up that kingdom of God within me
which is righteousness and peace and joy in the Holy
Ghost. Destroy the works of the devil within me, and
enable me in every hour of temptation to resist him, and so
put him to flight. May the same destruction which is to
sweep off the destroyers of the earth expel from my heart
the foul and rebellious influences which lurk and operate
there, and then shall I have boldness in looking onward
to that day when Thou shalt give reward unto Thy servant and Thy saints, and them who fear Thy name. That
the nations are to be angry is an intimation to us that we
shall incur the displeasure of the powers of this world;
but let us not fear what man can do unto us, for all his
wrath will be swallowed up in the day of the wrath of the
Lamb.

REVELATION XII.

Jedburgh.

The Church is now in the wilderness: and the state
of matters below is in some mysterious way connected
with the politics and the powers of a higher sphere. The
deep and universal deception that obtains throughout the
world is the work of the devil, who is the enemy and
accuser of all who believe in Christ. There is something
confirmatory in the thought, that in counterpart to each
other there is justification through Christ, and accusation
by him whose works and endeavours Christ came to destroy.
It lets us in somewhat to the opposition of interests between the Prince of Peace and the Prince of darkness—
that whereas on the one side so much has been done to

achieve our justification, on the other side, he who ac-
cuseth us before God day and night, seems bent on
thwarting and traversing this object—pleading against
the acquittal of the guilty, as if pleading for his own, and
that in virtue of their condemnation they may still remain within his power and under his jurisdiction. But
let us triumphantly say—It is God who justifieth, who
is he that condemneth? Let us build ourselves up in
the confidence that this our justification will be made
good; and let us be all the more confident when we
think of the devil as so bent in opposing it. Let us resist not merely his attempts to draw us into sin, but his
attempts to stir up those fears and misgivings of an ac-
cusing conscience which might drive us into unbelief.
Let us feel that in thus resisting we have God and His
Christ upon our side ; and placing all our reliance on the
Captain of our salvation, let us feel that His honour as
a conqueror, and our deliverance as His redeemed cap-
tives, are at one. But to whatever period the loud voice
from heaven may be referred—proclaiming salvation and
strength and the kingdom of God and the power of Christ
to have come—with us on earth at least the devil still
rages, and goeth about as a roaring lion, seeking whom
he may devour.—My God, save me from his wiles ; save
me from the might as well as the skill of this great adversary ; let me have help direct from Thine own sanctuary against him : and if need be to mitigate his temptations, and to save me from the power whether of his
allurements or his terrors—let me have help from the
earth below as well as from the heavens above. O give
me to be watchful when I think of the dangers that beset me, and that the contest, instead of being with flesh

and blood only, is with principalities and powers and spiritual wickedness in high places.   May I prevail, O God, in the warfare with the enemies of my soul.   Give me for this purpose to keep the commandments of God and to have the testimony of Jesus Christ.

REVELATION XIII.

Let me give earnest heed unto the words of this prophecy, to the effect of my strenuous opposition against Antichrist in all his forms.   Let me forget not the immutable and intolerant zeal of the God of heaven against idolatry in the Old Testament, and against that concentration of all that is idolatrous and blasphemous which is the subject of such solemn warning and denunciation both in this book of the Apocalypse and in various other places of the New Testament.   Let me feel a revolt in my own spirit from this corruption adequate to the terms of hideousness by which it is here characterized—as having on its head the name of blasphemy, and opening its mouth in blasphemy against God.   Let me feel the impressiveness of the repeated call—" He that hath an ear to hear, let him hear."   I must not turn away from the voice of this prophecy, but be prepared for taking a right part in what to all probability will be the great question and controversy of the years which are to come.   Let me confine myself to the proper warfare of saints, whose great armour is patience and faith.   Perhaps another victory is awaiting the Papal power; perhaps the friends of Scripture will be again overcome.   Certain it is that the policy of the greatest states in Christendom seems to be all on the side of a reviving and advancing Popery; and I earnestly pray, O God, for my own grace and guidance, and for the direction from on high of the Free Church, that we may resolve aright and do aright amid the difficulties upon which we have already entered. The weapons of our warfare are not carnal; and so far as those are concerned who wield such weapons, they are so much engaged to all appearance in behalf of the unprotestant and unscriptural, that it may well be said—" Who is able to make war against him ?" My God, we have no access to the book of life so as to read if our names be written there; but we are here told, that if we worship the beast our names are not written in that book; and therefore, O Lord, give me a more serious and practical sense than I have yet felt of the obligation under which I stand to study the sayings of this book, so as to compare them with the signs of the times, and to act accordingly.—And we are told of another or second or representative power, subordinate to the primary one, and helpful in confirming his ascendancy over the spirits of men. The plausibilities which are to mislead those of our own land might not issue as before from the monasteries and charitable institutes of the Middle Ages; but we have talking senators now, and their underlings, who would confound every distinction between truth and error—calling evil good, and good evil, and who would lull us into the delusion that there is no danger to be apprehended from the insidious and ever-plotting Jesuitism that is now everywhere at work. They might even deceive us by the marvellous results of their civilizing and educational processes. But let us not be deceived; and at the hazard of forfeiting all civil advantages—nay, even life itself, let us be enabled to stand up for the paramount claims of that knowledge which alone

can sanctify and save, even the knowledge of the one
Mediator between God and man, and to whom all power
has been given in heaven and earth. Come, Lord Jesus,
come quickly.

REVELATION XIV.

Grant, O Lord, that Thy name may be written on my
forehead. O Lord, redeem me from the love of all that is
in the world which is opposite to the love of the Father—
for how shall Thy name be on my forehead if the love of
Thee be not in my heart? Give me to be pure in heart,
and save me from the awful doom of those who defile the
temple of the Lord. Put truth into my inward parts,
and neither in my spirit nor in my mouth let there be
any guile; and speed forward, O Lord, the message of
Thy Son's salvation over the world. Let the everlasting
gospel be preached unto all nations; and let not the God
who presides over its economy be so alien as the artificial
forms and phrases of our orthodoxy have caused Him in
our minds to be from the God who made heaven and
earth, and the sea, and the fountains of waters. With the
downfal of Antichrist is associated the patience of the
saints and its reward—even of them who keep the obedience and the faith of Jesus. O Lord, may I look habitually onward to death, and let mine be a death in the
Lord. O that my works were such as to stand the judgment of the great day, so as that I may enter on that
rest which remaineth for the people of God. Let me receive not the mark of the name of the beast, else how
can I inherit along with those on whose foreheads is
written the name of the Father? Let the power of faith
and the fruit of obedience be alike realized upon me.

What an awful representation is here given of the last judgment, when Christ will come to be admired in them who believe, but will also come to take vengeance on them who know not God, and obey not the gospel of our Lord Jesus Christ! Such are the terrors of that day; and how shall I attain to boldness in the anticipation of it? There is one prescription for this: let me believe in the love which God hath to me, and then shall I love God; and with the consciousness of this love in my heart I shall look forward without trembling to the great and awful day of reckoning—and on the strength of this consideration, that I am like unto Him who is love, that as He is so am I in this world. (1 John iv. 17.) That will indeed be a day of decision, when the tares shall be cut down and cast into the fire, and the grapes in clusters upon the vine shall be cast into the great wine-press of the wrath of God. There are angels who are ministers of salvation, but there are angels also who are ministers of wrath. We know not the details of this world's closing history. I can say nothing in explanation of the wine-press trodden without the city, nor of the blood which overspread, and at such a depth, the extent which is here specified. But let me not forbear that attention to the Apocalypse which is so solemnly required of me, and let me even now take in and proceed upon the impression of its obvious sentiments. Let me bear an awful respect unto that day on which even the righteous scarcely shall be saved.

REVELATION XV.

Leadhills, August, 1846.

A most precious and impressive chapter, in which, amid the mysterious things of which we can give no explanation,

we have some weighty and sublime lessons on the character and ways of God. There is a wrath, in the discharge of which God eases Himself of His adversaries.
There is a consummation of vengeance, by which the
moral government of the Supreme is vindicated. There
is an anger in deep and intimate alliance with truth and
justice; for in connexion with these last plagues, and
seemingly because of God having judged thus, do we
find Him celebrated in the song of the righteous, not only
because of His works being great and marvellous, but because of His ways being just and true. Mark the appro-
priateness of the designations given first to works and
then to ways. Can this sea of glass—on which the saints
might stand and look on the execution of God's righteous
sentence on the earth at large—can it be what my friend
Edward Irving imagined it to be—one country in the
world that should stand exempted from the desolations
which are to go abroad over the face of it, and that country to be the evangelical and missionary Britain, aloof
from Popery, and actuated generally and throughout, or
at least influentially, though it might be partially, by a
pure, and scriptural, and Protestant faith? The song of
Moses, as commemorating the destruction of the enemies
of the Church and the Church's safety as well as prospects,
might well harmonize with the song of the Lamb; and
both together might harmonize with the circumstances
of that transition period, when plagues were to be sent
down from Heaven upon the earth, and, as the fruit of
God's judgments being made manifest, all nations were
to come and worship before Him. Hasten this final
result, O God, and prepare me for its appearance, that I
may be counted worthy on that day to stand before the

Son of man.   As Almighty Creator, Thy works, O God, are great and marvellous—as moral Governor, and more especially as King of Saints, Thy ways are just and true. May this kingdom, this kingship, this reign of Thine, be set up in my heart now—that I as one of Thy saints may join in the songs of eternity.   Let my place be on the sea of glass—for till the plagues be fulfilled no man can enter into Thy temple.   O save our beloved country—spare it, if it be Thy blessed will, from the visitations which are coming upon the earth.   The fire wherewith the sea of glass is mingled may perhaps betoken that here, too, there may be fierce contentions between the friends and enemies of Thy truth—with it may be such a prevalence of the former, as that they shall attempt and execute great things on the side of God and godliness.   Heaven grant us such a remnant of strength in the midst of us that we may bear a part in the toils and triumphs of the world's regeneration.

REVELATION XVI.

Strathleven.

The wrath of man worketh not the righteousness of God ; but the wrath of God Himself worketh out His righteousness.   The pouring out of His vials of wrath is for the execution of righteous judgments ; and so the pouring forth of the wrath is followed up by the solemn ascription of the angel of the waters.   Thou art righteous, O Lord, because Thou hast judged thus.   Like God may I be slow to anger ; like God when angry may I sin not, but do justly—and remembering well that vengeance is not mine but His.   God will recompense the sufferings of His servants ; and let us meanwhile acquiesce in the events of His providence, and look onward for a full

rectification and redress at the consummation of all things
—when the truth and righteousness of God will be echoed
and re-echoed throughout the high vaults of heaven. O
how possible it is to feel pain without penitence ; and
how often has this been exemplified in the history both
of individuals and nations ? Let me instance France
and its Revolution ; and also the judgments which, in the
shape of pestilence, and reverses, and famine, have from
time to time been inflicted on our own land—growing every year, it is to be feared, in ungodliness, and
the alienation of its public men from the spirit and
objects of the gospel of Christ. I fear that even now
we are on the eve of a calamitous visitation. Prosperity
has not mended us, but the nation has during its period
gone on to more ungodliness ; and adversity may not
soften or correct us. Sanctify Thine own chastisement,
O God. If it please Thee to send Thy plagues on man
and beast and the fruits of the earth, send, O Lord, a humbling and softening and life-giving spirit along with them.
O may the end of all Thy dispensations be the peaceable
fruit of righteousness.—A crisis is approaching, but we
know not when. Thou comest as a thief, let us be watchful and look for the coming of the Lord. May I keep my
garments pure, O Lord, and hate all that is spotted with
the flesh. What manner of man ought I to be in all
fear and holiness and godly conversation ? Thou knowest
my infirmities, O God. Solemnize me in the thought
of what I am, and of the things which are before me ;
O let me not awaken to shame and to everlasting contempt. There is a besetting sin which I pray to be
delivered from. May I cast aside every weight ; may I
mingle my prayers with my endeavours ; may I look at

all times to Thee as an ever present help in the time of temptation. Teach me to put in practice the new lesson in regard to this combination on which my mind has been dwelling of late ; and grant, O Lord, that taking Thy grace at all times along with me, I may ever work mightily according to that grace working in me mightily. Perfect Thy strength in my weakness, O God.

REVELATION XVII.

Morriston.

Surely events will clear up the obscurity of these pre-dictions. I can imagine a great tendency on the part of these higher beings, the angels, to reveal to men what they know must interest them—as represented by the coming of the angel to let John know these things. O, my God, let this hideous and revolting description of a fascinating vice deter me from the first and nascent inclinations to-wards it. I pray for purity of heart, and for this purpose create in me, O God, a clean heart. Let me *deny* un-godliness and worldly lusts. Let me exercise myself to keep my body under subjection, lest when I preach to others I myself should be a castaway. If lust and cruelty go together, as in the case of the woman of Babylon, then I hold myself free of cruelty ; and free me therefore, O God, of its guilty accompaniment. While I am in the flesh I am subject to the motions of the flesh ; but what I feel let me not follow after. Nay, cannot the evil affection be subdued at its source ? Can it not be pre-vented even from conceiving ?—and let me therefore, with all the dread of a sin which when finished bringeth forth death, shun with abhorrence and alarm the first approaches to it, and the first appearances thereof. O

Lord, give me to ascertain my name to have been written
in the book of life from the foundation of the world, by
this evidence of my being Christ's—even that I have
crucified the flesh with its affections and lusts.   It is
difficult to read this chapter without the conviction that
Popery is Antichrist.   True there are many Antichrists,
and perhaps many forms of Antichrist; but the Lamb
of God will overcome them all.   Give me, Almighty
Father, to be among His followers—called, and not only
called but chosen; and because chosen, faithful through
sanctification of the Spirit and belief of the truth.   Lord,
I believe, help mine unbelief.   Let me not be terrified
because of adversaries; let not the opposition of the
powers of this world overbear my constancy in the profession and practice of a pure gospel.   May I have grace
to be found faithful in that day, and to be counted worthy
of standing before the Son of man.   Keep me through the
power of faith unto salvation.   As the end of my faith
may I receive the salvation of my soul.

REVELATION XVIII.

What can be the city here spoken of?   It is much liker
London than Rome—a commercial than a mere ecclesiastical capital.—Is not this heart of mine a cage of every
unclean and hateful bird?   Let them be cast out of me,
O Lord.   But where is my resolution, where the systematic effort and aim at sanctification?   Enable me to keep
this heart with all diligence—seeing that out of it are
the issues of life.   Let me know, O God, when to apply
the injunction of—Come out from the companionships of
evil, lest I be partaker of their sins.   A book of remem-

brance is kept by God, and when the account has risen to a certain height, then comes the reckoning, and it will indeed be an awful one. The lamentation of the kings for Babylon points more to the ecclesiastical capital of their monarchies, whereas the description of her wealth and merchandise points greatly more to our own London; that may, however, be involved in the corruptions of Popery ere this fearful drama is consummated. The lamentation of the sailors points more to a place of great shipping interest than to Rome, or any place in Italy, and strengthens the argument for its being the capital of our own land. We cannot perceive that shipowners are much enriched by the traffic of Rome; and the lamentation seems far more applicable to London, lapsed, it may be, when the period of this fulfilment comes round, into Anti-christianism. The merchants of our land are far more the great men of the earth than those of any other nation—though the deception of all nations by sorceries and the shedding of the blood of saints, and the dealing in the souls of men, are as yet greatly more applicable to Rome, of which Babylon seems to be here spoken as the representative and the type. In the uncertainty of what is prophetical in this chapter let me not overlook the moral which obviously runs through it—the certainty of God's judgments on the wicked, and of the chastisements which He deals out collectively and nationally to corrupt societies of men. Let me shun all such societies, and keep myself pure in the midst of every surrounding contamination.

REVELATION XIX.

A further evolution of this wondrous history still en-

veloped in the future, and to us, in a great degree, the
unknown. We have here the song of gladness and victory over the destruction of those who were the enemies
of God and goodness—the sounds of jubilee and triumph
ascending from the lips of the now emancipated and
glorified saints set free from the persecutions and the
power of their adversaries. And mark the sympathy between heaven and earth, between the higher species of
being and our own, in the words uttered by the four living
creatures, and in the voice that came out from the
throne. O may I fear God and praise Him now, that I
may be qualified and prepared for joining in these high
acclamations. O may I be of the number of those who
shall be ready for the coming of the Lord, and be counted
worthy of standing before the presence of the Son of man.
Give me the fine linen, clean and white, of a perfect sanctification, that thus clothed upon with the wedding garment, I may be fit for partaking in the choirs and companies of the celestial. Let me worship God, yet honour
the Son even as I honour the Father—an honour not to
be rendered to any creature, not even to angels of the
highest order, the very highest of whom is but a fellow-
servant as ourselves, and looks up to Jesus. What a
lofty description of Him who is the Word of God!—O that
I could more adequately realize the glory of His person
and power, and then should He no longer be lightly
esteemed by me. What a significancy and worth and
grandeur it would attach to His work, did we only see
Him as He is—the Wonderful, Counsellor, The Mighty
God, The Everlasting Father, The Prince of Peace.—My
God, save me from the storm of that fierceness and wrath
which are in reserve for all who neglect Thy great salva-

tion.   May I flee to Him, the King of kings and Lord of
lords, who alone is able to save to the uttermost.   And
blessed be His name, He is as willing as He is able.
" Lord, if Thou wilt Thou canst make me clean."   " I will,
be Thou clean."   What a strenuous and athletic conflict
is here ; and how marvellous to us that such a conflict
should have been called for—seeing that we image of the
Deity, how He can achieve all and conquer all by the single word of His power, by the mere nod, as it were, of
His omnipotence.   What we know not now we shall know
hereafter, and meanwhile let us submit ourselves to the
solemnizing influence of the representations here set before us.   Let us stand in reverential awe before the august
spectacle of Him who is at once our Redeemer and our
Judge.   Let us flee to cover us under the ample canopy
of His Mediatorship—lest we incur the unescapable doom
of those who neglect the great salvation.   Let us avail
ourselves now of the meekness and gentleness of Christ
—kissing the Son while He is in the way—lest He be
angry and we fall on the day of His vengeance under the
wrath of the Lamb.

REVELATION XX.
September, 1846.

The world is protected from the deceitfulness of sin by
the confinement and binding of him who is the great De-
ceiver, the agent and originator of evil, the Prince of the
power of darkness.   The policy is to us inscrutable which
permits him at all, and which lets him forth again at the
end of a thousand years, to deceive the nations.   The time
is coming when we shall know this even as we are known ;
but meanwhile, in defect of theory, let us at least practise

up to the light of our own minds and of obvious duty. Let us resist the being whose place and significancy in the universe we cannot comprehend.—My God, save me from giving in to his temptations. Under the banner of Him who is the Captain of salvation, may I be delivered from the wiles and the strength of this formidable adversary—who, not yet chained in the bottomless pit, goeth abroad over the face of our world, seeking whom he may devour. O for a part in the first resurrection, and for the blessedness and holiness of him who is qualified and prepared for so high a preferment. But who shall prepare me?—who but He of whom it is said, that greater is He that is in you than He that is in the world—greater is the Spirit of God than the spirit who worketh in the children of disobedience. Grant me Thy Spirit, O Lord, that He may save me from the god of this world. He is again, and at a distant period, to be loosed from prison, and another battle is to be fought between the powers of light and darkness, leading to a final and decisive catastrophe—after which is the last judgment. O may I stand the reckoning of that day. Cause me to abound in the fruits of righteousness ; shed abroad in my heart the love of Thyself ; and then, under the consciousness of being like unto Thyself, who art love, I may with boldness look onward to the day of judgment. Let me never forget that though justified by faith I am judged by works ; and in all good works may I be made to abound more and more. Give me to walk worthy of Thee unto all well-pleasing. Under the regenerating power of Thy husbandry, may I become a good tree, giving forth good fruit. Give me holiness, without which I shall not pass through the ordeal of the final examination, and shall not see God.—Query,

Why should the Millennium be restricted to a literal thousand years any more than the three days and a half of the eleventh chapter? These are expanded into years by our interpreters, and it just requires the same degree of expansion to lengthen out the Millennium to three hundred and sixty-five thousand years—a great period; but in immensity and eternity there is room for cycles and periods of any magnitude.

REVELATION XXI.

The prophecy brightens onward to the final consummation of all things. Let me not overlook the materialism of the future state—the new earth as well as the new heaven. But what is of vastly more importance than the preparation—it may be by a geological catastrophe—of the new heavens and the new earth, is the moral preparation of the bride adorned for her husband. That I may have a part in the everlasting exemption from sorrow, O grant me, Lord, an exemption from sin. Give me a part and a foretaste now of the renovation of all things. Create a clean heart, renew a right spirit within me. Give me the Spirit as the earnest of my inheritance; and let me have some experience even now of God dwelling in me, and God walking in me. Pour on me even now the spirit of adoption, that I may not only be, but know myself to be, one of Thy reconciled children through the faith that is in Christ Jesus, and so at all times draw near with the full assurance of Thee as my reconciled Father. Give me full confidence in Thy words as true and faithful; and this will prove an inlet to me not only for all the hope and joy of the prospect here set in such bright and

illuminated characters before me, but also an inlet for all
the graces of the incumbent preparation. The faith in
God's faithfulness will work by love, and it is expressly said,
too, will overcome the world. Give me this faith, O Lord,
and give me to drink out of the fountain of life freely, even
of that living water given to all who shall believe ; for let
me not be deceived : all who are fearful because unbelieving, and all who are deformed by the vices whether of
violence or licentiousness or dishonesty—a fearful doom
awaits all these. Let me neglect Thy great salvation, O
God, no longer ; but forthwith embrace it and receive its
promises, and perfect my holiness, that I may participate
in the glories of the New Jerusalem, and rejoice for ever
in the immediate presence of God. What a magnificent
spectacle is here set before us in the capital of a regenerated world presiding over the nations, which in turn do
homage to the crowning city, inasmuch as the kings of
the earth bring their glory and honour into it. But sin
and sinners will be kept out of this New Jerusalem ;
neither defilement nor falsehood shall enter there. Even
they who are written in the Lamb's book of life must be
washed and sanctified ere they can find admittance there.
O may the contemplation here set forth sanctify and mo-
ralize me. Having the hope of this glorious exaltation
to a place of everlasting blessedness and triumph, let me
purify myself even as Christ is pure. They are not the
nations absolutely, but the nations of them which are
saved, that shall walk in the light of the city of God.
We know not the details either of the earthly Millennium,
or of the final and everlasting state in heaven ; but this
we know, that none but the sanctified as well as justified
shall have part in the inheritance of either.

REVELATION XXII.

Is this water of life—the living water, the Holy Spirit, who aliments our graces here? and do we continue to obtain from this aliment our spiritual sustenance through all eternity? and are there trees of life in the second Paradise, even as there was one in the first, and of which if Adam had partaken he should have become incapable of death? and how is it that the leaves of this tree minister to the healing of the nations? We are not able to reply to these things. Let us be satisfied to know that there will be no more curse, and that there we shall see the face of God, and serve Him without frailty and without a flaw. In the light of God we shall see light clearly. Let me ever aspire towards this heaven of glory; let me be ever preparing for it. In the confidence that these sayings are faithful and true, I would pray the Lord to come quickly. The sayings of this prophecy are, we conceive, on the eve of their fulfilment. I desire to be vigilant and observing, and to wait for the Lord from heaven. Him I honour as divine: He is God. The angel refused worship from John because a fellow-creature like himself; but let me yield unto Christ the honours which are due to Him, and be ever solemnized by the thought, that the time of His manifestation is at hand. And O let me set to the work of immediate repentance and reformation—seeing that as I die so shall I rise again. Give me, O Lord, to acquire the character of heaven now, that I may be found meet for heaven hereafter. May I cease to be impure; may I cease to be selfish—for of this latter vice I am making larger discoveries every day, and must struggle for its eradication. O in opposition to these may I henceforth

become a righteous and holy creature; and let no artificial orthodoxy overbear the authority of the sayings—
that Christ will reward and give to every man according
to his work, and that they are they who do the commandments who have a right to the tree of life.—My God, save
me from the doom of those who are without; save me
from their vices now, that I may have no part in that
dreary and everlasting exile in which they are to spend
their eternity.   Give me to be solemnized by this message
from the Lord Jesus, the root and offspring of David, the
bright and morning star.   O let me no longer hold out
against the invitations of a free gospel, but freely take of
that water of life which is there offered so freely and unto
all.   Let Thy Bible, O God, be henceforward my supreme
directory; nor let me incur the condemnation of those
who either add to its words or take away from them.—
Come quickly, Lord Jesus; and to prepare me for this
coming, let Thy grace be abundantly bestowed and Thy
power ever rest upon me.   In the attitude of habitual
service and of habitual supplication, would I wait for Thy
coming to our world; and O do Thou forgive the error
and bless the fruit of these scriptural devotions on the
New Testament, now brought to a close—devotions begun above five years since, and now ended on this twentieth of September, in the year of our Lord eighteen hundred and forty-six.

September 20, 1846.

John Eadie Titles

Solid Ground is delighted to announce that we have republished several volumes by John Eadie, gifted Scottish minister. The following are in print:

Commentary on the Greek Text of Paul's Letter to the Galatians
Part of the classic five-volume set that brought world-wide renown to this humble man, Eadie expounds this letter with passion and precision. In the words of Spurgeon, "This is a most careful attempt to ascertain the meaning of the Apostle by painstaking analysis of his words."

Commentary on the Greek Text of Paul's Letter to the Ephesians
Spurgeon said, "This book is one of prodigious learning and research. The author seems to have read all, in every language, that has been written on the Epistle. It is also a work of independent criticism, and casts much new light upon many passages."

Commentary on the Greek Text of Paul's Letter to the Philippians
Robert Paul Martin wrote, "Everything that John Eadie wrote is pure gold. He was simply the best exegete of his generation. His commentaries on Paul's epistles are valued highly by careful expositors. Solid Ground Christian Books has done a great service by bringing Eadie's works back into print."

Commentary on the Greek Text of Paul's Letter to the Colossians
According to the New Schaff-Herzog Encyclopedia of Religious Knowledge, "These commentaries of John Eadie are marked by candor and clearness as well as by an evangelical unction not common in works of the kind." Spurgeon said, "Very full and reliable. A work of utmost value."

Commentary on the Greek Text of Paul's Letters to the Thessalonians
Published posthumously, this volume completes the series that has been highly acclaimed for more than a century. Invaluable.

Paul the Preacher: A Popular and Practical Exposition of His Discourses and Speeches as Recorded in the Acts of the Apostles
Very rare volume intended for a more popular audience, this volume begins with Saul's conversion and ends with Paul preaching the Gospel of the Kingdom in Rome. It perfectly fills in the gaps in the commentaries. Outstanding work!

DIVINE LOVE: A Series of Doctrinal, Practical and Experimental Discourses
Buried over a hundred years, this volume consists of a dozen complete sermons from Eadie's the pastoral ministry. "John Eadie, the respected nineteenth-century Scottish Secession minister-theologian, takes the reader on an edifying journey through this vital biblical theme." - Ligon Duncan

Lectures on the Bible to the Young for Their Instruction and Excitement
"Though written for the rising generation, these plain addresses are not meant for mere children. Simplicity has, indeed, been aimed at in their style and arrangement, in order to adapt them to a class of young readers whose minds have already enjoyed some previous training and discipline." – Author's Preface

Call us Toll Free at 1-877-666-9469
Send us an e-mail at sgcb@charter.net
Visit us on line at solid-ground-books.com

Printed in the United States
206696BV00001B/123/A